D1257359

The Golden Book of Management

NEW EXPANDED EDITION

A Historical Record of the Life and Work of More Than One Hundred Pioneers

amacom

American Management Associations

To Lt. Col. Lyndall F. Urwick, management pioneer, eminent consultant, renowned scholar, and synthesizer of management thought

This book is available at a special discount when ordered in bulk quantities. For information, contact AMACOM, Special Sales Department, 135 West 50th Street, New York, NY 10020.

Library of Congress Cataloging in Publication Data

Main entry under title:

The Golden book of management.

Rev. ed. of: The golden book of management / Lyndall Urwick. 1956.
1. Management—Bio-bibliography. I. Urwick, L. F. (Lyndall Fownes), 1891– . Golden book of management.
Z7164.07G65 1984 [HD30.5] 658'.0092'2 [B] 82-71319
ISBN 0-8144-5561-1

First published in 1956 by Newman Neame Limited, 50 Fitzroy Street, London W1, for the International Committee of Scientific Management (CIOS). Printed in Great Britain by the Millbrook Press Limited, London and Southampton, and Sir Joseph Causton and Sons Limited, London and Eastleigh.

New expanded edition published in 1984 with the permission of Lyndall F. Urwick, by AMACOM Special Projects Division, American Management Associations, 135 West 50th Street, New York, NY 10020, for the International Academy of Management. All rights transferred to AMACOM by Lyndall F. Urwick.

First Printing

Preface to The New, Expanded Golden Book

THROUGHOUT the world, in both developed and developing countries, the past 50 years—and more especially the past 25 years—have been characterized by increasing concern with the task of managing and the scientific knowledge underlying it. No thinking person should be surprised that we have been experiencing through most of the world what might be called a "management revolution," a revolution in managerial techniques and approaches and in the extent of public interest in this field.

This growing interest in management is a reflection of the realization that managers at all levels, in all kinds of organizations, and in all kinds of societies have the same goal. The logical and socially desirable goal of all managers is so to manage their enterprises or departments as to achieve a desired mission with the least input of human and material resources or to accomplish as much of a mission as possible with the resources available.

With the early realization that effective managing can be best supported by seeking pertinent knowledge of the concepts, principles, theory, and techniques that underlie it and bringing this knowledge together on an international basis, the then President Masaryk of Czechoslovakia convened the first management congress in Prague in the year 1924. Out of this meeting came the Committee of Scientific Management (Comité International de l'Organisation Scientifique), familiarly known as CIOS. Since that time, congresses have been held triennially except for the period of the Second World War.

The members of CIOS, wishing to honor and record for posterity the pioneers of the scientific management movement, 30 years ago asked Lt. Col. Lyndall F. Urwick, of Great Britain, to compile an appropriate volume. Out of this came *The Golden Book of Management,* first published in 1956. It covered 70 management pioneers selected in accordance with strict criteria established by Col. Urwick and CIOS.

The entire management movement—and, indeed, all those interested in management, whether as scholars or as practitioners—owe Col. Urwick a deep and lasting gratitude for the care and dedication he displayed in developing the original *Golden Book* nearly three decades ago. He painstakingly researched the pioneers and their respective contributions to the management field and preserved for all time bio-bibliographical summaries, photographs, and brief comments on personalities—all of them no longer living by 1956—who had added significantly to management knowledge. This original book has long been out of print, and its lack of availability has been a source of deep regret to students of management and management history.

I am happy to say that we have received permission from Col. Urwick to republish his *Golden Book of Management,* without essential change, as Part One of the present volume. To fill the void left by the great pioneers who have passed from the scene in the past quarter-century and more, the Fellows of the International Academy of Management* fortunately were able to arrange with Professor William B. Wolf, of Cornell University, to collect the necessary data and incorporate them in a new section of the *Golden Book* which we have designated Part Two.

It is a pleasure for me to record the tremendous appreciation of the Fellows for the intelligence and diligence with which Professor Wolf has labored over several years to make Part Two of *The Golden Book of Management* a reality. It is also a pleasure to record our appreciation of the efforts of Professor Emeritus John F. Mee, of Indiana University, who served as Chairman of the Selection Committee which approved the persons to be included in Part Two. Likewise, we are indebted to the American Management Associations and to James L. Hayes, formerly AMA President and now President Emeritus and Chairman of the Board of Trustees, for undertaking the publication of this new and expanded *Golden Book,* including both the original version and the new Part Two. Finally, we of the Academy would like to express our gratitude to Ms. Elizabeth Marting, Vice-President Emerita of AMACOM, the publishing arm of AMA, for personally taking over the ultimate editing and preparation of this book for the press.

To me, as Chancellor of the Academy, it is a source of great pride to see the new, expanded *Golden Book* published. I sincerely believe that it will serve the needs of professors, students, researchers, and practitioners alike. It is certain to prove an invaluable tool throughout the management world.

HAROLD KOONTZ
Chancellor, International
Academy of Management
Encino, California

* For those who are not familiar with the International Academy of Management, the Fellows constitute an honorary organization, associated with CIOS, of some 176 persons from 32 countries who have been elected on the basis of internationally significant contributions to the management profession.

Master Contents

(in alphabetical order)

Frederick W. Taylor was once asked if he claimed any monopoly in scientific management. He replied, "I should say not. . . . My gracious, I do not believe there is any man connected with scientific management, who has the slightest pride of authorship in connection with it. Every one of us realizes that this has been the work of 100 men or more, and that the work which any one of us may have done is but a small fraction of the whole. This is a movement of large proportions, and no man counts for much of anything in it. It is a matter for evolution, of many men, each doing his proper share in the development, and I think any man would be disgusted to have it said that he had invented scientific management, or that he was even very much of a factor in scientific management. Such a statement would be an insult to the whole movement"—*Reply to a question from a member of the Special Committee of the House of Representatives, appointed in 1911–1912 "to investigate the Taylor and other systems of shop management." "Testimony," page 282, in* Scientific Management *by F. W. Taylor (New York, Harper & Bros., 1947 edition).*

As this book was about to go to press, the publishers were saddened to learn of the death of Lt. Col. Lyndall F. Urwick. We hope that this expanded edition of his book will serve as a fitting tribute to him, and we regret that time constraints do not allow us to include him as one of the management pioneers described within these pages.

Part One

Lyndall F. Urwick, Editor

Preface to Part One (1956)

The Significance of Management as a Body of Knowledge

WITHIN the past three quarters of a century, and principally within the past 40 years, a new branch of knowledge has claimed and won a foremost place in our social heritage. At different times and in different countries it has been described by various titles—management, scientific management, rationalization, the scientific organization of work, Stakhanovism, and so on. Primarily it was applied to the government of business undertakings. But from quite an early stage it was recognized that its principles, if well founded, must be equally applicable to all forms of organized human cooperation, to the business of government in any form as well as to the government of business.

This new department of learning, now usually called management, was based on the proposition that the methods of thought developed by the physical sciences, which have given to mankind so unprecedented a degree of control over material things, could and should be applied to human beings themselves, to the organization of their societies, small and large, and to the political, economic, and social problems to which those societies give rise. It postulated, as one of the greatest of its pioneers explicitly recognized, a "mental revolution"—the substitution of inductive thinking, thinking based on facts, for the old deductive thinking, thinking based on theories or opinions, in all matters concerning the organization of human groups.

That complete and exact knowledge is available as yet in management or in any of the underlying sciences bearing on human behavior—for instance, psychology, anthropology, or sociology—no one can claim. In these dynamic fields it is rather the approach or attitude employed that differs from older concepts. That attitude is based on the conviction that a greater degree of exact knowledge is possible and that, even today, truths are being developed by these comparatively young sciences which can be and are being applied with advantage to practical affairs. And, beyond the point where precision is possible, problems can still be handled—as in the comparable field of medicine—in the temper and spirit of science and with constant reference to organized clinical experience rather than in the halflight of custom and the limited data provided by individual empiricism.

Already, brief though management's history has been, this new branch of knowledge has profoundly changed people's ideas of how to conduct business and other enterprises in almost every country in the world. Where it has been applied consciously and completely, it has greatly increased individual productivity and made possible dramatic economies in human effort. In industrial and commercial undertakings it holds the best and, as many think, the only hope of a solution of those differences between capital and labor, between those who work and those who organize, which have hitherto prevented mankind from realizing anything but a fraction of the possibilities inherent in the use of power-driven machinery. Beyond the field of economic enterprise, it holds the yet undiscovered secret of how human beings may organize their national systems of government, and the relations between nations, so that the energies of each may be made available for the benefit of all and the curse of physical conflict between classes and nations may be removed forever, releasing the constructive impulses of mankind for new and beneficent enterprises.

The International Committee of Scientific Management (CIOS)

The first attempt to bring together persons from a number of countries with special knowledge of management took place in 1924. The late President Masaryk in that year invited a number of representative specialists to the First International Management Congress at Prague. There the decision was made to set up permanent machinery to maintain contact between individuals throughout the world who were devoting themselves to this new branch of knowledge. Then, at Brussels in the following year, the International Committee of Scientific Management (Comité International de l'Organisation Scientifique, or CIOS) was formally established. This Committee has since organized 19 triennial international congresses in various countries, with a break from 1938 to 1947 due to the Second World War.

The Decision to Issue "The Golden Book of Management"

So rapid and so varied, however, have been the developments in different countries and in the various sectors of management, that the machinery provided by CIOS is insufficient to keep the thousands of students and workers in touch with each other's efforts. There is always a danger that the contributions of many individuals who have added original and valuable ideas and discoveries to the corpus of knowledge as a whole may be lost to sight and even that their resources may be repeated by later workers. Moreover, it is impossible even today to appreciate the scope and possibilities of this growing body of knowledge without some acquaintance with its history and with the work of those pioneer thinkers who, no longer living, have each used their different viewpoints and specializations to add their fraction to the total structure.

As a contribution to the solution of this problem the International Committee of Scientific Management decided to issue *The Golden Book of Management: A Historical Record of the Life and Work of Seventy Pioneers.* The proposal to undertake such a project was first made by Lt. Col. L. Urwick, O.B.E., M.C., M.A., at the Ninth International Congress in Brussels in 1951. Later in that year, the Committee persuaded him to accept the honorary international editorship of the work and invited him to begin without delay the collection of documentary material, from all possible sources, about the individuals to be commemorated.

Considerations Governing the Choice of Names

The book contains the names only of those persons who, in the opinion of the International Committee of Scientific Management, have made original and outstanding contributions to the world body of knowledge about management and/or administration. *It does not contain the name of any person still living.* Service either to the "management movement" in the individual's own country or to the international management movement is considered one of the conditions for inclusion.

The existence of published work on a management subject is a further condition. The great practicing industrial managers of the world, outstanding though their immediate influence certainly is, therefore do not fall within the compass of the book unless they also have made an intellectual contribution to management through published work.

The majority of the individuals included by Lt. Col. Urwick were citizens of the United States. This apparent bias is merely a matter of chronology. Frederick W. Taylor, an American, was "the father of scientific management,"* although he was not the earliest of the pioneers. Even within his own lifetime his ideas began to gain recognition in every industrialized country, and in 1938 the International Committee engraved his portrait on its Gold Medal, awarded triennially for services to management. It was natural that, after Taylor's death, the ideas and skills which he had initiated should find their earliest and most widespread application among nationals of his own country, a tendency which both contributed to and was stimulated by the tremendous economic development of the United States in the first half of the twentieth century. National movements in other countries quickly got under way and have since flourished abundantly. Others have come still later. But, because the history of many of their movements is as yet in the making, it will find its record in future versions of this book.

The book is, moreover, in no sense a collection of competing national histories of management. It is presented as an evolving picture of an idea which is worldwide and transcends the particular nationalities of individuals. The extent to which each country has already enriched its own experience by the exchange of ideas with others will be apparent from a reading of the individual entries contained here.

In countries where there was doubt as to who should be included, the final choice of names was made by consultation between the Honorary International Editor and a small group of persons whose eminence in the management movements of their respective countries was long-standing. The International Committee of Scientific Management subsequently endorsed the choices arrived at.

It would be surprising if the selection of names commanded unanimous approval, and it is possible that exception may be taken to the inclusion or omission of certain individuals. The International Committee of Scientific Management found it unavoidable, in order to keep the publication within practical bounds, to limit the number of names severely. But any persons who feel that names which should have been included have been omitted should realize that this volume of the *Golden Book* is projected as only the first of many. It is hoped that later volumes will be published at appropriate intervals. Opportunities will thus be provided to add any individuals whose names should have been included in the first volume but who were overlooked. This first *Golden Book* contains the names of all persons selected by the International Committee of Scientific Management who died prior to 1955. For each individual there is

A portrait or photograph, with few exceptions.
The reasons, in the briefest possible form, for inclusion.
The main facts of the person's career.
A note on personal characteristics.

* Inscription on F. W. Taylor's tomb in Philadelphia.

The titles of the individual's most important written works on the subject of management.

* * *

The International Committee of Scientific Management wishes to take this opportunity of expressing its gratitude to those individuals in many countries who have contributed the work and information which have made this book possible and whose names are given in the "Acknowledgments."

CIOS Member Organizations

CIOS, the World Council of Management, is divided into three regional councils:

AAMO (Asian Association of Management Organizations)
Secretariat: Malaysian Institute of Management
15th Floor, Fitzpatrick's Building
86 Jalan Raja Chulan
Kuala Lumpur, Malaysia

CECIOS (European Council of Management)
Secretariat: Rationalisierungs-Kuratorium der Deutschen Wirtschaft e.V.
Düsseldorferstrasse 40
6236 Eschborn, West Germany

PACCIOS (Pan-American Council of Management)
Secretariat: Instituto para el Desarrollo de Empresarios en Argentina
Moreno 1850, 2e piso
Buenos Aires, Argentina

These regional councils contain the following member organizations:

AAMO

Australia	Australian Institute of Management
Hong Kong	The Hong Kong Management Association
India	All India Management Association
Indonesia	Perhimpunan Management Indonesia
Japan	International Management Association of Japan
Korea	Korea Productivity Center
Malaysia	Malaysian Institute of Management
New Zealand	The New Zealand Institute of Management Inc.
Papua/New Guinea	Papua Management Institute

Philippines	The Philippine Council of Management
Singapore	Singapore Institute of Management
Taiwan	China Productivity Center
Thailand	Thailand Management Institute

CECIOS

Austria	Management Institut der Industrie
Belgium	Stichting Industrie-Universiteit
Czeckoslovakia	Czeckoslovak Committee for Scientific Management
Finland	Finnish Institute of Management
France	Association Française de Management
Germany	Rationalisierungs-Kuratorium der Deutschen Wirtschaft
Ireland	Irish Management Institute
Israel	Israel Institute of Productivity
Italy	Associazione per la Promizione del Management e della Technica
The Netherlands	Nederlandse Vereniging voor Management Dutch Centre of Directors
Norway	The Norwegian National Committee of Scientific Management
Portugal	Associaçao Portuguesa de Management
South Africa	The National Development and Management Foundation of South Africa
Spain	Associacion para el Progreso de la Direccion
Sweden	The Swedish Institute of Management
Turkey	Turkish Management Association

PACCIOS

Argentina	Instituto para el Desarrollo de Ejecutivos en la Argentina
Brazil	Instituto de Organizaçao Racional do Trabolho
Chile	Instituto Chileno de Administración Racional de Empresas
Colombia	Instituto Colombiano de Administración
Ecuador	Centro de Ejecutivos
Guatemala	Instituto Tecnico de Capacitación y Productividad
Panama	Asociación Panamena de Ejecutivos de Empresas
Peru	Instituto Peruano de Administración de Empresas
Venezuela	Asociación Venezolana de Ejecutivos Federacion de Colegios de Administradores de Venezuela

In addition, CIOS has the following national member organizations:

Nigeria	Nigerian Institute of Management
U.S.A.	The American Management Associations

Acknowledgments

THE compilation of this book has been possible only because the Editor was privileged to draw on the willing aid of many individuals and organizations. Without this help he could not have assembled the extensive factual material given in the individual entries.

The introductory sections required judgment as to the nature and importance of the contribution of each pioneer. Here the Editor has sought to base his judgments on established facts, to preserve the utmost objectivity, and to secure approval in each case from persons in the respective countries qualified to comment. It has been equally his duty, however, to apply to each section, and throughout the book, a consistent interpretation of the history of management. Such an interpretation cannot be entirely free from subjective elements. For the text of the book, therefore, and for the judgments included in each introductory section in particular, he alone is responsible.

He wishes to record his deep gratitude in the first place to a number of organizations and individuals. An asterisk (*) indicates those who also aided the Editor in the selection of names from the country in question for inclusion in the book.

* The American Society of Mechanical Engineers (United States), in particular Mr. C. E. Davies (Secretary) and Mr. Alexander Kirk; The Department of Industrial Administration, Birmingham College of Technology (Great Britain), in particular Mr. D. H. Bramley (Head of Department); Mr. H. B. Maynard (United States), Past President of CIOS; Mrs. Rita Hilborn Hopf (United States), until 1955 Director of the Hopf Institute of Management, Ossining, N.Y.; and Mr. Hugo de Haan, Secretary-General of CIOS.

In addition, he extends his sincere thanks to organizations and individuals in various countries as enumerated below:

Australia

* The Australian Institute of Management (Mr. Walter Scott)

Austria
* The Oesterreichisches Kuratorium für Wirtschaftlichkeit

Belgium
* The Comité National Belge de l'Organisation Scientifique (M. Robert Caussin)

Brazil
* The Instituto de Organizaçao Racional do Trabalho (Dr. Moacyr E. Alvaro and Mr. M. Dos Reis Araujo)

France
* Comité National de l'Organisation Française (M. Louis Péhuet and M. L. Segonne)

Germany
* The Rationalisierungs-Kuratorium der Deutschen Wirtschaft (Dr. G. Freitag)
The Verein Deutscher Eisenhüttenleute (Dr. K. P. Harten)
Dr. E. Bornemann

Italy
* The Comitato Italiano di Rappresentanza Internazionale per l'Organizzazione del Lavoro (Prof. Ing. Luigi Palma)
Mme. Francesco Mauro

Switzerland
* The Comité National Suisse de l'Organisation Scientifique (M. Jacques Chapuis)
The Institut de Psychologie Appliquée, Lausanne (M. Charles Haurez and Dr. von Schnyder)
The International Association of Department Stores (Mr. Derek Knee)
M. Werner Kaufmann
M. Paul Silberer

United Kingdom
The Accountant
Messrs. W. & T. Avery Ltd., Birmingham
Reference Library, Birmingham Public Libraries
* The British Institute of Management (Sir Charles Renold, J.P., Mr. John Ryan, C.B.E., M.C., and Mr. Roland Dunkerley, J.P.)
Library and Archives Section, The General Post Office
The Institute of Industrial Administration
The Institution of Mechanical Engineers (Mr. R. T. Everett)
The National Institute of Industrial Psychology (Dr. C. B. Frisby)
Sir Isaac Pitman & Sons Ltd. (the late Mr. J. Hanley)

Messrs. David Rowan & Co. Ltd., Glasgow (Mr. Ewen H. Smith)
Messrs. Rowntree & Co. Ltd., York (Mr. W. Wallace, C.B.E., and Mr. Lloyd Owen)
The Royal Institute of Public Administration
Mr. P. J. Allen, Dr. G. H. Beaven, Miss Frances Bowie, Mr. E. S. Byng, Mr. J. R. Crane, Mr. J. K. Eastham, Mr. K. B. Elbourne, Major J. D. Gibson-Watt, Mr. J. C. Gilbert, Mr. Frank A. Heller, Mr. Walter Hewett, Mr. R. W. Isaacs, Professor J. H. Jones, Mr. F. W. Lawe, Mr. P. H. Lightbody, Professor C. A. Mace, Mr. H. W. Marsh, Mr. H. McFarland Davis, Mrs. George Elton Mayo and Mrs. Patricia Elton (Mayo) Curtis, Mrs. W. Nicholls, Mr. C. A. Oakley, Professor T. H. Pear, Mr. G. W. Perry, Professor Sir Arnold Plant, Mr. Allan Plowman, Mr. G. A. Robinson, Mr. T. G. Rose, Miss Anne Shaw, Mrs. Jean Sheldon, Dr. I. M. Shenkman, Dr. May Smith, Mr. N. A. H. Stacey, Mrs. C. (Meyenberg) Taylor, Mr. J. E. Wheeler.

United States

The American Management Association, New York, N.Y.
The Council for International Progress in Management (U.S.A.), Inc. New York, N.Y.
The Emerson Engineers, New York, N.Y. (Mr. Alonzo Flack)
The Edward A. Filene Good Will Fund, Inc., New York, N.Y. (Miss Betty W. Connors and Mr. Percy S. Brown)
La Salle Extension University, Chicago, Ill. (Mr. William Bethke)
Messrs. McKinsey & Co., New York, N.Y. (Mr. Marvin Bower)
The Stevens Institute of Technology, Hoboken, N.J.
The Twentieth Century Fund, New York, N.Y. (Miss Louise Field)
Mr. C. Canby Balderston, Mr. J. Christian Barth, Mrs. Wallace Clark, Mr. Fred H. Colvin, Mr. Morris L. Cooke, Mr. James T. Dennison, Mr. Theodore Diemer, Mrs. Henrietta C. Dodd, Mr. Kern Dodge, Professor Paul A. Freund, *Dr. Lillian Moller Gilbreth, Miss Marion S. Halsey, Mr. Paul A. Hasse, Mrs. C. E. Knoeppel, Professor Herbert S. Langfeld, Professor George F. F. Lombard, Professor Myles L. Mace, Dr. Raymond P. Marple, Mr. Joseph K. Milliken, Miss Winifred O'Brien, Mr. Allen H. Ottman, Dr. Harlow S. Person, Professor David B. Porter, Mr. John W. Punton, Professor Edwin M. Robinson, Professor F. J. Roethlisberger, *Professor Erwin H. Schell, Mr. Ordway Tead, Mrs. Sanford E. Thompson, Dr. L. W. Wallace, Mr. John A. Willard, Mrs. Edwin Williams

Members of the Editor's Staff

Miss Dorothy M. Adam (research), assisted by Miss Maureen C. Sandiford (collection of published sources), and Mrs. Fay L. Russell (secretarial work).

Contents

(Part One)

Names are arranged chronologically by date of birth. For an alphabetical listing, see Master Contents, pp. v–vii, for Parts One and Two combined.

James Watt, Jr
(1769–1848)
Great Britain

and

Matthew Robinson Boulton[1]
(1770–1842)
Great Britain

THE history of modern management is often considered to begin with the work of F. W. Taylor in the United States at the turn of the present century. Records preserved by unusual good fortune, however, show interesting anticipation of scientific management in one or two countries by a century or more. In Great Britain, in particular, it could be claimed that the first illustration of scientific management in action is to be found from 1795 on in the Soho Engineering Foundry, near Birmingham, of Boulton, Watt & Co. It has been shown, further, that this astonishing "early experiment in industrial organization" was the achievement not so much of founders Matthew Boulton and James Watt themselves, pioneers in the development of the steam engine, but rather of their respective sons, Matthew Robinson Boulton and James Watt, Jr.

In the Soho Foundry at that time, the following management techniques

[1] A portrait of Matthew Robinson Boulton is extant at Tew Park, Great Tew, Oxfordshire, the estate which he purchased after retiring from business. The Editor regrets that he was refused facilities for reproducing the portrait in *The Golden Book of Management*.

were being consciously applied—on a small scale but nevertheless no less systematically than in modern concerns today:

Marketing research and forecasting as the basis for the establishment of a new business.
Planned site location with provision for adequate communications by land and water and for possible extension of buildings.
Planned machine layout in terms of work-flow requirements.
Production planning.
Production process standards.
Machine-operating standards.
Standardization of product components.
Elaborate statistical records.
Advanced control records, including cost-accounting procedures that required keeping 22 standard books. It has been claimed that cost and profit for each engine manufactured, and profit and loss for each department, could be calculated.
A workers' training program.
Advanced division of labor.
Work study.
Payment by results based on work study.
Provision for personnel welfare, with a sickness-benefit plan administered by an elected committee of employees.
An executive development program.

The historian of the Soho Foundry has established the facts:

> The great development which Soho made after 1795 is . . . bound up with the names of Mathew Robinson Boulton and James Watt, Jr.; and it is to them that all credit must be ascribed. Combining a thorough education in the gentlemanly pursuits of the time with an early training as practical engineers in all stages of production, they brought to the task of organization an entirely new outlook. . . .[2]

> There is, in fact, nothing in the details of the most progressive factory practice of today that the two sons had not anticipated. Neither Taylor, Ford, nor other modern experts devised anything in the way of plan that cannot be discovered at Soho before 1805; and the Soho system of costing is superior to that employed in very many successful concerns today. This earliest engineering factory, therefore, possessed an organization on the management side which was not excelled even by the technical skill of the craftsmen it produced.[3]

From the little information which has come down to us, it would seem that the natures of the fathers were reproduced in the sons. Matthew Robinson Boulton was a brilliant conversationalist with a wide circle of friends,

[2] Erich Roll, *An Early Experiment in Industrial Organization* (London: Longmans, Green), 1930, p. 165.
[3] Professor J. G. Smith in his Introduction to Roll, *op. cit.*, p. xv.

the "external relations" partner. James Watt, Jr. was the "production" partner, concerned with the smooth running of the foundry and something of a disciplinarian although a liberal landlord and a man of culture. The two men shared a friendship based on sound character and on sincere devotion to their respective fathers. There can be few comparable instances in the history of British industry of so sustained a family relationship in business.

Matthew Robinson Boulton and James Watt, Jr. have a very special place in the early history of management.

SELECTED PUBLICATIONS

The only known writings of Matthew Robinson Boulton and of James Watt, Jr. are letters to their partners and business acquaintances. These are preserved in their original form in the historic Boulton & Watt Collection in the Reference Library of the City of Birmingham.

Watt Jr.'s letters are also quoted in the following publications:

Mathew Murray: A Centenary Appreciation. London: Newcomen Society. Reprinted in *The Engineer,* March 5, 1926; *Matthew Murray: Pioneer Engineer.* Edited by E. K. Scott. Leeds: Edwin Jowett, Ltd., 1928. 132 pp.

Watt, Jr. was the author of the article on James Watt Sr. in the sixth edition of the *Encyclopaedia Britannica* (1823).

Curricula Vitae

Matthew Robinson Boulton		**James Watt, Jr.**	
1770	Born in Midlands.	1769	Born in Glasgow.
1780–1786	Privately tutored by Rev. M. Stretch.		
1786–1788	Studied in Paris.		Studied chemistry, mineralogy, and natural philosophy.
1788	Invited by father to address Lunar Society on events in France.		
1788–1798	Again in Paris.		Studied in Paris and came to sympathize with some of leaders of French Revolution. Left France, however, because of excesses of the Terror. After short stay in Italy, returned to England

1790 Boulton, Jr. and Watt, Jr. appointed to take joint charge of business established some years previously by Watt, Sr. and devoted to manufacture of patented letter-copying press.

1794 Boulton, Watt & Sons formed to manufacture complete assembly for patented steam engine.

1796 Soho Foundry opened with management already in hands of junior partners. Watt, Jr. undertook much of organization and administration; Boulton, Jr. made self responsible for commercial activities.

1800 Boulton, Watt & Co. formed, sons taking complete control. Patents on Watt steam engine expired this year.

1802 Banking firm established: Matthew Robinson Boulton & James Watt & Co., London.

	1803 Contested competitors' patents on grounds of infringement.
1817 Became Squire of the Manor, Great Tew, Oxfordsire.	
	1820 Elected Fellow of Royal Society.

1833 Banking partnership dissolved.

	1840 Retired from active interests in Boulton, Watt & Co. to devote self to estates in Radnor and Brecon.
1842 Died at age 72.	1848 Died at age 79.

Courtesy National Portrait Gallery.

Robert Owen
(1771–1858)
Great Britain

THE name of Robert Owen—social reformer and philanthropist—is known far beyond his own country. Robert Owen—successful industrial executive and pioneer of management—is, however, much less well known. Yet it was in his managerial activities in the textile industry that Owen was most successful in achieving the lifelong aims which he set himself.

He was one of the earliest industrialists to set aside the undiluted technical and financial criteria of success characteristic of the age and to devote himself to management as a profession. To such professional managers as Owen may one day be attributed, by historians of the Industrial Revolution, more influence on the progress of events than that for which they now receive credit.

As a successful manager, Robert Owen was one of several among his contemporaries. The place in which he stands alone in the history of management is as "the pioneer of personnel management." He was virtually unique in his generation, not only in appreciating the immense importance of the human factor in industry, but in doing something to apply this knowledge. During the years 1800–1828 he developed, as manager of a group of textile mills in New Lanark in Scotland, what was then an unprecedented experiment. All through the period of his public activities as a propagandist and agitator for social change on a national and even on an international scale (activities which, however profound their influence on subsequent thought, currently appeared to be failures), this experiment was quietly transforming the actual lives of his New Lanark textile workers.

The transformation was gradual and characterized by two chief stages. In the first, Owen set himself to improve the factory and domestic conditions of his employees. Houses and streets were built. Workers' shops sold necessities at cost price. The minimum working age for children was raised and daily working hours decreased. Meal facilities were provided for the mills. The surroundings in the mills were made more attractive. The paternalism of a just employer shown in this and other respects brought about an improvement in the conduct and well-being of the New Lanark workers which was the wonder of the age.

In the second stage, Owen addressed himself to social reform in the community of which the factory was the center; from "a very wretched society" he created a model community. The New Lanark schools, where his educational reforms were in operation, had many visitors from home and abroad. Evening recreation centers met the problems created by the increased leisure given to the workers; and in this Owen was the forerunner, by a hundred years, of the work of Mary Follett in Boston. The "Village of Co-operation" became the prototype of a new basis of social life and inspired imitators in communities on both sides of the Atlantic.

The claim that Owen was the pioneer of personnel management is not based on an empty attribution of philanthropic principles and practices. The first syllable of "management" is "man." The essentials of personnel management are twofold, and they both found their first clear exemplification in the work of Robert Owen. First, a personnel policy must be considered an integral part of the management of an establishment in the economic sense. "Personnel management must pay." The purely "welfare" outlook on management can neither win wholehearted acceptance by employers in industry nor keep indefinitely the loyalty of employees. Its impact is tinged with charity, as though a factory were a proper place for "slumming." Owen wrote in an essay addressed to "the superintendents of manufactories":

> Many of you have long experienced in your manufacturing operations the advantages of substantial, well-contrived and well-executed machinery. If, then, due care as to the state of your inanimate machines can produce such beneficial results, what may not be expected if you devote equal attention to your vital machines, which are far more wonderfully constructed?

Secondly, the personnel function must not be a subordinate department of management, but must be identified with the purpose of good management itself. In our modern age we have adopted the belief that the workplace is a community and that the satisfactions which a person obtains there are an essential part of the conditions needed for harmonious social living within the democratic ideal. The community which Robert Owen built up around the workplace as the center, the partnership which he established between employer and worker, the justice which he dispensed simultaneously with measures of welfare, entitle him to be called the pioneer of truly modern personnel management.

SELECTED PUBLICATIONS

No summary of Owen's writings can give an adequate picture of the ground which he covered or of the diversity of the channels of which he made use. His first published papers appeared in 1812, and thereafter the literature that he produced mounted steadily to a tremendous volume, much of it repetitive or overlapping. A cross-section of his thought is the following:

1812	*A Statement Regarding the New Lanark Establishment.* Edinburgh.
1813–1814	*A New View of Society.**
1815	*Observations on the Effect of the Manufacturing System*—with hints for the improvement of those parts of it which are most injurious to Health and Morals. Dedicated most respectfully to the British Legislature. London: Hatchard. 20 pages.
1816	*Address to New Lanark*—delivered at the opening of the Institute for the Formation of Character.*
1817	Three addresses on a *Plan to Relieve the Country from its Present Distress.**
1821	*Report to the County of Lanark*—a plan for relieving public distress—by giving permanent productive employment to the poor—which will diminish the expenses of production and consumption and create markets coextensive with production.*

Curriculum Vitae

1771	Born in the little market town of Newton on the Welsh border. Robert Owen's father was a saddler and ironmonger and the local postmaster. He himself was the sixth of seven children.
1778	Employed as usher in the village school.
1781–1784	Apprenticed to a retail draper in Stamford, Lincolnshire.
1784–1787	Held post in a drapery house in London.
1787	Employed in textile mills in Manchester.
1781–1791	Became an employer. With Ernest Jones, set up his first partnership, manufacturing "mule"-type machines. After a few months Owen branched out in an independent spinning enterprise and made a financial success of it.
1791–1795	Managed a large spinning mill in Manchester. During these years he had many offers of partnership from textile manufacturers.
1795–1800	Was a partner in the Chorlton Twist Co., Manchester.

* These works are collected in a volume under the title *A New View of Society,* edited by G. D. H. Cole (London: Everyman, 1927). This volume gives a representative selection of Owen's writings, especially in his early and more constructive years.

1800–1828 Advanced to Managing Director of a group of textile mills in New Lanark, Scotland.
1828–1858 Retired from executive work and devoted the remainder of his life to campaigning in the press, and to public speaking, for acceptance of his projects of social reform.
1858 Died on November 17th at age of 87.

Owen was a gentle, kindly, and courteous man, one whose transparent honesty of purpose and genuine love of the entire human race inspired feelings almost of adoration in all those with whom he came in contact but particularly in children. He was a man of unalterable convictions. He "knew" himself to be right, although he was prepared to devote endless time to reasoning with those who differed from him. If he left them unconvinced, he would still persevere along his own path. If sometimes his friends thought him an autocrat and even a bore, such were his manners and his charm that he retained their respect and their affection.

Courtesy Science Museum, South Kensington, London.

Charles Babbage
(1792–1871)
Great Britain

CHARLES Babbage was not an industrialist or a manager. He was primarily a scientist and a teacher. But in connection with his mathematical studies he developed a "calculating" or "difference" engine and in the course of his work on this device he became very much interested in workshops and factories both in Great Britain and on the continent of Europe. Many of them he visited.

Babbage's studies of these workshops' and factories' methods led him to conclusions as to their problems of management, which in many respects anticipated some of the most important findings of F. W. Taylor in the United States, though Taylor was quite unacquainted with the other man's work. Babbage's own findings were embodied in his book *On the Economy of Machinery and Manufactures* (1832), which had, for those days, a wide circulation in Great Britain (over 10,000 copies) and was also published in the United States.

In particular, Babbage pointed out the possibility of developing general principles based on scientific analysis to govern the conduct of industrial undertakings. In this matter his thought and Taylor's were closely parallel:

CHARLES BABBAGE

Having been induced during the last ten years to visit a considerable num-

F. W. TAYLOR

When men, whose education has given them the habit of generalizing

ber of workshops and factories, both in England and on the Continent, for the purpose of making myself acquainted with the resources of mechanical art, I was insensibly led to apply to them those principles of generalization to which my other pursuits had naturally given rise.—*On the Economy of Machinery and Manufactures,* first edition (London: Charles Knight, 1832).

and everywhere looking for laws, find themselves confronted with a multitude of problems such as exist in every trade, and which have a great similarity one to another, it is inevitable that they should try to gather these problems into logical groups, and then search for some general laws or rules to guide them in their solution.—*The Principles of Scientific Management* (New York: Harper & Bros., 1911) and *Scientific Management* (Harper & Bros., 1947), p. 103.

Other directions in which Babbage anticipated modern management practice were:

- In the analysis of processes and manufacturing costs; e.g., in pin making.
- In the use of time study, on which he quotes with approval the observations of a French colleague, M. Coulomb. This is the first example of international collaboration on a management problem.
- In the use of printed standard information blanks for investigation.
- In the study of the comparative practice of business undertakings in the same field, as in his *A Comparative View of the Various Institutions for the Assurance of Lives* (1826).

Babbage's autobiographical *Passages from the Life of a Philosopher* shows him to have been a wit and a humorist, although fundamentally a man disappointed by the failure to attain full recognition for the fruits of his life work. The *Dictionary of National Biography* has a vivid paragraph in its article on him:

> In his latter years Babbage came before the public chiefly as the implacable foe of organ grinders. He considered that one-fourth of his entire working power had been destroyed by audible nuisances, to which his highly strung nerves rendered him peculiarly sensitive. In the decay of other faculties his interest and memory never failed for the operations of the extensive workshops attached to his house. There what might be called the wreckage of a brilliant and strenuous career lay scattered, and thence, after his death . . . some fragmentary portions of the marvellous engine, destined to have indefinitely quickened the application of science to every department of human life, were collected and removed to the South Kensington Museum.

SELECTED PUBLICATIONS

Books:

1816 Translation of Part I of *An Elementary Treatise on the Differential and Integral Calculus of La Croix.* Cambridge: Printed by J. F. Smith for J. Deighton & Sons. 728 pp.

1826 *A Comparative View of the Various Institutions for the Assurance of Lives.* London: J. Maurman, Ludgate Street. German translation: Weimar, 1827.

1830 *Reflections on the Decline of Science in England and on Some of its Causes.* London: B. Fellowes, Ludgate Street.

1831 *Specimen of Logarithmic Tables* printed with different-coloured inks on variously coloured papers. 21 vols. London. "The object of this work, of which one single copy only was printed, is to ascertain by experiment the tints of the paper and colours of the inks least fatiguing to the eye. One hundred and fifty-one variously coloured papers were chosen and the same two pages of my stereotype Table of Logarithms were printed upon them in inks of the following colours: light blue, dark blue, light green, dark green, olive, yellow, light red, dark red, purple and black. Each of these twenty volumes contains papers of the same colour, numbered in the same order, and there are two volumes printed with the same kind of ink. The twenty-first volume contains metallic printing in gold, silver and copper, upon vellum and on variously coloured papers."

1832 *On the Economy of Machinery and Manufactures.* First edition. 420 pp. London: Charles Knight, Pall Mall East. There were numerous English editions and American reprints and translations into German, French, Italian, Spanish, etc.

1837 *The Ninth Bridgewater Treatise.* London: J. Murray. 266 pp.

1848 *Thoughts on the Principles of Taxation, with Reference to a Property Tax and Its Exceptions.* London: J. Murray. 24 pp. Second edition, 1851; third edition, 1852. Italian translation: Turin, 1851.

1851 *The Exposition of 1851; or, Views of the Industry, the Science and the Government of England.* Second edition. London: J. Murray.

1864 *Passages from the Life of a Philosopher.* London: Longmans Green.

Articles:

Over 70 printed papers, pamphlets, etc., on mathematical, scientific, and philosophic subjects, including:

1822 "The Application of Machinery to the Calculation of Mathematical Tables," *Memoirs* of the Astronomical Society, Vol. I, p. 309.

____ "Observations on the Application of Machinery to the Calculation of Mathematical Tables," *Memoirs* of the Astronomical Society, Vol. I, p. 311.

1826 "On a Method of Expressing by Signs the Action of Machinery," *Transactions* of the Philosophical Society, Vol. II, p. 218.

1829 "Essay on the General Principles Which Regulate the Application of Machinery," *Metropolitan Encyclopaedia.*

Curriculum Vitae

1792	Born on December 26th in Teignmouth, Devonshire, the son of a banker. Babbage suffered from ill health as a child and was educated at private schools in Alpington (near Exeter) and Enfield.
1811	Student at Trinity College, Cambridge.
1812	A founder of the Analytical Society, which gave the impulse to a mathematical revival in England at that time.
1814	Received B.A. from Peterhouse, Cambridge (M.A. in 1817).
1815–1827	Lived in London, devoting himself to scientific activities.
1827–1828	Traveled in continental Europe, studying foreign workshops and factories.
1828–1839	Was Lucasian Professor of Mathematics (holding the chair of Isaac Newton) at Cambridge.
1832 and 1834	Stood unsuccessfully for Parliament on liberal principles.
1871	Died on October 18th at age of 79.

Babbage was a Fellow of the Royal Society at the age of 24; Gold Medalist of the Astronomical Society; prominent in the foundation of the British Association and the Statistical Society; and a member of scientific bodies in all parts of the world, including the Paris Academy of Moral Sciences and the Royal Irish and American academies.

Courtesy Solvay et Cie.

Ernest Solvay
(1838–1922)
Belgium

ERNEST Solvay was a great Belgian industrialist. Starting from modest origins, he built up a fortune and a business with worldwide connections for the manufacture of alkalis based on a new and economical process which he himself had brought to perfection. Solvay was a man who could perceive the broad trends in the industrial development of his day. He was a leader in progressive management in his own numerous factories, instituting the eight-hour day (1907), holidays with double pay (1913), and other liberal measures of personnel policy such as a profit-sharing scheme and medical and social assistance for employees. His great personal fortune was used to endow a series of foundations which, in Belgium, established the Institute of Social Sciences and of Sociology, strengthened the Workers' Educational Institute, and also created several institutes in the domain of the physical sciences.

Solvay was a pioneer of "productivity." Between 1947 and 1954 this word became, in Europe generally, the current popular synonym for "management." The European Productivity Agency was established in 1953 as part of the machinery for realizing the Marshall Plan, and many Western European countries set up "productivity centers." Managers and workers alike were exhorted by those controlling their political destinies to become more "productivity-minded."

Compatriots of Ernest Solvay must have learned of the "new religion" with a certain reserve, for in his writings of half a century before is to be found an astonishingly modern exposition of the need for productivity. He said that the improvement of human well-being depends on the achievement of an ever greater volume of goods and services produced along with a decrease in the effort required. This, he stated, can be made possible by the progressive installation of more and better machinery. It is to the interest of the worker equally with that of the manager to adopt the "productivist" state of mind.

If the need for productivity is universally accepted today, it was not so clearly apparent at the time Solvay enunciated his theories. They were in many respects original. Economists had for many years stressed the importance of *production* in the total well-being of a nation. The ideal of *productivity*, or more production for the same effort, was being developed by F. W. Taylor in America in terms of a single industrial unit. But from Solvay came the idea of productivity in terms of a nation as a whole, and in this he was certainly a pioneer of later thought.

When Solvay went on to use his productivist theories as the basis for a far-reaching plan of social reform, where the state would own shares in every factory and would regulate each man's fortune in terms of his productivity, he failed to win general support. Modern productivity theories differ from the productivism he advanced in restricting themselves to the economic sphere and in propounding no general solutions for political and social problems. Solvay's essential contribution, however, remains an interesting one; and it may be noted that the country of which he was a citizen is among the most highly productive in the world.

It is interesting to quote here from one of the last public addresses given by Henry Le Chatelier at a great scientific congress at the Sorbonne in 1935. Having reviewed the most recent advances in science and technology, he concluded:

> That is the past; we must now think of the future. I have always cherished the memory of a conversation I once had with the great Belgian engineer Solvay. "Today," he said to me, "science and technology have reached their peak; in this field there is nothing more to be looked for. The young engineers who follow us should have other and quite different preoccupations. Their duty is to study the human factor of which we know virtually nothing. Yet it is of capital importance in industry and will become continually more and more so." He did not wish to suggest, you will understand, that there will be no further technical progress, but merely that such progress would be achieved by methods already established. On the other hand, in dealing with the moral and social problems of industry, we have no method, we have not yet developed an established procedure, we do not know how to direct our enquiries. In this field, too, we should apply scientific method. But the problem is a complex one. . . . In short, the study of

the many different aspects of the human factor in industry demands special methods.

Though Ernest Solvay gained the fruits of worldly success, he remained an idealist for whom money making was incidental to the search for near-perfection in every activity, whether it was the processing of the materials of industry or the solution of the problems of society.

SELECTED PUBLICATIONS

1897 "Etude sur le progrès économique et la morale sociale," *Annales* de l'Institut des Sciences Sociales (Brussels), Vol. III, pp. 401–415.

1898 "Le productivisme social," *Annales* de l'Institut des Sciences Sociales (Brussels), Vol. IV, pp. 411–437.

1900 *Etudes sociales. Notes sur le productivisme et le comptabilisme.* Brussels: Lamertin. 172 pages.

1901 *Lettres relatives à la fondation de l'Institut de Sociologie.* Adressées le 12 février 1901 à MM. les Bourgmestre et Echevins de la ville de Bruxelles et à M. Charles Graux, Administrateur-Inspecteur de l'Université Libre de Bruxelles.

1910 *Industrie et science (biogénie et sociologie).* Discours prononcé à l'occasion du XXV anniversaire de la Société Belge des Ingénieurs et Industriels, le 30 octobre 1910.

—— *Questions d'energétique sociale.* Notes et publications de M. Ernest Solvay (1894–1910). Brussels: Institut de Sociologie Solvay. 229 pp.

Curriculum Vitae

1838 Born on April 16th at Rebecq, Brabant. Educated at the College of Malonne. Illness prevented Solvay from pursuing regular studies, and he was largely self-educated. He began his career in a technical post at a gas plant in Brussels. While still holding this post, he carried on the research which led to his development of the ammonia process for alkali manufacture.

1865 Founded Solvay & Cie. After a difficult initial period this family business gradually attained a position of international standing in the manufacture of alkalis by the Solvay process.

1892–1900 Served as Senator in the Belgian Parliament.

1893–1913 Founded and endowed in Belgium the Institute of Physiology, the Institute of Social Sciences, the School of Sociology, and the School of Commerce. Made large donations to the Workers' Educational Institute. Also founded the International Physical Institute and the International Chemical Institute.

1914	On outbreak of World War I, created the Comité National de Secours et d'Alimentation.
1918	Honored by King Albert of the Belgians, who, on the day of his return to Brussels, paid tribute to Solvay as the creator of the Comité National.
1922	Died on May 26th, aged 84, at Ixelles.

Ernest Solvay held the Liebnitz Medal for Distinction in Science.

Oberlin Smith
(1840–1926)
United States

WITH Oberlin Smith, the scene changes to the United States, to the germs of thought that were to bear fruit in the great contributions to management in that country. These fruits appeared first in the work of F. W. Taylor. One of Taylor's acknowledged precursors was, however, Oberlin Smith, whose original contribution to management was his system of mnemonic symbols for machine parts.

Oberlin Smith was the successful founder, and President for 63 years, of the Ferracute Machine Co., which manufactured dies and presses; and it was in this, his own company, that his system of order numbers was first applied. An engineer and inventor of note, he was one of the original members of The American Society of Mechanical Engineers. A number of the papers which he contributed to ASME in the 1800s had a management angle. Many of them were original in their presentation and in the force and humor with which he advanced his views. He was the ninth president of the Society (1890). As an engineer who was also an employer and a man of wide intellectual interests, he shared with H. R. Towne the credit for insisting that the scope of engineering was much wider than a narrow professional and purely technical view of the subject would suggest. Between them they prepared the Society to offer the nascent study of management that platform and that support which have been of such inestimable value in the development of the American business tradition.

F. W. Taylor based his own system of symbols for machine parts chiefly on the system devised by Smith. In *Shop Management* (1903) Taylor stated:

> Among the many improvements for which the originators will probably never receive the credit which they deserve the following may be mentioned. . . . The mnemonic system of order numbers invented by Mr. Oberlin Smith. . . .[1]

Oberlin Smith's paper entitled "Nomenclature of Machine Details" was presented at the second regular meeting of The American Society of Mechanical Engineers (1881). The requisites for a good system of names and symbols, he said, were these:

1. *Isolation* of each from all the others that did, do, or may exist in the same establishment.
2. *Suggestiveness* of what machine, what part of it, and if possible, the use of the said part—conforming, of course, to established conventional names, as far as practicable.
3. *Brevity,* combined with simplicity.[2]

The principles here set out (and by "suggestiveness" Smith meant "mnemonic") had considerable influence on all the later systems devised to meet the problem of nomenclature.

Taylor also credited to Oberlin Smith the basis of his routing scheme. Smith had made detailed drawings about 1875–1876 for his Bridgeton works. These contained the essential elements of classification, symbolizing, and routing and described the operations and suboperations to be performed in readying each piece and in assembling the machines to which the pieces belonged. The system then developed was not applied in full only because the work at the time involved little repetition of processes.

Smith's paper on order numbers established one of the earliest international links in management. In 1889 Emile Garcke and J. M. Fells published their *Factor Accounts,* one of the earliest management books to appear in Great Britain. In it they reprinted Oberlin Smith's paper in full. The paper was reprinted also in a number of American publications, notably C. Bertrand Thompson's *Scientific Management* (1914).

An outstanding characteristic of Oberlin Smith that may perhaps be singled out is the vivacity with which he pursued his many intellectual interests. He was particularly given to astronomical discussions. Mrs. Smith tells of bringing such a debate, which Mr. Smith was enjoying with a house guest, to an end at one o'clock on a Sunday morning. To her surprise and amusement, she heard the resumption of the heated discussion at six-thirty the same morning. Mr. Smith had got into bed with his guest, and the two were hard at it once more![3]

[1] *Shop Management* (New York: Harper & Bros., 1911), p. 201.

[2] "Nomenclature of Machine Details," ASME *Transactions,* 1881, Vol. 2, pp. 358–369.

[3] Anecdote from obituary in ASME *Journal.*

SELECTED PUBLICATIONS

Articles:

1881 "Experimental Mechanics," ASME *Transactions,* Vol. 2, pp. 55–69.

—— "Nomenclature of Machine Details," ASME *Transactions,* Vol. 2, pp. 358–369. Reproduced in *Scientific Management* by C. B. Thompson (Cambridge, Mass.: Harvard University, 1914).

1882 "The Systematic Preservation of Drawings," ASME *Transactions.*

1886 "Inventory Valuation of Machinery Plant," ASME *Transactions,* Vol. 7, pp. 433–439.

1887 "Intrinsic Value of Special Tools," ASME *Transactions,* Vol. 8, pp. 258–268.

1890 "The Graphical Analysis of Reciprocating Motions," ASME *Transactions,* Vol. 11, pp. 260–270.

1900 "Modern Machine Shop Economies," *Cassier's Magazine,* Vol. 27, pp. 295–299.

1911 "Impressions Regarding Foreign Shop Methods," *Iron Trade Review,* Vol. 48, pp. 826–828.

—— "Naming and Symbolizing," ASME *Transactions.*

Curriculum Vitae

1840 Born on March 22nd in Cincinnati, Ohio. Attended the public schools. During vacations Smith worked on farms and also learned carpentry. He continued at the West Jersey Academy and received his technical training at the Philadelphia Polytechnic Institute.

1863–1926 Was founder-president of a concern established in Bridgeton, N.J., for the manufacture of improved dies and presses which he had invented.

1877 Incorporated the business as the Ferracute Machine Co. It has for many years taken a leading part in the commercial development of the die-working of metals.

1901 Served as N.J. Commissioner to Pan-American Exposition in Buffalo.

1926 Died on July 19th, aged 86, in Bridgeton.

Courtesy R. Greenwood.

Henri Fayol
(1841–1925)
France

HENRI Fayol was the most distinguished figure contributed by Europe to the management movement up to the end of the first half of the present century. His deep scientific training and interest, both as engineer and as geologist, were brought to bear on 30 years of practical experience as chief executive of a great French mining and metallurgical combine—Commentry-Fourchambault-Decazeville ("Comambault"). When he took charge, this undertaking was on the verge of bankruptcy. When he retired, its financial position was impregnable, it had made a contribution of the greatest value to the national effort in the First World War, and it had an administrative, technical, and scientific staff famous throughout France.

Fayol always maintained that his amazing practical success was due, not primarily to personal qualities (though it is clear from the testimony of his contemporaries and the high honor in which he was held that he possessed these in abundance), but to the application of certain simple principles which could be taught and learned. These constituted his "theory of administration." This isolation and analysis of administration as a separate function was his unique and original addition to the body of management theory. It paved the way for the evolution of the whole modern approach to problems of higher management by way of functional analysis. It exercised and still continues to exercise a profound influence on all efforts to clarify and to organize thinking as to the qualities required for, the nature of, and the correct analysis of top management. It was and is supported and sustained by the great prestige both of Fayol's scientific work and of his achievements as a practical administrator.

After his retirement at the age of 77, in 1918, Fayol devoted the remaining seven years of his life to spreading an understanding of his theory and pointing out its application to fields other than business—military, naval, and governmental. For he maintained strongly that any theory of administration which is valid cannot be limited to business. It must be equally applicable to all forms of organized human cooperation.

While at first inclined to be unsympathetic about F. W. Taylor's work, Fayol quickly perceived that it was essentially complementary to his own field of study. Taylor had merely started at one end of the industrial hierarchy, the lathe worker at his bench, while Fayol himself had started at the other, the chief executive at his desk. Both were applying the same scientific principles. At the opening of the Second International Management Congress at Brussels in 1925, Fayol declared publicly how false he found the views of those who tried to discover conflict between his principles of administration and Taylor's.

This speech opened the way for Fayol's two eminent compatriots, Henry Le Chatelier and Charles de Fréminville, to propose a unification between the Centre d'Etudes Administratives, which he had founded, and the Conference de l'Organisation Française, which they had established to introduce Taylor's ideas to France. The two bodies were accordingly united in the Comité National de l'Organisation Française. The rapidity and friendliness with which this unification of effort took place were in themselves an instance of intellectual integrity and generosity, taking priority over possible organizational rivalry, which should long remain an example to the management movement.

With the foundation in 1925 of CNOF, France became the first country in the world to have an institution equipped, both by the intentions of its founders and by the work already done, to promote the study and application of scientific methods to business and other institutions *regarded as a whole.*

Someone who met Fayol in the last year of his life has described him as "still young—upright, smiling, with a penetrating and direct glance. M. Fayol meets you as a friend. His natural air of authority, his kindness, his youthfulness of spirit, which makes him interested in everything, enabling him to be a past master in the art of being a grandfather (and even a great-grandfather), are both impressive and, at the same time, most attractive."

SELECTED PUBLICATIONS

Books:

1916 "Administration industrielle et générale—prévoyance, organisation, commandement, coordination, contrôle," *Bulletin* de la Société de l'Industrie Minérale. Republished in book form (Paris: Dunod, 1925).

First English translation, *General and Industrial Administration*, by J. A. Conbrough (Geneva: International Management Institute, 1929). Second English translation, *General and Industrial Management*, by Constance Storrs (London: Pitman, 1949), with a foreword by L. Urwick.

1921 "L'Incapacité administrative de l'état—les postes et télégraphes," *Revue politique et parlementaire*, March. Republished in book form (Paris: Dunod, 1921).

1927 *L'Eveil de l'esprit public*. Paris: Dunod. A volume edited by Fayol but published after his death. It contains: "Importance de la fonction administrative dans le gouvernement des affaires"; "L'Enseignement de l'administration dans les écoles techniques supérieures"; "La Réforme administrative des services publics" (see below); and "L'Administration positive dans l'industrie," a short paper by Fayol published in *Technique moderne*, February 1918.

Articles:

1900 Paper on "Administration" presented to the Congrès des Mines et de la Métallurgie.

1908 Discourse on the "General Principles of Administration" presented to the Jubilee Congress of the Société de l'Industrie Minérale.

1917 "L'Enseignement de l'administration dans les écoles techniques supérieures," *Bulletin* de la Société des Ingénieurs Civils de France.

1918 "Importance de la fonction administrative dans le gouvernement des affaires," *Bulletin* de la Société d'Encouragement pour l'Industrie Nationale.

—— "La Réforme administrative des services publics," *Revue du commerce et de l'industrie*.

1919 "L'Industrialisation de l'état," *Bulletin* of the Société de l'Industrie Minérale.

1921 "La Réforme administrative des postes et télégraphes." Pamphlet.

1923 "La Doctrine administrative dans l'état," presented to Second International Congress of Administrative Science, Brussels, 1923. English translation, "The Administrative Theory in the State," by Sarah Greer, in *Papers on the Science of Administration*, edited by Luther Gulick and L. Urwick. New York: Columbia University Press, 1937.

Curriculum Vitae

1841 Born in France, probably at or near Lyons.

1856–1858 Attended the lycée at Lyons.

1858–1860 Attended the School of Mines, St. Etienne.

1860 Appointed Engineer of the Commentry pits of the S.A. Commentry-Fourchambault.

1866 Appointed Manager of the Commentry pits.

1872	Appointed General Manager of the Commentry, Montircq, and Berry group of mines.
1888	Appointed Managing Director of Commentry-Fourchambault.
1891	Purchased the Bressac mines for Comambault.
1892	Absorbed the mines and works of Decazeville.
1900	Purchased the Joudreville mines in the Eastern French coalfield.
1918	Retired as Chief Executive of Comambault but remained a director.
1925	Honored at dinner given in Paris by Old Students Association of the School of Mines, St. Etienne, to celebrate the 65th anniversary of graduation. Died at the age of 84.

Henri Fayol was awarded the Delesse Prize of the Academy of Sciences, the Gold Medal of the Société d'Encouragement pour l'Industrie Nationale, and the Gold Medal and the Medal of Honor of the Société de l'Industrie Minérale. He was appointed chevalier of the Legion of Honor in 1888, officier in 1913, and commander of the Order of the Crown of Rumania in 1925.

Courtesy The National Cyclopaedia of American Biography.

Henry Robinson Towne
(1844–1924)
United States

THE most significant contribution to management of Henry Robinson Towne, President of the Yale & Towne Manufacturing Co., was the leading part which he played in persuading his fellow engineers to extend the traditional scope of their professional interest to include management subjects. In 1886, at the time of his famous paper to The American Society of Mechanical Engineers—"The Engineer as an Economist"[1]—such a concept was revolutionary. Not until 1907 did the Society recognize the subject of management engineering, and up to 1915 a large and influential section of the membership continued vehemently to deny that there could be a science of management or, if there could, that it was any concern of an engineering society.

Towne's paper of 1886 was essentially a plea for the recognition and development of such a science. He said:

> The matter of shop management is of equal importance with that of engineering. . . . The management of works is unorganized, is almost without literature, has no organ or medium for the interchange of experience, and is without association or organization of any kind. . . . The remedy must not be looked for from those who are "business men" or clerks or accountants only; it should come from those whose

[1] ASME *Transactions*, Vol. 7, pp. 428–432.

training and experience has given them an understanding of both sides (the mechanical and the clerical) of the important questions involved. *It should originate from engineers!*

As President of ASME in 1889–1890 and as a leading member of its councils around this period, Towne's influence was constantly exercised to provide through the Society a platform and a professional environment where those interested in management could meet and encourage one another. This influence, along with Towne's strong support for the work of F. W. Taylor, were crucial in the growth of interest in management within the Society.

Towne was also a pioneer in the elaboration of an important management technique. In 1889 he presented to ASME the results of the "gainsharing" system operating in his own works.[2] This was a modified form of profit sharing on a group basis, the gains being awarded to departments on the basis of relative efficiency. An attempt at improvement on the traditional piece-rate system, it was the first of a number of pioneering experiments in wage-payment schemes, in the United States and elsewhere, as a means of stimulating output. Though Towne's scheme was soon to be superseded by Taylor's more scientific system, it did much to encourage other experiments, not least those of Taylor.

Almost to a unique degree, Towne combined technical engineering ability with executive capacity and economic vision. He became President of the Yale & Towne Manufacturing Co. at the age of 24. From then until his retirement the company *was* Henry R. Towne. As a great executive, he naturally possessed the art of surrounding himself with able associates. But he himself was always the leader, the moving spirit of that famous organization. A man of wide culture, he never appeared to better advantage than as leader of the American engineering delegation to England and France in 1889. In France, for example, he displayed a command of the language to be fully appreciated only by those who recall Towne's graceful and fluent response in French to the welcome extended at the reception tendered by M. Gustave Eiffel, as president of the Société des Ingénieurs Civils de France, upon the occasion of the luncheon given on the platform of the great tower on the Champ de Mars.

SELECTED PUBLICATIONS

1886 "The Engineer as an Economist," ASME *Transactions*, Vol. 7, pp. 428–432.

1889 "Gainsharing," ASME *Transactions*, Vol. 10, pp. 600–626.

1906 "Our Present Weights and Measures and the Metric System," ASME *Transactions*, Vol. 28, pp. 845–925.

1912 "Axioms Concerning Manufacturing Costs," ASME *Transactions*, Vol. 34, pp. 1111–1129.

[2] ASME *Transactions*, Vol. 10, pp. 600–626.

—— "General Principles of Organization Applied to an Individual Manufacturing Establishment," *Transactions* of the Efficiency Society, Vol. 1, pp. 77–83.

1915 "Frederick Winslow Taylor: A Sketch of His Life," *Engineering Magazine*, Vol. 49, pp. 161–163.

1916 "Tribute to F. W. Taylor at Annual Meeting," ASME *Journal*, Vol. 38, pp. 53–54.

Curriculum Vitae

1844 Born on August 28th in Philadelphia. Towne's father, a respected citizen of Philadelphia, was connected with several machinery-manufacturing industries. The son was educated at private schools and the University of Pennsylvania; he also completed a course at the Sorbonne in Paris.

1861–1865 Gained practical shop training in the Port Richmond Iron Works, in both the shop and the drafting rooms, leading to work (in charge of erection of machinery) in the navy yards of Boston, Portsmouth, and Philadelphia.

1866–1867 Studied engineering in Europe, accompanying a notable American engineer, Robert Briggs. One of the fruits of that association was an important investigation into the transmission of power by belting. The results appeared in a paper by Briggs and Towne in the Journal of the Franklin Institute (1868).

1867–1868 Employed as engineer with William Sellers & Co., Philadelphia.

1868 Had contacts with Linus Yale, Jr. leading to formation of the Yale Lock Co., which in 1883 became the Yale & Towne Manufacturing Co., Stamford, Conn. The sudden death of Yale in 1868, at the outset of the new enterprise, put Towne in sole control. He remained President until 1916, after which he was Chairman of the Board.

1882 Joined The American Society of Mechanical Engineers, founded two years previously. In 1884–1886 he was Vice-President; in 1889, President.

1889 Led delegation of the four American engineering societies to the Paris Universal Exposition.

1905 Had Taylor system initiated into Yale & Towne Manufacturing Co. under supervision of Carl Barth.

1924 Died on October 15th at age of 80.

Towne found time to take part in widely diverse activities. He was a president of the Merchants Association of New York; a president of the Morris Plan Co. of New York; and a director of the Federal Reserve Bank of New York, the Industrial Finance Corp., the American Dredging Co., and the Lincoln Safe Deposit Co. He was also Treasurer of the National Tariff Commission Association. He was made an honorary member of The American Society of Mechanical Engineers in 1921.

Courtesy The National
Cyclopaedia of American Biography.

Captain Henry Metcalfe
(1847–1917)
United States

IN the concluding paragraphs of his *Shop Management* (1903), F. W. Taylor wrote:

> Unfortunately there is no school of management. There is no single establishment where a relatively large part of the details of management can be seen, which represent the best of their kinds. The finest developments are for the most part isolated, and in many cases almost buried with the mass of rubbish which surrounds them. Among the many improvements for which the originators will probably never receive the credit which they deserve . . . may be mentioned . . . the card system of shop returns invented and introduced as a complete system by Captain Henry Metcalfe, U.S.A., in the government shops of the Frankford Arsenal. [This] represents . . . a distinct advance in the art of management. The writer appreciates the difficulty of this undertaking as he was at the time engaged in the slow evolution of a similar system in the Midvale Steel Works which, however, was the result of a gradual development instead of a complete, well thought out invention as was that of Captain Metcalfe.[1]

[1] *Shop Management* (New York: Harper & Bros., 1911), p. 202.

Metcalfe's book, *The Cost of Manufactures and the Administration of Workshops, Public and Private* (1885), recorded, in fact, the first example of a complete system of shop returns based on the unit principle—"The independence of a representative unit of record is the basis of the system I propose." That the author's general attitude corresponded with that subsequently propounded by F. W. Taylor appears in the following sentences from the Metcalfe book.[2]

> It may be stated as a general principle that while Art seeks to produce certain effects, Science is principally concerned with investigating the causes of those effects. Thus, independently of the intrinsic importance of the art selected for illustration, there always seems room for a corresponding science, collecting and classifying the records of the past so that the future operations of the art may be more effective. The administration of arsenals and other workshops is in great measure an art, and depends upon the application to a great variety of cases of certain principles which, taken together, make up what may be called the science of administration.

These sentences combine with the early date of his experiments (before 1885) to entitle Captain Metcalfe to a place among the pioneers of management.

Captain Metcalfe has been described by his contemporaries as "an able executive with a mind of his own, loyal, sincere, and with an all-encompassing desire for thoroughness. He was intuitive and had a keen sense of humor."

PUBLICATIONS

Book:

1885 *The Cost of Manufactures and the Administration of Workshops, Public and Private*. New York: Wiley & Sons.

Article:

1886 "The Shop Order System of Accounts," ASME *Transactions*, Vol. 7, pp. 440–488.

Curriculum Vitae

1847 Born in New York City on October 29th.

1868 Graduated from U.S. Military Academy at West Point and assigned to the Army Ordnance Department.

1873 Served as Recorder of the Small-Arms Board, which adopted the Springfield breech-loading rifle. Patented his cartridge block or detachable magazine. This was made of wood and was

[2] In his book Metcalfe also reproduced in full (pp. 110–118) Oberlin Smith's paper of 1881: "Nomenclature of Machine Details." See profile of Smith in Part One.

subsequently replaced by a metal clip, but was the origin of the principle of magazine loading. It was used in the Russo-Turkish War under the name Metkafomba.

1876 Superintended the erection of the U.S. government building at the Centennial Exhibition. Appointed Director of Inspection of small arms and ammunition made in New England for Turkey in the Russo-Turkish War.

1876–1893 Served as Superintendent successively of the Frankford Arsenal, the Benicia Arsenal, and the Watervliet Arsenal and as Instructor in Ordnance and Gunnery at West Point.

1893 Retired at age of 46 to Cold Spring on the Hudson, where he occupied himself with public affairs, becoming head of the Water Commission and President of the School Board.

1917 Died on August 17th, aged 70, at Cooperstown, N.Y.

Captain Metcalfe was awarded the Order of the Osmanic by the Turkish government.

Henry-Louis Le Chatelier
(1850–1936)
France

ALTHOUGH Henry Le Chatelier ranks as a pioneer of scientific management, he was not an industrialist nor was he in any way directly connected with industry. His distinguished career was primarily in industrial chemistry and metallurgy, a field in which he came to hold a worldwide reputation.

Le Chatelier's particular importance for scientific management is that he devoted the whole influence of his great scientific reputation to introducing the teachings of F. W. Taylor into France and French-speaking Europe. Though he was close on 50 years old when he first came into contact with Taylor's work, he immediately appreciated its significance. He soon became Taylor's friend. In 1904 he had founded the famous *Revue de métallurgie*, and in this journal in 1909 he began to publish extracts from Taylor's work and to teach how its principles could be applied to industry. This forceful and persistent elucidation secured widespread acceptance of Taylor's philosophy and methods and did much to prevent the misapplication which handicapped their introduction in other countries.

In 1920 Le Chatelier formed the French Conference on Scientific Management (Conférence de l'Organisation Française). A successful first French Management Congress was held in Paris in 1923. In 1926 the Conference was united with Fayol's Centre d'Etudes Administratives to form the Comité National de l'Organisation Française, which has remained ever since the chief management organization in France.

When Le Chatelier summarized his views concerning scientific management, he concluded that "the Taylor system is nothing else but the application of the principles of organization and the scientific method to tasks of every description." He firmly believed that there was no dividing line between pure and applied science; to him the scholarly approach was the only sound method of attack to be employed in the solution of new problems. Upon thousands of his students he impressed the validity of this credo, and sent them out, year after year, into the laboratories and the industrial world, fortified with knowledge that was to prove an inestimable asset in the work they were called upon to do."[1]

In the closing years of his life this great scientist became more and more preoccupied with the human and moral problems posed by a mechanized economy. His last public utterance was devoted to the effects of technological advance on the moral fabric of our society. It has been said of him that "his scientific and moral integrity were absolute; he was as modest in character as he was eminent in capacity, as disinterested in personal advantage as he was prodigal in invention, a man whose moral qualities do him even more honour than his intellectual gifts."[2]

SELECTED PUBLICATIONS

Books:

Le Chatelier's published work in the physical sciences was voluminous; much of it is in the *Revue de métallurgie,* which he founded in 1904. Of his 11 books, only 3 were concerned with aspects of management:

1925 *Science and Industry.* Paris: Library of Scientific Philosophy, Ed. Flammarion.

1934 *Taylorism.* Paris: Dunod.

1936 *Method in the Experimental Sciences.* Paris: Dunod. In effect, a new edition of *Science and Industry,* but with the examples drawn from the author's own work considerably changed.

Articles:

The bibliography of articles, lectures, and so on printed in the memorial volume *Henry Le Chatelier* covers 15 pages. Those on management subjects of special interest are:

1915 "The Principles of Organization," *Nature,* December 4th, p. 359 et seq.

—— Preface to French translation of *Scientific Management in the Home,* by Christine Frederick. *Revue de métallurgie* XII, pp. 348–350. Repub-

[1] Harry Arthur Hopf, *The Scholar in Management* (Ossining, N.Y.: Hopf Institute of Management, 1940), p. 36.

[2] M. L. Guillet in the memorial volume *Henry le Chatelier.*

lished in 1918 as a brochure with a preface and a conclusion. Paris: Dunod.

1919 "Our Enquiry into the Taylor System (Replies)," *Information ouvrière et sociale*, Vol. II, No. 57.

1920 "Advice to Students of the National Colleges Wishing to Familiarize Themselves with the Methods of Scientific Management in Industry." Paris: Société des Amis de l'Ecole Polytechnique. 15 pp.

1926 "Common Sense in Management," *Revue économique internationale* (Brussels), June.

1928 "The Development of Leaders," *Bulletin* de la Société Industrielle de Mulhouse, pp. 214–236.

1930 "Science—the Third Quality of the Executive." Lecture on the Tenth Anniversary of *X-Information*, March 25th. Paris: Association des Anciens Elèves de l'Ecole Polytechnique.

—— "Rationalization and the Economic Crisis," *Mon bureau*. Republished as a pamphlet entitled "Rationalization and Unemployment." Paris: Librairie Française de Documentation Commerciale et Industrielle. 47 pp.

—— "Industry, Science, and Organization in the Twentieth Century." Three lectures given at the Ecole Sociale d'Action Familiale de Moulin-Vert. Paris: Dunod. 88 pp.

1931 "The Problem of Industrial Employment," *Mon bureau*, September.

1934 "The Forty-Hour Week," *X-Information* (Association des Anciens Elèves de l'Ecole Polytechnique, Paris), June 25th.

Curriculum Vitae

1850 Born on October 8th. Le Chatelier's father was one of the early builders of the French railway system. The son was educated at the Collège Rollin, the Ecole Polytechnique, and the Ecole des Mines, Paris.

1878 Appointed to the Chair of General Chemistry at the Ecole des Mines.

1888 Was Professor of Mineral Chemistry, Collège de France.

1897–1907 Was Professor of General Chemistry, Collège de France.

1907 Appointed Inspector-General of Mines.

1907–1925 Was Professor of General Chemistry at the Sorbonne.

1914–1918 Commissioned by the Minister of Armaments to work in armaments-producing factories.

1924 Presided over the Second French Management Congress, and led the French delegation to the First International Management Congress at Prague in the same year.

1936 Died at age of 86. In the following year a memorial conference held in his honor was presided over by the President of the French Republic.

Le Chatelier was awarded the Gold Medal of the International Committee for Scientific Management at the Fourth International Congress held in Paris in 1929. He was an honorary member of the Comité National de l'Organisation Française, the Taylor Society (now the Society for the Advancement of Management), and The American Society of Mechanical Engineers; a member of the French Academy of Sciences; President of the Mineralogical Society, the Society for Encouragement of National Industry, and the Society of Physics; honorary president of the 1935 International Congress of Mining, Metallurgy, and Applied Geology; a foreign member of the Netherlands Society of Sciences and the Berlin Academy of Sciences; and a commander of the Legion of Honor. He was awarded the Prix Jerome Ponti (1892) and the Prix La Caze of the Academy of Sciences (1895).

James Rowan
(1851–1906)
Great Britain

ONE of the problems facing the historian of management is the comparatively minor part played by the representatives of British industry in the development of management thought at the beginning of the twentieth century. As the first of the industrialized countries, Great Britain supplied a number of the people who traced the first outlines of the philosophy subsequently developed by Taylor, Gantt, and the Gilbreths. Charles Babbage, Boulton and Watt, and Robert Owen all contributed important elements to the total picture. But, from 1900 till after the close of the First World War, Great Britain added little to the general interest in the subject which had been developing rapidly in the United States of America. Even at the latter date her original contributions were to the fields of industrial psychology and labor management rather than industrial management in general.

James Rowan was, however, an exception. Partner in a business of marine-engine manufacturers in Glasgow, Scotland, he made himself fully informed on developments in management in other parts of Great Britain and in America. One of the elements out of which scientific management was built up was the increasing interest, partly the result of disillusionment with some earlier experiments in profit sharing, displayed by practical engineers in incentives. Examples of this interest in the United States were H. R. Towne's "Gainsharing" (1889), F. A. Halsey's "The Premium Plan of Paying for Labor" (1891), F. W. Taylor's "A Piece-Rate System" (1895), and H. L.

Gantt's "A Bonus System of Rewarding Labor" (1902), all papers read to The American Society of Mechanical Engineers.

Rowan considered all these systems, but did not find them "suitable for the purposes of marine-engine manufacture." In a 1901 paper entitled "A Premium System of Remunerating Labor," he referred to "Mr. Fred W. Taylor's Paper on the Premium System, published in *Cassier's Magazine* of October 1897," and to "the objections to the ordinary piece-work system which were so well expressed by Mr. Slater Lewis in the *Engineering Magazine*."[1] He was impressed by the tendency of workers on piece rates to fix an arbitrary standard of output beyond which they would not put forward further effort for fear of rate cutting.

Rowan's own scheme, applied in his own works in 1898, was simple. It consisted of a fixed time allowance on each job at an hourly rate for that job. A job-data book was built up from which future hourly rates could be determined. The premium paid to the worker was calculated by adding to the hourly wage the same percentage as that by which he had reduced the time allowed for the job. This scheme worked well in practice. In Rowan's own works the original standard times were improved on by an average of 20 percent in the first year to 37 percent in the fourth year. The scheme is still being used in Glasgow at the present day, and has been applied with beneficial effects in many other engineering works in Great Britain.

An incentive scheme, especially when unsupported by time study and methods analysis, is only a fragment of scientific management as a whole, and its results can represent only a fraction of the problem facing every manager. Rowan himself realized this, and his interest in management went much further. It may be ascribed to his influence that at the International Engineering Congress in Glasgow, in 1901, papers on management subjects by British authors were for the first time presented at a function organized by the Institution of Mechanical Engineers. The three papers were:

"A Premium System of Remunerating Labor," by Rowan himself.

"Some Factors Affecting the Economical Manufacture of Marine Engines," by William Thomson.

"Workshop Methods: Some Efficiency Factors in an Engineering Business," by William Weir and J. R. Richmond.

James Rowan was a man of a genial and generous nature, popular with friends and fellow employers. He was known for his immense energy and enthusiasm in putting his new schemes into operation.

There is no doubt that his work gave a great stimulus to the use of the premium bonus in British engineering works. In 1902 *The Engineer* published a series of articles, reprinted in pamphlet form and running into several subsequent editions, supporting this method of remuneration. In the same year a national agreement regulating its application was signed at Carlisle by the Engineering Employers Federation and the Amalgamated Society of

[1] Vol. 18, 1899–1900, p. 203.

Engineers. And in 1903 a publisher thought it worthwhile to issue bonus tables for calculating wages on the bonus or premium system.[2]

It is equally clear that what attracted many employers about Rowan's plan was its avoidance of an awkward issue with labor over rate setting. Rowan's scheme was a memorable precedent which was to be followed by a reaction in Great Britain toward a more narrowly technical view of the functions of the engineer. It was to be a quarter of a century before the Institution of Mechanical Engineers again took up the serious study of management problems.

SELECTED PUBLICATIONS

1901 "A Premium System of Remunerating Labor." Paper presented to the Mechanical Section of the International Engineering Congress, Glasgow. *Proceedings* of the Congress. London: Institution of Mechanical Engineers.

1903 "A Premium System Applied to Engineering Works." Paper presented to Institution of Mechanical Engineers, London.

Curriculum Vitae

1851	Born on March 18th in Glasgow. Educated at Glasgow Academy and Glasgow University.
1870–1875	Served apprenticeship with David Rowan, Engineer (Marine Machinery), with further experience in yards of Fairfield Shipbuilding and Engineering Co.
1880	Was Assistant Manager, David Rowan.
1885	Made Partner; name of firm was changed to David Rowan & Son.
1888	Assumed complete control of firm.
1898	Introduced premium bonus system which bears his name soon after close of great engineering dispute of 1897–1898.
1906	Died on November 19th, at age of 55, in Glasgow.

Rowan served as President of the North-West Engineering Trades Employers' Association and as Vice-President of the Institution of Engineers and Shipbuilders in Scotland. He was a member of The American Society of Mechanical Engineers as well as the Institutions of Naval Architects, Civil Engineers, and Mechanical Engineers.

[2] Henry A. Golding: London, Charles Griffin & Co., 1903.

Courtesy The National Cyclopaedia of American Biography.

James Mapes Dodge
(1852–1915)
United States

JAMES Mapes Dodge was the first American industrialist to introduce the Taylor methods of shop management as a complete system into his concern. This was a signal triumph for scientific management, for the Link-Belt Co. was a concern of great standing in the American engineering industry of the time. The company had pioneered in the manufacture of the link-belt chain and had important manufacturing centers in Philadelphia, Chicago, and Indianapolis. Dodge had been President of one part of the concern since 1892.

He had first become interested in Taylor in connection with the latter's discovery of high-speed tool steel. Always a leader in introducing new developments, Dodge decided to tool up with high-speed steel in Link-Belt's Philadelphia plant, which was situated very near the Midvale plant where Taylor had worked from 1878 to 1890. Over a single weekend the line shaft speed was doubled in the entire plant, so that all machine tools with the exception of the grinders were operating on the Monday morning at twice the speed they had been running on the Friday night. The rapidity of the change brought many new difficulties. Finally Taylor's associate, Barth, was called in to reorganize the management of the tool room, a task which he accomplished successfully.

Dodge was finally converted to Taylor's management methods generally by Taylor's paper "Shop Management" in 1903. Soon thereafter Taylor was invited to apply his system completely in the Link-Belt Co. By that time Dodge was himself an eminent man in American industry, being already a past president of The American Society of Mechanical Engineers (ASME). It was greatly to the advantage of both men that he now became the first executive to accept Taylor's system as a whole, a stout champion of Taylor's general cause, and also one of Taylor's warmest personal friends.

> It took over two years [said Dodge] for our organization to surrender fully, and so change our mental attitude that we became really receptive. I mean by this that I found no difficulty at all in having the heads of various departments agree that the introduction of the Taylor system would be most desirable, but in each case it was [desirable] for everybody else in the establishment but entirely unnecessary for him.

The Link-Belt plant in Philadelphia was, in the later years of Taylor's life, one of the showpieces round which he conducted the many visitors who came to see his system in operation. With H. R. Towne, Dodge was one of those responsible for Taylor's election as President of ASME in 1906. Subsequently he was among the most open of Taylor's supporters, particularly during the hearings of the "Eastern rates case" in 1910 and the Committee of Congress inquiry in 1911–1912.

The following description of Dodge appears in the memorial volume of the Newcomen Society:

> With all his impressive qualities as gifted mechanician, a forceful executive, and a thoughtfully considerate employer, James Mapes Dodge combined yet another characteristic, that of a genial liveliness which distinguished him at once in every circle of society. His humorous pleasantries were ever fresh and seemingly inexhaustible. His drollery was never failing, his ready wit ever combined with penetrating wisdom, and his animated countenance was expressive of both. As a story teller he was simply inimitable, and was a constant source of merriment and glee. Mark Twain once said that "Jim" Dodge was "the greatest story teller in America."

SELECTED PUBLICATIONS

1903 "The Money Value of a Technical Training," ASME *Transactions.*

1906 "History of the Introduction of a System of Shop Management," ASME *Transactions.* Reprinted in *Scientific Management* by C. B. Thompson. Cambridge, Mass.: Harvard University, 1914.

1911 "The Spirit in which Scientific Management Should be Approached." Reprinted in *Scientific Management* by C. B. Thompson. Cambridge, Mass.: Harvard University, 1914.

1912 "The Present State of the Art of Industrial Management." Report of an ASME committee.

1913 "Industrial Management," *Industrial Engineering and Engineering Digest.*

Curriculum Vitae

1852	Born on June 3rd at Waverly, N.Y. Dodge's father was a prominent member of the New York City Bar, and his mother was a gifted writer of books, stories, and poems. Dodge was educated at Newark Academy, Cornell University, and Rutgers College. His first practical experience was gained at the Morgan Iron Works, New York City.
1873–1876	Successively journeyman, foreman, and superintendent of construction in the shipbuilding works of John Roach & Sons at Chester, Pa.
1876–1878	In partnership with E. T. Copeland for the manufacture of mining machinery in New York City.
1868	In partnership with William D. Ewart and his associates in Chicago for the technical and commercial development of Ewart's link-belt chain. Became superintendent of the Indianapolis Malleable Iron Works, where the chain was put into production.
1884	Returned to the East and established the firm of Burr & Dodge in Philadelphia as representatives of the Ewart Manufacturing Co. of Indianapolis.
1888	Instrumental in forming the Link-Belt Engineering Co. as a corporation to consolidate business operations in Philadelphia and New York.
1892 on	President and active manager of the Link-Belt Engineering Co. and the Dodge Coal Storage Co. (afterward called the J. M. Dodge Co.).
1906 on	Chairman of the Board of the Link-Belt Co., which in that year merged the Link-Belt Engineering Co. of Philadelphia, the Link-Belt Machinery Co. of Chicago, and the Ewart Manufacturing Co. of Indianapolis.
1915	Died on December 4th, aged 63, in Philadelphia.

Dodge received the honorary degree of Doctor of Science from Stevens Institute of Technology (1913). He was President of The American Society of Mechanical Engineers (1902–1903), Vice-President of the Franklin Institute (1903–1905), and a founder and first president of The Society to Promote the Science of Management. In addition, he was an engineering inventor of eminence. A report published by the U.S. Patent Office early in the century shows that at that time he, together with George Westinghouse, had been granted more patents by the U.S. government than any other two men in the country.

In 1904 Dodge was awarded the Elliott Cresson Gold Medal by the Franklin Institute of Pennsylvania for his invention of the Dodge system of conveying coal in and out of storage.

Joseph Slater Lewis
(1852–1901)
Great Britain

JOSEPH Slater Lewis played only a small part among the pioneers of British management. But he won his place by virtue of a single book: *The Commercial Organization of Factories* (1896). The book was the earliest comprehensive analysis, published in Great Britain, of the fundamentals of industrial administration with special reference to the control function. It appeared at a time when control in industry was mostly a matter of rule of thumb; there had been scant progress since 1869, when the British journal *The Engineer* described the engineer's attitude to commerce and administration in these words: "Right within twenty percent of the actual cost is regarded as a very good estimate, and one reflecting much credit on the Engineer and all concerned. . . . There is no good treatise on the subject."[1]

Slater Lewis's statement of the purpose of his book reads as follows:

> It is beyond question . . . that the largest and most successful industrial undertakings are those where minuteness of detail and perfection of organization have received paramount consideration: a fact which should, in itself, especially in these days of world-wide competition, make the commercial organization of factories a matter of the first importance in every country with any manufacturing pretensions.

[1] Leading article entitled "The Estimates of Consulting Engineers," *The Engineer*, September 3, 1869, p. 166.

And again:

> This book is intended as a practical handbook for the use of manufacturers who wish to adopt modern methods of organization. It is written throughout from the point of view of an organizer and manager, rather than from that of a professional accountant, and the author hopes that this feature will commend it to those who have to bear the responsibility of conducting large engineering and manufacturing undertakings.

The book is intensely interesting in detail. It reviews the whole field of production and cost control, providing the first known example in Britain of monthly profit and loss accounts; sets out the progress of work through the factory in a single chart, the first "flow chart" of its kind; makes use of graphic methods for management objects; elaborates a systematic theory of organization, presenting the first organization chart to be found in British business literature; and enlarges upon the dynamic aspects of organization and of management in describing how the manager must set the tone of the organization by his own leadership. This last comparatively small section of a voluminously documented work shows that even in detail Lewis was reaching out toward a general principle; namely, that management is to be regarded as a distinct profession that can be taught and learned.

The Commercial Organization of Factories is a truly remarkable book. Its arrangement and production set standards which have seldom since been equaled in the literature and were in themselves an example of the art of management. It was anything but typical of its time. It was too "modern," exhibiting a conception of workshop management and production control, set in a framework of general business management, comparable with that to be found in the best textbooks of later generations. It was published simultaneously in London and New York, and was hailed by the Institution of Electrical Engineers in Britain as "a monument to its author and a boon to all who desire to organize their manufacture on sound commercial lines."[2] The Institution of Mechanical Engineers in Britain also recognized the merits of what it described as "the standard book" on the subject it covered. That it did not win a popular reputation is due to the very fact that it was a textbook of *management* and not, as might appear from its title, one of the costing, estimating, and workshop procedures which were the subjects of contemporary emphasis. It is interesting to note that at the moment when the United States, under the influence of Taylor and his associates, was about to take a long step forward in the art of management, Slater Lewis was accepted as an English colleague in the forefront of the American movement. He contributed a number of articles to leading American journals in the management field.

Little is known of Slater Lewis's personality. The somewhat precise tone

[2] "Memoir on J. Slater Lewis," *Proceedings* of the Institution of Electrical Engineers, December 1901. p. 1286.

of the technical chapters of his book is lightened by his evident interest in the human problems of morale and leadership, and many phrases show him to have been keenly alive to what Oliver Sheldon called 30 years later "the philosophy of management."

SELECTED PUBLICATIONS

Book:

1896 *The Commercial Organization of Factories.* London and New York: Spon Books.

Articles:

Joseph Slater Lewis contributed a number of articles to leading American journals in the management field. For example:

1899–1900 "Works Management for the Maximum of Production," *Engineering Magazine,* Vols. 18 and 19.

1901 "The Mechanical and Commercial Limits of Specialization," *Engineering Magazine,* Vol. 20.

Curriculum Vitae

1852 Born in Helsby, Cheshire. After a preliminary private education, spent some years at the Mechanics Institution in Manchester.

1868–1872 Apprenticed to a land agent in Norwich.

1872–1879 In the coal trade.

1879- Set up in Helsby as an electrical engineer on his own account.

1880 Visited United States to dispose of the rights to his patented self-binding insulator.

1881–1889 Was managing director of a small company manufacturing the insulator and other electrical products.

1889 Did consulting and service work as an electrical engineer in Birmingham.

1892 Was General Manager, W. T. Goolden & Co., London, electrical engineers.

1895 Headed Dynamo and Electrical Engineering Department, Salford Rolling Mills, Manchester.

1900 Was Director of British Electrical Engineering Co.

1901 Died in July at age of 49.

Lewis was a member of the three Engineering Institutions (Civil, Mechanical, and Electrical) and a Fellow of the Royal Society of Edinburgh.

Hans Renold
(1852–1943)
Great Britain

IT has been said in the preceding sketch that Slater Lewis's book, *The Commercial Organization of Factories*, was too "modern" in the Britain of 1896. It remained too modern for a considerable time, since in Britain the new concept of management developed slowly. Not until the years of the First World War and later did signs appear that a British "scientific management" was taking root which assimilated the American contribution and was yet peculiarly British in character. A pioneering practical experiment in British scientific management was, however, being carried out prior to the war of 1914 by at least one engineering firm—Hans Renold Ltd.

In 1913 Hans Renold, by birth a Swiss, described the management practices of his own Lancashire firm, which had been developed in the years since its foundation in 1879, in an address to the Manchester Association of engineers entitled "Engineering Workshop Organization." The salient achievements of the firm in management, as presented in this paper, were an enlightened staff recruitment policy; an organization structure based on functional specialization and recorded on charts published with the paper; the existence of written standard management instructions and practices prepared and administered by functional departments; and an interlocking committee system acting as a consultative mechanism among the management staff.

The Renold system of carefully conceived monthly cost-control returns was particularly interesting. These returns covered not only financial matters but also manufacturing activities and stocks. The system had been developed by Renold with the aid of the costing expert A. H. Church, and it became the foundation of modern scientific costing in Great Britain.

Renold was probably the first British industrialist to appreciate the work of F. W. Taylor and to adapt it to British management practice. He was certainly the only industrialist prior to the First World War who experimented deliberately and comprehensively with Taylor's methods. In his paper of 1913 he adopted the simple standpoint of defining scientific management as "neither more nor less than common sense tabulated and applied with fact and reason when facing the everyday problems as they arise." He went on to expound the achievements of Taylor and took care to distinguish between sound principles and their unsound application.

In another part of his paper Hans Renold showed great understanding of the true nature of management. ". . . There is no denying that the working of an efficient system requires men of tact and power to lead. . . . More often than not, when difficulties arose it was because the common respect which every man, especially superiors, owes to his fellow workers was wanting, and therefore the necessary tact for a successful management could not exist." Renold had grasped not only the mechanics of management but its dynamics. It is only now, decades later, that this line of thought is finding widespread acceptance.

In the remarkable organization that he created—a generation ahead of its time and an outstanding illustration of British scientific management in practice—the place of Hans Renold as a pioneer can be measured.

A few days after Hans Renold's death his son, addressing the staff and workers, tried to explain the secret of his achievement.

> I think that the keynote of his whole life was a passion for good work. He enjoyed money when it came, but commercial success was of quite secondary interest. What drove him on was the joy of creation—of doing something just as well as he knew how. "Good enough" was a sentiment that was quite unknown to him. It might well have been written of him, "Whatsoever thy hand findeth to do, do it with thy might." His relations with other people were based on this same deep instinct. . . . That also was at the root of his relations with his employees. . . . His respect went out to the good workman. He collected good workmen around him, and the mutual respect between good workmen knows no social distinctions.*

PUBLICATION

1913 "Engineering Workshop Organization." Paper presented to Manchester Association of Engineers.

* C. G. (later Sir Charles) Renold, *Hans Renold, a Memorial Address*. Privately printed, 1943.

Curriculum Vitae

1852	Born at Aarau, Switzerland. Educated in district and county schools; during vacations worked as apprentice in mechanics' shops.
1870	Received technical training at Polytechnic School, Zurich.
1873	Came to England and worked with machine-export firms.
1879	Bought a small business in Salford, Lancashire, and began, on his own account, the manufacture of roller chains.
1903	Formed Hans Renold Ltd.
1916–1918	Served as a member of the Manchester Armaments Output Committee.
1928	Resigned, at age of 76, from chairmanship of Hans Renold Ltd. but continued in office as a director.
1943	Died at age 91 in Grange-Over-Sands, Lancashire.

Renold received an honorary D.Sc. degree from Manchester University in 1940.

Courtesy R. Greenwood.

Harrington Emerson
(1853–1931)
United States

THE highlight of Harrington Emerson's career and, perhaps, his most important contribution to the development of management was his statement made during the hearings of the Interstate Commerce Commission in 1910–1911 when the shippers on the Eastern seaboard opposed an application by the railroad companies to raise rates. He gave evidence on oath that the railroads could save "a million dollars a day" on their operating costs. This claim hit the headlines. In 24 hours "scientific management," hitherto an obscure technology practised by a few unknown engineers, became national news across America.

This sudden publicity had important consequences, not all of them desirable. The attention of businessmen throughout the nation was attracted to scientific management. But the publicity probably stimulated the opposition from certain sections of organized labor which seriously handicapped its subsequent development.

Emerson was an engineer whose thought had developed independently along the lines of scientific management and who had used analogous methods to reorganize the workshops of the Santa Fe Railroad. There he had devised a system for integrating shop procedures which had most successful results in terms of cost savings. When called by L. D. Brandeis as a principal witness for the shippers in the "Eastern rates case," he was the only one who testified with firsthand experience of the particular industry in dispute: namely, railroad transport. He thus spoke with authority when he said flatly in court that if the American railroads improved their management as had been done in Santa Fe, the total savings would indeed total more than a million dollars a day.

Both before and after this episode, Harrington Emerson was one of the limited number of genuinely qualified persons who practiced the profession of "efficiency engineer," a term of which he himself was the originator. He was a popularizer of scientific management in his active consultancy work, in his prolific writings on different aspects of "efficiency," and in his education of a vast following of businessmen in his methods. He expounded the concepts of standard times, standard costs, and preventable wastes, and he indicated how scientific methods could be applied to many different activities—even potato growing, where he stressed the importance of the psychological factors which could influence people to increase output. He was also the first individual to call attention to the lessons which business management could learn from military experience. Part of his education was in Germany, and in his writings he drew freely on the examples of brilliant army staff organization provided by the campaigns of 1866 and 1870.

Later in his career, Emerson became particularly interested in the selection and training of employees—an aspect of scientific management which had not hitherto been greatly developed. In his writings on this subject he was concerned to justify scientific management to the worker, emphasizing its value in finding the place for which the individual is best fitted.

Harrington Emerson made a particularly original contribution to the early development of scientific management. For, though he was in close touch with the Taylor group, he was not part of it and his additions to the body of management principles were independent.

Harrington Emerson was not only the man of action implied by the description "efficiency engineer" but also an intellectual and a scholar. He is especially remembered for a personality which gave him considerable power to influence those with whom he came in contact, whether they were business leaders in industry or younger men seeking to learn his own profession.

SELECTED PUBLICATIONS

Books:

1900 *Efficiency as a Basis for Operation and Wages.* New York: Engineering Magazine Co.

1912 *The Twelve Principles of Efficiency.* New York: Engineering Magazine Co.

1913 *The Scientific Selection of Employees.* New York: The Emerson Co.

1921 *Course in Personal Efficiency:* New York: The Emerson Co.

Articles:

1904 "A Rational Basis for Wages," ASME *Transactions.*

—— "Tool Room Practice in a Railroad Repair Shop," *Engineering Magazine*.

1905 "Shop Betterment and the Individual Effort Method of Profit Sharing," *Engineering Magazine*.

1907 "Methods of Exact Measurement Applied to Individual and Shop Efficiency at the Topeka Shops of the Santa Fe." New York: The Emerson Co.

1908 "The Efficiency Method of Determining Costs to Eliminate all Waste from Foundry Operations," *Iron Trade Review*.

—— "The Modern Theory of Cost Accounting," *Engineering Magazine*.

—— "Preventable Wastes and Losses on Railroads," *Railway Age Gazette*.

1911 "Standards of Efficiency in Shop Operation," *Iron Age*.

1912 "Comparative Study of Wage and Bonus Systems." New York: The Emerson Co.

—— "Practicing Efficiency and Knowing Costs." New York: The Emerson Co.

1915 "Personality in Organization," Efficiency Society *Journal*.

Curriculum Vitae

1853 Born on August 2nd in Trenton, N.J. Educated in England, France, Germany, Italy, and Greece.

1876 Headed Modern Language Department, University of Nebraska.

1882 Left the university to engage in banking and real estate operations in Milford and Ulysses, Nebr.

1885–1891 Did special economic and engineering research work for the Burlington Railroad.

1895–1899 Served as U.S. representative of a British syndicate investing in America: investigated finances and operations of many industrial plants and mines in Mexico, the United States, and Canada.

1899–1901 Managed a glass-manufacturing company.

1901–1907 Active as professional consulting management engineer.

1904–1907 Carried out the reorganization of the Atchison, Topeka & Santa Fe Railroad; introduced a bonus plan, standard costs, accounting by tabulating machines, and planned maintenance for equipment and rolling stock.

1907–1923 Was President of The Emerson Co., efficiency engineers, New York City.

1910–1911 Called one of the principal witnesses in the "Eastern rates case."

1911 Named to Civilian Expert Board on Industrial Management of the U.S. Navy Yards (with Gantt and Day) to investigate the functions and conditions of the yards.

1921 Appointed member of the Hoover Committee for the Elimination of Waste in Industry; assigned to cover the coal and railroad industries.

1929 Attended the International Management Congress in Paris.

1931 Died on September 2nd, aged 78, in New York City.

Courtesy Michelin Tire Corp.

The Michelin Brothers
(André: 1853–1931; Edouard: 1859–1940)
France

IF scientific management was introduced into France and continental Europe by the Frenchmen Fayol, Le Chatelier, and de Fréminville, all of whom appear in this book, it was popularized by the Michelin brothers. As a result of the series of booklets, entitled *Prospérité*, which André and Edouard Michelin published during the period 1928–1936, the ideas of Taylor came to be common knowledge in France.

Because the partnership of the Michelin brothers was lifelong, their work is described here as a single achievement. Everyone knows the jolly Michelin tire man "Bibendum" and the Michelin road maps, but fewer know the extent of the Michelin contribution to modern management. The early success of the brothers was due to their development of the detachable pneumatic bicycle tire and their introduction of the automobile pneumatic tire, which gained for their concern the lead in world developments in tire manufacture.

By the turn of the century the Michelins were, in their own business, applying methods very close to the principles of scientific management, although the work of Taylor was as yet unknown to them. In 1912, however, Edouard Michelin first read of Taylor's work in Le Chatelier's *Revue de métallurgie*. In a matter of a few weeks he had established contact with Taylor. Then, in 1913, André Michelin first met Taylor at a dinner given for Taylor in Paris by Le Chatelier. André relates that on leaving the restaurant he hurried at once to buy two stop-watches, one of which he sent off that very evening to his brother at the factory in Clermont-Ferrand. Such was the effect of Taylor's "timid exposition" of his methods on that occasion.

After 1918 the brothers set themselves the task of making Taylor's work known throughout France in the interest of national prosperity. The Taylor-Michelin Committee was created in 1921 in collaboration with Le Chatelier. During ten years 860 students from the engineering and technical colleges were sent to take training courses. Le Chatelier wrote a booklet for their use: *Advice to Students of the National Colleges Wishing to Familiarize Themselves with the Methods of Scientific Management in Industry.* The Committee published informative articles in the press, showed documentary and propaganda films, organized conferences and lectures, and above all reached a very wide public through the *Prospérité* booklets, supplied free of charge by Michelin & Cie.

After 1931 the brothers continued to apply scientific management in their own business; and Edouard's periodical notes to his staff, which have been collected in a booklet, make an interesting comparison with the notes by which Fayol used to record the administrative mistakes he observed and the remedies he applied. Their public activities decreased from this time on, but it was for the good reason that scientific management was becoming more widely understood.

The brothers were complementary personalities, dissimilar in many ways. André was the "public relations" man. He lived in Paris and made the social contacts required. Edouard remained in Clermont-Ferrand and managed the factory; he was a quiet-spoken man with a peremptory manner.

The two were, however, both noteworthy for their clarity of mind, practical good sense, rapidity of thought, and passionate love of work. Both were painstakingly accurate in detail. Their tremendous faith in the future was accompanied by genuine humility regarding their own achievements. Above all, the *Prospérité* booklets are redolent of the Michelin brothers' sense of fun.

SELECTED PUBLICATIONS

1928–1936 *Prospérité.* Clermont-Ferrand: Editions Michelin. A trimonthly review devoted to scientific management. The subjects were of three kinds:

Popular

Sam et François

Le Succès

Celà vaut-il la peine de s'occuper de la méthode Taylor? (first published in 1927, second edition in 1930)

Ce que Taylor dit de sa méthode

Sa majesté le client

Sur le tas ou conseils pour débuter dans la méthode Taylor

L'Automobile source de richesse—l'auto contre la crise

Technical:

Pourquoi et comment chronométrer?

Comment nous avons Taylorisé nos ateliers de mécanique d'entretien

La Préparation du travail
Suggestions
Un Exemple de travail continu, ou la construction de nos maisons ouvrières
Deux exemples d'application de la méthode Taylor chez Michelin
La Construction de maisons ouvrières en série chez Michelin
La Méthode Taylor dans l'étude d'une machine Le Chronographe
Remarques sur la formation professionnelle

Miscellaneous (chiefly on social subjects):
Une Dépense qui paye: un service médical
Oeuvres sociales de Michelin & Cie
Une Expérience de natalité
Allocations et rentes pour familles nombreuses
Comment alimenter vos bébés
L'Autobus de Lempdes
Une Expérience d'education physique

Curriculum Vitae

André: Educated at the Ecole des Arts et Manufactures and the Ecole des Beaux Arts (architecture).
Edouard: Educated at the Ecole des Beaux Arts (painting).

The brothers both abandoned their chosen careers to save the family business (rubber products) from bankruptcy. Edouard settled in Clermont-Ferrand to manage the factory. André lived in Paris and conducted the external affairs of the business.

1891 Patent lodged by Michelin & Cie for a detachable rubber tire.
1895 First motor vehicles on pneumatic tires entered by Michelin & Cie in Paris-Bordeaux race.
1899 A motor vehicle equipped with Michelin tires was first to reach speed of 100 kilometers per hour.
1909 Michelin & Cie financed building of 3,000 workers' houses.
1911 Michelin Prize won by first aircraft to fly from Paris and land on the Puy de Dôme in central France.
1914 Michelin factory began to manufacture aircraft.
1916 Family allowances established for Michelin employees and their widows.
1929 First pneumatic tire created for railway carriages by Michelin.
1931 André died at age of 78.
1938 First tire of metallic rubber fabric created by Michelin.
1940 Edouard died at age of 81.

André was an honorary president of the Aero-Club de France, a chevalier of the Legion of Honor, and an officer of the Academy. Edouard's last years were overcast by the tragic deaths of his two sons: Etienne in an aircraft accident (1932) and Pierre in an automobile accident (1937).

Courtesy Brandeis University.

Louis Dembitz Brandeis
(1856–1941)
United States

LOUIS D. Brandeis made his total contribution to management in less than two years. He was a famous lawyer who ultimately became an associate justice of the U.S. Supreme Court; and his contribution to management, important though it was, is but a small segment of his total achievement in his own sphere. This contribution was, however, to bring the Taylor system of industrial management to the forefront of public interest during the hearings of a single legal case.

The story cannot be better told than in F. W. Taylor's own words. As Taylor wrote to a friend in January 1911:

> A very extraordinary thing has happened through a Boston lawyer named Louis D. Brandeis. . . .
>
> Brandeis has for many years devoted a considerable part of his time to serving in the capacity of, as he calls it, "the people's lawyer." He has taken a great variety of cases, notably brought about the ten-hour law for women in Oregon and then in Illinois, and all public work of this sort he has done for nothing.
>
> When the Eastern railroads asked the Interstate Commerce Commission for an increase in the freight rates. Brandeis took up the case of the shippers to prevent this arbitrary increase in rates, and adopted a very ingenious and what I think will prove to be a successful course in

> at least modifying the increase in freight rates which the railroads asked for. He went before the Interstate Commission in Washington, claiming that the practical management of the railroads was completely out of date and inefficient, and that they could save, through efficient management, far more than they could accomplish through an increase of freight rates; manifestly to the great benefit of both themselves and the whole country.
>
> In proving his case, he brought before the Interstate Commerce Commission the various managers and owners of the companies which are running under our type of management—Mr. Dodge, of the Link-Belt; Hathaway, of the Tabor; Towne, of the Yale and Towne Co., and a lot of others; and he was so successful in setting forth the merits of scientific management that he has awakened the whole country, and the interest now taken in scientific management is almost comparable to that which was aroused in the conservation of our natural resources by Roosevelt.

Taylor's view of the importance of the incident was correct. Although the case argued by Brandeis was rejected by the Commission as being insufficient proof, the decision nevertheless went against the railroads, and it is believed that the Commission was influenced by Brandeis more than it cared to acknowledge. At any rate, Brandeis had brought the Taylor system to a place in the sun, and Taylor received visits and letters from hundreds of people as a result of the hearings. The American Society of Mechanical Engineers has pointed out that although the hearings caused an uproar, "Brandeis's masterly analysis of the principles of scientific management in his brief was scarcely noticed."*

Moreover, Brandeis is to be remembered in the history of management in another respect. In October 1910 he called together a small group of engineers in the apartment of H. L. Gantt in New York to choose the most suitable designation for the new philosophy of management which they were to expound and defend at the forthcoming hearings. A number of titles were suggested, including "Taylor system," "functional management," "shop management," and "efficiency." Finally the group decided unanimously to adopt the term "scientific management" for the purpose of the hearings. Thus, for good or bad, the term was coined which has most constantly been used to describe the "mental revolution" which Taylor postulated for our times.

Documents left by Taylor show that the question of railroad costs continued to interest both him and Brandeis for several years. The stubborn opposition of the railroad managements, however, persuaded Taylor to dissuade Brandeis from contemplating further action in this sphere.

* In ASME's *History of Scientific Management in America.* New York: *Mechanical Engineering.* September 1939. 10pp.

Brandeis was a brilliant public figure. Through his law partnership he attained financial independence by the age of 30, and frugal living and conservative investment later made him a wealthy man. He used this independence to take up enthusiastic public service without payment, finding an absorbing outside interest in the causes which interested him.

He had a lifelong opposition to "bigness" and the many crusades of which he was the storm center were directed chiefly against monopolies and trusts. But most of the progressive social-reform projects of his day claimed his services at one time or another and he gave these services generously. His unifying passion was to preserve individual freedom. The special importance of his combination of active law practice with unpaid public service lay in the fact that, unlike many apostles of reform, he was thoroughly immersed in the realities of business and finance; he brought to bear on public issues the zeal for facts and the highly trained analytical faculty characteristic of a lawyer. This discipline permitted his idealistic liberalism to exert an impressive influence on affairs.

SELECTED PUBLICATIONS

Books:

1911 *Scientific Management and the Railroads.* New York: Engineering Magazine Co. 92 pp.

1914 *Business—A Profession.* Boston: Small, Maynard & Co. 327 pp.

1918 *Case Against Night Work for Women.* With J. C. Goldmark. New York: National Consumer's League. 452 pp.

Articles:

1910 "Can the Principles of Scientific Management Be Applied to Railway Operation?" *Engineering News,* Vol. 64, pp. 600–601.

—— "Evidence in Matter of Proposed Advances in Freight Rates." Brief submitted to Interstate Commerce Commission. Senate Document 725, 61st Congress, 3rd Session, Vol. 8 (Scientific Management), pp. 4752–4845.

1911 "The New Conception of Industrial Efficiency," *Journal of Accountancy,* Vol. 12, May, pp. 35–43.

—— "An Aid to Railroad Efficiency," *Engineering Magazine,* October. Reprinted in *Business—A Profession* (see "Books").

—— "Organized Labor and Efficiency," *Survey,* Vol. 26, April 22nd, pp. 148–151.

1912 "Efficiency in Your Home and in Your Business," *American Magazine,* December 10th.

—— Foreword (2 pp.) to *Primer of Scientific Management,* by F. B. and L. M. Gilbreth. New York: D. Van Nostrand Co.

1915 "Efficiency Systems and Labor," *Harper's Weekly,* Vol. 59, Aug. 15th, p. 154.

Curriculum Vitae

1856	Born on November 13th in Louisville, Ky.
1874–1875	Studied at Annen-Realschule, Dresden.
1875–1878	Studied at Harvard Law School; subsequently admitted to the St. Louis Bar.
1879–1897	Employed as lawyer, Warren & Brandeis, Boston.
1889	Admitted to Bar of U.S. Supreme Court.
1897–1911	Served as "people's attorney" for Public Franchise League and Massachusetts State Board of Trade.
1897–1916	Active as Senior, Brandeis, Dunbar & Nutter, Boston.
1907–1913	Was unpaid counsel for William B. Lawrence in New Haven merger controversies.
1907–1914	Was unpaid counsel for the State in defending hours of labor and minimum wage statutes of Oregon, Illinois, Ohio, and California.
1910–1911	Was unpaid counsel for commercial organizations in Interstate Commerce Commission "Eastern Rate Case."
1910–1916	Served as unpaid chairman, Arbitration Board, in case of New York Garment Workmen's strike and under subsequent protocols.
1911–1915	Prominent as worker and adviser in progressive politics.
1912	Joined Zionist Movement.
1913–1914	Served as special Interstate Commerce Commission counsel in "five-per-cent rate case."
1916	Confirmed by Senate as an associate justice, U.S. Supreme Court.
1939	Retired on February 13th.
1941	Died on October 5th, at age of 85, in Washington, D.C.

Charles de la Poix de Fréminville
(1856–1936)
France

CHARLES de Fréminville was the collaborator of Henry Le Chatelier in bringing scientific management to France. An engineer in railways and then in the motor industry, interested in management from the beginning of his career, de Fréminville was from 1907 on in close touch with Le Chatelier. It was not till he made Taylor's acquaintance in 1912, however, that de Fréminville became an enthusiastic exponent of Taylor's methods. In 1913 he began to write for Le Chatelier in the *Revue de métallurgie* and to launch a campaign by means of addresses to economic and industrial organizations. These activities are regarded by Frenchmen as the turning point of the French management movement. It was de Fréminville's special achievement to interpret Taylor's doctrines faithfully and yet to adapt them to French industry and to the French temperament.

In 1920 his efforts, jointly with those of Le Chatelier, were materially responsible for the creation of the Conférence de l'Organisation Française, of which de Fréminville became President in 1924 and which was united in 1926 with Fayol's Centre d'Etudes Administratives. When Fayol, during the opening session of the Second International Management Congress in Brussels in 1925, announced his belief in the unity between his own work and that of Taylor, it fell to de Fréminville to grasp the hand thus warmly extended as a symbol of the fusion of two complementary lines in the evolution of management thought. De Fréminville's capable presidency, from 1926 to 1932, ensured that the activities of the new Comité National de l'Organisation Française would be many and fruitful; and his election to the presidency of CIOS in 1929 was the culminating international tribute to his work.

De Fréminville's simplicity, kindliness, and generosity of spirit were at the service of all and sundry who showed the least interest in the subject of which he was a master. At international meetings—not always distinguished for their freedom from national intrigues—his integrity of purpose, his preoccupation with the advancement of the scientific method, was a beacon only slightly dimmed by a most disarming modesty. As a chairman in his own rightful domain—the meetings of the National Committee in Paris—he would welcome the stranger from another country with the same combination of warmth and dignity which marked the atmosphere of his private apartment. Even the massacre of his beloved language which sometimes followed was forgiven as, courteously, he gave a clear and stimulating lead to the discussion. Many young people owed their progress in the art of management to the guidance that de Fréminville gave to their first steps. A compatriot has called him, not only a great engineer, but an honest man in the sense which this expression implied in the century of Louis XIV. He was a man of culture, and his leisure moments were devoted to the arts: to sculpture, in particular, and to the art he considered most important of all—that of living.

SELECTED PUBLICATIONS

Book:

1918 *The Fundamental Principles of the Taylor Method.* Paris: A. Maréchal.

Articles, Addresses, etc.:

From among the many important contributions made by de Fréminville, the following will serve as an indication of the scope of his writings:

1914 "Le Système Taylor" (The Taylor System), *Bulletin* de la Société d'Encouragement pour l'Industrie Nationale, March.

1915 Introduction to "Le Facteur humain dans l'organisation du travail" (The Human Factor in Scientific Management). A French translation by Perrot and de Fréminville of a work by James Hartness, a former president of The American Society of Mechanical Engineers.

1917 "L'Utilisation des mutilés pour l'organisation du travail" (The Employment of Disabled Persons in Scientific Management), *Revue de métallurgie*, July–August.

1918 "Quelques aperçus sur le système Taylor" (Some Impressions of the Taylor System). Edition de l'Association Industrielle, Commerciale et Agricole de Lyon et de la Région.

1919–1920 "Cinq conférences sur l'organisation du travail" (Five Lectures on Scientific Management). Paris: Ecole des Hautes Etudes Commerciales (Stage de l'Intendance).

1920 "The Appreciation of H. L. Gantt in France." Paper read at the Gantt Memorial Conference of The American Society of Mechanical Engineers.

—— "The Manager's Responsibility for Production," *Proceedings* of the Academy of Political and Social Science, June.

—— Preface to "Sur la pratique de l'organisation des ateliers modernes" (On the Practice of Management in Modern Factories), by Caillant and Warin.

1921 "Analyse et préparation du travail dans les ateliers" (Analysis and Preparation of Work in Factories), "Conférence aux élèves de l'enseignement technique feminin," *Mon bureau* (Paris), July 15th.

1923 "L'Organisation méthodique du travail dans la papeterie en Amérique" (The Methodical Organization of Work in the Paper Industry in America), *Chimie et industrie,* July.

1926 "Evolution de l'organisation scientifique du travail" (Evolution of Scientific Management), paper read to the International Management Congress, Brussels, 1925. *Revue de métallurgie,* April and May.

1927 "The Evolution of Scientific Management," paper presented to the Third International Management Congress, Rome.

1934 "Discours de prise de présidence de la Société des Ingenieurs Civils de 12 Janvier 1934" (Inaugural speech on assuming the presidency of the Society of Civil Engineers on January 12, 1934), *Fascicule bimensuel des Ingénieurs Civils (Paris). No. 1, January.*

Curriculum Vitae

1856 Born at Lorient in France. Graduated from Ecole Centrale as Engineer of Arts and Manufactures.

1878 Worked as engineer in the Equipment Section, Paris-Orléans Railway.

1885 and 1887 Visited the United States to study developments in electric transportation.

1899 Was Technical Director and subsequently Assistant Managing Director, Panhard & Levassor Motor Co.

1914–1918 Active as consulting engineer in military factories and naval yards; reorganized, among others, Penhoet Naval Construction Co. and Schneider Co.

1919 Was member of French Government Economic Mission to the United States.

1927–1933 Was member of Council, International Management Institute, Geneva.

1929 Served as President of the Fourth International Management Congress, Paris, and of CIOS.

1936 Died in June, at age of 80, after a short illness.

De Fréminville was awarded the Cross of the Legion of Honor in 1929. He was President of the Society of Civil Engineers (1934); an honorary vice-president of The American Society of Mechanical Engineers (1913); and a member of the Taylor Society (United States).

Courtesy The National Cyclopaedia of American Biography.

Frederick Arthur Halsey
(1856–1935)
United States

FREDERICK A. Halsey originated in American industry the first successful incentive system of wage payments to improve upon the ordinary piece-rate system. The question how to increase the output of labor was of great interest to engineers at the close of the 1800s. Before Halsey presented his paper to The American Society of Mechanical Engineers in 1891, three wage-payment systems were known, all of which had important defects. Day rates had the fault of not being based on the incentive principle. Ordinary piece rates failed because they were constantly associated by the worker with rate cutting by the employer as soon as the worker had achieved any substantial rise in his or her output. Lastly, the gainsharing plan presented by H. R. Towne to the Society in 1889 was deficient, as Halsey showed, in that the increased output, no doubt due to the efforts of the better workers, provided rewards without distinction between good workers and bad.

Halsey's "premium plan of paying for labor" was an original contribution to management from many points of view. His avowed aim was to eliminate rate cutting with all that it implied in antagonism between worker and employer. The plan called for a guaranteed daily or hourly rate for a fixed quantity of work, agreed upon with the worker on the basis of his or her customary performance in the past. Then there would be a premium payment, for any additional work, of about one-half to one-third of the sum the employer would have paid for this work under the daily or hourly rate. Under this scheme the worker's earnings would not be excessive even if output were doubled. Hence the employer, who would gain the most from the additional output, would be dissuaded from cutting the rate.

The premium plan had a very great influence, not only in the United States but also in Great Britain, where it was, together with Taylor's piece-rate system, the model for many incentive schemes. The Halsey premium plan was introduced, for example, into Taylor, Taylor & Hobson, lens and optical instrument makers of Leicester, England, in 1900. (James Rowan's premium system of 1901 was undoubtedly based upon Halsey's premium plan.) In the United States Halsey influenced Taylor's work on incentives; and, although the premium plan was overshadowed by Taylor's piece-rate system, it continued to be used in cases where its advantages remained evident. At the Watertown Arsenal in 1911, for instance, one of Taylor's followers installed a variant of the Halsey plan because it was considered a better incentive than the piece-rate system for mainly nonrepetitive types of work.

The important limitation of Halsey's premium plan, a limitation found in all schemes prior to the piece-rate system of Taylor, was that it took the customary output of workers as the basis of calculation. Taylor's new contribution was to show how the scientific measurement of work could do much more to increase and improve management output than could any methods of payment, however they might be manipulated. The application of both these plans in subsequent years, however, showed that there were good points in each.

Though Taylor's desire to improve the workers' earnings was as genuine as Halsey's, his systematic planning of every movement of every worker in the shop made high output depend more on the planning department than on the initiative and constructive cooperation of the individual worker. Halsey's plan depended more on the latter element. Suggestion schemes came more frequently into existence under Halsey's plan than under Taylor's; and the improved methods which tended to emerge continuously from this form of positive alliance with the worker on the job have been the basis of some of the most successful examples of modern management. Taylor's was the system of the greatest significance for the future of management, but some have said that Halsey knew human beings better than Taylor. Halsey had a forceful personality. That he was also a generous man was made apparent in his reaction to Taylor's criticism of his premium plan. At the reading of Taylor's paper "A Piece-Rate System" in 1895, where Taylor's comments on "Messrs. Towne and Halsey's plans" must have been painful hearing for him, Halsey rose at once to say:

> If Mr. Taylor can determine the maximum output of the miscellaneous pieces of work comprised in the everyday operation of the average machine shop, he has accomplished a great work, and the present

paper should be followed at once by another giving the fullest details of his method.

It was yet long before Halsey could accept that maximum output could be determined, but when he finally did so he generously acknowledged Taylor's achievement.

Halsey showed in his own working relations that he was a leader of men. He is remembered particularly as a chief who never allowed his own clear-cut views to intrude on the maximum freedom of action accorded to every individual working under him.

SELECTED PUBLICATIONS

1891 "The Premium Plan of Paying for Labor," ASME *Transactions.*
1897 "Some Special Forms of Computers,"ASME *Transactions.*
1899 "Administration of the Premium Plan," *American Machinist.*
—— "Experience with the Premium Plan of Paying Labor," *American Machinist.*
1900 "Economics of the Premium Plan," *American Machinist.*
1902 "Origin of the Premium Plan: A Personal Statement," *American Machinist.*
1903 "The Metric System," ASME *Transactions.*
1909 "From Piece Work to the Premium Plan," *American Machinist.*

Curriculum Vitae

1856 Born on July 12th at Unadilla, N.Y.
1878 Awarded Bachelor of Mechanical Engineering degree by Cornell University. Elected a member of Sigma Xi.
1878–1880 Worked in various machine shops.
1880–1890 Employed as draftsman in the Rand Drill Co., later by merger the Ingersoll-Rand Co. of New York. He soon became Chief Engineer, in which capacity he designed numerous straightline air compressors and invented the Slugger rock drill.
1890–1904 Employed as Engineer and General Manager, Canadian Rand Drill Co., Sherbrooke, Quebec.
1894 Named Associate Editor, *American Machinist,* New York. Editor from 1907; later Editor Emeritus.
1911 Retired from editorship owing to ill health.
1911–1914 Was Associate Professor in Mechanical Engineering, Columbia University, New York City.
1916 Served as Commissioner of the American Institute of Weights and Measures, a body which he had established as one means

of successfully defeating the movement to introduce the metric system into the United States.

1935 Died on October 20th, aged 79, in New York City.

In 1923 Halsey was awarded the first Gold Medal of The American Society of Mechanical Engineers for his 1891 paper on the premium plan. The citation stated that the adoption of the methods proposed in the paper had been profoundly effective in harmonizing the relations of worker and employer.

Courtesy R. Greenwood.

Frederick Winslow Taylor
(1856–1915)
United States

FREDERICK Winslow Taylor's tomb at Germantown outside Philadelphia bears the simple phrase "The Father of Scientific Management." It is a title which has been accepted not only by his compatriots but by management movements the world over. His writings have been translated into a score of languages. Since 1938, the Gold Medal of the International Committee for Scientific Management has borne his portrait. In 1918, Lenin wrote in *Pravda* with reference to Russian industry, "We should immediately introduce piece work and try it out in practice. We should try out every scientific and progressive suggestion of the Taylor system." The very ubiquity of his influence has led at times to misunderstanding of his work. But the historian, after careful examination of the evidence, can only conclude that the emergence in the twentieth century of a science of business management, directed toward enhancing the economic and social contribution of business to the democratic way of life, was an achievement which owed more to Taylor than to any other single individual.

That Taylor benefited from the work of some earlier pioneers he was the first to acknowledge, and this will be evident to readers of this book. When he began his career, efforts had already been made, on both sides of the Atlantic, toward drawing together the work of the two principal technical professions concerned with the management of a factory—engineering and accountancy. Interest had developed in various labor-incentive schemes.

Several devices for better managerial control of production processes had been worked out. The subject of cost accounting was being actively discussed. From these slender beginnings, however, F. W. Taylor developed, at first almost single-handed and by thinking the problem through from its basic element—the process carried out by a single worker at a particular time—a whole new attitude toward the art of managing business enterprises. This attitude he himself described as "a mental revolution." From it the philosophy of the best and most modern management in the twentieth century has taken its inspiration.

At the time Taylor began his work, business management as a discrete and identifiable activity had attracted little attention. It was usually regarded as incidental to—and flowing from knowledge of or acquaintance with—a particular branch of manufacturing, the technical know-how of making sausages or steel or shirts. Those called on to conduct the aggregates of capital, plant, equipment, materials, and human beings by which these articles were made "picked up" their management skill by experience and by trial and error. They overlooked the fact that in this particular context the learner's errors are other people's trials. The idea that a person needed any training or formal instruction to become a competent manager had not occurred to anyone.

It was through the gradual elaboration of techniques for analyzing and measuring elementary processes that Taylor progressed toward a new philosophy of management. His earliest concern, as a gang boss at the Midvale Steel Works, Philadelphia, was to end the practice of "soldiering," or restriction of output, by the workers for whom he was responsible. From his own practical experience as a lathe operator, he knew that much higher outputs were possible without unreasonable effort. He decided that the difficulty was due to ignorance on both sides. Management demanded, and the men were ready to give, "a fair day's work for a fair day's pay." But neither side had a clear idea of what, quantitatively, constituted a fair day's work. Both were relying on vague impressions and traditions which led to constant disputes.

Taylor reached a solution of this problem through the exact and detailed measurement, which yielded "standard" times, of the movements used on every process; through the reorganization of tasks; and through changes in the system of payment in the light of these data. Inevitably such work led to many other developments in planning, in the flow of materials and jobs, in tool supply, and so on, all designed to make it possible for each worker to achieve "standard" or better at all times. Taylor thus arrived at the two principles which he believed to be the essence of his philosophy of management—"scientific management," as it came to be called. These principles were:

> Both sides (management and men) must take their eyes off the division of the surplus as the all-important matter, and together turn their attention towards increasing the size of the surplus.

And:

> Both sides must recognize as essential the substitution of exact scientific investigation and knowledge for the old individual judgment or opinion, either of the workman or the boss, in all matters relating to the work done in the establishment.[1]

In short, if men are to cooperate effectively (and every business is essentially a system of human cooperation), all concerned must have (1) a common purpose and (2) a common method. Taylor devised many new techniques as the instruments of his work. His inventive genius and fertility of ideas were such that he could have achieved eminence on this count alone. Forty technical patents stand to his credit, including the revolutionary discovery of high-speed steel. He was equally productive of new management methods and devices. Many, if not the majority, of the methods characterized as "modern" today can be traced to ideas initiated by him and his followers more than half a century ago. Though they have been refined and developed almost out of recognition, the germ can usually be found in Taylor's writing and practice. In 1902 he decided, however, that he "no longer could afford to work for money."[2] He devoted the rest of his life to advocating, not particular techniques, but the new principles which he believed were his real contribution to the world.

As is the case with most innovators, Taylor was much misunderstood. Many who called themselves his "disciples" imitated his methods while remaining blind to the principles behind them and indifferent to the sense of social responsibility essential to their successful application. Thus his ideas were bitterly opposed both by big business and by the trade unions.

Nor was the written statement of his philosophy complete. The activity of management is partly a matter of mechanics, of creating and controlling a structure, and partly one of dynamics, of inspiring and energizing the group of people who work within this framework. Because Taylor was preoccupied with the first and indispensable preliminary task, clarifying the mechanics, some critics accused him of lacking an appreciation of—or any constructive approach to—the dynamics. It is true that some of his devices, such as functional foremanship as he described it, may not stand the test of time. His own life and writing, however, provide ample evidence of the integrity and essential rightness of his personal attitude toward those who worked with him and his concept of the obligations of management to society as a whole. There was never a strike in any plant where he personally was operating. It was in accord with his whole outlook that his immediate followers, particularly Gantt and Gilbreth, made a larger contribution to the

[1] Testimony before the Special Committee of the U.S. House of Representatives, 1912. Published in F. W. Taylor, *Scientific Management* (New York: Harper & Bros., 1947).

[2] F. B. Copley, *Frederick W. Taylor* (New York: Harper & Bros., 1923), Vol. II, Foreword, p. xviii.

dynamics of management. One of his major preoccupations toward the end of his life was the fear that those who came after would mistake the methods he had developed for the spirit which had made them possible. And in that spirit, that philosophy, his passion for the well-being of his fellow human beings was the outstanding element. His outburst in 1912, when he was stung by hostile criticism from a Committee of Congress, epitomizes his contribution to a new democratic philosophy of fundamental importance for our century:

> Scientific Management is not an efficiency device, nor is it any bunch or group of efficiency devices; it is not a new system of figuring costs; it is not holding a stop-watch on a man, and writing things down about him; it is not time study; it is not motion study; it is not the printing and ruling and unloading of a ton or two of blanks by a set of men saying, "Here's your system, go to it"; it is not divided foremanship, or functional foremanship; it is not any of the devices which the average man calls to mind when Scientific Management is spoken of. Now, in its essence, Scientific Management involves a complete mental revolution on the part of the working man engaged in any industry, and it involves an equally complete revolution on the part of those on the management's side—the foreman, the superintendent, the owner, the board of directors, and without this complete mental revolution on both sides Scientific Management does not exist. . . .[3]

And replying to the question whether the management principles he had developed could not be abused:

> I have never said that Scientific Management could be used for bad [ends]. It is possible to use the mechanism of Scientific Management for bad [ends] but not Scientific Management itself. It ceases to be Scientific Management the moment it is used for bad [ends].[4]

By "bad" ends he meant, as his whole life work testified, purposes which were selfish or sectional, harmful to the well-being of a democratic society or of any important segment of such a society. He started his working life as a laborer on the shop floor at Midvale, and he was faithful as long as he lived to what he believed to be the ultimate interests of working men and women.

Taylor was a blend of opposing impulses; his genius was "sparked" by internal conflict. His father was of an exceptionally gentle and retiring disposition. His mother was a woman of the liveliest intellectual curiosity and strong personality; from her side of the family he probably inherited his taste for mechanical invention. Both were Quaker in background and nonconformist and independent in principle.

From this common feature came the strongest element in Taylor's

[3] Copley, *op. cit.*
[4] *Idem.*

character, his intense sense of duty and of social obligation. He neither smoked nor drank, regarding even tea and coffee as stimulants to be avoided. He has been described as possessing "a whale of a New England conscience." He liked to say that it was more worthwhile in life to make a pleasure of duty than a duty of pleasure.

Taylor might have had a brilliant career purely as an inventor. But he would have regarded that as self-indulgence. Whenever he had invented a useful device or perfected a new idea, his social conscience stepped in and insisted that he must persuade his contemporaries to adopt it. He once described his interest in inventing things as "something of a temptation." He was exceptionally quick-minded and his patience, infinite in technical research, was not inexhaustible in human relations. Nor was he, for all his zeal, perfectly equipped as a propagandist; he often found difficulty in expressing himself in writing. He was primarily an engineer.

Yet for all his personal austerity Taylor was full of human sympathy and fun. His record at Midvale indicates that he was an outstanding practical executive. Despite his early struggle with his workers, his complete integrity won their respect and his intense enthusiasm swept them along. One of his colleagues said of him, "He would have filled up a corpse with enthusiasm, if only the corpse could hear."

It was tragic that the evening of his days should have been shadowed by the loss of personal friends and misunderstanding of his work. That this work should be identified with a type of management designed to oppress the workers does a grave injustice to his memory. He was as democratic in his attitudes as he was dedicated in spirit; from dawn to dusk his intensely hard-working life was devoted to the service of his fellow human beings.

SELECTED PUBLICATIONS

The best known of Taylor's writing were in the form of papers given to The American Society of Mechanical Engineers, many of them subsequently reproduced in book form.

1886 "The Relative Value of Water-gas and Gas from the Siemens Producer for Melting in the Open-Hearth Furnace," ASME *Transactions*, Vol. 7, pp. 669–679.

1893 "Notes on Belting," ASME *Transactions*, Vol. 15, pp. 204–259.

1895 "A Piece-Rate System," ASME *Transactions*, Vol. 16, pp. 856–903. Reproduced by, for example, *Engineering Magazine*, Vol. 10.

1903 "Shop Management," ASME *Transactions*, Vol. 24, pp. 1337–1480. Reproduced in book form (New York: Harper & Bros. 1911).

1905 *Concrete, Plain and Reinforced*. With S. E. Thompson. New York: Wiley & Sons.

1906 "On The Art of Cutting Metals," ASME *Transactions*, Vol. 28, pp. 31–350. Later published as a book.

1907 "A Comparison of University and Industrial Discipline and Method," *The Stevens Indicator*, Vol. 24, pp. 37–46.

1909 "Why Manufacturers Dislike College Graduates," *The Sibley Journal of Engineering*, Vol. 24, reproducing a paper presented to the Society for the Promotion of Engineering Education.

1910 Contribution to the Joint Meeting of ASME and the Institution of Mechanical Engineers, Birmingham, July. Reproduced *in extenso* in the *Proceedings* of the Institution and in summary form in *Engineering*, London, August 5th.

1911 "The Gospel of Efficiency," *American Magazine*, Vols. 71–72. Reproduced in three articles in *World's Work*. London edition issues of May, June, and July.

——— *The Principles of Scientific Management*. New York: Harper & Bros. Also in *The American Journal of Accountancy*, Vol. 12, 1911, as well as subsequent editions and translation.

1912 *Concrete Costs*. With S. E. Thompson. New York: Wiley & Sons.

Curriculum Vitae

1856 Born on March 20th in Philadelphia.

1872–1874 Studied at Phillips Exeter Academy. Taylor received an excellent general education, which included European travel and attendance at French and German schools. He intended to study law and qualified for Harvard, but temporary eye trouble led him to turn to engineering.

1875–1878 Apprenticed in the Enterprise Hydraulic Works, a small machine shop in Philadelphia, to the trades of pattern maker and machinist.

1878–1890 Joined Midvale Steel Works, Philadelphia, as a machine-shop laborer. He became successively shop clerk, machinist, gang boss, foreman, maintenance foreman, head of the drawing office, and Chief Engineer. In 1883 he obtained a degree in engineering, by evening study, from the Stevens Institute of Technology, Hoboken, N.J.

1890–1893 Employed as General Manager, Manufacturing Investment Co., manufacturers of paper fiber.

1893–1898 Active as consulting engineer in management. Among his clients were William Deering & Co., Northern Electrical Manufacturing Co., Lorain Steel Co., and Simonds Rolling Machine Co. At this time he mastered accounting by private study.

1898–1901 Employed by Bethlehem Steel Co., Bethlehem, Pa. During this period he and White made the discoveries leading to the development of high-speed tool steel that was first demonstrated at the 1900 Paris Exposition.

1901–1915 "Retired" from working for payment. From now until his death he devoted his energies as unpaid consultant, lecturer, etc., to furthering acceptance of scientific management in the United States and abroad.

1910 Owing to Brandeis's handling of the "Eastern rates case" nationwide attention was attracted to scientific management.

1911 Appeared before Congressional Committee of Enquiry, as a result of a strike at the Watertown Arsenal, to investigate "the Taylor and other systems of shop management." The use of time study and the payment of premium bonuses was banned on all government work.

1915 Died on March 21st, aged 59, in Philadelphia.

Taylor was President of The American Society of Mechanical Engineers (1906) and was awarded an honorary Sc.D. by the University of Pennsylvania (1906) and an honorary LL.D. by Hobart College (1912). He received an award (1900) from the Exposition Internationale Universelle, Paris, and, jointly with White, the Elliott Cresson Medal of the Franklin Institute of Pennsylvania (1902) for his work on high-speed cutting tools.

Courtesy R. Greenwood.

Carl Georg Lange Barth
(1860–1939)
United States

"BARTH was one of the two greatest management engineers that the United States has produced." These words, written by another pioneer of management,[1] may surprise the many people to whom the name of F. W. Taylor is familiar but the name of Carl Georg Lange Barth is unknown.

Barth was, in fact, the earliest, ablest, and closest associate of Taylor. The first contribution he brought to Taylor's work was his exceptional ability for engineering mathematics.

> When Barth became Taylor's assistant at the Bethlehem Steel Co. in 1899, the latter was in possession of a vast accumulation of experimental data relating to machine operations which no one had been able to analyze successfully. Taylor had submitted the data to several university professors of mathematics who had been unsuccessful in getting anything of value out of them. Taylor submitted them to Barth who soon developed the famous formula of twelve variables described in Taylor's *Shop Management*. On the basis of this formula he then developed the Barth slide rule.[2]

[1] H. S. Person, in *Advanced Management*, Vol. 4, No. 5, Section 1, 1939.
[2] *Idem.*

The slide rule enabled the person preparing the instruction card for the machine operator to utilize the formula easily, in the setup of a machine, for the best performance of any operation within the capacity of the machine.

After this achievement Barth became Taylor's right-hand man. The new slide rule, which Barth claimed as an important advance in the art of slide rule construction in general, proved to be the solution to most of Taylor's metal-cutting problems. Indeed, many of the standardized tools on which Taylor's system depended were the fruit of Barth's personal ingenuity. "If they became known as Taylor tools, they were so only in the sense that Taylor had inspired and directed the course of the experiments. If he avoided singling out Barth for special attention, it was for the good of the movement just as he subordinated his own part. But he came to recognize that this operated to do Barth not a little injustice."[3]

Barth was of value to Taylor not only as a mathematician. He rendered much service in Taylor's other researches into time study, fatigue study, and so on and in Taylor's work of introducing scientific management into manufacturing concerns. He was adept at devising practical procedures by which the Taylor principles could be implemented. In 1903, when progressive managers like James Mapes Dodge were impatient to use the new high-speed tool steel, Barth was appointed on Taylor's suggestion to supervise the application of the new methods in Link-Belt's Philadelphia plant. This was the first of many assignments which Barth undertook to install the Taylor methods either in part or as a complete system of management. In the early days Taylor was the outside consultant, charging no fee, and Barth was what was later termed the "system man" who was responsible for the actual installation. Barth soon became a consultant in his own right, and his slide rules were often the means of bringing about conversions to Taylor's methods. Taylor frequently introduced Barth as "the man who solves impossible problems." In his testimony before the Special House Committee he said:

> Mr. Barth here has been perhaps the most efficient man of all the men who have been connected with scientific management in devising new methods for turning out work fast. I can remember a number of—one or two—instances in which almost overnight he devised a method for turning out almost twenty times as much as had been turned out before with no greater effort to the workman.[4]

Barth continued, up to the time of Taylor's death in 1915, to work with Taylor in the plants which were the models of the new system. When the Harvard School of Business Administration was inaugurated in 1908, it was Barth who convinced the dean that the school should accept the Taylor system as the standard of modern management.

[3] F. B. Copley, *Frederick W. Taylor* (New York: Harper & Bros., 1923), Vol. II, p. 253.

[4] F. W. Taylor, *Scientific Management* (New York: Harper & Bros., 1947).

The words of Dr. Person may appropriately close this outline:

> Taylor had the vision. . . . But he did not like to handle the details. Here he needed able associates. Barth was the ablest among them. . . . It appears fair to say that the association of these two types of genius made each more creative than he might otherwise have been.[5]

Carl Barth was short and slender, with a severe professorial look. He was easily excitable and haughty of manner, although a look of great animation compensated for the absence of smiles.

> Some of the biggest business men this country has produced have had the lesson taught them that Carl Barth courts no one. When in his younger and more frisky days he would walk into a shop to report on what could be done to reorganize it on a Taylor basis, he had no hesitation in letting it appear how forcibly he was struck by the contrast between it and what he was used to. It was as if he had said, "My God! So this is what you call a machine shop!" Hearing of this, Fred Taylor would beseech him not always to find that everything was wrong—would beseech him to have a little tact. Whereupon Carl Barth would experience all the emotions of a pot called black by a kettle. What Homeric laughter would pass all down the line of the Taylor following at the bare mention of the word "tact"! And the spectacle of Fred Taylor and Carl Barth locking horns over this issue—that surely was the limit.[6]

SELECTED PUBLICATIONS

Books:

1919–1920 *Supplement to F. W. Taylor's "On the Art of Cutting Metals."* Series of 12 articles published in *Industrial Management* in 12 monthly issues between September 1919 and November 1920. These articles constitute the equivalent of a complete book on the development of the complete Feed and Speed slide rule.

Articles:

1903 "Slide Rules for the Machine Shop as Part of the Taylor System of Management," ASME *Transactions*, Vol.25.

1912 "Betterment of Machine Tool Operations by Scientific Metal Cutting," *Engineering Magazine*, Vol. 42.

1916 "Standardization of Machine Tools," ASME *Transactions*, December.

1918 "The Income Tax, An Engineer's Analysis with Suggestions,"

[5] Person, *op. cit.*

[6] Copley, *op. cit.* Vol. II, p. 27.

Philadelphia Chapter of ASME, *Journal* of the Engineers Club of Philadelphia, June–July.

1919 "Labor Turnover, A Mathematical Discussion," *Bulletin* of the Taylor Society, Vol. V, No. 2.

1922 "The Improved Belt Slide Rule," *Management Engineering*, June.

1924 "A Suggestion for a Premium System," *Management and Administration*, July, Vol. 8, No. 1.

1925 "A New Graphical Solution for Time Allowances in Task Setting," *Management and Administration*, Vol. 9, No. 2.

1926 "The Barth Standard Wage Scale," *Manufacturing Industries*, Vol. 11, No. 5.

Curriculum Vitae

1860 Born on February 28th in Christiana (now Oslo), Norway. He received a high school education and then entered the Horten Technical School, run under the auspices of the Navy Department.

1877–1881 Apprenticed in the navy yard, also acting in the last two years as a part-time, then a full-time instructor in mathematics at the Horten School.

1881 Emigrated in April to the United States.

1881–1895 Employed as draftsman with William Sellers & Co., Philadelphia, machine-tool manufacturers, ultimately rising to chief designer.

1895–1897 Employed as chief draftsman, Rankin & Fritch Foundry & Machine Co., St. Louis; later a designer of special machinery in the St. Louis Water Department.

1897 Taught mathematics and mechanical drawing at International Correspondence Schools, Scranton, Pa.

1898–1899 Taught mathematics and manual training, Ethical Culture School, New York City.

1899 Active as machine-shop engineer and special assistant to F. W. Taylor at Bethlehem Steel Co., Bethlehem, Pa.

1901 Left Bethlehem to work again with William Sellers & Co., Philadelphia.

1903 on Became consulting engineer in private practice, often collaborating with Taylor in the earlier years in plants such as those of the Tabor Mfg. Co. and Link-Belt Co. (both Philadelphia). Also worked independently—for instance, in the Yale & Towne Mfg. Co., Stamford, Conn.

1911–1916 Lectured on scientific management at Harvard University.

1912 Founded Carl G. Barth & Son in Philadelphia as a firm of consulting engineers. Most of the firm's work was to train clients' personnel in the techniques of the Taylor system.

1914–1916 Lectured on scientific management at the University of Chicago.

1919–1922 Lectured again at Harvard on scientific management.
1923–1939 In semi-retirement, always available for consultation when called on. He devoted much of his time to higher mathematics.
1939 Died on October 28th, aged 79, in Philadelphia.

Barth was made an honorary member of the Taylor Society in 1920, the only other honorary members being Taylor and Le Chatelier. He was a life member of The American Society on Mechanical Engineers.

Courtesy The Twentieth Century Fund.

Edward Albert Filene
(1860–1937)
United States

EDWARD Albert Filene was the founder of the Twentieth Century Fund and the architect of the International Management Institute. He was also a pioneer of retail management.

Filene began the practice of management from the bottom in a small retail business in Boston. Basing his policy on principles first stated in the nineteenth century by the Frenchman Boucicaut (the "father" of the department store), Filene developed his business, through efficient organization and a series of dramatic innovations in sales methods, into one of the first great American department stores on the modern pattern. The principles that guided him were, in effect, "small profits and quick returns" and "the customer is always right." He wrote authoritative books and articles on these principles of retail management. In them he affirmed that the long-term aims of business coincide with those of social progress. "The merchant's true function, he said, is not making money at the expense of the customer, but satisfying genuine wants adequately." Thus a "social" policy was also good business, and he made a fortune to prove it. His book *The Model Stock Plan* (1930) probably had a greater impact on retail management than any other book written on the subject of distribution.

In addition to innumerable other business and public activities, Filene used his fortune to endow the Twentieth Century Fund, a research institution conducting its own studies in economic and social problems. Many of these studies have had a close bearing on management both in the United States and in other countries of the world. The Fund aims at rigorous and impartial fact finding, by intelligent researchers, presented in book form and in pithy news items which are publicized to keep the American people aware of the facts of their economy. Its pioneering work along the lines laid down by Filene has made it famous. Others among the many organizations he helped to create did not observe his principles and have been less enduring. Of one of them he said, "They assemble their own opinions instead of facts to solve business problems. I was forced to the conclusion that neither the ends of business nor the ends of democracy can be served by such a policy."

Filene, through the Fund, took the decisive initiative in creating the International Management Institute, which operated from 1927 to 1933. The Institute's establishment came as a new achievement of the international management movement shortly after the successes of the first international conferences. For the first time the movement was not represented by a permanent body with its own international secretariat. Financed jointly by the Twentieth Century Fund and the International Labor Office and located in Geneva, the Institute acted as an international clearing house for the exchange of information on better methods of management. It published a monthly bulletin in three languages, held a number of technical conferences, issued many reports on special subjects, assisted in the reorganization of a number of international bodies, and—perhaps most important of all—helped to bring into personal contact individuals in many countries who shared a common interest in the technique of business organization.

The Institute was the only body to be entrusted with international research and communication on management problems either before or since the six years of its existence. It fell victim to Hitler's rise to power in Germany and the depression of the early 1930s, which cut by two-fifths the purchasing power of the dollar in terms of Swiss francs. The conjunction of these two events destroyed, for the time being, Filene's interest in Europe, but not before the Institute had justified his idea by much useful pioneering work in management.

> Ten years after his death men whose judgment is equally good and whose opportunities of observing Edward A. Filene were equally adequate still disagree flatly about what manner of man he was. He was a paradox in a dozen ways. . . . He prided himself on a marked indifference to the ordinary charities, yet he gave away his entire fortune. He contended that selfishness is the basic motive of human activity and stripped himself to improve the lot of mankind. He was a large employer and in many respects an autocratic one who fought consistently for the rights of wage earners. He could be startlingly mean in small matters and as startlingly generous when thousands or millions were involved. . . .
>
> There was the big man who built up an obscure women's speciality shop into the greatest store of its kind in the world, who played a large

> part in establishing the United States Chamber of Commerce and the International Chamber of Commerce, who apprehended—"comprehended" is rather too strong a word—the trend of modern economics long before his contemporaries, who understood mass distribution before Ford understood mass production, who grasped the principles of the New Deal before Roosevelt did, who set up two great foundations and became the counselor of statesmen and potentates all around the earth.
>
> That man deserved the respectful consideration of mankind and got it.*

But though he was basically thoughtful and generous he was not a happy man. He never married. He quarreled readily with friends and associates and drove those who worked for him. This personal isolation deprived him, in the opinion of those who knew him well, of some of the sympathy and understanding that his work merited.

SELECTED PUBLICATIONS

1924 *The Way Out*. New York: Doubleday, Page & Co. 139 pp.
1925 *More Profits from Merchandising*. Chicago: A. W. Shaw & Co. 159 pp.
1930 *The Model Stock Plan*. New York: McGraw-Hill. 253 pp.
1932 *Successful Living in this Machine Age*. New York: Simon & Schuster. 274 pp.
1934 *The Consumer's Dollar* (pamphlet). New York: The John Day Co. 29 pp.
1935 "*Morals in Business*" (Reprint of lecture). Berkeley: Committee on the Barbara Weinstock Lectures, University of California. 45 pp.
1937 *Next Steps Forward in Retailing*. With Werner K. Gabler and Percy S. Brown. New York: Harper & Bros. 309 pp.
1939 *Speaking of Change*. Selection of speeches and articles. Kingsport, Tenn.: Kingsport Press. For associates of Edward A. Filene—material selected during his lifetime but published after his death.

Curriculum Vitae

1860 Born on September 3rd in Salem, Mass. Filene's father had emigrated from German-held Poland to settle in New England and had started several retail stores. Filene had an elementary and high school education, and planned to attend Harvard, but his father's failing health obliged him to enter the family business (1879) with his brother Lincoln Filene. Throughout his career he was President of William

* Extracts from Gerald W. Johnson, *Liberal's Progress* (New York: Coward McCann, 1948), pp. 1–35.

Filene's Sons Co., though from 1928 on he had no active part in operating the store.

1909 Organized the credit-union movement of the United States.

1919 Founded the Twentieth Century Fund.

1921 Founded the Credit Union National Extension Bureau to direct a mutual association of credit unions throughout the United States.

1933 Served as Chairman, Massachusetts State Recovery Board.

1935 Founded the Consumer Distribution Corporation.

1936 Founded the Good Will Fund (now the Edward A. Filene Good Will Fund).

1937 Died on September 26th, aged 77, in Paris.

Filene was awarded honorary degrees by Lehigh University (1931), Rollins College (1932), and Tulane University (1935). He was an officer of the Legion of Honor (France), cavaliere, Order of the Crown (Italy), and commander of the Order of the White Lion (Czechoslovakia). In addition, he held the Austrian Gold Cross of Merit. He was active in many political, social, and economic societies, including the Society for the Advancement of Management. Not the least of his international services was his invention of the simultaneous-translation device (the Filene-Finlay Simultaneous Translater) used at the Nüremberg war-criminal trials and subsequently at every international gathering of importance.

Courtesy R. Greenwood.

Henry Laurence Gantt
(1861–1919)
United States

HENRY Laurence Gantt was one of the earliest members of the scientific management group in the United States to direct his major interest toward the human being in industry. "In all problems of management," he wrote, "the human element is the most important one."

In its first years the movement had had a different emphasis. Taylor, although his ultimate objective had undoubtedly been to improve the lot of the working man, had sought the solution of industrial problems through the analysis of processes, the planning of work and organization; for individual motivation he had relied largely on financial incentives. His was an essential first step. But Gantt's methods, applied when "Taylorism" was under a cloud owing to labor opposition, were undoubtedly a further step. He has been called the forerunner of modern industrial democracy, and his work is only today being fully recognized. To many familiar with modern management methods he is known only by the one particular chart that bears his name—though he evolved many charts. Yet his contributions of detail—the bonus plan, the charts, the methods of production control—were, as with Taylor, no more than tools, the methods through which he expressed his central philosophy.

For many years a close associate of Taylor's, Gantt made his first original contribution to management with his "task and bonus" system of wages, the results of which were presented in a paper to The American Society of

Mechanical Engineers in 1901. This system was working successfully at the Midvale Steel Co. earlier than Taylor's differential piece-rate system, and it won acceptance long afterward because it was simple, generally applicable, and less severe than Taylor's on failure to attain standard. Its advantage was to assure to the worker a definite reward for finishing a task in the time allotted and an extra reward if he or she could do still better. The system had the same essential basis as that of Taylor: namely, that of a scientifically measured task.

Gantt's next contribution was to evolve graphic charts for production control. The "daily balance chart," the forerunner of the later but better-known "Gantt chart," was designed to give a picture of the results of the day's work by noon of the following day and thus to facilitate continuous preplanning of production. From the daily balance chart Gantt went on to graphic cost-control and idle-expense charts. The final evolution, the bar chart for which he became famous, made the important change of planning production programs in terms of *time* instead of in quantities. Nothing could be simpler than the Gantt chart, yet nothing could at the time have been more revolutionary.

In his later years, Gantt's influence in bringing American industry, and particularly the American engineering profession, to accept the new concepts of management was enhanced by his success in insisting that the training of workers should become a responsibility of management. In 1908 he was putting forward views not generally accepted until the end of the First World War. By then he was already thinking further ahead, to "democracy in industry" and the humanizing of the science of management. In his later writings he rose to philosophical stature in his proposals for equality of opportunity in industry and for the identification of the interests of employers and employees on the basis of scientifically ascertained facts.

He was, of all the leading pioneers of management, possibly the most sensitive to the importance of acceptable leadership as the primary element in the success of any business undertaking. He was, indeed, called "an apostle of industrial peace."[1] His famous Yale lecture in 1915, which bears the title "Industrial Leadership," is one long plea for the wider recognition of the human factor in management and of the fact that the financial incentive is only one among many of "the motives which influence men." In common with Harrington Emerson, Gantt suggested that business should not restrict its "case studies" to its own limited experience of this particular problem. It might with advantage draw on the much longer records of military and government organizations which had been handling large numbers of employees for many more centuries than the few decades in which business enterprises had been dealing with "big battalions."

In 1929 it was decided by The American Society of Mechanical Engineers and the Institute of Management (the latter eventually replaced by the

[1] By Fred J. Miller, Past President, The American Society of Mechanical Engineers, at first award of Gantt Medal in 1929.

American Management Association) to establish a Henry Laurence Gantt Gold Medal, which would be awarded "for distinguished achievement in industrial management as a service to the community." The first award went posthumously to Gantt himself—"for his humanizing influence upon industrial management and for invention of the Gantt chart."

Gantt was the temperamental opposite of Taylor, although they were close associates for many years. "Taylor was thoroughgoing. Gantt did not wish to go any further than you were willing to have him. Taylor was profound, revolutionary; Gantt adaptable, opportunist. . . . At Bethlehem, as elsewhere, Gantt's ready ability to make the best of whatever situation arose was of great service in supplementing Taylor's bulldog ability."[2] We are told that he won Taylor's confidence by promptly solving a mathematical problem which had baffled Taylor, "Gantt reaching his solution by emphasizing the coincidences and minimizing the differences, and so tracing out a law, a method highly characteristic of his fluent, adaptable nature."[3]

In his later years Gantt attained the stature of a leader and thinker in industry. The many tributes paid to him at the memorial meeting of The American Society of Mechanical Engineers made clear that his high ideals for harmony within the industrial community were the reflection of genuine gifts of leadership and of the ability to enlist the enthusiasm of others in a worthwhile endeavor. The greatest tribute to his memory is the number of leaders in management in the next generation who ascribed their inspiration to his example and teaching.

SELECTED PUBLICATIONS

Books:

1910 *Work, Wages and Profits*. New York: Engineering Magazine Co. 312 pp.

1916 *Industrial Leadership*. New Haven, Conn.: Yale University Press. 128 pp.

1919 *Organizing for Work*. New York: Harcourt, Brace and Howe.

Papers.

Gantt read 12 papers to The American Society of Mechanical Engineers, two early ones on technical subjects and the rest on aspects of management. Among the most important are:

1901 "A Bonus System of Rewarding Labor," ASME *Transactions*, Vol. 23, pp. 341–372.

1903 "A Graphical Daily Balance in Manufacture," ASME *Transactions*, Vol. 24, pp. 1322–1336.

1908 "Training Workmen in Habits of Industry and Co-operation," ASME *Transactions*, Vol. 30, pp. 1037–1063.

[2] Copley, *Frederick W. Taylor, op. cit.*, Vol. II, p. 23.
[3] *Ibid.*, Vol. I, p. 252.

1915 "The Relations Between Production and Costs," ASME *Transactions*, Vol. 37, pp. 109–128.

1918 "Efficiency and Democracy," ASME *Transactions*, Vol. 40, pp. 799–808.

Articles, Addresses and Reports:
Gantt was a prolific writer and an active speaker. Most of his early writings were on technical problems, but from about 1902 on he produced an almost continuous flow of publications and pronouncements on the various aspects of management in which he was currently interested as his principles and methods developed. Over 150 titles are listed in the official biography by Alford.

Curriculum Vitae

1861 Born on May 18th on a plantation in Maryland. His family were prosperous farmers, but their fortunes were dissipated in the Civil War while Gantt was still in early childhood, and his early years were marked by some privation. Gantt was educated at the McDonagh School and at Johns Hopkins University (A.B., 1880).

1880–1883 Taught natural sciences and mechanics at McDonagh School.

1884–1886 Worked as a draftsman with a firm of iron founders and qualified at Stevens Institute (1884) as a mechanical engineer.

1887–1893 At Midvale Steel Co., Philadelphia. From Assistant in the Engineering Department, became Assistant to the Chief Engineer (F. W. Taylor) and then Superintendent of Casting Department.

1893–1901 Held a succession of technical executive posts except for one year (1894–1895) as a consultant in Philadelphia. Most of the time he was in close contact with Taylor—for instance, in consulting work at the Bethlehem Steel Co.

1902–1919 Active as consultant. In 1917 he relinquished private activity to accept a government assignment in the Frankford Arsenal and, later, one in shipbuilding for the Emergency Fleet Corporation.

1919 Died on November 23rd, aged 58, at his home in Montclair, N.J.

Gantt was Vice-President of The American Society of Mechanical Engineers (1914–1915) and received the Distinguished Service Medal for his assistance in the war effort.

Courtesy Institut des Hautes Etudes de Belgique.

Paul Sollier
(1861–1933)
France/Belgium

WITH Sollier of Belgium the contribution of psychology to the management of industry appears for the first time in this book. In continental Europe, the pioneering years were the 1920s, when academic psychologists first began to look beyond their clinics to explore the practical application of psychology to problems of the human being at work in the factory. From the application of physiology on one hand and psychology on the other, the science of "psychotechnics" or, in Anglo-Saxon terms, industrial or occupational psychology, grew in continental Europe.

Paul Sollier was the pioneer of psychotechnics in Belgium. He was by training a psychiatrist and was, for many years, Professor of Pathology at the Belgian Institute for Advanced Studies in Brussels. He gradually, however, became interested in the practical application of psychology in industry, and in 1923 he founded the Section d'Ergologie at the Institute. This developed into the Ecole Belge d'Ergologie, which, with its associated laboratory, became the center of research into industrial psychology in Belgium and a model for other countries. Sollier greatly developed the activities of the school in the ten years which followed and which ended with his death. He instituted numerous new courses, undertook research projects, secured the collaboration of Belgian industry in his studies and laboratory experiments, and himself invented several mechanical research devices. Out of this work came the Belgian contribution to vocational guidance and selection, operator training, merit rating, rehabilitation of disabled workers, and the other techniques of industrial psychology which have today so profoundly modified the understanding of people in many countries of the "human factor" in industry.

Sollier was a prolific writer, first in the French *Journal de psychologie* (1925 on) and then in two specialized journals which he was largely instrumental in founding: *Revue de la science du travail* (1929 on) and *Bulletin ergologique du Comité National Belge de l'Organisation Scientifique* (1931 on). Today the titles of his articles seem to us familiar, often outmoded, subjects for research. But at the time their novelty was great, for these journals did much to disseminate and develop knowledge of a scientific nature about the human factor in industrial work.

Sollier summarized his life work in his book *La Psychotechnique* (1933), finished after his death by his colleague and successor Professor José Drabs. The Association Internationale de la Psychotechnique is today a flourishing and active institution which can count on the participation of organizations of applied psychology in most countries of the Free World. The name of Sollier should not be forgotten as one who did much to make psychotechnics an accepted branch of management studies.

Sollier is remembered as having been physically robust. He also is said to have possessed, in addition to his more serious qualities, great charm.

SELECTION PUBLICATIONS

Book:

1933 *La Psychotechnique* (Psychotechnics: Introduction to a Technique for Studying the Human Factor in Work). With José Drabs. Brussels: Editions du Comité Central Industriel de Belgique. Paris: Alcan.

Articles:

Sollier wrote more than 150 articles, the greater part of which, from 1926 to 1933, dealt with psycho-physiological subjects related to the study of the human factor in industry and were published in the new journals devoted to psychotechnics: *Revue de la science du travail* (1929 on) and *Bulletin ergologique du Comité National Belge de l'Organisation Scientifique* (1931 on). The following are some of the titles:

"Automatization in Work"

"Experiment in Functional Classification of Looms for the Purpose of Vocational Guidance"

"Fatigue and Energy Expenditure"

"Medicine of Industry and the Factory"

"Practical Study of Attention"

"The Prediction of Accurate Motor Performance"

"Preselection of Morse Telegraphists"

"Problem of Aptitudes"

"Psychotechnical Research on Filing Clerks"

"Rational Choice of Typists and Stenographers"
"Reaction Time to Stop Signals"
"Scientific Choice of Chauffeurs"
"Technical Aptitude and Apprenticeship"
"Technique of Vocational Guidance"

Curriculum Vitae

1861	Born in France of French nationality.
1890	Received Doctor of Medicine degree in Paris. Subsequently served as intern in the Paris hospitals. Director of the Sanatorium of Boulogne-sur-Seine, France, and Professor of Hygiene in the Paris Schools of Nursing.
1897	Was Professor of Pathology, Institut des Hautes Etudes de Belgique (Belgian Institute for Advanced Studies), Brussels.
1915–1919	Was Director of the Centre Neurologique Militaire, Lyons, France.
1923	Created the Section d'Ergologie at the Belgian Institute for Advanced Studies.
1924	Created the Laboratory for Industrial Psychology at the Belgian Institute for Advanced Studies.
1925	Saw the Section d'Ergologie become the Ecole Belge d'Ergologie, annexed to the Institute, with the Laboratory undertaking the research work of the School.
1933	Died at age of 72.

Sollier was a laureate of the Belgian Academy of Sciences (Lallemand Prize, 1920); commander of the Legion of Honor, the Order of Leopold, and the Order of Orange of Nassau; knight of Christ of Portugal; and knight of Saint-Anne of Russia.

Hugo Münsterberg
(1863–1916)
Germany/United States

HUGO Münsterberg was the father of industrial psychology—the first man to propose that the new knowledge which inductive psychology was developing in universities and experimental laboratories could be put to use to further the objectives of industry. He was also the first to define the scope and method of this new applied science.

Not only was Münsterberg foremost among theoretical psychologists of his time, but he had also, early in his career, been initiating the use of psychology for practical purposes—education and crime detection, for example. About 1910 he and his students began experimental research into application of psychology to industry, trying out their tests in many large industrial plants. The outcome was Münsterberg's pioneering book *Psychology and Industrial Efficiency*, published in German in 1912 and in English in 1913.

Münsterberg distinguished two significant social movements in America, to both of which psychology could make a contribution: "the effort to furnish to pupils leaving school guidance in their choice of a vocation, and the . . . movement toward scientific management in commerce and industry."[1] After paying a perceptive tribute to the work of F. W. Taylor and stressing that applied psychology is concerned with means, not ends, Münsterberg put forward in this book his program for the contribution of the psychologist to industry:

[1] Münsterberg, *Psychology and Industrial Efficiency* (Boston: Houghton, Mifflin Co. 1913), p. 39.

> We select three chief purposes of business life, purposes which are important in commerce and industry and every economic endeavor. We ask how we can find the men whose mental qualities make them best fitted for the work which they have to do; secondly, under what psychological conditions we can secure the greatest and most satisfactory output of work from every man; and finally how we can produce most completely the influences on human minds which are desired in the interests of business. In other words, we ask how to find the best possible work, and how to secure the best possible effects.[2]

Münsterberg supported this systematic formulation of the aims of the new science by giving the results of his experiments under each of the three heads. One of these experiments, his tests for the selection of streetcar drivers, was entirely novel. It marked the beginning of vocational guidance along scientific lines in industry.

Münsterberg's book stimulated the development of the new science, not only in Germany and the United States, but elsewhere also. Great numbers of business people came to consult Münsterberg at Harvard. In the First World War, his influence was immeasurably extended when nearly every combatant nation used psychology to select and train its armed forces. The United States, on entering the war in 1917, developed and applied army tests for two million men—an unprecedented experiment in the use of psychology. In great measure owing to Münsterberg's work, industrial psychology was, by the end of the war, firmly established as one of the most important aspects of the science of management.

Hugo Münsterberg was in every sense an outstanding figure. It has been said that from the outset of his brilliant career he was "a storm center, the object of both vehement attacks and unstinted praise."[3] His "non-Aryan" parentage, and the personal antagonisms he aroused, blocked his career in Germany; and although he achieved greatness in his adopted country, the United States, he never relinquished his German nationality and continued to hope for acceptance in his native land.

A great publicist, Münsterberg sought to influence affairs. His books and articles written in popular style, and his many public activities, brought psychology to the attention of the world at large and greatly advanced its acceptance by practical men in industry. It was no mean achievement for one who was also recognized as a foremost authority on the theory of the subject. His ingenuity in suggesting new fields for experiment was extraordinary. As he became more and more a public personage, he had less time to give his students. ". . . Students were too awed by his extracurricular activities to bother him; for surely they would not be expected to intrude when he was closeted with the Argentine ambassador, or was serving as host to a German prince, or giving an interview to a metropolitan editor, or

[2] *Ibid.*, p. 24.

[3] Quoted in A. A. Roback, *History of American Psychology* (New York: Library Publishers, 1952). p. 200.

advising the head of a detective bureau, or entertaining a wealthy brewer, who might be enlisted as a patron of a projected museum."[4]

Perhaps because he did not achieve a real bond with his students, Münsterberg left no disciples and his reputation did not endure as long as it deserved, being marred toward the close of his life by his political activities in Germany and the United States. Yet he was "of a kindly spirit, hospitable, generous, appreciative of others. His mental energy seemed limitless, his industry tireless, his optimism unquenchable."[5] Above all, his contemporaries recognized in him a giant of originality, and his students have testified to his influence upon them: "In his seminary, he was at his best, and there we got the meat of our work. Never did any loose conclusion or faulty method get by him. . . . We were all drawn to Harvard by the same force—it was *the* center for psychology at the time. . . . He radiated scientific impulses, and profoundly altered the course of American psychology. . . .[6]

SELECTED PUBLICATIONS

Münsterberg wrote, in all, more than 20 volumes, besides a prodigious number of articles in periodicals. Only those publications relating to applications of psychology to industry are noted here.

1910 *American Problems—From the Point of View of a Psychologist.* New York: Moffatt, Yard and Co. Contains chapters on "The Choice of a Vocation" and "The Market and Psychology."

1912 *Psychologie und Wirtschaftsleben.* Leipzig: J. A. Barth. Republished with modifications as.

1913 *Psycyhology and Industrial Efficiency.* Boston: Houghton, Mifflin Co.; London: Constable & Co. 320 pp.

1914 *Grundzüge der Psychotechnik.* Leipzig. Not translated into English.

—— *Psychology, General and Applied.* New York: Appleton.

1918 *Business Psychology,* Chicago: La Salle Extension University in the series of texts issued to students of the Business Administration course.

Curriculum Vitae

1863 Born on June 1st in Danzig, Germany. His father was a lumber merchant.

1872 Attended gymnasium of Danzig.

1882 Attended University of Geneva (one semester), then University of Leipzig, studying medicine and psychology.

[4] *Idem.*

[5] "Minute on the Life and Services of Professor Hugo Münsterberg," *Harvard University Gazette,* reporting a meeting of the Faculty of Arts and Sciences on January 16th, 1917.

[6] K. Dunlap, *History of Psychology in Autobiography,* Vol. II, p. 42; quoted in Roback, *op. cit.,* p. 199. It should be mentioned that the magnetic attractions at Harvard at this time included not only Münsterberg but also his senior colleague William James.

1885	Awarded Ph.D. in psychology, University of Leipzig, under Wundt.
1887	Awarded Doctor of Medicine degree, University of Heidelberg.
1887–1892	Employed as Lecturer, then Assistant Professor (in philosophy) at University of Freiburg, teaching psychology privately in his spare time.
1892–1895	At age of 29 went to Harvard University, at invitation of William James, to take charge of psychological laboratory as Professor of Experimental Psychology.
1895–1897	Again teaching at Freiburg.
1897	Returned permanently to Harvard as Professor of Psychology.
1903	Largely instrumental in having cornerstone laid for Emerson Hall at Harvard University, the third floor of which was used as a laboratory especially equipped for experimental psychology.
1910	Served as exchange professor from Harvard to University of Berlin, where he helped to create the Deutsch-America Institute.
1912	Attended meeting of German experimental psychologists in Berlin.
1916	Died on December 16th, aged 53, at Harvard.

Münsterberg received the honorary degrees of A.M. from Harvard (1901), LL.D. from Washington University, St. Louis, (1904), and Litt.D. from Lafayette Collete (1907). He was President of the American Psychological Association in 1898 and of the American Philosophical Association in 1908; a Fellow of the American Academy of Arts and Sciences and a member of the Washington Academy of Sciences; organizer and Vice-President of the International Congress of Arts and Sciences at St. Louis (1904); and Vice-President of the International Philosophical Congress at Heidelberg.

Dexter Simpson Kimball
(1865–1952)
United States

DEAN Dexter Kimball's earliest contribution to management, of the many he made in a long life of service to the American engineering profession, was his decision in 1904 to offer an elective course of lectures in works administration to senior students in mechanical engineering at Cornell University. This was the first course in any American university to teach the principles of management with full reference to the pioneering work accomplished up to that time by F. W. Taylor.

As Kimball himself recognized in his autobiography, the course was the fruit of his immediate appreciation of Taylor's paper *Shop Management*, read to The American Society of Mechanical Engineers the previous year. Kimball recorded his view that "this remarkable paper was . . . the first effort to apply logical methods to the problems of production and management. No other single document has had such a profound effect upon American industry and management." He had wished to call his new course at Cornell Economics of Production,

> but Dean Smith thought that was a little high-brow, and so we settled on works administration as more likely to get by the Committee on Courses. For the first time I as a teacher experienced the skepticism that many educators display toward new educational ideas. One of the older professors remarked that he saw no reason why I should not offer such a course, but for the life of him he could not see what I could put in it. . . . Anyway, the Committee on Courses agreed that

> no serious harm could be done by my course in works administration. . . . So far as I know, these were the first lectures on the economics of production given in any university in this country. There had been books and lectures on shop systems, costs, etc., but I believe this was the first effort to inform engineering students of the economic basis of modern production.[1]

The lead which Cornell University thus took in teaching the new science of management was long maintained. Four years later, in 1908, the new Harvard School of Business Administration hesitated for some time before deciding to adopt the Taylor system as the basis for its teaching of shop management.

The Kimball book which grew out of these lectures at Cornell, *Principles of Industrial Organization* (1913), was a pioneering effort in management literature and became a standard textbook. Almost 40 years later it was still being issued in a new edition to meet the steady demand from students and from practicing engineers and managers. Scholarly yet practical in its review of the whole field of management principles and practice, it has been the basis of many engineers' management education in Europe as well as in America.

Kimball was a happy example of that blend of practical experience with academic work which has enriched American teaching of management. He lived to a ripe old age and rendered outstanding services to American engineering, to engineering education, and to the science of management. At Cornell University he influenced hundreds of undergraduates, among them many future leaders of industry. In his public and consulting work he was in contact in speeches and writings with very many teachers, college administrators, and engineers, and he actively participated in most of the societies and organizations concerned with the advancement of management. His achievement may be measured by the many honors which came to him and the unique collection of management medals of which he was the recipient.

> There exists in memory a portrait of this dynamic Dean. He enters with cheery welcome and quick, sure step. He perches his active and slender body on the corner of a desk or table, one foot dangling and swaying to and fro. From his hands hangs a not too elegant hat. He chuckles good-naturedly, head cocked on one side. The intense piercing eyes sparkle with interest and good humor. His manner and language are simple, unaffected. Here is a warm, genial, kindly and friendly person, repeating, like Homer of old, stories that are dear to him.
>
> One such story called for a bit of acting. It was the Dean's impersonation of the serious-minded but dreary college professor at a faculty meeting. Standing behind a table and leaning on his right arm, the Dean would begin a finely spun academic argument with the opening words "On

[1] Dexter S. Kimball, *I Remember* (New York: McGraw-Hill, 1953), p. 85.

the one hand." After covering all the points on that side of the case he would shift his weight to the left arm and take a new lease of his theme by saying, "But on the other hand." Thus the objective and analytical mind of the professor would exhaust all the possibilities of debate on both sides of the question without arriving at a single clear-cut conclusion. . . .

Here, in these and other stories, is wisdom disguised in homespun, and the best of life recaptured and retold by an optimist who had found most things and most people good and hid from his friends the memories of events that were evil or sad. . . . With stories told and farewells spoken, there was a quick movement of the hand to put in place the sparse locks across a balding head, and he was gone, having refreshed and enriched the lives of those he left behind.[2]

SELECTED PUBLICATIONS

Books:

1909 *Elements of Machine Design*. With John H. Barr. New York: Wiley & Sons.
1911 *Industrial Education*. Ithaca: Cornell University Press.
1913 *Principles of Industrial Organization*. New York: McGraw-Hill, 478 pp.
1914 *Elements of Cost Finding*. New York: Alexander Hamilton Institute.
1919 *Plant Management*. New York: Alexander Hamilton Institute.
1929 *Industrial Economics*. New York: McGraw-Hill.
1953 *I Remember*. New York: McGraw-Hill. 259 pp.

Articles:

A complete list of the 269 pamphlets, magazine articles, and miscellaneous items written by Dexter S. Kimball is given in his autobiography *I Remember*.

Curriculum Vitae

1865 Born on October 21st in New River, New Brunswick, Canada. The family went to California to settle during his boyhood.
1881–1887 Worked as apprentice and journeyman with Pope & Talbot, Port Gamble.
1887–1893 Worked in shops of Union Iron Works, San Francisco.
1893–1896 Studied mechanical engineering at Stanford University.
1896 Received A.B. in Engineering.
1896–1898 Worked in Engineering Department of Union Iron Works, San Francisco.
1898–1901 Was Assistant Professor of Machine Design, Sibley College, Cornell University.

[2] From *Mechanical Engineering*, December 1952.

1901–1904 Employed as Works Manager, Stanley Electric Manufacturing Co., Pittsfield, Mass.

1904–1905 Was Professor of Machine Construction, Sibley College, Cornell University.

1905–1915 Was Professor of Machine Design and Construction, Cornell University, also undertaking consulting work in industry.

1913 Received M.E. degree from Stanford University.

1915–1920 Was Professor of Industrial Engineering, Sibley College, Cornell University.

1920–1936 Served as first dean of the unified College of Engineering, Cornell University (subsequently emeritus).

1918 and 1929–1930 Served as Acting President, Cornell University.

1941 Was Chairman, Tools and Equipment Group, Priorities Division, Office of Production Management, Washington, D.C.

1944 Was special lecturer in industrial organization and management in the Federal War Training program and in the Postgraduate School of the U.S. Naval Academy.

1952 Died on November 1st at age of 87.

Kimball held the following degrees: LL.D., Rochester University (1926); D.Sc., Case School of Applied Science (1930); D.E., Kansas State College (1933), Northeastern University (1934), and Lehigh University (1939). He was President of The American Society of Mechanical Engineers (1922) and honorary member from 1939; President of the American Engineering Council (1926–1928); and President of the Society for the Promotion of Engineering Education (1929). He was awarded the following medals:

1933 Lamme Gold Medal of the Society for the Promotion of Engineering Education.

1933 Worcester Reed Warner Gold Medal of The American Society of Mechanical Engineers.

1943 Gantt Medal of The American Society of Mechanical Engineers and the American Management Association "for outstanding attainment in the teaching and practice of industrial management and for distinguished contributions to its literature."

1948 Taylor Key of the Society for the Advancement of Management.

Karol Adamiecki
(1866–1933)
Poland

KAROL Adamiecki distinguished himself among the pioneers of management by his original contribution to management theory, by the part he took in the Polish and international movements for scientific management, and by his striking practical success.

His original contribution to management theory was contemporary with, but initially quite independent of, that of F. W. Taylor. From 1895 on he was using his experience as an engineer in Polish and Russian rolling mills to formulate principles of organization and in particular his "theory of harmonization," which set out a law governing the planning and control of teamwork in production. To apply this theory, Adamiecki developed the "harmonogram," a graphical device for simultaneously charting several complicated operations and thus ensuring the harmonization of a large number of activities. He constructed the first harmonogram in 1896. In rolling mills and mechanical-engineering factories in the chemical industry, agriculture, and mining, within Poland and abroad, the introduction of harmonograms led to increases in output between 100 and 400 percent.

Adamiecki continued to develop his theory with remarkable results until his death. He described it and the results of its application for the first time in 1903 before the Society of Russian Engineers in Ekaterinoslaw; it caused a sensation in Russian technical circles. Its general principles, as well as the techniques associated with their application, follow the same lines that Taylor laid down for scientific management. Thus, in the same year when F. W.

Taylor was establishing a landmark in the management movement of the West with his paper *Shop Management*, Adamiecki was preparing the East to receive the new ideas, although the name of Taylor was yet unknown either to him or to his audience. Had this contribution been made in a language more accessible to the West, it would have achieved the still wider recognition that it well merited.

From 1903 on, Adamiecki pioneered the Polish management movement. While continuing his work as an engineer and a consultant, he pursued this self-appointed task for some years by the writing of articles on aspects of organization and management. Then, in 1919, he was appointed to lecture in management at Warsaw Polytechnic, later becoming the first professor of management. In the same year he set up an Institute for Propaganda in Favor of Rationalization. Between 1919 and 1924 he fostered, in a large number of towns in Poland, the establishment of groups of engineers for the study of scientific management, and in 1925 his efforts resulted in the foundation of the Polish Institute of Scientific Management in Warsaw. He became the first chairman and director of the Institute.

Already by the end of the First World War, Adamiecki's reputation had spread far beyond the frontiers of Poland, and in 1926 the International Committee for Scientific Management (CIOS) appointed him its first vice-president. Soon after, he was offered a seat on the Board of the International Management Institute which was set up in Geneva in 1927.

At the Fifth International Management Congress in Amsterday in 1932, Karol Adamiecki received the Gold Medal of the International Committee. It would have made him sad to know that Poland, a country in the vanguard of the management movement of his generation, no longer takes her place among the members of the International Committee for Scientific Management.

Adamiecki's career was one of unusual struggle, for it was not politically easy for a Pole of his generation to achieve a leading position in the industry of Eastern Europe, and in his later years he was tragically afflicted with the physical infirmity of paralysis. This illness, which was to cause his death, prevented him from coming to Amsterdam to receive his Gold Medal in person in 1932.

The memory which Adamiecki's friends retain of him is of a man of great courage. He is remembered, also, for his perfect courtesy and broad-mindedness as a teacher, as a friend, and lastly as a citizen of Europe by virtue of the wholehearted support he gave to the international management movement.

SELECTED PUBLICATIONS

Beginning in 1903, Adamiecki contributed a very large number of papers and articles to Polish and foreign reviews on the social and economic effects of rationalization, on the part played by the engineer in industry, on methods of wage payment, and on the humanization of work. For instance:

1903 "Principles of Collective Work," paper presented to the Society of Russian Engineers at Ekaterinoslaw.

1909 "The Graphical Method of Organization of Work in Rolling Mills," *Przeglad techniczny*, Nos. 17–20.

He was also very active in an editorial capacity, from 1925 on, as director of the Polish Institute of Scientific Management. Here he promoted the translation into Polish of foreign works on management, particularly the writings of Taylor.

Book:

1948 *Harmonizacja pracy* (Harmonization of Labor). Posthumously published collection of articles by Adamiecki on his theory of harmonization. Warsaw: Instytut Naukowy Organizacji i Kierownictwa. 118 pp.

Curriculum Vitae

1866 Born on March 18th in Dabrowa Gornicza, Poland. Son of a mining engineer. He was educated at the Higher Technical School, Lodz, and took an engineering degree in St. Petersburg, Russia, in 1891.

1891–1899 Employed as an engineer in the Bank Smelting Works, Dabrowa Gornicza, working after 1896 on the problem of increasing rolling-mill output.

1899–1905 In charge of the Rolling Department of the Hartman Smelting Works, Lugansk, and then Technical Director in the rolling mills for pipes and iron in Ekaterinoslaw. During this period he carried out technical research, incorporated in various papers, and designed several important constructional installations.

1906–1918 Worked in Poland and Russia as a consulting engineer and, at the same time, was Director of a smelting works in Ostrow (1906) and Managing Director of The Ceramic Works at Korwinow (1907–1911). During this period he built several ceramic furnaces of his own design.

1919–1922 Lectured at Warsaw Polytechnic.

1922–1923 Became first professor to hold the newly created chair of industrial organization and management, Warsaw Polytechnic.

1825–1933 Was co-founder, first chairman of the board, and first director, Polish Institute of Scientific Management, Warsaw.

1933 Died on May 16th, aged 67, after a long illness.

Adamiecki held the Commodore Cross of the Order of Polonia Restituta and the Czechoslovakia Order of the White Lion. He was an honorary member of the Masaryk Academy of Arts (Czechoslovakia, 1928) for his theory of harmonization and of the Academy of Technical Science, Warsaw. He was President of the Executive Committee of the Association of Organizing Engineers in Poland.

Alexander Hamilton Church
(1866–1936)
United States

A. Hamilton Church's contribution to management is the more worthy of mention in this book because it has been neglected. It was twofold: Church was, first, a pioneer in both Britain and America of modern cost and works accounting and, secondly, author of one of the earliest standard textbooks on scientific management.

Church spent his early career in England before moving permanently to the United States. In 1901, while still living in England, he published a series of articles in the *Engineering Magazine* of New York entitled "The Proper Distribution of Establishment Charges." These articles took rank as reference works in accounting literature both in Britain and in the United States.[1] At that time the rudimentary costing methods in use for allocating overhead charges were beginning to be displaced by the "machine-hour rate" method, whose adoption would be described years later as the greatest single step forward in costing techniques of modern times.[2] Church made important improvements in the machine-hour rate and combined with it his "supplementary rate" and his "general establishment charges."

[1] See preface to the articles, which were reprinted in book form under the title *The Proper Distribution of Expense Burden* (New York: Engineering Management Co., 1916).

[2] Harry Arthur Hopf, *Soundings in the Literature of Management: Fifty Books the Educated Practitioner Should Know* (Ossining, N.Y.: Hopf Institute of Management, 1933).

Subsequent application of his methods in the Hans Renold concern in England and elsewhere proved that they were not, in practice, the solution in line with future development. But his pioneering work has been acknowledged by a sometime president of the Institute of Cost and Works Accountants (England and Wales) who has said that Church "probably did more than anyone, both directly and indirectly, to promote costing as it is now known, chiefly because he promoted thought."[3] In effect Church had, in his articles, been the first to define the real aims of cost accounting, and in his emphasis on the conception of normal costs and abnormal losses he had pointed the way to the technique of "standard" costs on which cost accounting is so extensively based today.

Church had from the outset of his career been interested in the more general questions of organization and management. No doubt his interest was in part aroused by his early association with J. Slater Lewis. At B. & S. Massey in England, between 1898 and 1900, he is credited with having introduced into the office something closely resembling work study as we know it today. For example, he had castors fixed on the juniors' chairs to ease the task of sorting job cards in the works' order bins. In 1900 he published his first article on organization. By 1906 he was probably living in the United States and was enthusiastically supporting the work of F. W. Taylor. A little later he was undertaking consultancy work in management in all its aspects, and in 1914 he published his book *The Science and Practice of Management.*

On this work rests Church's second claim to the title of pioneer. It has been called on high authority "in every sense of the word a pioneering effort of fundamental importance and value."[4] In it Church explained that, just as in his earlier articles on establishment charges he had been endeavoring to ascertain the fundamental facts of production from the viewpoint of *costs,* he was now pursuing the same air from the viewpoint of *management* and seeking to substitute, for the disconnected ideas initially represented by the elements of scientific management, an approach to the reduction of the regulative principles of management to their simplest terms. In his preface to the book, Church claimed that these principles, in the form he presented them jointly with L. P. Alford in an article in 1912, were afterward adopted by the well-known committee which was appointed by The American Society of Mechanical Engineers to investigate the new systems of management and whose eventual report was entitled "The Present State of the Art of Industrial Management." It appears that Church's book did not attract lasting attention, owing perhaps to lack of aggressive publicity. It deserved a better fate, for it presents an early and most remarkable synthesis of management.

A better fate might also have attended the memory of Church himself. Although he is recognized as a pioneer of management both in Great Britain

[3] Roland Dunkerley, "A Historical Review of the Institute and the Profession," an address to the Institute of Cost and Works Accountants, Great Britain, 1946.

[4] *Ibid.*

and in the United States, and although he lived to a ripe age, the facts of his life and work are hidden in obscurity. Fortunately, much patient research by The American Society of Mechanical Engineers has shed new light on the memory of this well-nigh forgotten pioneer of the management movement.

Church was an exceptionally timid and lonely man. Though he was an authority on accounting and on management, he never joined any of the recognized accounting societies, the Taylor Society, ASME, or any other engineering society. He refused all invitations to speak in public, for he lacked the courage to face a group of people. Yet those few who knew him say he was an unusually charming man, one with whom it was a pleasure to work; that he had gifts, not shared by all the early "efficiency experts," for drawing out useful contributions from those with whom he worked and for finding compromise solutions which won general satisfaction. He was a perfectionist in work, almost an artist, yet he could not bear daily routine. Sometimes he would vanish for weeks at a time and then reappear with a new, constructive idea.

Church never married. Gradually, as he grew older, he became more and more reclusive. It was rumored that he had wealthy relatives, but there is no indication that he ever saw them, or they him. He died alone, with no obituary notices in either the local or the metropolitan journals. Yet his contribution to management was as great as or greater than that of many whose names are famous in the movement. This shy, solitary, and forgotten man takes a place in *The Golden Book of Management* that he doubly earned.

SELECTED PUBLICATIONS

Books:

1914 *The Science and Practice of Management.* New York: Engineering Magazine Co. Later republished by John R. Dunlop. 535 pp.

1916 *The Proper Distribution of Expense Burden.* New York: Engineering Magazine Co. (Reprint 144 pages in book form, with an added preface, of the series of articles published in 1901 with the title "The Proper Distribution of Establishment Charges.")

1917 *Manufacturing Costs and Accounts.* New York: McGraw-Hill.

1923 *The Making of an Executive.* New York: D. Appleton & Co.

1930 *Overhead Expense in Relation to Costs, Sales and Profits.* New York: McGraw-Hill.

Articles:

1900 "The Meaning of Commercial Organization," *Engineering Magazine,* Vol. 20. No. 3, December, pp. 391–398.

1901 "British Industrial Welfare," New York: *Cassier's Magazine,* Vol. 19, pp. 404–408.

—— "The Proper Distribution of Establishment Charges," *Engineering Magazine,* Vols. 21 and 22 (articles in six issues).

1906 "Cost and Time-Keeping Outfit of the Taylor System," *American Machinist,* Vol. 29, Part 2, pp. 761–763.

1910 "Organization by Production Factors," *Engineering Magazine,* Vol. 38 (in 6 parts).

—— "Production Factors in Cost Accounting and Works Management," *Engineering Magazine.*

1911 "Distribution of the Expense Burden," *American Machinist,* Vol. 34, Part 2, pp. 991–992, 999.

—— "Has 'Scientific Management' Science?" *American Machinist,* Vol. 35, pp. 108–112.

—— "Intensive Production and the Foreman," *American Machinist,* Vol. 34, Part 2, pp. 830–831.

—— "The Meaning of Scientific Management," *Engineering Magazine,* Vol. 41, pp. 97–101.

1912 "The Principles of Management" (with L. P. Alford), *American Machinist,* Vol. 36, pp. 857–861.

1913 "Practical Principles of Rational Management," *Engineering Magazine,* Vols. 44 and 45 (3 parts in each volume).

—— "Premium, Piece-Work and Expense Burden," *Engineering Magazine,* Vol. 46, pp. 7–18.

1914 "The Scientific Basis of Manufacturing Management," Efficiency Society *Journal,* Vol. 3, February, pp. 8–15.

—— "What Are Principles of Management?" Efficiency Society *Journal,* Vol. 3, Febuary, pp. 16–18.

1916 "Industrial Management with Discussion," *Transactions* of the International Engineering Congress, San Francisco, 1915.

Curriculum Vitae

1866 Born on October 11th in England. There is no certain record of where Church was born or who his parents were. One report would indicate he was born in the British West Indies. Another, more probable, states he was born in Brooklyn, that his father was a wealthy ship merchant, that his family moved to England in Church's boyhood, and that he was educated at Oxford. He practiced as an electrical engineer for the National Telephone Co. and then for P. & R. Jackson & Co. (Salford, Lancastershire), there working with J. Slater Lewis, from whom he learned a great deal. Later became a consultant and a specialist in costing systems.

1898–1900 With B. & S. Massey, Manchester, where he reorganized the costing and financial accounting methods used and made improvements in office management.

1900–1905 Introduced his own costing methods into Hans Renold Ltd., Manchester. He had already transferred his chief activities to the United States and probably about this period he became an

	American resident. An early supporter of scientific management, he spent the rest of his career as a consultant and a writer on management.
1912–1915	Was a consultant engineer with Patterson, Teale & Dennis of Boston.
Late 1920s or early 1930s	Was a consultant to the Mt. Hope Finishing Co., North Dighton, Mass., converters of cotton cloth, where he set up the production lines and established a realistic cost system.
1936	Died on February 11th, aged 70, in Taunton, Mass.

John Lee
(1867–1928)
Great Britain

JOHN Lee was the editor of an outstanding reference work on management published in Great Britain—Pitman's *Dictionary of Industrial Administration* (1928). This massive two-volume "Comprehensive Encyclopaedia of the Organization, Administration and Management of Modern Industry" contained contributions from more than a hundred of the best-known contemporary authorities on management in both Britain and America. The work marked an epoch. Its only fault was to be in advance of its time. A reprint did not prove commercially possible, and much of the influence the book could have had was lost by the fact that copies were not easily to be found. It continues to be used today by those fortunate enough to possess it.

The editorial task of codifying the best management thought of the day was congenial to John Lee, who was particularly gifted in clear exposition. Himself the author of several of the articles, he handled with great skill the problem of harmonizing the contributions of so many authorities without imposing a meaningless conformity. His editorial preface was an illuminating analysis of the interest in management to be observed at the time. The compilation of the work must have absorbed the greater part of his leisure time during his last years, for he retired from executive work only in 1927.

Although this editorial feat was Lee's greatest single achievement, he had long been a writer of originality on management. His books had a philosophical quality too often lacking in management literature. His writings on organization, administration, and personnel subjects were a serious contribution to thinking, particularly in interpreting American scientific management in British industrial terms. Lee reinforced the influence of his books and articles by much public speaking. He lectured regularly at the Rowntree management conferences and elsewhere, and he was active in the Institute (now Royal Institute) of Public Administration in its early days. His pronouncements carried respect by virtue of his own practical achievement, for he was manager of a large-scale enterprise with many international connections—the Central Telegraph Office of the British Post Office.

In the advancement of truth, the clear definition of terms is important. In making his final contribution to management in this field, Lee rendered a substantial service.

"Joined to a quick and perceptive mind, Lee possessed imagination and a rare gift of sympathy, which won for him in a high degree the affection of subordinates and colleagues and of a wide circle of friends. He possessed a native and genuine eloquence, and few could tell a story better.* His conciliatory spirit and balanced outlook were of immense service to many younger people who were struggling to realize the new concepts of management in industrial practice.

Lee was interested in the application of psychology to administrative problems. Another of his special interests was the reconciliation of the demands of industrial efficiency with the principles of Christianity, and he wrote several important books on this subject. He carried on his management activities in addition to his full-time duties in the Post Office, where he had risen from the ranks to a leading executive position, and it is certain that this ceaseless activity led to the permanent impairment of his health. When he retired, he received remarkable personal tributes from business colleagues in Australia, Canada, the United States, France, Italy, and Germany.

SELECTED PUBLICATIONS

Books:

1913 *Pitman's Economics of Telegraphs and Telephones*. London: Pitman. 93 pp.

1917 *Telegraph Practice: A Study of Comparative Methods*. London: Longmans, Green. 111 pp.

1921 *Management: A Study of Industrial Organization*. London: Pitman. 134 pp.

—— *Plain Economics: An examination of Essential Issues*. London: Pitman. 118 pp.

1923 *Industrial Organization: Developments and Prospects*. London: Pitman. 130 pp.

1924 *The Principles of Industrial Welfare*. London: Pitman. 124 pp.

1925 *An Introduction to Industrial Administration*. London: Pitman. 202 pp.

* *The Times*, December 28, 1928 (obituary).

1928 *Letters to an Absentee Director*. London: Pitman (first published in *The Times Trade and Engineering Supplement*). 112 pp.

—— *Dictionary of Industrial Administration*. Editor. London: Pitman. Vol. 1, 543 pp.; Vol. 2, 607 pp. Lee was the author of articles under the following headings—"Discipline"; "Specialization and Coordination"; "Employee Share Holding"; "Significant Reports"; "Labor Banks"; "Trade Schools"; "Distribution of Processes"; "Byproducts"; "Census of Production"; and "Migration of Industries."

Articles:
Lee was a frequent contributor to *The Economist* and to *The Times Trade and Engineering Supplement*. In addition, he edited the *Journal* of the Institute (now Royal Institute) of Public Administration. The following proceedings included are of interest:

1922 "Works Councils and Similar Institutions in America, France, Germany and England," papers of the Rowntree Lecture Conference, Oxford, September 21st–25th.

—— "Ideals of Industry" (with Sydney Pascall), papers of the Rowntree Lecture Conference, Oxford, September 21st–25th.

1923 "The Ethics of Industry," papers of the Rowntree Lecture Conference, Oxford, September 20th–24th.

1926 "The Developments of Industrial Administration in Europe: An Attempt at Comparison," papers of the Rowntree Lecture Conference, Oxford, September 30th–October 4th.

1928 "The Pros and Cons of Functionalization," papers of the Rowntree Lecture Conference, Oxford, September 27th–30th. Reproduced as a chapter in *Papers in the Science of Administration* by Gulick and Urwick, eds. (New York: Columbia University, 1937).

Curriculum Vitae

1867 Born on June 16th in Liverpool, of Irish parents. Later received M.A. and M.Com.Sc. (Belfast).

1883 Entered Post Office as a telegraphist in Liverpool.

1901 Became Assistant Superintendent.

1907 Became Assistant Traffic Manager for Telephones at Post Office Headquarters, London.

1909–1910 Helped to reorganize the Indian Railway Telegraph System.

1916 Became Deputy Chief Inspector of Telegraph and Telephone Traffic.

1917 Served as member of Committee on High-Speed Telegraphy. Helped to organize the employment of women as telegraphists and telephonists behind the Allied lines in France.

1918 Employed as Postmaster of Belfast, where he introduced a system of staff consultation on the Whitley model.

1919 Became Controller of the Central Telegraph Office.

1920 Served on Post Office delegation to a European conference on the restoration of communications organized by the League of Nations.

1925 Headed British delegation to the International Telegraph Conference, Paris.

1926 Served on International Committee investigating code language in telegrams.

1927 Retired; joined the boards of the Automatic Telephone Co. and some of its associated companies.

1928 Died on December 24th, aged 61, on the ship *Laconia* while returning from the United States.

John Lee was made a C.B.E. in 1923. He was a founder-member of the Institute (now Royal Institute) of Public Administration and Chairman of its Council (1925–1926).

Walther Rathenau
(1867–1922)
Germany

WALTHER Rathenau is chiefly remembered in Germany as a captain of industry who became a government servant and a stateman. But he was also an important forerunner of the German management movement by virtue of his writings on industrial organization and on the place of industry in society.

Rathenau was preoccupied with the economic problems of Germany arising out of her great increase in industrialization at the turn of the century. He became prominent before 1914 as a writer with radical though constructive political views. An able administrator in the industries which he controlled, he showed himself equally able as a government administrator during the war, and his writings on economic and social subjects in 1917 and 1918 made him a passionately discussed figure and drew him into the political life which was to end in his assassination.

Rathenau set out his theories on industrial organization in his books *Things to Come* (1917) and *The New Economy* (1918). It was through changes in the management of industry that Germany's economic and social problems could be solved. In the structural aspect of industrial organization, all the unnatural barriers—such as monopolies and customs tariffs—to the rational interplay of industrial forces must be removed. When this had been done, the rational application of scientific method and planning and the use of the new power-driven machinery, whose advent was still recent in Germany, would permit the creation of limitless industrial wealth; and by this means many political problems could in turn be solved.

But the effectiveness of industry could not be built on mechanized efficiency alone. There was needed an inspiration for industry's workers, a soul to infuse industry's life. So, in the dynamic aspect of industrial organization, Rathenau urged the sublimation of the profit motive by depersonalizing the ownership of industry; enterprises were to be transformed into democratic institutions by giving the workers a share in the management. He declared:

> As there is so little room for the rise of responsibility within the actual limits of his labor, the worker must be able to find this outside those those limits by having a share in the management. The provisional solution of the problem is the cooperation of the workers and officials in the conduct of the undertaking.

The final solution was to be the form of organization that Rathenau postulated as the foundation of all industrial progress—the uniting of each industry into a self-governing body in which each worker would have a voice. The transformation was to be gradually and peaceably carried out by the state.

It is instructive to compare these suggestions of Rathenau with the subsequent evolution of industrial organization in Germany. In 1919, self-governing corporations were set up in the coal and potash industries under the new German constitution. In the interwar period *Mitbestimmungsrecht* (joint management), or the representation of workers on the top executive board in important German industries, became law and was further extended after 1945. Rathenau's method for "motivating" industrial groups, although it has made little impact on the theory of industrial organization in Anglo-Saxon countries, accurately anticipated German developments.

As a thinker on industrial organization, Rathenau differed from the Frenchman Fayol in looking outward to the community around him rather than inward to the administrative processes he directed, and he differed from the American Mary Parker Follett in leaving untouched the psychological foundations of management in favor of its social implications. He was, however, at one with both these thinkers in perceiving that the rational organization of industry according to principles of social responsibility holds the secret of progress for a democratic community.

Strangely enough, Rathenau was not popular in democratic circles in spite of his radical advocacy of democratic principles both for politics and for industry. Probably he was an incomprehensible figure—a businessman who preached the need of a soul; a rich man who built himself an expensive villa yet attacked luxury; a captain of industry whose political views were more socialistic than those of any of the agitators among the employees of his own factories. His family has said that at heart he was much more a poet and philosopher than a man of affairs and that he entered business life more through feelings of duty than because he really wished it. The highlights of his later political career were his speech as Foreign Minister at the Genoa Conference in 1922, when he obtained the first diplomatic concessions for

Germany, and the conclusion of the peace treaty with Russia in the same year. His assassination was a tragic end for one who had been the pioneer of an idealistic philosophy for German industry and society.

SELECTED PUBLICATIONS

Books:

1902	*Impressionen* (Impressions). Leipzig: Hirzel-Verlag. 255 pp.
1908	*Reflexionen* (Reflections). Leipzig: Hirzel-Verlag. 270 pp.
1912	*Zur Kritik der Zeit* (Contemporary Criticism). Berlin: S. Fischer-Verlag. 260 pp.
1913	*Zur Mechanik des Geistes* (Mechanics of the Mind). Berlin: S. Fischer-Verlag. 348 pp.
1916	*Deutschlands Rohstoffversorgung* (Supply of Germany's Raw Materials). Berlin: S. Fischer-Verlag. 52 pp.
1917	*Eine Streitschrift vom Glauben* (A Polemic of Faith). Berlin: S. Fischer-Verlag. 42 pp.
——	*Vom Aktienwesen* (Corporate Shares). Berlin: S. Fischer-Verlag. 62 pp.
——	*Von kommenden Dingen* (Things to Come). Berlin: S. Fischer-Verlag. 344 pp.
——	*Probleme der Friedenswirtschaft* (Peacetime Economic Problems). Berlin: S. Fischer-Verlag.
1918	*An Deutschlands Jugend* (To Germany's Youth). Berlin: S. Fischer-Verlag. 126 pp.
——	*Die neue Wirtschaft* (The New Economy). Berlin: S. Fischer-Verlag. 86 pp.
1918–1925	*Gesammelte Schriften [Werke] in 5 Bänden* (Collected Writings [Works] in 5 Volumes). Berlin: S. Fischer-Verlag.
1919	*Der Kaiser* (The Emperor). Berlin: S. Fischer-Verlag. 60 pp.
——	*Der neue Staat* (The New State). Berlin: S. Fischer-Verlag. 74 pp.
——	*Kritik der dreifachen Revolution [Apologie]* (Critique of the Triple Revolution [Defense]). Berlin: S. Fischer-Verlag. 125 pp.

Articles and Letters:
Rathenau was a prolific writer; his articles and letters, as noted, fill five volumes. These deal with problems of social and industrial organization, political issues, German aspirations and their implications, etc. A representative selection of titles is given in Count Kessler's biography.*

Curriculum Vitae

1867	Born of a well-connected family; son of Emil Rathenau, founder of the Allgemeine Elektricitäts-Gesellschaft (General Electric

* Harry Graf Kessler, *Walther Rathenau. Sein Leben und sein Werk* (London: Gerald Howe, Ltd., 1929).

	Co.). Educated in classics at a gymnasium; obtained a doctor's degree at the University of Berlin after studying mathematics, physics, and chemistry.
1890	Continued studies in mechanical and electrical engineering in Munich.
1891–1893	Employed by Aluminium-Industrie, AG, Neuhausen, Switzerland.
1893–1899	In charge of the Elektrochemische Werke, GmbH, with administrative headquarters at Bitterfeld, Saxony.
1899–1902	Served as member of the Board and head of the Department for construction of Power Stations, Allgemeine Elektricitäts-Gesellschaft.
1902–1907	Member of the Board, Berliner Handels-Gesellschaft.
By 1909	Associated, as director or managing director, with more than 80 large concerns centering mainly on the Allgemeine Elektricitäts-Gesellschaft.
1914	Appointed to the War Office to organize the German system of raw-material supply.
1915	Named President of the Allgemeine Elektricitäts-Gesellschaft.
1919	Shared in preparations of the German government for the Versailles negotiations.
1920	German expert at the conference at Spa (Belgium).
1920–1921	Member of the Socialization Commission for the reorganization of Germany's economic system.
1921	Appointed Reichsminister for Reconstruction.
1922	Appointed Reichsminister for Foreign Affairs in the Wirth cabinet.
——	Assassinated on June 24th, at age of 55, by a Nationalist extremist.

Courtesy R. Greenwood.

Sanford Eleazer Thompson
(1867–1949)
United States

SANFORD E. Thompson was one of the group of associates who helped F. W. Taylor to develop the principles and techniques of his system of management. The independent contribution of Thompson was substantial. Among its most significant aspects were, first, the application of the Taylor system of management to the building industry and, secondly, the development of time study as a management tool.

It was at the suggestion of Taylor that Thompson began his work in the building industry. Taylor had developed his ideas of management in terms of the engineering shops in which he himself had always worked. From the beginning, nevertheless, he had been concerned to prove that his methods had general application in any industry, and he even hoped to bring about the publication of a series of books on management, each written in terms of a different basic industry. The building industry was a suitable one with which to start, since many of its processes were already repetitive and detailed time study could at once be put in hand.

In 1896 Thompson, acting as an independent consultant but guided by Taylor, began the study of work in the building industry which he was to pursue with infinite thoroughness for almost 17 years. By 1903 Thompson's material for a book was well advanced. In his paper *Shop Management* Taylor said:

> Mr. Sanford E. Thompson, C.E. (Civil Engineer) started in 1896 with but small help from the writer, except as far as the implements and

> methods are concerned, to study the time required to do all kinds of work in the building trades. In six years he has made a complete study of seven of the most important trades—excavating, masonry (including sewerwork and paving), carpentry, concrete and cement work, lathing and plastering, slating and roofing, and rock quarrying.

And further on:

> The writer's chief object in inducing Mr. Thompson to undertake a scientific study of the various building trades and to join him in a publication of this work was to demonstrate on a large scale, not only the desirability of accurate time-study, but the efficiency and superiority of the method of studying elementary units as outlined above. He trusts that his object may be realized and that the publication of this book may be followed by similiar work on other trades and more particularly on the details of machine shop practice, in which he is especially interested.

The two books incorporating the results of these studies were *Concrete, Plain and Reinforced* (1905) and *Concrete Costs* (1912), published under the joint authorship of Thompson and Taylor. Their success was immediate and their effect revolutionary. They put forward, to replace the pure guesswork which was the only existing method of computing building labor costs, an analysis and a method which was to constitute the turning point of modern development in this field.

The technique most used by Thompson in the building industry was time study. To him belongs the credit for perfecting this "tool" of management, and to him is attributed the invention of the decimal-dial stop-watch. The stop-watch became, years afterward, a symbol hated by the opponents of scientific management. It is important to record here that throughout Thompson's career he was repeatedly called upon by labor groups to give professional advice in problems relating to the measurement of work. His and Taylor's integrity in their attitude toward the use of the stop-watch was shown in 1908, when Dean Gay of the new Harvard School of Business Administration suggested that the teaching of the Taylor system should begin with a course on time study conducted by Thompson. "This idea Taylor combatted with vehemence; he said it would be like teaching architecture by putting cornices on houses."[1] The idea was abandoned. Thompson did not teach time study until 1910, and then only to advanced students and in the context of building operations. The incident demonstrates once again that the accusations made against scientific management can often be refuted most easily by reference to the words of the pioneers themselves.

Like several of Taylor's other followers, Thompson became in later life a management consultant, advising on many different aspects of management and being entrusted with several assignments of public importance. An

[1] Frank B. Copley, *Frederick W. Taylor* (New York and London: Harper & Bros., 1923), Vol. II, p. 290.

anecdote may illustrate the genuine idealism which motivated him as it did the others of the Taylor group. In 1913 the magazine *Collier's Weekly* was running a series of articles on "everyday heroes." Taylor received a letter suggesting that he himself would be a suitable subject. He replied:

> My feeling is that the heroes such as are called for by *Collier's Weekly* are men who are really making great sacrifices for the good of their kind. . . . I have always in my work had the satisfaction of seeing tangible results accomplished within a reasonably short time, and having these results appreciated at least by the men whom they most concern.
>
> It is a very different story for a man to work through a term of years . . . with no recognition whatever. In fact, my friend Sanford E. Thompson, of Newton Highlands, Mass., who for a great many years worked in a tireless manner and for a very small salary, and refused to publish any of his colossal time study until it was in really a very magnificent form, is far more of a hero than I ever was.[2]

Sanford E. Thompson's real energy and imagination were sometimes hidden by a New England reticence, and he was not a commanding speaker. He was a devoted family man, known for his high ethical standards.

The special quality that F. W. Taylor valued in Thompson was his tireless patience. This was shown in the earliest days of his association with Taylor at the Manufacturing Investment Co., when Thompson was at one time assigned a 40-hour observation stretch of a woodpulp-"cooking" process. When the results proved unsatisfactory, Thompson at once cheerfully volunteered for another stretch. This demonstration of a capacity for sustained application, together with infinite thoroughness, gained him Taylor's permanent friendship.[3]

SELECTED PUBLICATIONS

Books:

1901 *Taylor Differential Piece-work System.* New York: Engineering Magazine Co.

1905 *Concrete, Plain and Reinforced.* With F. W. Taylor. New York: Wiley & Sons.

1907 *Reinforced Concrete in Factory Construction.* New York: Atlas Portland Cement Co.

1909 *Concrete in Railroad Construction.* New York: Atlas Portland Cement Co.

1912 *Concrete Costs.* With F. W. Taylor. New York: Wiley & Sons.

1939 *Reinforced Concrete Bridges.* With F. W. Taylor and E. Smulski. New York: Wiley & Sons.

[2] *Ibid,* Vol. II, p. 434.

[3] Anecdote from Copley, *op. cit.,* Vol. I, p. 376.

Articles:

1902 "Quality of the Production in Piece Work," *Cassier's Magazine*, Vol. 23, pp. 233–237.

1913 "Time Study and Task Work." *Industrial Engineering and Engineering Digest*, Vol. 13, pp. 347–350.

1914 "A Study of Cleaning Filter Sands with No Opportunity for Bonus Payments," ASME *Transactions*, Vol. 36, pp. 693–706.

1915 "Construction Management" (with W. O. Lichtner), *Journal* of the Western Society of Engineers, Vol. 20, pp. 109–151.

1916 "Scientific Methods in Construction." with W. O. Lichtner. *Proceedings* of the Engineers Society of Western Pennsylvania, Vol. 32, pp. 433–465.

1928 "Smoothing the Wrinkles from Management: Time Study the Tool," *Bulletin* of the Taylor Society, Vol. 13, pp. 69–86.

1935 "Opportunities for Cost Reduction in Textile Manufacturing and Selling," *Rayon and Melliand Textile Monthly*, Vol. 16, pp. 314–316, 435–436, 549, 576, and 585.

1936 "Improved Pulp and Paper Quality Through Incentives," *Paper Trade Journal*, Vol. 102, March 19th, pp. 39–43.

1937 "Brief Survey of Management Methods in Paper Mills," *Paper Trade Journal*, Vol. 104, March 11th, pp. 31–36.

1938 "History of Scientific Management in America." With others. Prepared for the 1938 International Management Congress. *Mechanical Engineering*, Vol. 69, September, pp. 671–675.

1939 "Standards in Their Relation to Production Control," *Paper Trade Journal*, Vol. 109, November 9, pp. 31–35.

1940 "Increased Production for Defense Needs," *Advanced Management*, Vol. 5, pp. 153–158.

1941 "Synchronized Arms Production," *Army-Ordnance*, Vol. 21, March–April, pp. 475–476.

1944 "Postwar Cost Reductions," *Paper Trade Journal*, Vol. 119, August 17th, pp. 40–47.

Curriculum Vitae

1867 Born on February 13th in Ogdensburg, N.Y.

1889 Graduated from Massachusetts Institute of Technology with a B.Sc. degree in civil engineering. Later took graduate course in chemistry.

1889–1890 Employed as engineer and draftsman on design and construction, Moosehead Pulp and Paper Co., Solon, Maine.

1890–1893 Was Superintendent of Construction and Assistant Superintendent of Production, Manufacturing Investment Company, Madison, Maine.

1893–1894 In charge of operating department, Mt. Tom Pulp and Paper Co.

1894–1895	Resident engineer, waterworks construction, Arlington, Mass.
1895–1896	Assistant engineer on hydraulic and mill design, J. P. Frizell, Boston, Mass.
1896–1917	In private practice as consulting engineer and executive, Newton Highlands, Mass.
1917	Served as lieutenant colonel, Army Ordnance Department.
1917–1949	Was Senior Partner, Thompson and Lichtner Co., Brookline, Mass.—a management and engineering consulting firm. President from 1925 on.
1921	Served as member of Hoover Committee on Elimination of Waste in Industry.
1922	Served as member of Economic Advisory Board to the President of the U.S. Unemployment Conference.
1931	Served as member of Elimination of Waste Committee of the National Construction Conference.
1938	Represented International Industrial Relations Institute at Oxford Management Conference.
1942–1943	Served as consultant to Secretary of War.
1949	Died on February 25th, aged 82, in Phoenix, Ariz.

Sanford E. Thompson was President of the Taylor Society (1932), Fellow of The American Society of Mechanical Engineers, an honorary life member of the American Society of Civil Engineers, and an honorary member and Vice-President (1917–1919) of the American Concrete Institute.

Courtesy R. Greenwood.

Mary Parker Follett
(1868–1933)
United States

MARY Parker Follett was a political and social philosopher of the first rank. Her contribution to management, among the most outstanding recorded in this book, was to apply psychological insight and the findings of the social sciences to industry and, through this, to offer a new conception of the nature of management and of human relationships within industrial groups.

Before Mary Follett, industrial groups had seldom been the subject of study of political or social scientists. It was her special merit to turn from the traditional subjects of study—the state or the community as a whole—to concentrate progressively on the study of industry. In this context she not only evolved principles of human association and organization, specifically in terms of industry, but also convinced large numbers of business people of the practicality of these principles in dealing with their current problems. Her approach was to analyze the nature of the *consent* on which any democratic group is based by examining the psychological factors underlying it. This consent, she suggested, is not static but is a continuous process, generating new and living group ideas through the interpenetration of individual ideas.

Starting from this conception of the pattern which social relationships should take within human groups, Mary Parker Follett showed that *conflict* can be constructive. It can be harnessed to the service of the group much as an engineer uses friction. The most fruitful way of resolving conflict is not domination, nor even compromise, but *integration* in which the parties concerned examine together new ways of achieving their conflicting desires. Again, it is demonstrable that *authority,* in terms of the subordination of one person to another, offends human emotions and cannot be the foundation of good industrial organization. The concept of final authority inhering in the chief executive should be replaced by an authority of function in which each individual has final authority for his or her own allotted task. By this means, personal power gives place to "the law of the situation" in which a *decision,* though it may appear to crystallize in an act of the chief executive, is only a "moment in a process" which may have started with the office boy. *Leadership* is not a matter of a dominating personality. The leader should be the one most able to secure interpenetration within the group of the best ideas of both leader and led. The leader must have the insight, not only to *meet* the next situation, but to *make* it. Moreover, leaders are not only born but can also be made through training in the understanding of human behavior.

It will be seen that with Mary Parker Follett the key words in the terminology of industrial organization, which up to now had been static or structural words, became active and dynamic. The four principles of organization at which she finally arrived were all active, implying the need of four kinds of coordination as the basis of good management:

1. Coordination by direct contact of the responsible people concerned.
2. Coordination in the early stages of a situation.
3. Coordination as a reciprocal relation of all the features in a situation.
4. Coordination as a continuous process.

These ideas are clearly of great importance for the problems of industry, where the possibilities of conflict are so numerous and where the authority concept has been so highly developed.

Miss Follett's final principles were expressed in terms of industry alone, and so she earned a place among the philosophers of management. But her contribution was more significant still in that, for her, the principles of organization were universal and the choice of industrial groups as the subject of study was incidental. She found more liveliness of thinking, more courage for experiment, more impulse for "integration" in her sense of the word among business managers than among administrators in any other kind of group. But her philosophy was equally valid for any kind of purposeful human association. Thus she was one of the earliest political scientists to enable those whose lot is cast in business to see their work, not only as a means of livelihood, not only as an honorable occupation with a large content of professional interest, but as a definite and vital contribution toward the building of that new social order which is the legitimate preoccupation of every thinking citizen.

Mary Parker Follett's thinking was and still remains in advance of the times. Her influence has yet to reach its peak. The extent of her immediate practical influence on many business people must, however, also be mentioned here. From 1924 on she was lecturing to business audiences in both the United States and England, and many managers sought her advice on their problems of securing and maintaining human cooperation in their concerns. She had a strong bent for the practical. The illustrations with which her writings are liberally scattered are drawn from almost every phase of life. Business people learned from her forthright and lucid suggestions how to approach their difficulties by taking into account the motivating desires of individuals in relation to their working groups, and how to aim in their businesses, as government must do in the larger community, at the integration of points of view. Many successful business administrators, not least B. S. Rowntree, have testified to the help afforded them in their immediate difficulties by this modest individual who had never managed a business in her life.

Although Mary Parker Follett was so distinguished a philosopher, and although she never married, she was no blue-stocking. She left in her Boston social work a practical achievement as distinctive as her contribution in the realm of ideas. Her outstanding characteristic was a facility for winning the confidence and esteem of those with whom she came in contact; she established a deeply rooted understanding and friendship with a wide circle of eminent men and women on both sides of the Atlantic. The root of this social gift was her vivid interest in life. Every individual's experience, his or her relations with others and with the social groups—large or small—of which that individual was a part, was food for her thought. She listened with alert and kindly attention, she discussed problems in a way which drew the best out of the individual with whom she was talking. She did not force her learning on the business executives who called on her to assist them with their problems. "Often," she is reported to have said, "they could only spare time for luncheon, but I never had such interesting meals. One of those men gave me . . . the threads of a tangle he had with his employees. He wanted me to straighten it out. I answered him straight from Fichte; he didn't know that, of course, but . . . it seemed to meet the case."*

She was in herself an example of the principle which she found basic for every form of human organization, from each individual life to world relations—coordination. For she was a person of universal mind and viewpoint and of rounded culture, combining an interest in religion, music, painting, nature, history, and travel with her consuming lifetime absorption in her work. She had no taste for power or prestige at all. Even her intellectual output was limited by her rigid self-criticism, her determination to be simple and understandable at all costs, her great modesty, and her wish to be of practical use in quite humble capacities.

* Quoted by F. M. Stawell in her memoir in the Newnham College *Letter* for January 1935.

SELECTED PUBLICATIONS

Books:

1909 *The Speaker of the House of Representatives.* New York and London: Longmans, Green.

1920 *The New State.* New York and London: Longmans, Green.

1924 *Creative Experience.* New York and London: Longmans, Green.

Papers on business organization and administration:
The majority of these papers, presented between 1924 and 1933, have been collected in two books as follows:

Dynamic Administration: The Collected Papers of Mary Parker Follett. Edited by H. C. Metcalf and L. Urwick. 320 pp. London: Pitman, 1941. This volume contains the following papers, given to audiences either in the United States or Great Britain.

"Constructive Conflict"
"The Giving of Orders"
"Business as an Integrative Unity"
"Power"
"How Must Business Management Develop in Order to Possess the Essentials of a Profession?"
"How Must Business Management Develop in Order to Become a Profession?"
"The Meaning of Responsibility in Business Management"
"The Influence of Employee Representation in a Remolding of the Accepted Type of Business Manager"
"The psychology of Control"
"The Psychology of Consent and Participation"
"The Psychology of Conciliation and Arbitration"
"Leader and Expert"
"Some Discrepancies in Leadership Theory and Practice"
"Individualism in a Planned Society"

Freedom and Co-ordination: Lectures in Business Organization by Mary Parker Follett. Edited by L. Urwick. 89 pp. London: Pitman, 1949. This volume contains the following papers, the first given to the Taylor Society in New York and the remainder to the London School of Economics.

"The Illusion of Final Authority"
"The Giving of Orders"
"The Basis of Authority"
"The Essentials of Leadership"
"Co-ordination"
"The Process of Control"

Curriculum Vitae

1868	Born in Boston, Mass. Educated at Thayer Academy, Boston. Studied philosophy, history, law, and political science at Radcliffe College (Cambridge, Mass., U.S.A.) and Newnham College (Cambridge, England) and did graduate study in Paris.
1891	On returning to the United States, took up active life of social work in Boston.
1900	Set up Roxbury Debating Club in Roxbury Neighboring House in Boston, later expanding it into centers providing social, recreational, and educational facilities in this depressed locality.
1909 on	Became chairman of a group, renamed in 1911 the Committee on the Extended Use of School Buildings, which developed the well-known "Boston evening centers," for educational and recreational activities, which were taken as a model by other cities throughout the United States.
1912	Was a member of the first Boston Placement Bureau Committee, which became later the municipal Department of Vocational Guidance; then served as a member representing the public on the Massachusetts Minimum Wage Board.
1920	Gained wide recognition as a political philosopher upon publication of *The New State.*
1924	Began giving papers on industrial organization, especially to the annual conferences for business executives held in New York by the Bureau of Personnel Administration. As her experience of industry grew, Miss Follett came to be consulted by many business managers on problems of organization and human relations.
1926 and 1928	Visited England to read papers at the Rowntree Lecture Conference and to the National Institute of Industrial Psychology.
1929	Returned to live quietly in England until shortly before her death. She shared a home in Chelsea, London, with Dame Katherine Fruze of the Girl Guide movement.
1933	Died on December 18th, aged 65, in America.

Frank Bunker Gilbreth
(1868–1924)
United States

FRANK Bunker Gilbreth's distinctive contribution was to develop motion study as a primary tool for managers and as a basis for new thinking about some of the aims of management.

Scientific management, as Taylor and Gantt developed it, was a series of principles for analyzing the routines and procedures surrounding the worker on the job. Gilbreth began his contribution to management with the publication of *Field System* and *Concrete System* in 1908, describing the lines of authority and the responsibilities of different jobs within his own business as a building contractor. His earliest work was thus in the wider field of general management. His unique contribution was, however, his emphasis on human effort and the methods he devised for showing up wasteful and unproductive movements. He felt that if the "one best way to do the work" could be discovered for each and every element in a worker's movements and surroundings, the resulting gains in productivity could add significantly to the gains which Taylor was making by revising the system of management in the productive unit as a whole.

Gilbreth had already, as a builder, proved the truth of this theory. He had simplified the motions used in bricklaying, reducing their number from 18 to 5, increasing the hourly number of bricks laid from 175 to 350, and thus increasing productivity 100 percent over the previous system. Later, during the First World War, he was to have similar success in using his methods for training recruits and for rehabilitating disabled men. From 1912 until his death in 1924, he devoted himself to the steady development of the science of motion study. He was the first to apply the motion-picture camera to the recording and analysis of performance, the first to classify the elements of human motions, or "therbligs" (the word "Gilbreth" spelled backward). Out of this work grew the laws of motion economy, looking to the systematic elimination of inefficiencies and waste and the idea of estimating performance times as the sum of the times normally taken for the performance of the elementary motions used in an operation.

Thus far the contribution of Gilbreth has been described as pertaining to the mechanics of management. Motion study was, however, the means by which he made a contribution of the greatest importance to the dynamics of management. For whereas Taylor's emphasis had been primarily on the external factors affecting the worker, Gilbreth began by looking at the worker first, and this led him to apply the knowledge available from physiology and the various social sciences—psychology, education, and the rest—to the task of improving and broadening the worker's capacity to contribute to the productivity of industry. This search for "the one best way" was no narrow regimentation of the worker's movements. It was the means by which individual workers' personal potential could be maximized with benefit both to themselves and to the unit in which each worked. It included the workers' training, the methods they used, the tools at their disposal, and the physical and mental environment which surrounded them.

Gilbreth's particular contribution was therefore to develop management as a social science in which the human being is the center of interest, around which research and experiment revolve and toward whose development they are directed. In 1916 he and his wife contributed jointly to the *Annals* of the American Academy of Political and Social Science an article on the "Three-Position Plan of Promotion." It was based squarely on the proposition that "no organization can hope to hold its members that does not consider, not only the welfare of the organization as a whole, but also the welfare of the individuals composing that organization." The authors emphasized three points:

1. The necessity of attracting desirable job applicants.
2. The necessity of holding, fitting, and promoting those individuals already employed.
3. The interdependence of these two necessities.

And they insisted that "no worker who is constitutionally able to become a permanent member of an organization will wish to change if he or she is receiving adequate pay *and* has ample opportunity for advancement." The Gilbreths' plan for achieving this objective practically with its person "in charge of promotion," its "master promotion chart," its "individual promotion charts" or "fortune sheets," and its regular meeting between promotion staff and worker to discuss the latter, was—allowing for differences in nomenclature—precisely the plan so often sold to corporations in the 1950s as something of a novelty under the title of "executive" or "management" development.

That Frank Gilbreth should have loved and married a woman who was herself a psychologist and a teacher can only be described as providential. As he fired her enthusiasm and strengthened her self-confidence, so she broadened his outlook on management and widened the scope of management inquiry to include the whole range of the social sciences. In awarding its Gold Medal to Lillian Moller Gilbreth in 1954 on the occasion of its Tenth Congress, the International Committee for Scientific Management paid tribute to the work of the husband to whom she owed her initial inspiration.

Because two of his children have written one of the most amusing books in modern American literature, which has been made into a film that has enjoyed wide popularity, there is a real danger that the depth and value of Frank Gilbreth's achievement may be underestimated by future generations. Both families and films need laughter; however, the fact that the originality of Gilbreth's mind and his total lack of self-consciousness added to the gaiety of life should never be allowed to diminish our appreciation of his high seriousness of purpose or of the courage, energy, and devotion which he brought to the service of management and of society. As a man of 44, with a large and growing family, he abandoned his very lucrative and successful contracting business in order to concentrate on the new science of management because he believed it was of importance to the community. That, in itself, is evidence of an unusual depth of character and indifference to personal advantage where it appeared to conflict with social purpose.

In a very real sense Gilbreth's was a "dedicated" life, and his having won and held the abiding love of one of "the first women of America" is witness to his qualities as a man. Though his children may have often laughed with him and at him, and sometimes found his forthright enthusiasm extremely embarassing, the picture of a small boy sobbing his heart out because "he had lost his Daddy" is a truer record of their relations. Frank Gilbreth was lovable as well as laughable and, above all, a real pioneer who added greatly to our knowledge and understanding of management in the early days when its novelty as an idea was often deeply suspect.

SELECTED PUBLICATIONS

Books:

1908 *Concrete System.* New York: The Engineering News Publishing Co.

—— *Field System.* New York and Chicago: The Myron C. Clark Publishing Co.

1909 *Bricklaying System.* New York and Chicago: The Myron C. Clark Publishing Co.

1911 *Motion Study.* New York: D. Van Nostrand Co.

1912 *Primer of Scientific Management.* New York: D. Van Nostrand Co. 108 pp.

1916 *Fatigue Study.* New York: Sturgis & Walton Co.

1917 *Applied Motion Study.* New York: Sturgis & Walton Co.

1920 *Motion Study for the Handicapped.* New York: The Macmillan Co.; London: Routledge.

Contributions to the Proceedings of Learned Societies:

1910 "Fires: Effects on Building Material and Permanent Elimination," ASME *Journal,* Vol. 32, p. 754, and Vol. 33, p. 577.

1915 "Motion Study for the Crippled Soldier," ASME *Journal,* Vol. 37, p. 669.

—— "What Scientific Management Means to America's Industrial Position." With Lillian Gilbreth. *Annals* of the American Academy of Political and Social Science, Vol. 61, p. 208.

1916 "Graphic Control of the Exception Principle for Executives," ASME *Transactions,* Vol. 38, p. 123.

1921 "Process Charts." With Lillian Gilbreth. ASME *Transactions,* Vol. 43, p. 1029.

—— "Symposium. Stop-Watch Time Study. An Indictment and a Defence." With Lillian Gilbreth. *Bulletin of* the Taylor Society, Vol. 6, p. 97.

1922 "Ten Years' Progress in Management." With Lillian Gilbreth. ASME *Transactions,* Vol. 44, p. 1285.

1924 "Scientific Management in Other Countries than the United States." With Lillian Gilbreth. The Taylor Society *Bulletin,* Vol. 9, p. 132.

Curriculum Vitae

1868 Born on July 7th in Fairfield, Maine. Though he lost his father in early childhood, F. B. Gilbreth had a good schooling at Andover Academy and then at Boston Grammar School. He qualified for entry to the Massachusetts Institute of Technology but decided to start practical work at once.

1885 Apprenticed to a building contractor, within ten years had become chief superintendent of the company. He also achieved technical distinction with a new design for scaffolding, a new method of waterproofing cellars, and several innovations in concrete construction.

1895 Resigned to set up his own contracting business in Boston. Patented many technical inventions and perfected many administrative improvements in the methods of the business, which tended to develop from contracting to consulting work in construction. On this basis he could run, not only a busy New York office with American branches, but also a London office. His first three books on building were based on this experience, but he also began to be interested in the general science of management.

1903 Became a member of The American Society of Mechanical Engineers.

1910 Became intensely interested in the "Eastern rates case" and joined the scientific management group. Also was one of the ASME team that paid a formal visit to the Institution of Mechanical Engineers in England.

1912 Gave up his contracting business and turned to "management engineering," specializing in physical working methods. Became friendly with Gantt and Taylor and, in collaboration with his wife, began to develop the distinctive Gilbreth contribution to the science of management. The New England Butt Co. of Providence was the scene of his experimental work during the next five years. There he established the Taylor system of management as a whole and carried out his own research into motion study. He quickly gained a reputation as an expert on management.

1917–1918 Major of engineers in U.S. Army, assigned to general staff concerned with training of recruits. He also did special work on rehabilitation of crippled soldiers till his war effort was cut short by a severe illness.

1919–1924 Returned to management consulting and development of motion study.

1924 Died on June 14th, aged 56, when preparing to attend the Prague International Management Congress.

In 1943 the Gantt Medal was awarded to Lillian M. Gilbreth and Frank B. Gilbreth jointly by The American Society of Mechanical Engineers and the Institute of Management "in recognition of their pioneer work in management, their development of the principles and techniques of motion study, their application of those techniques in industry, agriculture, and the home, and their work in spreading that knowledge through courses of training and classes at universities."

Robert Franklin Hoxie
(1868–1916)
United States

In 1915 Robert F. Hoxie published a book entitled *Scientific Management and Labor.* This book is significant in the history of management because it was the first attempt to define the relationship between scientific management and organized labor.

Formal labor opposition to scientific management crystallized immediately, once the movement became popular. This was perhaps inevitable, for scientific management had gained numerous adherents whose understanding of its principles was imperfect and who lacked both the social outlook of the early pioneers and their practical skill in dealing with people. The labor strike at the Watertown Arsenal precipitated a strong political movement to ban the use of the stop-watch in all government factories. This was followed by the Congressional inquiry of 1912. In 1914 public feeling on the matter was so aroused that the Federal Commission on Industrial Relations decided to make a special investigation into scientific management in relation to labor. This it entrusted to Hoxie, a professor of economics at the University of Chicago who had made a special study of labor problems although he had not hitherto been concerned with scientific management.

Scientific Management and Labor records the results of Hoxie's investigations and is full of interest. He attempted two things: first to define formally the trade unions' objections to scientific management and the labor claims of scientific management; and, secondly, to persuade the parties concerned to reconcile their views on the points of conflict which he had elicited. His success on the first count was noteworthy. For his statement of labor objections he obtained the official approval of the American Federation of Labor. For his statement of the scientific managers' side of the case he obtained the approval of Harrington Emerson and other practicing exponents of the new management—with the exception of one person. The father of scientific management himself would not give his approval. After protracted discussion an appendix had to be added: "The Labor Claims of Scientific Management according to Mr. Frederick W. Taylor."

Taylor's opposition was based on his distrust of the well-meaning efforts of Hoxie and his colleagues to reconcile the aims of scientific management with those of trade-unionism, for Taylor believed that Hoxie did not see the issues correctly. However, even though he did not agree with Hoxie's proposed solutions, he is known to have fully appreciated the importance of the investigation, and he is quoted as saying that he and his associates would use every possible effort to make good come out of it.

The impartial reader of *Scientific Management and Labor* must conclude that it is a fair and penetrating analysis of the issues between management and labor as they then appeared, documented by many facts exhaustively investigated. As a first attempt to take stock of issues which were new in 1914 but which have remained fundamental sources of conflict in our society down to the present time, the book merits a place in the history of management. One significant phrase shows the quality of Hoxie's understanding of what was at stake:

> Because of its youth and the necessary application of its principles to a competitive state of industry, it [scientific management] is, in many respects, crude, many of its devices are contradictory of its announced principles, and it is inadequately scientific. Nevertheless, it is to date the latest word in the sheer mechanics of production and *inherently in line with the march of events.*[1]

It has been said that Hoxie was an inquirer.

> He could not satisfy a demand for honest truth by accepting authority: he had to test what the books say by reference to the facts. Yet he was no devotee of mere description; he dealt with facts in relation to problems, and demanded both facts and consistent theory. He was painstaking in analyzing his problem, diligent in gathering data, and painfully conscientious in determining what it all meant. In his mind there was endless conflict between the cautious student and the bold adventurer.

> . . . He cared little for public reputation or academic recognition. His students were his public; to him inquiry and teaching were inseparable; he was forever following the quest wherever it led, in utter disregard of academic frontiers, with a pack of cubs at his heels. His distinctive

[1] *Scientific Management and Labor* (New York: D. Appleton & Co., 1915), p. 137. The italics are those of the Editor of *The Golden Book.*

work was in raising questions, in blazing trails, in sending youngsters adventuring.[2]

Hoxie suffered from ill health almost all his life. This made him subject to moods of deep depression, and it was during one such mood that he ended his own life at the age of 48.

SELECTED PUBLICATIONS

1915 *Scientific Management and Labor.* New York: D. Appleton & Co.
1916 *Scientific Management and Social Welfare.* New York: Survey.
—— *Why Organized Labor Opposes Scientific Management.* Chicago: Journal of Political Economy.
1917 *Trade Unionism in the United States.* Posthumous collection of lectures at the University of Chicago, edited by E. H. Downey.

Professor Hoxie also wrote several books on sociological subjects.

Curriculum Vitae

1868	Born on April 29th at Edmeston, N.Y.
1893	Received Ph.B. at Cornell University, Ithaca, N.Y.
1896–1898	Employed as Instructor in Economics at Cornell College, Iowa.
1898–1901	Employed as Instructor in Economics at Washington University, St. Louis, Mo.
1901–1902	Still an Instructor in Economics, taught at Washington and Lee, Lexington, Va.
1903–1906	Returned to Cornell University as Instructor in Economics.
1905	Received Ph.D. at University of Chicago.
1906–1916	Returned to University of Chicago as Associate Professor of Political Economy.
1914–1916	Served as special investigator for U.S. Commission on Industrial Relations.
1916	Died on June 22nd at age 48.

[2] *Dictionary of Modern Biography.*

Hugo Diemer
(1870–1939)
United States

HUGO Diemer was the author of a classic textbook, published in 1910, on factory management. He was also a pioneer in the teaching of management in American colleges.

Diemer was an early and original writer on management subjects, as is shown by a comparison of the titles of his books and articles with their dates. His early perception of the new principles of management was supported by experience as a consulting engineer in applying the management methods of F. W. Taylor, supplemented by procedures of his own, in a number of factories. As a result, his textbook of 1910, *Factory Organization and Administration*, was an immediate and sustained success. It ran through many editions. In that of 1935 Diemer wrote:

> The author has had many letters from readers stating that after they had mastered the interrelation and universal application of management principles this has affected every important action in their lives as well as their outlook and attitude in their work and even their private lives and personality. Numerous executives and officials attribute less waste, more profits, and better understanding of employees to their mastery of management principles, science and philosophy. Surely the study is worthwhile.

The later books which he wrote and edited, those on foremanship in particular, were similarly in the vanguard of management thinking.

Diemer occupied an important place in the American management movement over many years. A self-made man, he became a professor but retained an active connection with industry. In 1909, as a professor at Pennsylvania State College, he was one of the early pioneers in sponsoring a course whose syllabus centered about industrial management. Soon after came vocational courses for foremen, again very early in the field.

Hugo Diemer spent the last 19 years of his career at LaSalle Extension University in Chicago (a correspondence institution) as Director of Management Courses and Personnel. At LaSalle, he dealt with thousands of students who were educating themselves "the hard way" in the theory of management while keeping up their full-time jobs in its practice. He therefore had an important influence on the development of management education in America. The publicity engendered by his writings, original experiments in teaching, platform speaking to management organizations, and consultancy work did much to stimulate national interest in management education and to gain eminence for LaSalle as a teaching institution in this sphere.

Col. Diemer was a kind and likable man who made friends easily and who did not obtrude his formidable engineering and managerial gifts in his personal relationships. He gave much leisure time to neighborly work in his community—the Beverly Hills area of Chicago—and was an active church worker. He is remembered for his constant interest in people, and one of his colleagues has used the lately coined term "a human engineer" as a happy epitome of his personality.

In 1938, Diemer's long and pioneering services to management were recognized when the Society for the Advancement of Management awarded him its Taylor Key.

SELECTED PUBLICATIONS

Books:

1910 *Factory Organization and Administration*. New York: McGraw-Hill. 412 pp.

1918 *Industrial Organization and Management*. Chicago: LaSalle Extension University. 308 pp.

1920 *Personnel Administration*. With Daniel Bloomfield. Chicago: LaSalle Extension University. 560 pp.

1921 *Modern Foremanship and Production Methods*. With Meyer and Daniel Bloomfield. Chicago: LaSalle Extension University. 1036 pp.

1925 *Principles of Production*. Chicago: La Salle Extension University. 449 pp.

1927 *Foremanship Training*. Chicago: LaSalle Extension University. 56 pp.

1929 *Wage Payment Plans That Reduced Production Costs* (Editor). New York: McGraw-Hill. 275 pp.

1930 *How to Set Up Production Control for Greater Profits* (Editor). New York: McGraw-Hill. 312 pp.

Articles:

1899 "Functions and Organization of the Purchasing Department," *Engineering Magazine.*

1902 "Aids in Taking the Machine Shop Inventory," *Engineering Magazine.*

1903 "Essentials of Shop Management," *American Machinist*, Vol. 38.

1905 "A Combined Bonus and Premium System," *Engineering Magazine.*

1912 "The 'Efficiency Movement' in 1911," *Iron Age*, Vol. 89.

____ "Factory Organization in Relation to Industrial Education," *Annals* of American Academy of Political and Social Sciences, Vol. 44.

____ "Industrial Management," *Journal of Accountancy*, Vol. 3.

1915 "Education in Scientific Management," *Efficiency Society Journal.*

1917 "Executive Control in the Factory," *Factory.*

____ "Industrial Organization and Management." Chicago: LaSalle Extension University.

Curriculum Vitae

1870	Born on November 18th in Cincinnati, Ohio.
1888–1892	Employed at Addyson Pipe & Steel Co., Cincinnati.
1892–1896	Studied at Ohio State University (earning M.E. in Electrical Engineering), University of Chicago, and Pennsylvania State College (studying history and political science).
1896–1900	Worked as production engineer at Bullock Engineering & Manufacturing Co., and Westinghouse Electric & Manufacturing Co.
1900–1901	Was Assistant Professor of Mechanical Engineering, Michigan State College.
1901–1904	Was Associate Professor of Mechanical Engineering, University of Kansas.
1904–1906	Was Superintendent, National Motor Vehicle Co., Indianapolis.
1904–1907	Active as consulting engineer in Indianapolis and Chicago.
1906–1908	Employed as production manager, Goodman Manufacturing Co., Chicago.
1907–1909	Was Professor of Mechanical Engineering, Pennsylvania State College.
1909–1919	Was Professor of Industrial Engineering, Pennsylvania State College.
1917	Was Major, Ordnance Department, U.S. Army, in charge of U.S. Cartridge Co., Lowell, Mass., and then on staff of commanding officer at Bethlehem Steel Co., Bethlehem, Pa. Later lieutenant colonel in U.S. Army Reserve.
1919–1920	Personnel Superintendent, Winchester Repeating Arms Co.
1920–1921	Was President and Director, Indianapolis Furniture Co.
1920–1939	Was Director, Management Courses and Personnel, LaSalle Extension University, Chicago.
1939	Died on March 3rd, aged 69, in Chicago.

Diemer served as President, Chicago Chapters, The American Society of Mechanical Engineers, and as President of the Taylor Society; he was also National Director and Vice-President of the Society of Industrial Engineers and National Vice-President of the Society for the Advancement of Management.

Carl Köttgen
(1871–1951)
Germany

CARL Köttgen was a leader of the rationalization movement in Germany in the 1920s and a founder of the Reichskuratorium für Wirtschaftlichkeit (German Institute of Management, or RKW).

Köttgen was an electrical engineer who, entering at the bottom, won his way to the position of chief executive in the firm of Siemens, the greatest concern in the German electrical-equipment industry, while also gaining a high reputation in the technical field through his published work. As an engineer and sometime president of the Verein Deutsche Ingenieure (Association of German Engineers, or VDI), Köttgen viewed the responsibilities of his profession in their broadest terms. Like the early members of The American Society of Mechanical Engineers in the United States, he urged a close relationship between engineering and executive management, whether in business or government, since he himself had successfully made the transition from the one activity to the other.

A visit to the United States after the First World War gave Köttgen the opportunity to observe scientific management as it was being applied there. Upon his return home, he was determined to promote rationalization, as scientific management was then known in Germany, among German industrialists. By persuading Carl Friedrich von Siemens to interest himself in rationalization and by enlisting the support of the German government and of important industrial firms, Köttgen in 1921 brought about the creation of RKW, backed by sufficient support to ensure its progress. The introduction and early development of the rationalization movement in Germany were therefore inspired in great measure by this distinguished engineer. He became RKW's Vice-Chairman, then its Chairman (1930–1934), and upon its reconstitution after the Second World War he was awarded honorary membership in it (1950).

Dr. Köttgen was a man who devoted most of his waking hours to his work. Notwithstanding its heavy claims, he always had time for the enjoyment of conversation and for various hobbies. He was a keen gardener and a skilled amateur photographer, and he was fond of hunting.

SELECTED PUBLICATIONS

Books:

1897 *Elektrotechnik und Landwirtschaft* (Electrical Engineering and Agriculture). Berlin: Paul Parey.

1925 *Das wirtschaftliche Amerika* (Productive America). Berlin: VDI (Verein Deutsche Ingenieure).

1928 *Das fliessende Band* (The Assembly Line). Berlin: J. Springer.

Articles:

1925 "Rationalization of Economic Activity," *Industrie und Handelszeitung*, June 24th.

—— "The Tasks of German Rationalization in Government and in Private Business," *Technik und Wirtschaft*, No. 5.

1926 "Rationalization." Address to the Association for the Promotion of Industry, *Gewerbefleiss*, No. 3.

1927 "The Assembly Line." Report to the Berlin Chamber of Industry and Commerce, October.

1929 "Fundamentals of Assembly-Line Work," *ZVDI* (Journal of the Society of German Engineers), p. 125.

Curriculum Vitae

1871	Born on August 29th at Barmen; son of an engineer. Köttgen was educated at Barmen Realgymnasium and the Polytechnic Academy of Berlin-Charlottenburg (student of Professor Slaby).
1894	Joined firm of Siemens.
1897	In charge of power-transmission office of Siemens.
1903	Became confidential clerk to the lately formed Siemens-Schuckert-Werke (SSW).
1905	Became deputy member of the Executive Board, SSW.
1907	In charge of Siemens Brothers' heavy-current plant in Great Britain.
1914–1919	Interned in Great Britain during First World War.
1919	Returned to Germany to take charge of SSW's central administration.

1920 Named Chief Executive, Siemens-Schuckert-Werke.
1939 Retired.
1951 Died on December 12th, aged 80, in Düsseldorf.

Köttgen was awarded an honorary Doctor of Engineering degree by Berlin Polytechnic Academy (1920). He was President of the Association of German Electrical Engineers (1926–1927), of the Association of German Engineers (1929–1931), and of the Third World Power Conference in Berlin (1930).

Courtesy Rowntree Mackintosh Ltd.

Benjamin Seebohm Rowntree
(1871–1954)
Great Britain

B. SEEBOHM Rowntree was the British management movement's greatest pioneer. If his manifold contributions had to be summed up in a few words, it could be said that he gave purpose to the search for effective management. He had two underlying principles in his approach to the problems of industry. First: "Whatever may be the motives which induce any given individual to engage in industry, its true basic purpose must be the service of the community." And second: "Industry is a human thing, in which men and women earn the means of life, and from which men and women are entitled to expect the means to a life worth living." Rowntree's career was devoted to realizing this philosophy in his own family business and in British industry as a whole.

His early work was primarily social, directed toward improving industrial welfare. His discoveries in his first famous study of poverty (1901) led him, as Labor Director of Rowntree & Co., the chocolate and confectionery manufacturers of York, to introduce there what was probably the most advanced provision for employee welfare of any factory in Britain. During the First World War, he founded at the Ministry of Munitions a new welfare department offering an advisory service to employers in difficulties over the unfamiliar human problems arising out of war production. Largely through Rowntree's work and influence in this capacity there became firmly established in British industry, by the end of the war, an interest in industrial welfare and in the human aspects of industry.

After the war Rowntree's work for industrial welfare expanded. Within his own firm he had early set out to remove the principal "fears" which depress the outlook of employees and to achieve that enhanced status for the worker which, he knew as a sociologist, was among the most important of the satisfactions arising from work. This covered a wide range of developments. As early as 1904 the company had established a medical department; then, in 1905, a day continuation school. The year 1919 saw the introduction of a 44-hour, 5-day week, the question of whether the 44 hours should be worked in 5 or 5½ days being left to a ballot of employees. Also in 1919, a comprehensive system of Works councils was set up.

The many pioneering measures introduced into the Cocoa Works in the 1920s included family allowances, unemployment pay, higher education, the employment of trained industrial psychologists, and further provision for health, canteens, and recreation. In 1919 there had been a comprehensive investigation of all profit-sharing experience up to that time; and, as a result, management in 1923 introduced a profit-sharing scheme which again was widely regarded as a model.

Beyond the confines of his own firm, Rowntree gave substantial support to the foundation of the Industrial Welfare Society and the National Institute of Industrial Psychology. He continued his research into social problems. He devised a "human needs standard" which was used for every social survey made in Britain between the two wars. Although he had no political ambitions, he had considerable political influence, and he came to enjoy the firm trust of the trade unions and to mediate significantly in more than one national industrial dispute. He played a leading part in the Liberal Industrial Inquiry of 1927–1928 which published "Britain's Industrial Future."

Rowntree was, however, never a paternalist in his industrial philosophy. He insisted from the outset that an industrial concern could not afford to pay high wages and provide good conditions of employment unless it was efficiently organized and managed. Because of this conviction he became a pioneer, also, in the science of management. From 1923 on, the Rowntree Works were systematically reorganized according to the new principles, which Rowntree culled from every source available to him both in Britain and the United States. Many of these principles became the foundation for accepted textbooks in the study of management,[1] and it should not be forgotten that Mary Parker Follett chose the Rowntree Works as one of the "cases" for her study of the social philosophy of business.

Rowntree's energy and zeal for advancing scientific management overflowed into the national movement in Britain. In 1919 he founded those meetings for works directors, managers, and foremen which became the annual Oxford Management Conferences. Beginning with the theme of

[1] O. Sheldon, *Philosophy of Management* (London: Pitman, 1923). Also, C. H. Northcott and others, *Factory Organization* (London: Pitman, 1927); W. Wallace, *Business Forecasting and Its Practical Application* (London: Pitman, 1927); and L. Urwick, *Organizing a Sales Office* (London: Pitman, 1929).

industrial relations, they came to be a national forum for the widest exchange of knowledge bearing on the principles and practice of management. Again, in 1926 Rowntree founded the Management Research Groups with a different aim—the exchange of confidential management information for the mutual benefit of senior executives from noncompeting firms. The groups have become a permanent institution. In fact, these two movements started by Rowntree marked virtually the inception of the study of scientific management in Great Britain. Moreover, no organization connected with the advancement of management was formed between 1918 and the Second World War which did not owe much of its origin and progress to Rowntree's enthusiasm and interest.

Separate mention should be made, finally, of B. S. Rowntree's work in a sphere halfway between welfare and scientific management—that of communications in industry. The immediate postwar years were the era of the Whitley Councils and new gospels of the ideal relationship between management and worker. Rowntree led the way in the York Works toward a new concept of successful joint consultation, setting this out in his book *The Human Factor in Business: Experiments in Industrial Democracy* (1921). A full-time company-paid shop steward, a works council, a joint appeal committee for disciplinary matters, and the regular supplying of management information to the employees—these were only a few of the innovations that made the Rowntree organization the model of good industrial relations which it has remained. The joint appeal committee, in particular, was a lone instance of a recognition in industry of the distinction between the executive and judicial aspects of authority.

Rowntree was a force, the full impact of which is yet to be felt, for better relations between managers and workers. Some of the experiments which he initiated and applied with outstanding practical success still read like "moonbeams from the larger lunacy" to the more conservative element among business managers. He was, in the considered judgment of this editor (whose chief he was during important formative years), a greater influence than any other business executive who has lived in our time toward guiding his country to a wider, wiser, and more enlightened view of the task of business leadership. Indeed:

> For those of us who were privileged to work alongside him—and with him it was always "alongside" and never "under"—it is the memory of the man, the human being, that endures like a spring of water in a thirsty land. I have known a few men in my lifetime (my own father was another of them) whose attitude to life was so ordered that one was never tempted, even for an instant, to doubt their integrity, to start that search for a secondary motive behind the outer pattern of their deeds and words which implies that their yea is not wholly yea and their nay means "it depends." He was a man, too, of perfect loyalty. To these may be added other virtues—a kindliness to others, a generous and sensitive sympathy with their feelings, a readiness to

share in the ordinary joys and sorrows of every man, regardless of rank or station, which made him a very able practitioner of what he preached. That sounds dull, "unco' guid." But the whole was irradiated by a most delightful and constantly unexpected sense of humour.

I am sure that the last thing he would have wished is that our proceedings should be in any way saddened by the thought of his passing. Rather, it would accord with his lifelong attitude that we should go forward with renewed vigour in the task of developing better management as an essential preliminary condition to better relations not only between the parties to industry but also between the nations—the task to which he devoted the major portion of his working life.[2]

SELECTED PUBLICATIONS

Books:

1901 *Poverty: A Study of Town Life*. London: Macmillan. 437 pp.

1910 *Land and Labor: Lessons from Belgium*. London: Macmillan. 633 pp.

1911 *Unemployment: A Social Study*. With Bruno Lasker. London: Macmillan. 318 pp.

1913 *How the Laborer Lives*. With May Kendall. London: Thos. Nelson. 342 pp.

1914 *The Way to Industrial Peace*.

1918 *The Human Needs of Labor*. London: Longmans, Green. 168 pp.

1921 *The Human Factor in Business: Experiments in Industrial Democracy*. London: Longmans, Green. 188 pp.

—— *The Responsibility of Women Workers for Dependents*. With F. D. Stuart. London: Oxford University Press. 68 pp.

1922 *Industrial Unrest: A Way Out*. London: Longmans, Green. 48 pp.

1930 *The Agricultural Dilemma*. With Viscount Astor. London: P. S. King & Son, Ltd. 101 pp.

1939 *British Agriculture*. With Viscount Astor. London: Penguin Books. 284 pp.

1941 *Poverty and Progress—A Second Social Survey of York*. London: Longmans, Green. 540 pp.

1946 *Mixed Farming and Muddled Thinking*. With Viscount Astor. London: Macdonald. 143 pp.

1951 *Poverty and the Welfare State—A Third Social Survey of York*. With G. R. Lavers. London: Longmans, Green. 104 pp.

—— *English Life and Leisure: A Social Study*. With G. R. Lavers. London: Longmans, Green. 482 pp.

[2] From the text of the short address given by L. Urwick at the European Management Conference, Torquay, October 20–22, 1954, as Gold Medalist of the International Committee for Scientific Management.

Articles, etc.:

B. S. Rowntree wrote many articles for English and American periodicals and addressed numerous conferences. Many of his articles and papers have been reproduced in pamphlet form. The following small selection of titles will give some idea of the subjects covered:

"The Board of Directors and the Purpose of a Business"
"Christianity and Industrial Relations"
"The Conditions of the People"
"Economic Conditions in Industry"
"Industrial Unrest—A Way Out"
"The Prospects and Tasks of Social Reconstruction"
"A Solution of the Unemployment Problem"

Curriculum Vitae

1871	Born on July 7th, second son of Joseph Rowntree, founder of Rowntree & Co., the chocolate and confectionery firm at York. Educated at Bootham, the Quaker School at York, and trained in chemistry at Owen's College, Manchester.
1889	Began his career as a chemist at the York Works, soon becoming a departmental manager.
1897	Became Labor Director. In this position Rowntree was able to undertake experiments directed toward improving conditions among the workers. For example, he was responsible for the establishment of a pension fund for workers in the company.
1913–1914	Served as a member of Lloyd George's Land Enquiry Committee.
1916–1918	Directed a new industrial welfare department created by Lloyd George at the Ministry of Munitions, London.
1917	Appointed to the Government's Reconstruction Committee.
1918	Organized at Scarborough the first of a series of weekend lecture conferences, for works executives and foremen, which settled down in 1922 to two conferences a year at Balliol College, Oxford.
1919	Founded the Central Works Council at Rowntree & Co. Standard factory hours reduced to 44; a five-day week subsequently established by workers' ballot.
1921	Visited the United States (and repeated the visit almost annually up to 1939).
1923	Succeeded his father as Chairman of Rowntree & Co. but retained the post of Labor Director until 1936.
1927	Founded the first management research group in Britain, an association of noncompeting firms.
1931	Advised Lloyd George on a study of unemployment under Ramsay Macdonald's government.
1936	Relinquished executive responsibilities, remaining Chairman of the Board.

1941 Retired from the Board.
1954 Died on October 7th, aged 83, at his home in High Wycombe, Buckinghamshire.

Rowntree was made a Companion of Honour in 1931. He was named to the Royal St. Olaf Order of Norway and a justice of the peace, an honorary LL.D. of Manchester University, and the first honorary fellow of the British Institute of Management.

Robert Grosvenor Valentine
(1872–1916)
United States

ROBERT G. Valentine was, like Robert F. Hoxie, one of the earliest persons who endeavored to interpret scientific management in a form acceptable to organized labor.

Many of F. W. Taylor's closest adherents had become troubled, about the year 1912, by the absence of any provision for the role of labor unions in Taylor's conception of management. Taylor believed that the advantages of scientific management were, if correctly and systematically pursued, mutually beneficial to both employers and workers, but that the employers alone should be responsible for applying scientific management in their concerns. The labor unions, with their tendency to restrict output and their insistence on collective bargaining, were, to him, acting in opposition to his principles. Valentine was a sincere admirer of Taylor and, in his practice as a consultant, had been introducing the Taylor system into manufacturing plants. Valentine, however, came to hold the view that the interests of employer and worker are not necessarily identical in the matter of dividing the profits arising from increased production; thus workers need the collective bargaining power provided by union organization. He therefore voiced the criticism that scientific management was misguided in not enlisting the cooperation of the unions.

Valentine was able, because of his sympathy with both Taylor and the labor-union movement, to mediate in some of the potential conflicts with labor of Taylor's last years. In his own consulting work he specialized in the labor-relations aspect of any changes in management. In some assignments he acted as the agent jointly of the employers' association and the union and was able to devise practical patterns of cooperation, furnishing the necessary assurance of protection to the workers while promoting the advantages to be obtained from improved management. He devised a technique for a "labor audit" which was an early approach to a body of principles of personnel management. He assisted Hoxie in the federal inquiry which led to the publication of Hoxie's *Scientific Management and Labor* (1915), a landmark in the effort to reconcile the two philosophies involved.

Finally, Valentine himself published papers which were contributions to this vital issue. The title of one, "The Progressive Relationship of Efficiency and Consent," indicates that he was a thinker of vision in that transitional period in industrial philosophy. Studying the controversy today, one can recognize that the criticisms of Taylor reported by Valentine in his articles were less than just and that Valentine's hopes for "joint control" by employers and labor in dividing the production surplus were too far ahead of the times. Yet the part played by Valentine and his collaborators in exploring the common ground between management and labor, and in working for the development of cooperation instead of conflict in industrial relations generally, was a contribution of importance.

Robert G. Valentine is remembered as a man of deep sincerity who had a liberalizing and democratizing influence over those with whom he came in contact. He is said, in fact, to have influenced in this way several of the other pioneers commemorated in this book.

SELECTED PUBLICATIONS

1915 "New Certificates of Character for Manufacturers," *Industrial Engineering and Engineering Digest.*

—— "The Progressive Relationship of Efficiency and Consent," Society to Promote the Science of Management.

—— "Scientific Management and Organized Labor," Society to Promote the Science of Management.

Curriculum Vitae

1872 Born on November 29th in West Newton, Mass.

1896 Awarded A.B. by Harvard University.

1896–1899 Employed as Assistant in English, Massachusetts Institute of Technology.

1899–1901 With the National City Bank, New York City, part of the time in the Accounting Department.

1901–1902 At Massachusetts Institute of Technology again as Instructor in English.

1902–1904 With Farmers Loan and Trust Co., New York City.

1905–1908	Served as private secretary to Commissioner Francis E. Leupp of the Indian Service.
1908	Became Supervisor of Indian Schools.
1909–1912	Held position of Assistant Commissioner for Indian Affairs.
1912–1916	Active as investigator and consultant in labor problems, Boston.
1913	Acted as voluntary chairman of first Massachusetts minimum-wage board during the economic depression of the period.
1916	Died on September 15th at age of 44.

Charles Samuel Myers
(1873–1946)
Great Britain

CHARLES Samuel Myers pioneered industrial psychology in Great Britain. His practical contribution was to found and develop the National Institute of Industrial Psychology.

Until the First World War Myers had been an academic psychologist at Cambridge University; there he had gained a considerable reputation for his development of experimental psychology. In 1918, following his wartime work of promoting applications of psychology in the Armed Services, he delivered two important lectures to the Royal Institution of Great Britain. In these he declared that the time had come to "take psychology out of the laboratory and carry it over into the field of everyday life"—in particular into industrial life. One of his listeners was H. J. Welch, a businessman who had for some time been wondering whether psychological methods could not be applied to industry and commerce along the lines described by Hugo Münsterberg in some of his popular American writings. The two men decided to collaborate in organizing the subscription of funds for a suitable project, and in 1920 their efforts met with success with the founding of the National Institute of Industrial Psychology.

Since its foundation, the Institute (NIIP) has been one of the focal points in Great Britain for the study and application of better methods in dealing with the human factor in management. Its object is defined as the application of psychological and physiological knowledge to the problems of industry and commerce. Its activities include research, advisory services to individuals and firms, training, and dissemination of information through lectures, discussions, publications, and the maintenance of a reference library. Its growth was Myers's lifework. Gaining recognition from British industry, however, was no easy matter; the quiet life devoted to scientific research which had always been Myers's ambition was exchanged for a plunge "into the arduous task of organization, administration, making contacts with private individuals, public bodies, and commercial firms, securing financial support, and seeking to introduce scientific ideals and methods into the world of commerce and manufacture. . . . Much of the support the Institute received was the direct result of his capacity for communicating to others his own enthusiastic belief in the great part industrial psychology has still to play in the life of the nation."[1] By the end of the interwar period, the Institute had helped to build up a remarkable corpus of knowledge in regard to the work and reactions of the human being in industry and commerce, and its program was wider than that of any comparable body in the world.

Myers's conception had been noble from the outset. Though he had given full weight to the specialized techniques which psychology could contribute to management in such fields as vocational selection and training, he did not restrict the claims of industrial psychology to narrow confines. Industrial psychology in his view was the means by which the whole process of management could be thought through in order to take its rightful place as a social science. It was with this aim in mind that he mastered the principles of F. W. Taylor and F. B. Gilbreth, made himself familiar at first hand with every aspect of industry, and undertook so wide a program for the Institute. In his earlier years he had helped to take psychology from the lecture room into the laboratory. In his later career he took it from the laboratory into the manager's office and onto the factory floor.

Myers is remembered with affection by his fellow psychologists. He radiated good humor and enthusiasm. "A humane cultured scientist"[2] of the eighteenth-century British tradition, he combined scientific integrity with many social graces and had a large circle of friends into which he readily welcomed newcomers, especially the young. The turning point in his life was his abandonment of the gracious way of living he had followed at Cambridge to install himself in two rooms in Holborn and set out to establish relations with the world of business. At times the setbacks of his new activities depressed him, for he was modest and not by nature assertive. "Indeed, it was his personal qualities, which he himself often regarded as defects rather than as assets, that enabled him to succeed where the more usual kind of pioneer would have failed. His quiet and cultured manner, his diffident speech, his complete freedom from push or gush, his self-criticism and reserve, his amazing kindliness and tolerance, combined with a dogged resistance wherever the interests of the Institute were threatened, enabled

[1] Quoted from obituary by Professor Sir Cyril Burt in *Occupational Psychology*, January 1947, p. 4.

[2] *Ibid.*

him, in spite of much opposition and scepticism, to win his way alike in the world of business and the world of high science. From the first to the last, the key to his success was his own unflagging self-sacrifice."[3]

SELECTED PUBLICATIONS

Books:

1918 *Present-Day Applications of Psychology*. Originally two lectures given to the Royal Institution. London: Methuen. 47 pp.

1921 *Mind and Work*. London: University of London Press. 176 pp.

1925 *Industrial Psychology in Great Britain*. London: Jonathan Cape. 164 pp.

1928 *Industrial Psychology*. Editor. London: Home University Library of Modern Knowledge Series: Oxford University Press. 252 pp.

1932 *Business Rationalization*. London: Pitman. 76 pp.

—— *Ten Years of Industrial Psychology*. With H. J. Welch. London: Pitman. 146 pp.

Articles:

Myers contributed numerous papers to scientific journals. He was one of the founders, in 1904, of the *British Journal of Psychology*.

Curriculum Vitae

1873 Born in London on March 13th. Myers's father and grandfather were businessmen in the City of London. He was educated at the City of London School.

1891–1898 At Cambridge University (Gonville and Caius College), taking a B.A. and then a medical degree.

1898–1899 On Cambridge Anthropological Expedition to New Guinea and Borneo.

1899–1900 Employed as a house physician at St. Bartholomew's Hospital, London.

1900–1902 In Egypt for health reasons.

1902 Assisted W. H. R. Rivers, at Cambridge, with his classes in experimental psychology.

1906 Employed part-time as Professor of Psychology, King's College, London.

1909 Lectured at Cambridge University on experimental psychology. His important *Text Book of Experimental Psychology* was published in this year.

1912 Became Director of the Psychological Laboratory, Cambridge University.

1915 Commissioned in the Royal Army Medical Corps in France.

[3] Memoir by Professor T. H. Pear in *British Journal of Educational Psychology*, February 1947, p. 5.

1916	Acted as consultant psychologist to the British armies in France.
1918–1922	At Cambridge as Reader in experimental psychology.
1918–1929	Active as member of Industrial Fatigue Research Board.
1919	Organized a summer school on industrial administration at Cambridge under auspices of University Laboratory.
1922–1938	Left academic life to become Director of NIIP on full-time basis.
1930	Became Principal of NIIP.
1938	Retired from NIIP with title of Honorary Scientific Adviser.
1941	Appointed member of War Office Advisory Committee on Personnel Selection.
1946	Died on October 12th, aged 73, at Winsford, Somerset.

Myers was one of the first Fellows of the Royal Society to be elected for psychological work (1915), President of the British Psychological Society (1920), President of the Psychology Section of the British Association (1922 and 1931), and President of the Seventh International Congress in Psychology (1923). He served on the Education Committee of the British Management Council throughout its existence (1937–1947). He was made a Companion of the British Empire in 1919 and held the following academic degrees: M.A., M.D., Sc.D. (Cambridge), honorary D.Sc. (Manchester), honorary LL.D. (Calcutta), and Honorary D.Sc. (Pennsylvania). In addition, he was an honorary Fellow of Gonville and Caius College, Cambridge.

John Howell Williams
(1873–1941)
United States

JOHN Howell Williams is remembered as an early thinker on scientific management and the originator of the "flexible budget" as an instrument of general administrative control.

His first contribution to management, however, was the concept he termed "visualization of management." In papers presented to the Taylor Society in 1915 and 1916, he drew attention to the importance of *recording* in the development of a body of knowledge. Just as in engineering the drawings and plans precede the physical work and make it easier to execute, so in the Taylor system of management, said Williams, it was becoming customary to make indexes and instructions of increasing precision which could be executed in the way an engineer executes the blueprints of the drawing office. The science of management could in this respect learn from engineering, and the efforts of those in the movement should be directed toward increasing the precision of the indexes, instructions, and symbols used. Williams himself originated several devices of this sort which were subsequently found useful in practice.

Williams put forward his concept of the flexible budget in 1922 and published the authoritative statement on it in 1934. The flexible budget has proved to be one of the most effective devices of general administrative control in the management of enterprises.

Interestingly, John Howell Williams was the subject of a new development in the admission policy of The American Society of Mechanical Engineers.

In 1920 he was the first person to be admitted to the Society entirely on evidence of managerial ability—that is, without having any engineering qualifications.

Distinguished management friends have recorded that Williams's upbringing in the school of hard knocks made him a rugged, energetic individualist, depending almost too much on himself. Yet he was outstandingly honorable and dependable, charming, loyal and appreciative, sensitive to beauty in every form, tolerant in argument, and unusually courageous in the face of failing health.

SELECTED PUBLICATIONS

Book:

1934 *The Flexible Budget.* New York: McGraw-Hill.

Articles:

1915–1916 "The Index as a Factor in Industry," *Bulletin* of the Taylor Society, Vol. I, No. 3, May 1915, pp. 2–6; and Vol. II. No. 2, July 1916, pp. 6–14.

1922 "A Technique for the Chief Executive," *Bulletin* of the Taylor Society, Vol. VII, No. 2, April, pp. 47–68.

1923 "The Ways and Means of the Chief Executive," *Bulletin* of the Taylor Society, Vol. VIII, No. 2, April, pp. 53–58.

1924 "Management as an Executive Function," *Bulletin* of the Taylor Society, Vol. IX, No. 2, April, pp. 66–71.

1926 "Top Control," *Bulletin* of the Taylor Society, Vol. XI, No. 4, October, pp. 199–206.

1928 "The Budget as a Medium of Executive Leadership," *Bulletin* of the Taylor Society, Vol. XIII, No. 4, August, pp. 166–169.

1929 "General Administrative Control." Chapter XIX in *Scientific Management in American Industry,* edited by H. S. Person for the Taylor Society. New York: Harper & Bros.

Curriculum Vitae

1873 Born on January 22nd in Baltimore, Md. Williams had no formal education, and his early life was marked by economic struggle.

1899–1900 Started a small printing business in Baltimore. This prospered through his efforts and evolved into Williams, Wilkins & Co., the leading business of its kind in Baltimore, which was later noted as an example of scientific management.

1900–1907 Moved to New York and, for a period, was connected with different aspects of the printing business.

1907–1917 Employed by Trust Co. of America as investigator of new enterprises seeking loans.

c. 1909	Began undertaking management-consultancy work.
1917–1921	In charge of organization and methods in the Quartermaster Corps of the U.S. Army.
1921–1935	Was New York manager for Day and Zimmerman, Inc., of Philadelphia.
1928	Retained to report to the Interstate Commerce Commission on railroad costing procedures. This report disclosed important new information on costs and was widely read.
1935–1941	Retired because of severe ill health.
1941	Died on May 23rd at age of 68.

Ernst Streer, Ritter von Streeruwitz
(1874–1952)
Austria

ERNST Streeruwitz was the founder of the Austrian Board of Efficiency (1928) and the author of one of the classics of management literature in the German language.

Rationalisierung und Weltwirtschaft (Rationalization and the World Economic System), published in 1931, was a picture of contemporary affairs so comprehensive as to merit the term "encyclopedic." As Director of the Austrian Board of Efficiency, Streeruwitz was in the closest touch with every management activity in his country and with the international management movement. In the course of his varied career he gained a wealth of experience in every field of economic life, to which he could apply the yardstick of rationalization obtained from his close contact with the management movement. It is not surprising that he should have applied this standard to the highest and widest field of his manifold activities—national and international statecraft. *Rationalization and the World Economic System* was written by the founder and leader of the Austrian Board of Efficiency, but it was the politician and statesman (for Streeruwitz had been Federal Chancellor of Austria) who guided the pen. Much of the book was controversial in both its technical and its political aspects, but the whole was illuminated by a powerful personality, by a wide general knowledge not cramped by specialization, and by a characteristic temperament.

The author's chief aim was to lead the reader through the successive stages from the narrower rationalization of undertakings and national industries to the rationalization of the world economic system and of politics.

That a rationalization expert should venture into the realm of general politics was novel in 1931. "Politics and rationalization—is there any connection between the two things? There is, for politics may hinder and hamper economic rationalization."[1]

In this view Streeruwitz was in agreement with the ideas underlying the discussion on "The Pros and Cons of Rationalization" at the Second Conference of the International Management Institute in July 1931. His view was that the leaders and experts in the rationalization movement had "the right" to concern themselves with "bigger things than conveyors, automatic lathes, and stop-watches, and thereby lift the discussion of rationalization to a higher plane and give it a wider scope; namely, the rebuilding and reorganization of the world as a whole by leading it back to the source from which our movement took its name—*ratio* or reason."[2]

In 1928 Streeruwitz devised the constitution of the Oesterreichisches Kuratorium für Wirtschaftlichkeit (Austrian Board of Efficiency). Not only has this constitution stood the test of time in Austria, but at the 1931 International Rationalization Conference in Geneva it was specially commended as a model which other countries might adopt in creating their own institutes. The OeKW, during the years up to the Second World War, accomplished significant work under Streeruwitz's leadership, applying the principles of rationalization to trade, the health and insurance services, timber and coal utilization, and road and rail transport.

Streeruwitz was an idealist and a nobleman in the best sense of the term. His closing years were devoted to the consolations of private study in the uncertain surroundings of the danger center of postwar Western society in which he lived. The sage remark of the old Austrian philosopher Carneri, with which Streeruwitz closed his book of 1931, reflected the philosophy of this statesman of prewar Austria.

> There are times when the proper leader cannot be found and in which conscience fails to act. But a people is not on that account doomed. The work is taken over by necessity, and it never fails. But before necessity can accomplish anything it must grow—grow until, like a horrible spectre, it brings men to their senses, so that the idle are aroused from their idleness, the cranks cured of their perversity and the despairing imbued with fresh courage. Then folly and incompetence are driven out of the field, and the world once more resumes, as it always has done, its steady forward march.[3]

SELECTED PUBLICATIONS

1931 *Rationalisierung und Weltwirtschaft* (Rationalization and the World Economic System). Vienna: Julius Springer.

[1] Ernst Streeruwitz, *Rationalisierung und Weltwirtschaft* (Rationalization and the World Economic System). Vienna: Julius Springer, 1931, p. 147.
[2] *Ibid.*, pp. 356–357.
[3] *Ibid.*

1934 *Wie es war . . .* (The Way It Was . . .). Vienna.
1937 *Springflut über Oesterreich* (Springtide over Austria). Vienna.

Curriculum Vitae

1874	Born in Mies, Bohemia. Educated at grammar school, Vienna; military academy, Wiener Neustadt; Vienna University (Law); and Vienna Technical High School (Engineering).
1900–1902	Employed as steward of the Lissa Estate, Bohemia.
1902–1903	Employed as Director, Franz Leitenberger Textile Mills, Bohemia.
1904–1913	Employed as Director, Cosmanos AG, textile mills, Bohemia.
1914–1919	Volunteered for army service; was cavalry captain and major.
1919	Named Director of Neunkirchner Druckfabriks AG, textile printers.
1923	Elected Christian Socialist Deputy to the National Assembly.
1928	Became Founder-President of Oesterreichisches Kuratorium für Wirtschaftlichkeit (Austrian Board of Efficiency).
May–September 1929	Served as Federal Chancellor of Austria.
1930–1938	Held office of President, Vienna Chamber of Commerce, until his retirement. Served as parliamentary rapporteur for the reform of the Austrian Federal Railways.
1952	Died at age of 78.

Streeruwitz received a Doctor of Political Science degree from Vienna University (1939) and during the First World War was decorated with the Franz Joseph Order, Signum Laudis with Cross D, and the Iron Cross.

Courtesy The National Cyclopaedia of American Biography.

George De Albert Babcock
(1875–1942)
United States

GEORGE D. Babcock pioneered in introducing the Taylor system of management into the American motor-vehicle industry between 1908 and 1912. This work, begun by Carl Barth as a consultant and continued by Babcock as a plant executive, was the first application of scientific management in a major American industry.

Babcock made several original contributions to the Taylor methods: the earliest known employee counseling program of the kind later made famous by Elton Mayo, an improved formula for base wage rates, and an integrated planning system visualized from a single control board. The employee counseling program in the Franklin Co. was developed as an integral part of Babcock's system of management. An early and original experiment, it anticipated the Hawthorne investigations by many years and has been called "management's first attempt to direct human processes within an industrial structure."[1]

Of the wage-rate formula which Babcock introduced into the plant manufacturing the Franklin automobile, Carl Barth wrote: "In Mr. Babcock's

[1] Article in *National Cyclopaedia of American Biography*, Vol. 31. This profile is largely based in that article.

formula in determining a man's base rate, we have the first attempt to consider this matter from all possible angles with a view to absolute justice."[2] The formula automatically adjusted the base wage rate in accordance with changes in the cost of living and the personal record of the employee.

Babcock's visualized planning system made use of a control board showing the exact location of every project in the plant. It introduced such features as the use of pneumatic tubes for issuing and returning orders and the preservation by photography of progress records. The net result of the system in the Franklin plant was a great saving of capital through reduction of the volume of work in progress.

Later in his career Babcock put into practice other remarkable applications of his system. In a tractor-and-road-machinery plant he laid out a two-year time schedule for more than two million detailed operations, each of which was without exception completed on time. In his work for the Rural Electrification Administration he codified a very large number of government construction projects on a single sheet of paper, producing the first clear picture to be obtained of this heterogeneous field. His methods here saved the government several million dollars in construction costs.

The work of Babcock, combining pioneering advances in the science of management with advances in the field of morale and human relations, is yet another piece of evidence refuting those who accuse the Taylor group of having dehumanized management. For, although George D. Babcock was a protagonist of the scientific approach to management, he was also noted for his capacity for seeing management as a whole. Science, in his outlook, occupied only its due place and was harnessed to a sincere interest in the welfare of his workers and to a kindly and generous personality.

SELECTED PUBLICATIONS

Book:

1917 *The Taylor System in Franklin Management.* New York: Engineering Magazine Co. 245 pp.

Articles:

1914 "Results of Applied Scientific Management." Series of 7 articles: in *Iron Age*, Vols. 93 and 94.

—— "Routing Schedule and Despatch," *Industrial Engineering and the Engineering Digest*, Vol. 14, pp. 228–233, 275–283.

—— "Making an Efficient Plant More Efficient," *Industrial Engineering and the Engineering Digest*, Vol. 14, pp. 427–431.

1915 "Exact Control of Manufacture in Practice," *Iron Age*, Vol. 96, pp. 1410–1413.

[2] Preface to George Babcock, *The Taylor System in Franklin Management* (New York: Engineering Magazine Co.).

1916 "Fixing Individual Wage Rates on Facts," *Iron Age*, Vol. 97, pp. 1375–1379.

1921 Part of *Waste in Industry*. New York: McGraw-Hill, for Federated American Engineering Societies.

1924 Section on "Production and Control" in *Management Handbook*, edited by L. P. Alford. New York: Ronald Press.

Curriculum Vitae

1875 Born on October 18th in Corinne, Utah. Educated at public schools in Syracuse, N.Y., later attending Fairfield Military Academy, N.Y.

1897–1900 Taught physics, chemistry, and mechanical drawing at Fairfield Military Academy.

1900–1904 Attended Purdue University, graduating with B.S. degree in electrical engineering.

1904–1907 Associated with William Kent as Professor of Mechanical Arts and Industrial Engineering at Syracuse University.

1907–1912 Employed as Assistant Superintendent, H. H. Franklin Automobile Manufacturing Co., Syracuse.

1912–1917 Rose to Factory Superintendent and General Production Manager, H. H. Franklin Automobile Manufacturing Co.

1917–1919 Served as Chief Ordnance Supply Officer of the American Expeditionary Force in liaison with the General Staff.

1919–1925 Became manufacturing executive with the Holt Manufacturing Co., Peoria, Ill., producers of caterpillar tractors and road machinery.

1921–1922 Collaborated with others in organizing the Division of Simplified Practice in the U.S. Department of Commerce.

1925–1928 Was manufacturing engineer and Assistant to the Vice-President of Manufacture, Dodge Bros., automobile producers, Detroit, Mich.

1928–1934 Operated his own lumber manufacturing plant in Fletcher, N.C.

1934–1937 Entered service of U.S. government as regional engineer with the Civil Works Administration, holding various positions of increasing authority.

1937–1939 Served as management engineer for the Rural Electrification Administration.

1939–1942 Was Director of Engineering Management, Federal Works Agency.

1942 Died on January 12th, aged 67, in Washington, D.C.

Babcock was a charter member of the Taylor Society and a lecturer on industrial management at the University of Chicago, Harvard University, and other American institutions as well as in Germany, France, and Czechoslovakia.

Edward Tregaskiss Elbourne
(1875–1935)
Great Britain

EDWARD Tregaskiss Elbourne was the pioneer in Great Britain of management viewed as a profession in its own right. To this end he founded the Institute of Industrial Administration, a body which has striven in Great Britain through many years and against many obstacles to establish recognized professional standards. The Institute's qualification has long been the sole British equivalent of the many degrees to which the student of management may aspire in other countries, notably the United States.

Elbourne's own career demonstrated the logic upon which his aims for management were based. If management was a science (and early in the course of his work as an engineer and factory manager he became convinced that it was), its principles and practice could be the subject of analytical definition. So in 1914 he published *Factory Organization and Accounts*, perhaps the most comprehensive one-man textbook on the whole field of management (with the exception of selling) to appear in any country up to that time. Largely through the instrumentality of a high official in the Ministry of Munitions, some 10,000 copies of this book were sold during the course of the First World War, principally to the executive staffs of government contracting firms. Elbourne's principles of management were thus provided with an avenue leading to their immediate translation into practice, and the book may well have been among the main stimuli giving rise to the marked progress in applied scientific management which was one of the features of British industry between 1914 and 1920. A comprehensive British textbook of management published in 1953 included it in a list of authoritative books on management restricted to seven publications.*

If management was a field which could be analytically defined, it was a subject that could be taught and could be made the basis of a professional qualification. Elbourne conceived a plan for creating a corporate body devoted to the study and teaching of management; the body would be designed, also, to impart that special responsibility associated with the word "profession" to the status of those practicing management. In 1920, he founded the Institute of Industrial Administration. Essentially concerned with education, the Institute from the outset took as one of its objects the development of a syllabus and the awarding of a certificate of qualification to those attaining a required standard of knowledge, training, and experience in management. In 1928, Elbourne's advocacy resulted in the initiation by the Regent Street Polytechnic, London, of a four-year part-time course in industrial administration according to the Institute's syllabus—the most extensive syllabus so far in existence.

The focal point having been established for the development of management as a profession, Elbourne's remaining years were spent in the endeavor to gain support for the Institute from a skeptical industrial world. His vision proved justified, although progress was slow. In 1924, the Institution of Mechanical Engineers adopted the subject "engineering economics" as part of its professional-examination scheme. In 1934, the Institution of Electrical Engineers joined the older organization in a common syllabus for this subject, whose title was now changed to "Fundamentals of Industrial Administration." Elbourne lived, moreover, to see other bodies—the Federation of British Industries and the University of London, for example—recognize management as a valid subject for systematic study.

Finally, Elbourne was the precursor of a second major stage in education for management: provision for a period of mental reinvigoration for experienced executives midway through their careers at a "staff college for industry" on the army model. His ten full-time study conferences for executives at Loughborough College in 1934 foreshadowed many of the essential features of the Administrative Staff College, which was not founded until more than a decade later.

Elbourne had chosen the most difficult task among those who strove to found institutes in the field of management in Britain. For, though others were successful in specialized fields (for example, Myers in industrial psychology), he was seeking recognition for the study of management viewed as a whole. In so doing he had to struggle against the many prejudices of managers who had "learned the hard way" and who found it difficult to accept the idea that younger men might train themselves in management by more systematic and rational means. In Great Britain there are still those

* *Principles and Practice of Management.* Edited by E. F. L. Brech. (London: Longmans, Green, 1953). 750 pp. See p. 742.

who refuse to recognize that the art of business can be based on science, but many younger managers have cause to be grateful to Elbourne for the start he gave them in making their business careers not only more effective but more satisfying and creative.

Elbourne was a man more interested in ideas than in money making. He needed a colleague to give a practical direction to his visionary plans, and the early death of his friend Sir Harry Brindley was a setback not only for his work but also for the development of the Institute which they had founded together. His intellectual endowments were so abundant that they sometimes tripped him in matters of exposition. The thoughts tumbled over each other. He could see what he meant; he did not always succeed in making other people see it.

That almost single-handed Elbourne should have succeeded as an unpaid officer in establishing the Institute while continuing to practice his own consultancy work is a tribute to his unflagging energy and patient courage in the face of difficulties and disappointments. On his death the management movement in Britain sincerely lamented the loss of one of its most devoted pioneers. And in 1951 the Institute of Industrial Administration established the Elbourne Memorial Lecture, to be given periodically, at the Institute's invitation, by an individual whom the Institute would thus honor in association with the name of its founder.

SELECTED PUBLICATIONS

Books:

1914 *Factory Organization and Accounts*. London: Library Press. 654 pp. Revised and much enlarged in 1921 and subsequent editions as *Factory Administration and Cost Accounts*. 831 pp.

1919 *The Costing Problem*. London: Library Press. 148 pp.

1920 *The Management Problem*. London: Library Press. 153 pp.

1926 *The Marketing Problem*. London: Longmans, Green. 216 pp.

1934 *Fundamentals of Industrial Administration*. London: Macdonald & Evans.

Articles:

1918 "The Story of Ponders End Shell Works: Its Labor Problems and Their Solution," *The Engineer*. Series of 13 articles, later circulated privately in book form.

1921 "Staff Organization in Factories," *Journal of the Institute of Industrial Administration*, October.

1924 "The Organization of Brains in Industry." Papers of Rowntree Lecture Conference No. 19, Oxford, September.

1927 "Trade Association Statistics." Paper read before the Royal Statistical Society. *The Accountant*, Vol. LXXVII, October 1st, p. 437 *et seq.*

1928 "The Technique of Industrial Administration." Series of articles under this title published in *The Accountant*, January–October.

Curriculum Vitae

1875	Born in Hampshire on June 12th. Educated in Birmingham; apprenticed successively in three engineering concerns.
1896	Began his engineering career as a draftsman and an associate member of the Institution of Mechanical Engineers.
c. 1900	Visited the United States to study machine tools and factory organization.
1900	Became works organizer and accountant, John I. Thorneycroft & Co., moving progressively to higher posts. Also was Assistant General Manager to Mr. (later Sir) Harry Brindley at the Ponders End Shell Factory of the same company.
1919	Joined Brindley as partner in consultancy work in engineering and factory administration. In June and July gave three series of lectures on industrial administration to audiences of industrial executives.
1920	On Brindley's death, continued the consultancy practice alone, relinquishing the technical side and concentrating on organization. Named first honorary secretary and honorary director of education of the Institute of Industrial Administration.
1925	Visited the United States to study marketing and publicity.
1927	Served as joint director of studies for lecture course at Regent Street Polytechnic, London.
1935	Died on October 18th at age of 60.

Elbourne received the M.B.E. in 1919 in recognition of his work at Ponders End.

Friedrich-Ludwig Meyenberg
(1875–1949)
Germany/Great Britain

THE name of Professor F. L. Meyenberg is linked, like that of Kurt Hegner, with the formative period of the Reichsausschuss für Arbeitszeitermittlung (German Institute of Work and Time Study, or REFA).

Professor Meyenberg was one of the earliest pioneers of management in Germany. From 1919, by which time he was an engineer of mature industrial experience, he began publishing articles on management, popularizing the work of F. W. Taylor in the United States and interpreting it in terms applicable to German industry. In 1925 he became the first managing director of REFA, founded the previous year. In this capacity he made many contributions to the dissemination in Germany of the science of work study and of management. In particular, he was among the first in Germany to insist on giving foremost place to the human factor in management. During his period with REFA, he was also Professor of Industrial Administration and head of the Institute for Scientific Management at the Polytechnical Academy of Brunswick, and he took a leading role in different societies for the furtherance of the German management movement. He was co-editor of the successful *Second REFA Book,* a manual of the principles and practice of work study, which sold over 100,000 copies within a short time of its publication in 1933.

In the same year, Professor Meyenberg left his native country for Great Britain. This major change did not stop his career in management. By 1938 he had become a management author in the English language, and he eventually published in England four management books dealing with the subjects on which he was an authority—work study and management, particularly from the engineering viewpoint. He lectured in technical colleges and was active in the management group of the Institution of Mechanical Engineers. In addition, he helped to found the Institute of Economic Engineering, an association of work-study engineers.

After the Second World War Meyenberg returned to Germany to forge a new bond with his old colleagues of REFA. He helped them to set up their organization again after the changes caused by the war, and in the year of his death in Germany he was awarded an honor which must have meant much to him—REFA's honorary membership.

A man of first-class intellect who won the respect of the engineering profession in both Germany and Great Britain, Meyenberg had many of the traditional characteristics of the professor—modesty, a quiet manner of speaking, short sight, indifferent health during the last years of his life, and a simple manner of living. The start of a new life in England, made necessary by his enforced departure from Germany, was not easy for him; it disturbed his work and brought economic difficulties which he never entirely surmounted. His return home after the Second World War was a great joy to him, and one must admire the fortitude with which he had adapted himself and pursued his life work in England during those troubled years.

SELECTED PUBLICATIONS

Books:

1924 *The Place of Standardization in the Organization of an Engineering Plant.* Berlin: Julius Springer.

1938 *The New Management.* With H. T. Hildage and T. G. Marple. London: Macdonald and Evans. 358 pp.

1942 *Economic Control of Iron and Steel Works.* London: Chapman and Hall. 332 pp. Based on two series of articles originally published in *Metallurgia* and *Iron and Steel.* (See articles for 1938–1940 and 1940–1941).

1945 *Time Study and Rate-fixing.* London: Pitman, for the Institute of Economic Engineering.

1951 *Industrial Administration and Management.* Posthumously published. London: Pitman.

Articles:

1919 "The Basic Principles of Scientific Management—An Aid in Economic Reconstruction," *Technik und Wirtschaft,* Vol. 12, pp. 353–365.

1921 "A Critical Review of Taylorism. An analysis in the Light of Two New Publications in the Managerial Literature," *Technik und Wirtschaft,* Vol. 14, pp. 402–413.

1924	"Factory Management and Factory Organization," *ZVDI*, Vol. 68, p. 34.
1929	"The Adoption of Standards in Practice," *Masch-Bau Betrieb*, Vol. 8, pp. 465–466.
——	"Training of Engineers at Technical High Schools," *Masch-Bau Betrieb*, Vol. 8, pp. 3–6.
1930	"The Significance of Scientific Management," *Technik und Wirtschaft*, Vol. 23, pp. 1–3.
1931	"The Finances of a Technical-Scientific Association and Publishing House," *Technik und Wirtschaft*. Vol. 24, pp. 141–146.
——	"The Human Factor in Factory Operation," *Masch-Bau Betrieb*, Vol. 10, pp. 614–616.
——	"Industrial Costing; the Engineer and Industrial Costing," *ZVDI*, Vol. 75, pp. 61–62.
1932	"Evaluation of Operating Costs per Electric Truck Conveying," *Der Betrieb*, Vol. 11, p. 95.
1938–1940	"Industrial Administration and Production Control." Series of articles in *Metallurgia* (England).
1940–1941	"Features of Costing and Accountancy in Iron and Steel Industry," *Iron and Steel* (England).

Professor Meyenberg was Editor of the journal *Maschinenbau*, published by the Verein Deutscher Ingenieure, for the period 1925–1933 and of the *Engineers' Digest*, in London, during the years 1945–1947.

Curriculum Vitae

1875	Born at Hanover on October 22nd. Educated at the Goethe Gymnasium and the Polytechnical Academies of Hanover and Berlin. Graduated with degree of Dipl.Ing.
1894–1898	Served apprenticeship during college vacations at Royal Railway Main Works, Hanover.
1898–1900	Assisted Professor Eugen Meyer at the Institute of Physical Engineering, University of Göttingen.
1900–1925	Employed as designing engineer in the Gasmotorenfabrik Deutschland, later, as tending and shipping engineer with Maschinenbau AG, Balcke, Bochum. Still later, became Chief Engineer, Eisenbahn-Signal-Bauanstalt Max Judel & Co., Brunswick; Technical Director, Waffenwerk Oberspree Kornbusch & Co.; Director of Factory Management, Knorrbremse AG, Berlin-Lichtenberg; and Technical Director, Riebe Kugellager- und Werkzeug-fabrik, Berlin-Weissensee. Finally, he was in charge of internal organization, business statistics, and standardization for Deutsche Werke AG, Berlin.
1925–1933	Was Managing Director, Reichsausschuss für Arbeitszeitermittlung (German Institute of Work and Time Study, or REFA).

1926–1933	Was Professor of Industrial Administration and head of the Institute for Scientific Management at the Polytechnical Academy of Brunswick.
1933	Emigrated to Great Britain; later became a naturalized British subject.
1934–1935	On technical staff of British Iron and Steel Federation.
1935–1941	Employed as work study engineer and management expert with Appleby-Frodingham Iron & Steel Co. and then with Samuel Fox & Co., Stocksbridge.
1941–1949	Active as author, translator, and lecturer on work study and management at Polytechnics, etc.
1946	Became member of a BIOS technical mission to Germany.
1949	Died on October 1st, at age of 74, in Frankfurt.

In Germany Meyenberg was Chairman of the Committee on Practical Application of Standards, German Standards Association; Chairman of the Committee on Industrial Accounts, Association of German Engineers; and Member of Council, German Institution of Production Engineers. In Great Britain he was a full member of the Institution of Mechanical Engineers (1939 on) and an honorary member of the Institute of Economic Engineering (1941 on).

Courtesy Administrative Management Society.

William Henry Leffingwell
(1876–1934)
United States

W. H. LEFFINGWELL was the first person to demonstrate that the principles of scientific management, as they had been applied to production, could be applied with equal success in the office. His writings are still standard works.

Leffingwell's first major contribution to the literature was his book *Scientific Office Management* (1917), the forerunner of all modern studies in office management. In 1921 he published his eight principles of scientific office management. In 1925 came *Office Management Principles and Practice*, a comprehensive treatise presenting his philosophy of management and expounding its application to office work. It too earned a place in the general literature of management.[1] And Leffingwell's third book, *Textbook of Office Management* (1932), was included in H. A. Hopf's selection of 50 leading management books in 1949.[2]

Leffingwell's influence through his books and his many articles was widened by much practical success, beginning with his first application in

[1] Its importance is noted, for instance, in "A History of Scientific Management in the United States of America," by H. P. Dutton, in *Advanced Management*, October 1953.

[2] Harry Arthur Hopf, *Soundings in the Literature of Management—Fifty Books the Educated Practitioner Should Know*. Publication No. 9 (Ossining, N.Y.: Hopf Institute of Management, 1949). 28 pp.

his own office of the methods of F. W. Taylor and continuing throughout his distinguished career as a consultant. The essence of the new attitude he brought to office management was the replacement of forms and systems by the intelligent application of universal management principles. He was a prominent figure in the management movement at home and abroad, and his work was recognized in 1933 by his election to an important general management honor in America—the presidency of the Taylor Society.

Leffingwell endowed a medal during another presidency—that of the National Office Management Association. The medal is awarded annually, not for inventing a machine, appliance, or device, not for writing a book, but for outstanding accomplishment of practical value in office management. This criterion was the one by which he also measured his own achievement.

W. H. Leffingwell is remembered for his generosity in sharing the results of his researches with others and for his unfailing goodwill and courtesy. One cannot but admire the man who, beginning his career as a male shorthand typist, succeeded by his independent endeavors in originating a whole new branch of management knowledge and in becoming an internationally known authority on its practice.

SELECTED PUBLICATIONS

Books:

1917 *Scientific Office Management*. Chicago: A. W. Shaw Co. 262 pp.

1918 *Making the Office Pay*. Editor. Chicago: A. W. Shaw Co. 389 pp.

—— *Automatic Letter Writer and Dictation System*. Editor. Chicago: A. W. Shaw Co. 308 pp.

1925 *Office Management Principles and Practice*. Chicago: A. W. Shaw Co. 850 pp.

1926 *Office Appliance Manual*. Editor. Chicago: A. W. Shaw Co. 836 pp.

1932 *Textbook of Office Management*. New York: McGraw-Hill. 649 pp. Revised in 1943 and 1950 by E. M. Robinson.

Articles:

Beginning in 1916 and continuing to the time of his death, Leffingwell contributed many articles on scientific office management to management periodicals, especially the Taylor Society *Bulletin* as well as *System* and its successor publications. His first published article, entitled "My Plan for Applying 'Scientific Management' in Offices," appeared in *System* in October 1916. Nearly all his addresses to national and international management societies were published, including three to congresses of the International Committee of Scientific Management.

A comprehensive bibliography of Leffingwell's writings appears on pp. 14–15 of *A Bibliography on Office Management*, compiled by Dorothy B. Goldsmith and published by the National Office Management Association in 1931.

Curriculum Vitae

1876	Born on June 14th in Woodstock, Ontario, Canada. His father was a woodworker. The son attended high school in Grand Rapids, Mich.
1893	Started work as a stenographer.
1895	Became a stenographer in an engraving house in Chicago.
c. 1897	Worked as a stenographer in a stockyards commission house.
1900	Was private secretary to a manufacturing superintendent; then worked in the advertising business in Erie, Pa.
1903–1910	Starting as a stenographer in a mail-order publishing house in New York, became successively Circulation Manager, Office Manager, and General Manager.
1910–1914	Visited England, France, Belgium, and Germany, establishing branches for his employer and studying management practices and office methods.
1914	Returning to the United States, joined the management engineering firm of L. V. Estes, Inc.
1916	Became Manager, Office Efficiency Department, L. V. Estes, Inc.
1918–1934	Headed W. H. Leffingwell Co., a professional consulting organization (after 1920 the Leffingwell-Ream Co).
1934	Died on December 19th at age of 58.

Leffingwell was a member of The American Society of Mechanical Engineers, the Taylor Society (President, 1933 and 1934), the American Management Association, and the National Office Management Association (President, 1929–1932). In 1927 he was Chairman of the Society of Industrial Engineers' national committee on the elimination of waste in offices.

Courtesy Nation-Wide News Service.

Leon Pratt Alford
(1877–1942)
United States

L. P. ALFORD was the pioneer of "management handbooks." These manuals, published by Ronald Press and edited by Alford, who was a distinguished engineer, interpreted the work of the earlier management pioneers and did much to disseminate knowledge about management at a time when few textbooks were available for the use of engineers. They aroused interest at all levels of industry and became standard works both in the United States and in Europe.

Alford's second major contribution to management was his work for The American Society of Mechanical Engineers. From 1912 until his death he served continuously on ASME committees. He was the first chairman of the Management Division on its creation in 1920. Two years later he produced the first of the decennial reports by ASME on "Ten Years' Progress in Management." He was the author of the second in 1932, and his preparations for the third were well advanced when he died in 1942. These reports, covering a period of 30 years and prepared under the unifying influence of a mind deeply versed in management literature and practice, form a unique contribution to our knowledge, a brief yet authoritative guide among the many more ponderous volumes which exist.

Alford made several original contributions to the literature of industrial economics, particularly on the collation of quantitative data. He showed in this way how a qualified engineer could bridge the gap between technology and business affairs. Above all, however, his contribution was interpretative. He passed on to later generations, through his handbooks and reports, a better understanding of the work of the early pioneers. His wide influence was due to the singular breadth of view, balance of judgment, and clarity of expression with which he fulfilled this task.

> L. P. Alford possessed the industrious and solid virtues of his New England background. His customary modest manner and softly spoken voice accentuated the sincerity and logic of clear thinking, lucidly expressed. The orderliness of his mind was fertile ground for the principles of management which he unearthed, studied, practiced, formulated, and taught. His fair, benevolent, and bespectacled countenance is best remembered as being lightened with an infectious and disarming smile. . . . He spoke forcefully and lucidly with an economy of words and an abundance of sound sense and wrote in like manner.*

Above all, Leon Pratt Alford knew how to stimulate and direct the best efforts of other people.

SELECTED PUBLICATIONS

Books:

1924 *Management's Handbook.* Editor. New York: Ronald Press Co. 1607 pp.

1928 *The Laws of Management Applied to Manufacturing.* New York: Ronald Press Co. 266 pp.

1934 *Cost and Production Handbook.* Editor. New York: Ronald Press Co. 1544 pp.

—— *Henry Laurence Gantt, Leader in Industry.* New York: The American Society of Mechanical Engineers. 315 pp.

1940 *The Principles of Industrial Management for Engineers.* New York: Ronald Press Co. 531 pp.

1944 *Production Handbook.* Co-editor with J. R. Bangs. New York: Ronald Press Co. 1650 pp.

Papers:

Alford's contributions to the papers and reports of The American Society of Mechanical Engineers are too many to be enumerated. The scope of his papers included high-speed drilling, industrial relations, preferred numbers, factory construction and arrangement, production control, and the evaluation of manufacturing operations. In addition, he wrote papers for the Society for the Promotion of Engineering Education, the American Management Association, and the American Engineering Council, as well as others which were given in England, Japan, and Germany.

* Quoted from obituary in *Mechanical Engineering,* 1942.

Curriculum Vitae

1877	Born on January 3rd at Simsbury, Conn.
1896	Educated at Plainville (Conn.) High School. Received B.S. in Electrical Engineering, Worcester Polytechnic Institute.
1905	Received M.E., also from Worcester.
1896–1907	Entered McKay Metallic Fastening Association, Winchester, Mass., rising from Assistant Machine-Shop Foreman to Chief of Mechanical Engineering Departments for the various McKay companies, which united to form part of the United Shoe Machinery Co.
1902	Was materially responsible for the design and building of the United Shoe Machinery plant at Beverly, Mass., at that time the largest reinforced-concrete machine shop in the world.
1907–1917	Employed as an editor of *The American Machinist.*
1911	Became Editor in Chief of *The American Machinist.*
1917–1921	Continued career as Editor, *Industrial Management.*
1921–1942	With Ronald Press Co. as Editor of its journals in the management field (*Management Engineering, Management and Administration*, etc.).
1922–1934	Held position of Vice-President at Ronald.
1925–1942	Served on Board of Ronald Press Co.
1935–1937	Undertook two management studies for government departments as a consulting engineer.
1937–1942	Active as Professor of Administrative Engineering at New York University and head of the Industrial (later Administrative) Engineering Department.
1942	Died on January 2nd, aged 65, in New York City.

In 1931 Alford was the recipient of the Gantt Gold Medal "for long and distinguished service in the field of industrial engineering," and in 1927 he was awarded the first Melville Prize Medal by The American Society of Mechanical Engineers. He was a member of the Society from 1900 and was elected an honorary member one month before his death. He was made an honorary Doctor of Engineering by Worcester Polytechnic Institute in 1932.

Courtesy R. Greenwood.

Henry Sturgis Dennison
(1877–1952)
United States

HENRY Sturgis Dennison was an industrialist who, between the two world wars, played a creative part in many aspects of the management movement, both in the United States and internationally.

He first became known for making the management of his own medium-size manufacturing company among the most progressive in America. In 1911 he and his uncle put through a profit-sharing and management-sharing plan in the company. Two hundred employees were brought into partnership in management as "voting shareholders" with a share in choosing directors. Since then the destiny of the company has been completely in the hands of the current "industrial partners"; i.e., the principal employees. Also, Dennison pioneered in the 1920s with an unemployment-insurance scheme and an elaborate pattern of executive development. Dennison's aim was to convince American business, through his own example, that it should serve employees and the community at large no less than the shareholders, the traditional beneficiaries of business effort. He sought to establish high employee morale through teamwork, honorable dealing, and the use of the scientific method.

> It is the Company as a Fellowship which alone is really worth dreaming and hoping for. . . . There can't be much fun very long in working for yourself alone; to work with and for others who are working with and for you is what can lift you and swing you along so that the

> Monday morning start of the week is as keen as the Saturday end. . . . The absolute measure of men is the extent to which they have operated to capacity—be that capacity what it may—in the service of their fellows.[1]

In preaching this philosophy, Dennison helped to lead American business to a new conception of its place in society. He could, in this and other respects, be called "the Seebohm Rowntree of America"—the enlightened manager of a private business contributing his experience ever more prodigally to public affairs.

In 1924 Dennison initiated the Manufacturers Research Association with headquarters in Boston. This was a group of noncompeting firms that conjointly established a small research staff as a center on which to base the exchange of detailed information about their respective management methods. The Association represented a new concept of frankness and cooperation between businesses which was of lasting importance. Although it was dissolved in the depression years of 1929–1931, it served as the model for the Management Research Groups in Great Britain, which have there become permanent.

Dennison was active in the organized management movement in America, particularly in the Taylor Society and the American Management Association. In the international sphere he was a prominent supporter of the International Management Institute along with his friend E. A. Filene. He served as its Vice-Chairman throughout its six years' existence.

Dennison wrote, among other works, a short book—*Organization Engineering* (1931)—which has been called "one of the clearest and most fundamental expositions of the subject of which our American literature may boast."[2] His efforts were recognized in 1932 by the award of the Gantt Medal (by The American Society of Mechanical Engineers and the Institute of Management) as "one of the leading contributors to the development of the science and art of management" and, in 1940, by the award of the Taylor Key (by the Society for the Advancement of Management).

> Henry S. Dennison . . . was certainly not a typical businessman. . . . His business acumen built the paper products company . . . into one of the most successful of its kind in the world. Yet he never appeared to be interested in money or even power. It was the "operation" and the "team" behind it that concerned him. Like E. A. Filene who was his good friend, he had a strong bent for the social. . . . He was a "liberal" in the old-fashioned usage of the word.[3]

[1] From the *Memorial Booklet* published by the Dennison Manufacturing Co. in 1952.

[2] By Harry Arthur Hopf in a book review of *The Making of Scientific Management* by L. Urwick and E. F. L. Brech. *Management Review* (American Management Association, N.Y.), January–February 1947.

[3] Editorial in *The Boston Herald,* March 3, 1952.

The many who were privileged to know Dennison remember, not only the kindness and vitality of a broad human character, but also the wisdom of a distinguished mind. Interested in every field of knowledge, whether philosophy, literature, or the arts, he was a man who understood the art and science of management not just in their application to business but, even more, in the living of a constructive and gracious life.

Perhaps the dominant impression that Dennison left in the minds of many of his friends was the inexhaustible sense of fun with which he illuminated alike the most profound argument and the simplest social occasion. It was this which prevented his high seriousness of purpose from ever tempting him to become, even for a moment, pompous. It was fun to work with him and fun to play with him.

Probably it was this ultimate simplicity which left his memory enshrined in the hearts of many much younger people, in no way related to him, as "Pop" Dennison.

SELECTED PUBLICATIONS

Books:

1926 *Profit Sharing and Stock Ownership for Employees.* With others. New York: Harper & Bros.

1931 *Organization Engineering.* New York: McGraw-Hill.

1938 *Modern Competition and Business Policy.* With others. New York: Oxford University Press.

—— *Toward Full Employment.* With others. New York: McGraw-Hill.

The three last-named books were anticipated, in briefer form, in the chapter on "Management" in *Recent Economic Changes,* the report presented to President Hoover's Conference on Unemployment in 1929.

Articles:

The following is only a brief selection from the very large number of papers and lectures delivered over a considerable period:

1922 "Management and the Business Cycle," *Proceedings* of the American Statistical Association.

1924 "Who Can Hire Management?" Taylor Society *Bulletin.*

1925 "Business Management and the Professions," *Proceedings* of the American Academy of Political and Social Science.

1926 "How Manufacturers Can Cooperate with Each Other to Secure Maximum Efficiency in Industry." Papers of the Rowntree Lecture Conference, Oxford, England.

1929 "Probable Effects on Mechanization in Industry," *Proceedings* of the American Economic Association.

1931 Chapter contributed to *Restriction of Output Among Unorganized Workers,* by S. B. Mathewson. New York: The Viking Press.

1932 "Ethics in Modern Business." Weinstock Lectures.

Curriculum Vitae

1877	Born on March 4th at Roxbury, Mass. Educated at Roxbury Latin School and Harvard University (A.B., 1899).
1899	Joined family business, Dennison Manufacturing Company, Framingham, Mass., a medium-size concern producing paper products such as jewelers' boxes, tags, labels, sealing wax, and crepe paper.
1906	Became Manager of Works, Dennison Manufacturing Co.
1917–1952	Held office as President of Dennison Manufacturing Co.
1917–1918	Contributed to war effort as Adviser to the Chairman of the War Industries Board and Assistant Director of the Central Bureau of Planning and Statistics.
1919	Served on President Wilson's Industrial Conference.
1921	Served on President Harding's Unemployment Conference.
1922–1928	Served as Director, Service Relations Division, U.S. Post Office Department.
1926–1952	Served as Trustee of the Twentieth Century Fund.
1934	Appointed Chairman, Industrial Advisory Board, U.S. Department of Commerce.
1935–1943	Active as adviser to National Resources Planning Board.
1935–1939	Became first American employers' representative to International Labor Office, Geneva.
1937–1945	Was a director and Deputy Chairman, Federal Reserve Bank of Boston.
1951–1952	Held membership on National Manpower Council, Columbia University.
1952	Died on February 29th, aged 75, at Framingham, Mass.

Dennison was President of the Taylor Society and a member of the Council of the American Management Association. He was an honorary Sc.D. of the University of Pennsylvania (1927) and an honorary Doctor of Business Administration, University of Michigan (1929).

Courtesy R. Greenwood.

Horace King Hathaway
(1878–1944)
United States

HORACE K. Hathaway was, along with Barth, Gantt, and Cooke, one of the four close associates with whom, over a period of years, F. W. Taylor worked out his system of management. Taylor considered Hathaway to be "the best all-round man in the movement."[1]

Hathaway's personal achievement was the application of scientific management to the Tabor Manufacturing Co. of Philadelphia, manufacturers of molding and other machine-shop products. When he went there in 1904, the company was in bad financial straits. In 1910 the remarkable improvement in its position was used by Brandeis in the "Eastern rates case," dealing with a proposed rise in railway rates, as the strongest argument for the efficiency of scientific management. The material value of the company's output had grown to fully three times that of 1904, while the size of the factory and the amount of capital equipment had remained substantially the same and the labor force had been reduced. The Tabor plant became, with the Link-Belt plant as managed by J. M. Dodge, "the most celebrated demonstration ground and school connected with the scientific management movement."[2]

[1] H. B. Drury, *Scientific Management: A History and Criticism* (New York: Columbia University/Longmans, Green, 1915), p. 249.
[2] *Ibid.*, p. 148.

This was the essence of Hathaway's contribution to management, and it was recognized in 1942 when he received the Taylor Key from the Society for the Advancement of Management. He is also to be remembered, however, for important articles contributed to journals. Those on the planning department and on elementary time study were in particular regarded as classics. Hathaway's 1912 report to the Newton Machine Tool Company, which dealt with flow charts of accounting procedures, made an important contribution to that new field.

In the Taylor group Hathaway was, although the youngest member, perhaps the calmest and most evenly balanced. A tireless and meticulous worker, he was nonetheless gregarious and genial; he was known for a dry vein of humor. Able to gain the complete confidence of his workers, he always seemed to be enthusiastically enjoying whatever he happened to be doing. A comment of Taylor's upon him in the early days was as follows:

> For about three years past I have been very intimately thrown with Mr. Hathaway. Time after time, when the decision rested with him, I have seen him choose the straightforward, honest, and direct way of dealing with men and the square way of treating them. It is needless for me to add that I look upon Mr. Hathaway as one of the most able and brilliant young men that I know of.[3]

SELECTED PUBLICATIONS

Articles:

1906 "Discussion of Mr. Taylor's 'Art of Cutting Metals,'" ASME *Transactions*, Vol. 28, pp. 287–290.

1911 "Prerequisites to the Introduction of Scientific Management," *Engineering Magazine*, Vol. 41. Reprinted in *Scientific Management*, edited by C. B. Thompson and published by Harvard in 1914.

1912 "Elementary Time Study as a Part of the Taylor System of Scientific Management," *Industrial Engineering*, Vol. 11, pp. 85–95.

____ "The Planning Department, Its Organization and Function," *Industrial Engineering*, Vol. 12. Reprinted in *Scientific Management*, edited by C. B. Thompson and published by Harvard in 1914.

1915 "Scientific Management and Its Relations to the Foundry Industry," *Transactions* of the American Foundrymen's Association, Vol. 24, pp. 83–120.

1916 "Proposed Plan for Activities of Machine Shop Sub-Committee of ASME," ASME *Journal*, Vol. 38, p. 972 *et seq*.

In his later years Hathaway was a frequent contributor of articles on applied scientific management to the transactions of various technical societies. Many of them were translated into foreign languages.

[3] Written by Taylor to the President of The American Society of Mechanical Engineers in 1907. See F. B. Copley, *Frederick W. Taylor* (New York: The Taylor Society; London: Harper's), Vol. II, p. 181.

Curriculum Vitae

1878 Born on April 9th in San Francisco. Educated in San Francisco public schools, Williamson Trade School, and Drexel Institute, Philadelphia.

1896–1902 Associated with the Midvale Steel Co. of Philadelphia, starting as apprentice and working up to journeyman machinist, draftsman, inspector, gang boss, and finally tool-room foreman.

1902–1904 Employed as Superintendent of the Payne Engine Co., Elmira, N.Y., manufacturer of boilers, steam engines, and special machinery.

1905 Engaged by James Mapes Dodge to assist in the installation of the Taylor system in the Philadelphia plant of the Link-Belt Co.

1905–1907 At the request of F. W. Taylor, and at first on loan from the Link-Belt Co., installed the Taylor system in the Tabor Manufacturing Co. of Philadelphia. Acted first as Superintendent and later became Works Manager and Vice-President.

1907–1917 While continuing to be Vice-President of the Tabor Manufacturing Co., took up consulting practice in Philadelphia in association with Taylor. During this period, lectured regularly at the Harvard Business School, at the Wharton School of the University of Pennsylvania, and on various occasions at New York University and the Massachusetts Institute of Technology.

1917–1919 Commissioned in the U.S. Army; saw service in Europe.

1919–1923 Resumed consulting practice in Philadelphia.

1923–1926 Active as consulting engineer to Industrial Association of San Francisco.

1927–1928 Held position of General Manager of the Schlage Lock Co., San Francisco.

1929–1941 Retained for a short period by Manning, Maxwell and Moore, New York City (makers of railway and machine tools) and then, for a number of years, by the Mallinckrodt Chemical Works of St. Louis.

1937–1944 Was a consulting professor at the Graduate School of Business, Stanford University.

1941–1944 In private consulting engineering practice in San Francisco.

1944 Died on June 12th, aged 66, in Palo Alto, Calif.

For his services in the First World War Hathaway was made an officer of the Ordre de l'Etoile Noire by the French government. He was a member of The American Society of Mechanical Engineers and of the Society for the Advancement of Management.

Gustave-L. Gérard
(1879–1949)
Belgium

GUSTAVE-L. Gérard was a pioneer of the management movement in Belgium during more than three decades.

In his early career, beginning in 1906, he was one of Europe's first professional management consultants—a specialist in organization and in the encouragement of engineering standardization. This latter work led him to found the Belgian Standards Organization and then win appointment to the Central Industrial Committee, a key policy-forming body in the industrial economy of Belgium. From this position Gérard played for many years an important part in the industrial development of his country.

To this engineer, imbued with a sense of order and logic, the development of better management in industry was a fundamental preoccupation. In 1922, with Edmond Landauer and Robert Caussin, he made the first contacts with a view to creating an organization devoted to management studies. In 1925, the year in which he was a chief organizer of the Second International Management Congress in Brussels, these contacts bore fruit in the creation of the Comité National Belge de l'Organisation Scientifique (CNBOS). This group had his influential support throughout the rest of his life, and from 1940 to 1948 he held its presidency. In addition, he aided its work from outside. He was responsible for the creation of the Science-Industry Fund (1929) for ensuring cooperation between research establishments and the leaders of industry; of the Coordinating Committee for Distribution Studies (1932) under the aegis of the International Chamber of Commerce; and of the Committee for Professional and Technical Education (1926). He was the author of an excellent book containing a collection of recommendations on good management, the writer of regular articles on management for a wide audience over many years in the journal *L'Etoile belge*, and the editor of a series of special publications on management subjects.

Gérard had all the genius required for making an individual and a profound contribution to the principles and practice of management. He deliberately chose, nevertheless, to make a contribution of another kind. He was a born organizer, with the gift of enlisting support for projects of many kinds likely to benefit the Belgian economy on the national industrial level. He concentrated his energies on the constant creation of study groups, committees, research organizations, funds, and so on, staffing them with teams of individuals giving voluntary service and drawn from the same circles likely to benefit from the results of their efforts. In this way, inspiring enthusiasm in others while effacing himself, he set in motion over the years a volume of collective activity exceeding by far the compass of one man's possibilities. Since he was a man of high social purpose, his endeavors did much to bring Belgian industry to a new realization of its social responsibilities. He displayed, in a word, an example of good management as the art of "getting things done through people."

The Belgian management movement recognized Gérard's achievements in 1948 by appointing him to the honorary presidency of CNBOS and by instituting the Gustave-L. Gérard Prize, awarded for a contribution to the advancement of management.

> What one noticed in him at once was his direct way of seeing things, of penetrating to the heart of a problem. This clarity of thought emanated from an upright character, from a complete integrity.
>
> He gave himself inexhaustibly to his work and seemed never to pause for an instant, drawing his associates with him in his tireless drive, demanding much from them but more from himself. He called on industry for effort, effort in the economic sphere, effort in the technical sphere, effort toward science, effort toward progress.
>
> The multiplicity of his interests did not give his work the stamp of careless improvisation. He practiced his own maxim: "Everything worth doing is worth doing well," and this pride in a job well done showed itself in his writing, to the simplicity of which was added the charm of a naturally elegant style. If another trait characterized him it was his gift for synthesis. He would crystallize in a few words, objectively and accurately, the conclusions of a whole meeting's debate. As an employers' representative he was particularly appreciated for his humanity in social problems. And, finally, he expended himself without stint in the moral and social purposes which guided his lifework.*

* Extracts translated from "Gustave-L. Gérard," by R. Caussin, in *Organisation scientifique*, Monthly Bulletin of CNBOS, January 1949.

SELECTED PUBLICATIONS

1929 *L'Art de l'organisation* (The Art of Management). Brussels: La Renaissance du Livre. 90 pp. Second, revised edition (1943), 102 pp.

From 1932 to 1947, with the aid of the Solvay Fund, Gérard edited some 50 publications entitled "Etudes du Comité Central Industriel" (Studies of the Central Industrial Committee). Among these were certain noteworthy contributions to management knowledge in Belgium on the subjects of social security, factory hygiene and health, accident prevention, industrial organization, distribution, purchasing power and salaries, work qualification, budgetary control, technological unemployment, the proportion of labor in different industries, professional organizations, and the activity of industrial federations.

Gérard also published an article each week for 20 years (totaling more than a thousand) in *L'Etoile belge* under the pseudonym "Observer."

Curriculum Vitae

1879	Born on April 24th in Liège.
1902	Received degree of Civil Engineer (Mines) at Liège University.
1902–1906	Employed as engineer in the design department of a large rolling stock and metallic structure manufacturing company, traveling several times to South Africa on the company's behalf.
1906–1914	Worked as a consultant in mechanical engineering factories.
1918	Became a member of the Comité Central Industriel (Central Industrial Committee) of Belgium, which became in 1946 the Federation of Belgian Industries; from 1927 to 1946 he was Managing Director.
1919	Founded the Association Belge de Standardisation (Belgian Standards Organization), after 1946 the Institut Belge de Normalisation. Was successively Secretary-General, Vice-President, and President (1946–1949).
1921–1949	Served as secretary of the Belgian Committee of the International Chamber of Commerce.
1926	Became Technical Counselor of the Bureau International du Travail (International Labor Office).
1928	Joined Board of Bureau International du Travail; subsequently helped to found the Association des Employeurs Industriels (Association of Industrial Employers).
1949	Died on January 11th, aged 70, in Brussels.

Gérard was President of the Association of Engineers of Liège University (1934–1937) and President of the Federation of Belgian Engineers Associations (1934–1935).

Courtesy The National Cyclopaedia of American Biography.

Wallace Clark
(1880–1948)
United States

WALLACE Clark is responsible for one of the greatest single contributions, made by any American, toward popularizing American methods of management and promoting their use outside his own country.

During many years he worked in European countries as a management consultant, advising both private and public concerns. That the older societies of Europe appreciated his exceptional understanding of their problems is shown by the offices and honors which came to him and by the number of languages into which his writings have been translated.

> Wallace Clark possessed many of the natural attributes of leadership: poise, knowledge, simplicity of expression and bearing, helpfulness, objectivity, direct but tactful utterance, discretion, devotion to long-range aims, and carelessness of self. Small wonder, then, that he exercised a strong and lasting influence over thinking and planning in management and related fields.

Thus wrote a leading American engineer and consultant. And an engineer in Europe declared:

> The greatest achievement of Wallace Clark, in my opinion, his greatest contribution, consists in the men he trained . . . the people who came

under his influence in the various countries where he worked and who represent a living tribute to his great work. By his role as a guide and leader of men, Wallace Clark has ensured for himself a permanent place in the history of the scientific management movement.

Americans also recognized his achievements. The Gantt Medal was awarded to him by The American Society of Mechanical Engineers and the Institute of Management in 1934 "in recognition of his distinguished service in the development and promotion of scientific management in the United States and abroad." On his death four leading American management bodies* established the Wallace Clark International Management Award for "a distinguished contribution to scientific management in the international field."

The basis of the management philosophy which Wallace Clark introduced into Europe was the principles and methods of Henry Laurence Gantt, under whom he had begun his career. He developed and adapted the work of Gantt, adding in his maturity contributions of his own. His industrial gospel for Europe was "to remove all obstacles to a free flow of work, starting from the bottom up, considering nothing as static or impossible." This implied, of course, more production and better quality in less time and at lower cost; but, even more, it connoted better working conditions and the philosophy characteristic of Gantt with regard to human beings in their work. It was nothing else than the "mental revolution" postulated by Taylor. In Europe it merged into the productivity drive which has become an integral part of the effort for economic recovery after the Second World War. Wallace Clark, in short, helped to lay the foundations on which the European productivity movement is based.

In 1952 Clark's wife, Pearl, who had long been his business partner, retired to establish at New York University the Wallace Clark Institute of International Management, where the reports and other records incorporating his international experience have been collected for use in research and education in the international management field.

Among many tributes to Wallace Clark is the following:

> He was always the quiet, unassuming colleague and generous friend, never seeking the limelight or the transient glamour of public recognition, but always applying that penetrating intelligence and fine understanding to the consideration of problems presented and striving for solutions which, when attained, owed much to his commonsense approach and marked powers of analysis.

* The American Society of Mechanical Engineers, the American Management Association, the Society for the Advancement of Management, and the Association of Consulting Management Engineers. The award is presented annually through the Council for International Progress in Management (U.S.A.).

SELECTED PUBLICATIONS

Books:

1921 *Foremanship*. Contributing author. New York: The Association Press.

1922 *The Gantt Chart*. New York: Ronald Press. Since its first appearance, this book has been translated and published in numerous countries.

1924 "Plant Layout." With Fred J. Miller. Chapter in *Management's Handbook*. New York: Ronald Press.

1925 *Shop and Office Forms*. New York: McGraw-Hill.

1926 *Report on Polish Monopolies*. Included in report of the Kemmerer Commission to the Republic of Poland.

1944 *Production Handbook*. Contributing editor. New York: Ronald Press.

Articles:

Clark contributed numerous articles to the proceedings of various engineering and management societies and to technical and management journals.

Curriculum Vitae

1880 Born on July 27th in Cincinnati, Ohio.

1902 Graduated from University of Cincinnati; B.A. degree.

1902–1908 Held clerical positions in Cincinnati and the Philippines.

1908–1913 Employed as private secretary to the President of the Remington Typewriter Co., New York City.

1913–1915 In charge of office work at Remington. Attended night classes in industrial management at New York University.

1915–1917 Retained by Remington as a member of Henry L. Gantt's management consulting staff.

1917–1920 Continued with Gantt.

1918–1920 Headed Scheduling Section of U.S. Shipping Board.

1920–1948 Headed his own consulting firm, Wallace Clark & Co.

1926 Went to Poland as industrial member of Kemmerer Finance Mission. Returned the following year at the invitation of the Polish government to organize the modernization of several state industries.

1927–1939 Maintained offices in London and Paris, installing his methods in private and government industries in 12 countries.

1939 Was consultant to the French Purchasing Mission in New York City.

1940–1942 Was consultant to U.S. Signal Corps and several other government agencies in Washington.

1942–1948 Resumed his private consulting practice, chiefly in the United States and Canada.

1946–1948 Served as Chairman of the International Committee of the National Planning Association, which presented his report and recommendations on "The Export of Technology," preceding "Point Four."

1948 Died at age of 68 in New York City.

Wallace Clark was awarded the Order of Polonia Restituta in 1926. He was an honorary Doctor of Engineering of the Stevens Institute of Technology; Fellow of The American Society of Mechanical Engineers; Fellow of the Society for the Advancement of Management; and a member of the Institute of Industrial Administration (Great Britain), the Institution of Civil Engineers (France), and the Masaryk Academy (Czechoslovakia). He served as adviser on scientific management to the International Labor Office and as American representative on the International Committee of Scientific Management.

Raoul Dautry
(1880–1951)
France

THE name of Raoul Dautry is to the French railways what the name of Fayol is to the French mining and metallurgical industries.

The extent of Dautry's great personal achievement with the railways is widely acknowledged in France. An able engineer and a born organizer, he was an early convert to the science of management. His initial career successes included his 1918 completion in record time of a strategic railway line, the reconstruction in 1919–1921 of the Northern Railway network with the use of disabled men, and the rapid building of new homes for 60,000 railway employees and families. In 1928, as Chief Engineer of the Northern Railways, he created "management commissions" instructed to reorganize the technical and administrative services. Appointed Director of the State Railways later in the same year, he there instituted similar commissions. By this and other means, Dautry transformed administrative procedures and reorganized the management of stations, factories, depots, and warehouses. When he retired in 1937, the State Railways, which had been the subject of much popular criticism, were among the most efficient of the different networks. His book *Métier d'homme,* a record of talks given over a long period, has served as a textbook on management to many engineers both in Dautry's own industry and in others.

Dautry participated from the outset in the management movement. In 1926 he was among the first engineers to give support to the newly created Comité National de l'Organisation Française (CNOF). In 1934, when CNOF instituted the School of Scientific Management, Dautry enrolled a number of State Railway men in the opening course and persuaded his colleagues in the private railway companies to do the same thing. Since then railway personnel have regularly attended the School. Also, Dautry was a member of the CNOF Council in 1935–1937, and in 1948 he took a leading part in the CNOF International Management Conference.

Dautry was further distinguished as a social reformer. His campaign for slum clearance, his famous garden cities for railway employees, medical welfare services, children's holiday camps, apprenticeship centers, schools—all these testify, as do many passages in his book, to the importance he attached to human beings in all his managerial work. For he had an intense social consciousness. Sometimes his intimate colleagues would expect to surprise him by proposing some splendid new objective at which to aim. Instead, Dautry would show them that their vision had not been great enough. When he himself had conceived one of his many ideas, nothing would shake his determination to realize it in record time. And although, all his life, he had no interest in wealth for himself, he found the most ingenious means of obtaining financing for the projects he had at heart. His door was open to the humblest visitor, and his somewhat cold and severe manner hid much sensitivity to social misfortune.

Dautry was not an orator, but spoke with clarity. He was a man of wide culture as a result of much reading, especially during hours of insomnia. His capacity for work was great. He was first at his desk each morning when not out on a site, in this respect setting the pace for all fellow workers. At the end of his life, at 71 years of age, he was still the most eager—in any group of his colleagues—to make progress with the projects on hand.

PUBLICATION

1937 *Métier d'homme* (A Man's Profession). Paris: Libraire Plon.

Curriculum Vitae

1903	Graduated from the Ecole Polytechnique and entered the Northern Railway Co.
1928–1937	Was Director of the State Railway Co.
1931	Reorganized the General Transatlantic Co. and the Aeropostal Co.
1934	Served as Chairman of Technical Public Works Commission for dealing with unemployment.
1937	Retired from government service and entered private industry for a short time (in General Electricity Co.).
1939	Named Minister of Armaments.
1940	Retired from public life.
1944	Became President of the French Mutual Aid Movement.
1944–1946	Named Minister of Reconstruction and Town Planning.

1944–1951	Served as Vice-President, International Wagon-Lit Co.
1945–1951	Elected Mayor of Lourmarin (Vaucluse).
1946–1951	Served as French government delegate to the Atomic Energy Commission.
1948–1951	Served as President of the Council, Cité Universitaire de Paris.
1951	Died at the age of 71.

Dautry was named to the Légion d'Honneur in 1918.

Waldemar Hellmich
(1880–1949)
Germany

WALDEMAR Hellmich's name is honored by two great German organizations: the Verein Deutscher Ingenieure (Association of German Engineers, or VDI) and the Organisation der Deutschen Normung (German Standards Association).

Hellmich, as Managing Director of VDI from 1916 to 1933, guided it through the difficult years after the First World War in its work for the German engineering profession. Gifted both as an originator and as a stimulator of effort in others, Hellmich achieved progress for VDI notably by the creation of many study groups and committees, both in engineering and management. Among groups in the latter sphere owing their inception to him were the Arbeitsgemeinschaft Deutscher Betriebsingenieure (Study Group of German Efficiency Engineers), the Reichsausschuss für Arbeitszeitermittlung (German Institute of Work and Time Study, or REFA), and the Ausschuss für Wirtschaftliche Fertigung (Study Group for Productivity). He is perhaps best known for his leadership in establishing the conception of engineering as a profession with moral responsibilities not less than those of the medical profession. His article "The Cultural Mission of the Engineer" (1949) defined an ideal of which German engineers are justly proud.

Hellmich made many contributions to the progress of standardization. A year after he assumed directorship of VDI he became Founder-Director of the German Standards Association, and he set the movement securely on the path of progress by public speaking and writing. His "Ten Years of Standardization in Germany" (1927) and "Twenty-five Years of Standardization in Germany" (1942) were considered landmarks in the movement.

Later in his career, Waldemar Hellmich received many tributes of honor from the two organizations he served, not only for his activity in the material aspects of their work, but also for the spiritual leadership he gave them and the German engineering profession as a whole. Vision, judgment, fertility of mind, ceaseless energy, and a noble spirit were the qualities which animated Hellmich's career and gained him his privileged place in the history of German engineering.

SELECTED PUBLICATIONS

1910 "Pension Schemes for Employees in Private Business," *Technik und Wirtschaft*, Vol. 3, pp. 488–494.

1911 "The Question of the Competition Clause," *Technik und Wirtschaft*, Vol. 4, pp. 39–43.

—— "Law Relating to the Terms of Association of Municipal Bodies," *Technik und Wirtschaft*, Vol. 4, pp. 187–190.

—— "The Law Relating to Compulsory Vocational Training Schools," *Technik und Wirtschaft*, Vol. 4, pp. 269–271.

—— "The Administration of Public Works in Prussia from 1900 to 1910," *Technik und Wirtschaft*, Vol. 4, pp. 544–551.

1913 "State Control and State Intervention in Private Business," *Technik und Wirtschaft*, Vol. 6, pp. 37–45.

1923 "The Concept of Labor Value in the Production of Commodities in Germany," *ZVDI* (Journal of the Society of German Engineers), Vol. 67, pp. 965–969.

1925 "Economic Conveying in Works with Particular Reference to the Use of Trackless Haulage Trucks," *Masch-Bau Betrieb*, Vol. 4, pp. 472–477.

1927 "Ten Years of Standardization in Germany," *ZVDI*, Vol. 71, pp. 1525–1531.

—— "The Nature of German Standardization," *ZVDI*, Vol. 71, No. 44.

1929 "The Professional Consciousness of the Engineer," *ZVDI*, Vol. 73, pp. 1073–1074.

1930 "The Need for Research!" *ZVDI*, Vol. 74, pp. 1525–1526.

—— "Ten Years' Cooperation among German Industrial Engineers," *Masch-Bau Betrieb*, Vol. 9, p. 188.

1931 "The Responsibility of an Engineer," *ZVDI*, Vol. 75, pp. 1–4.

1932 "Pros and Cons of Technology," *Der Betrieb*, Vol. 11, No. 1.

1942 "Twenty-five Years of Standardization in Germany," *Stahl und Eisen*, Vol. 62, No. 45, pp. 937–941.

1943 "The Meaning of Standardization," *ZVDI*, Vol. 80, pp. 2–7.

1948 "The Spiritual Division among German Engineers," *ZVDI*, Vol. 80, pp. 65–67.

1949 "The Cultural Mission of the Engineer," *VDI Nachrichten*, Vol. 3, No. 8, pp. 1–2.

Curriculum Vitae

1880 Born on August 21st in Berlin. Educated at the Humanities Gymnasium, the University of Breslau, and the Polytechnical Academy of Charlottenburg.

1910 Joined staff of the Association of German Engineers (VDI).

1916–1933 Served as Managing Director of the Association of German Engineers.

1917–1933 Helped to found, and was Director of, the German Standards Association, and was Director of the Study Group of German Efficiency Engineers, the Study Group for Engineering in Agriculture, and the German Metallurgical Society.

1924 Awarded the honorary degree of Doctor of Engineering by the Polytechnical Academy of Braunschweig for his work in promoting the progress of industry.

1933 Was Managing Director of the German Hoffmann-La Roche AG, at Grenzach. Also, served as a trustee of the German Standards Association.

1942 Awarded the VDI Medal of Honor for his contribution to engineering and to standardization.

1948 Named honorary member of the Association of German Engineers and honorary President of the German Standards Association.

1949 Died on October 1st, aged 69, at Grenzach.

Courtesy R. Greenwood.

George Elton Mayo
(1880–1949)
Australia/United States

ELTON Mayo's main contributions to management were, first, his revelation of the importance of the human and particularly the social factors in industrial relationships, and, second, his emphasis on the immense difficulty of developing true scientific techniques applicable to the study of social behavior.

Although he was by birth Australian, Mayo did his most significant work in the United States, at the Harvard Department of Industrial Research, between 1927 and 1947. He was invited in 1928 by the Western Electric Co. to examine the material generated from the Hawthorne experiments, by far the most comprehensive study ever attempted of the attitudes and reactions of groups of workers under practical conditions. The resulting data justified Mayo's new concept of the motives which influence industrial relationships.

Mayo believed that logical, economic factors are far less important, even in economic relationships, than emotional and nonlogical attitudes and sentiments. Moreover, of the human factors influencing employees' attitudes and sentiments, the most powerful are those arising from their participation in social groups. Thus, not only must arrangements for work satisfy the objective requirements for realizing the purpose toward which the effort is directed, but the arrangements will be effective only if, simultaneously, they satisfy for the workers concerned this subjective requirement of social satisfaction in the working process. Our society in the past 100 years, however, has changed its nature. Formerly it was an established society in which individuals acquired both technical skill and the capacity for collaboration slowly, by "living into" a prescribed set of traditional routines—in short, through the apprenticeship system. For that society we have substituted "an adaptive society," dedicated to continuous technical change. This technical change disturbs the social routines of the primary working groups and rouses the deepest resentment among the workers. Our capacity to collaborate with each other appears to be diminishing steadily.

The remedy Mayo proposed is that we learn new "social skills." "If our technical skills are to make sudden and radical changes in our methods of working, we must develop social skills that can balance these moves by effecting social changes in methods of living to meet the altered situation. We cannot live and prosper with one foot in the twentieth century and the other in the eighteenth."[1] Mayo pointed out that whereas high administrators have accepted responsibility for training workers in new technical skills, no one has taken responsibility for training them in the new (adaptive) social skills.[2] That involves primarily a new concept of authority as dependent, not on the formal right to require action of others, but on the degree to which individuals assent to orders. And that in its turn depends upon "a cooperative personal attitude of individuals on the one hand and the system of communications in the organization on the other."[3]

Above all, we must learn to study actual social situations, not theoretical formulations. We must practice what Mayo called "the clinical approach." Finally, we must remember that although Mayo's work was based primarily on industrial examples, it applies to any form of human cooperation.

Many people who write of social skill are far from word-perfect; in actual situations they require incessant prompting. Not so Elton Mayo. To watch him handle a strange and sometimes initially suspicious audience was in itself an invaluable lesson in practical psychology. With his slight figure leaning against a table, his fingers busy interminably building up his cigarette holder of many quills and disassembling it again, he just talked; he never made speeches. It is hard to do justice to the quality of those "talks"; their casualness, their clarity, and their humor were the perfect expression of the charm, the persuasiveness, and the humanity of the man himself.

A friend who worked as his assistant over a number of years wrote about him:

> My colleagues will understand me when I say that without Elton Mayo's genius for integrating the activities of a working group, and without his unfailing generosity in putting his ideas and wisdom at the disposal of his followers, some of us, I in particular, would have had no insight by which to approach the critical problem of a civilization committed

[1] *The Human Problems of an Industrial Civilization* (Boston: Division of Research, Harvard Business School, 1933), p. 30.

[2] *Ibid.*, p. 32

[3] *Ibid.*, p. 50.

for the first time to a continuous technological evolution with all that implies in the way of skilled social readjustment.[4]

SELECTED PUBLICATIONS

Books:

1933 *The Human Problems of an Industrial Civilization.* Boston: Division of Research, Harvard Business School. Second edition published by Macmillan in New York, 1946. English edition published by Routledge and Kegan Paul, Ltd., in London, 1952, with an appendix on "The Political Problem," reproducing two lectures delivered at Harvard in 1947.

1948 *Some Notes on the Psychology of Pierre Janet.* Cambridge, Mass.: Harvard University Press.

Articles:

The following are some of the most noteworthy of Mayo's many articles:

1929 "Maladjustment of the Industrial Worker," a chapter in *The Wertheim Lectures on Industrial Relations,* a volume of lectures on various phases of industrial relations published by the Jacob Wertheim Fellowship for the Betterment of Industrial Relations (Cambridge, Mass.: Harvard University Press, 1928).

—— "What Is Monotony?" *The Human Factor* (Boston: Massachusetts Society for Mental Hygiene, January).

1930 "Changing Methods in Industry," *Personnel Journal,* Vol. XX, No. 1.

—— "The Work of Jean Piaget," *Ohio State University Bulletin,* Vol. XXXV, No. 3.

1937 "What Every Village Knows," *Survey Graphic,* Vol. XXVI, No. 12.

1939 "Frightened People," *Harvard Medical Alumni Bulletin,* Vol. XIII, No. 2.

—— "Routine Interaction and the Problem of Collaboration," *American Sociological Review,* Vol. IV.

1941 "The Descent into Chaos." Privately printed by the Harvard Business School.

1945 "Group Tensions in Industry," in *Approach to National Unity,* a paper prepared for the fifth symposium of the Conference on Science, Philosophy, and Religion in Their Relation to the Democratic Way of Life, Inc. Edited by Lyman Bryson, Louis Finkelstein, and Robert M. MacIver. New York and London: Harper.

—— "Supervision and What It Means," *Studies in Supervision,* a lecture given at McGill University, Montreal, on January 30th. Montreal: McGill University.

[4] T. N. Whitehead, *Leadership in a Free Society* (London: University of London Press, 1936).

At least seven books on the Hawthorne investigations by other authors have been published. Among them may be mentioned:

Management and the Worker, by F. J. Roethlisberger and W. J. Dickson. Cambridge, Mass.: Harvard University Press, 1939.

The Industrial Worker, by T. N. Whitehead. London: Oxford University Press, 1938.

Management and Morale, by F. J. Roethlisberger. Cambridge, Mass.: Harvard University Press, 1942.

Leadership in a Free Society, by T. N. Whitehead. London: University of London Press, 1936.

The Making of Scientific Management, Vol. III, The Hawthorne Investigations, by L. Urwick and E. F. L. Brech. London: Pitman, 1948.

Curriculum Vitae

1880	Born on December 26th in Adelaide, Australia. Educated at St. Peter's College, Adelaide, and at Adelaide University, where he took a degree in logic and philosophy. Mayo studied medicine in Edinburgh, Scotland, and was associated with W. H. R. Rivers in his work on psychopathology.
1911–1919	Lectured on logic, ethics, and philosophy at Queensland University. During the First World War he undertook in his spare time the psycho-therapeutic treatment of shell-shocked soldiers, the first person in Australia to use this treatment.
1919	Occupied Chair of Philosophy, Queensland University.
1922	Went to United States.
1923–1926	Undertook industrial research for the Rockefeller Foundation as a Research Associate of the University of Pennsylvania.
1926	Was Associate Professor, Department of Industrial Research, Graduate School of Business Administration, Harvard University.
1929–1947	Awarded Chair of Industrial Research without limitation on tenure.
1949	Died on September 7th, aged 69, in Surrey, England.

George Elton Mayo was a Fellow of the American Academy of Arts and Sciences and held the title "Emeritus" on retiring from Harvard in 1947.

Charles Edward Knoeppel
(1881–1936)
United States

CHARLES Edward Knoeppel was one of the exponents of the Taylor system of scientific management in the years immediately following the most active period of Taylor and Gantt. In his understanding of management he was noticeably ahead of his time. He is to be remembered for adding several original contributions to the principles and methods already established. By 1907 he had done much work in cost accounting, including the development of standard costs, in the foundry industry and elsewhere. By 1908 he had developed methods of factory organization and administration based on the Taylor system. He is credited with probably the earliest application (1908–1909), as part of his original work in the use of graphs for management purposes, of the cross-over "break-even" chart, which is now a standard tool of management. Later in his career he became the original exponent of "profit engineering" and coined the name "profit-graph" as more descriptive of the purpose of the break-even chart.

Knoeppel was an early and prolific writer of books and articles on the science of management. As soon as he had satisfied himself with regard to the practical worth of a development in management, he published a book or an article about it. A glance at the list of his titles is sufficient to show his originality. Since his publications were popular by reason of their lucidity, Knoeppel therefore helped significantly to focus attention on the science of management at a crucial time in its struggle for acceptance by American industry.

As a contribution to public service, Knoeppel played a remarkable part in the work of the Committee on Waste in Industry, organized under Herbert Hoover by the Federated Engineering Societies in 1920–1921. To this committee he furnished, for the use of its engineers in making analyses of industry, a complete and specific questionnaire which he and his staff had evolved through years of study and practice. This was used by the committee as the basis for its method of work. Knoeppel was himself the author of the chapter of the committee's report entitled "Purchasing and Sales Policies."

A man who owed his worldly success to his own efforts from the time he began his working life as a laborer, C. E. Knoeppel deservedly earned the high esteem of his contemporaries. He was a man of charm and candor. Perhaps because his own early difficulties had imbued him with a feeling for the importance of the community, he had an acute sense of public duty and he gave very generously of his time and experience to many causes.

SELECTED PUBLICATIONS

Books:

1911 *Maximum Production in Machine Shop and Foundry.* New York: Engineering Magazine Co. 365 pp.

1915 *Installing Efficiency Methods.* New York: Engineering Magazine Co. 258 pp.

1916 *Industrial Preparedness.* New York: Engineering Magazine Co. 145 pp.

1917 *Organization and Administration.* New York: Factory Management Course, Industrial Extension Institute. 446 pp.

1920 *Graphic Production Control.* New York: Engineering Magazine Co. 477 pp.

1921 *What Industrial Engineering Includes—for Industrial Executives: 101 Things to Do; 1001 Results Others Secured.* New York: C. E. Knoeppel & Co. 154 pp.

1933 *Profit Engineering—Applied Economics in Making Business Profitable.* New York and London: McGraw-Hill. 326 pp.

1937 *Managing for Profit—Working Methods for Profit Planning and Control.* With the collaboration of E. G. Seybold. New York and London: McGraw-Hill. 343 pp.

Papers (selected from a very much longer list):

1907 "Cost Reduction Through Cost Comparison." Series of three articles in *The Engineering Magazine*, March, April, and May.

1908 "Maximum Production Through Organization and Administration." Series of four articles in *The Engineering Magazine*, April–June.

1918 "Industrial Organization as it Affects Executives and Workers," ASME, *Transactions.*

____ "Women in Industry," *Miscellaneous Publications* of the Society of Industrial Engineers, Vol. 1, February.

1920 "The Future of Industrial Engineering," *Publications* of the Society of Industrial Engineers, Vol. 3, No. 5, February.

1928 "Human Development as Industry's Real Task," *Proceedings*, 9th Annual Southern Conference on Human Relations in Industry, August.

1929 "Dividend Requirements from Waste Elimination," *Bulletin* of the Society of Industrial Engineers, January. An address delivered at the 15th National Convention of the Society, Rochester, N.Y., October 1928.

1930 The following series of seven articles appeared in *Factory Management and Maintenance*, during the months January through July, in the order stated:
"Wanted—the Profit Engineer"
"Profit Planning and Control"
"Profit-making Policies"
"Plotting the Profit Course"
"Isolating Industrial Loss Germs"
"Industrial Pilot House"
"Profit Engineering: The Cure for Marginitis"

Curriculum Vitae

1881 Born on April 15th in Milwaukee, Wis. Educated in the public schools of Buffalo, N.Y. Prevented by economic difficulties from going to college, although he had prepared to do so.

1899–1904 Employed as a newspaper reporter, then successively as a laborer and molder at the Ames Iron Works, Oswego, N.Y. Progressed to become draftsman and then designer at the Buffalo Forge Co. Later was Office Manager, then Systematizer, at the Parkhurst Boiler Works, Oswego.

1905 Was a member of the expert systematizing staff of the Library Bureau, Boston, Mass. Also did personal consulting work in cost accounting and industrial engineering.

1908 With his father, organized Knoeppel & Knoeppel, foundry specialists.

1909 Joined staff of Emerson Engineers, New York City.

1911 Joined staff of Suffern and Son, New York.

1912 Organized Van Gelder, Knoeppel & Young, cost accountants and industrial engineers, New York.

1914 Organized C. E. Knoeppel & Co., industrial engineers, New York.

1917–1918 Made an eight-month study of shipyard conditions for the Emergency Fleet Corp. and investigated the employment of women in war work.

1925–1929 Associated with Bigelow, Kent, Willard and Co., management

	engineers in Boston, as Managing Director of a division called Waste Eliminators, Inc.
1929–1932	Organized Knoeppel Industrial Counsel, Cleveland, Ohio.
1933–1936	Engaged in individual consulting practice in Philadelphia, advising on profit planning, economic pricing, and variable budgeting.
1936	Died November 29th, aged 55, in Philadelphia.

Knoeppel was an active member of several management societies and one of the organizers of the Society of Industrial Engineers (1917). He lectured on organization and management for two years at New York University.

Kurt Hegner
(1882–1949)
Germany

KURT Hegner served the German management movement by his lifelong support of many management associations and by his original contributions to the development of work study and standardization.

The introduction of time study and method study into Germany, using the principles of Taylor and Gilbreth, was not easy and required years of teamwork by those who understood the potentialities of the new science. Hegner was a leader among them. He was from 1928 to 1945 chairman of the first work-study organization to be created in Germany—the Reichsausschuss für Arbeitszeitermittlung (German Institute of Work and Time Study, or REFA).

In 1923, before the founding of REFA, Hegner had already adapted case-study material on elementary management accounting, from his own machine-tool factory, to serve as the basis of short courses which he organized. In 1924, he published the book, *Manual of Standard Processing Times,* which became the leading text on the principles and practice of time study. It served as material for the extended teaching which Hegner now undertook and in which he was the pioneer of the well-known REFA teachers. He directly inspired the successful "first" and "second" REFA books (1928 and 1933, respectively), manuals dealing with the principles and practice of work study.

From the start, Hegner took an active interest in the German standardization movement. Himself Chairman of the Machine Tool Committee of the German Standards Association, he did much to further the general progress of the movement, helping to overcome the considerable resistance with which it had to contend.

In addition to all these activities, Hegner devoted time and energy to the Reichskuratorium für Wirtschaftlichkeit (German Institute of Management, or RKW), the Ausschuss für Wirtschaftliche Fertigung (Study Group for Productivity), and the Arbeitsgemeinschaft Deutscher Betriebsingenieure (Study Group of German Efficiency Engineers).

Hegner was a gifted speaker, yet he had the modesty needed by a good teamworker. Though he was a busy executive in a great machine-tool concern, his work for REFA was always something of a crusade to him. He considered the great events in REFA's progress to be the highlights of his life. He died at his desk while working on a speech for a REFA function. In it he demanded systematic principles for the conduct of REFA courses and termed the talk itself a "sort of confession."

SELECTED PUBLICATIONS

Books:

1924 *Lehrbuch der Vorkalkulation von Bearbeitungszeiten* (Manual of Standard Processing Times). Berlin: Springer.

1939 *Die Werkzeugmaschine* (The Machine Tool). Report to the 77th General Meeting of the Association of German Engineers at Dresden. Berlin: Publishing House of VDI (Association of German Engineers).

Articles:

1922 "Basic Time Units for the Calculation of Operating Time," *Der Betrieb,* Vol. 4, pp. 323–329.

—— "Means of Reducing the Cost of Assembly Work," *Der Betrieb,* Vol. 4, pp. 244–249.

1923–1924 "Costing Problems," *Masch-Bau Betrieb,* Vol. 3, p. 701.

—— "The Costing Problem and Its Solution," *ZVDI,* Vol. 68, pp. 821–824.

1926 "Manual on the Evaluation of Operating Times," *Masch-Bau Betrieb,* Vol. 5, p. 176.

1928 "Piecework and Rate Fixing," *Masch-Bau Betrieb,* Vol. 7, pp. 97–103.

1933 "A more Detailed Study on the Evaluation of the Operating Time," *Second REFA Book.* Berlin: Beuth-Vertrieb.

1937 "Appraisal of Standard Values for Milling on the Basis of Practical Examples from Milling." Report of the Milling Committee of the Corporation of German Industrial Engineers (ADB), pp. 387–388, 437–438.

—— "Standardization in Machine Tool Making," *Der Betrieb,* Vol. 19, pp. 169–172.

——	"Standard Values for Milling" and "Assessment of Milling Examples." Reports of the Mills Committee of the Corporation of German Industrial Engineers (ADB), pp. 287–288.
——	"The Working Committees of the Corporation of German Industrial Engineers (ADB)," *Der Betrieb,* Vol. 21, p. 64.
1944	"New Operating Units in German Machine Tool Making," *ZVDI,* Vol. 88, pp. 633–637.
——	"Future Tasks for German Machine Tool Making," in *Werkstattstechnik und Maschinenbau.* Berlin: Springer.

Curriculum Vitae

1882	Born on December 9th at Zeitz.
1899	Apprenticed to Ludwig Loewe & Co., Berlin (machine-tool manufacturers).
1908	Became Works Manager of Loewe's standard-products plant.
1919	Became Works Manager of the milling-machine-manufacturing plant.
1926–1949	Rose to be Loewe's Technical Director and a member of the Board.
1949	Died on September 17th, aged 67, in Berlin.

Hegner was awarded VDI's Gold Medal of Honor in 1941, particularly for his services as Chairman of the Arbeitsgemeinschaft Deutscher Betriebsingenieure (Study Group of German Engineers).

Courtesy R. Greenwood.

Harry Arthur Hopf
(1882–1949)
United States

HARRY Arthur Hopf was an outstanding figure in the history of the management movement. His lifework was recognized in 1938 when CIOS awarded him its Gold Medal.

His was the contribution of both a doer and a thinker. In his chosen career as a management consultant, he was in his early days the pioneer, along with W. H. Leffingwell, in applying the methods of scientific management, hitherto confined to the factory, to the domain of the office. In life insurance companies between 1908 and 1917 he made some of the earliest studies and applications of techniques now universally adopted in scientific office management. Among them were procedure analysis, standardization of clerical operations and output, production control, and job analysis. Somewhat later, Hopf did much original work on executive compensation. The advances made in many aspects of office organization and management during the three decades from 1918 through 1948 were largely of his inspiration. In the final phase of his career he became a consultant of national and international repute in the broader field of business administration and organization.

As a teacher, Harry Arthur Hopf influenced many of those who went on to be leaders in the world of management. As a worker for the management movement, he helped to create many management societies now prominent in the United States. When these societies ultimately came together, largely through his influence, to found the National Management

Council and so unify the American management movement, he served as its first chairman (1933–1936). He was one of the founders of CIOS and contributed to its expansion, serving as Deputy President from 1935 to 1938.

It was, however, as a scholar and philosopher of the science of management that Harry Arthur Hopf accomplished his most outstanding work. The booklets which he published between 1915 and 1947 surveyed the whole field of management thought and may be classified by subject as follows: office management, compensation, and incentives; the human factor in management; the evolution of management thought and future education for management; management engineering and means of measuring managerial accomplishment; the nature of management and of organization.

The last-named category entitled Harry Arthur Hopf to a place with Fayol and Mary Parker Follett among writers of classics on the philosophy of management. His papers "Adapting the Industrial Organization to Changing Conditions" and "Evolution in Organization During the Past Decade" must, in particular, be read by all serious students of organization. Perhaps the best summary of his philosophy of management as a whole is contained in "New Perspectives in Management." His general approach was essentially simple:

> It is because of a profound conviction that, for an indefinite period to come, the solution of the economic problems of this country will have to be sought through reconstitution of all types of organized human enterprise on levels of simplicity and scope low enough to permit readily of coordination and control, that consideration of the role of management and what it can and should do to create and preserve optimal conditions in the individual business enterprise appears to be a timely and worthwhile undertaking.

Hopf emphasized the dynamic aspects of management and contributed to the analysis of leadership. Lastly, he put forward the all-inclusive concept of "optimology, or the science of the optimum."[1]

It was his thesis that management, whether of individual enterprises or of social and political entities, should strive always for attainment of the optimum, or "that state of development which, when reached and maintained, tends to perpetuate an equilibrium among the factors of cost, size and human capacity, and thus to promote, in the highest degree, regular realization of its objectives."

In 1938, he founded the Hopf Institute of Management. As he put it:

> The stimuli derived from the many activities to which I was devoting myself crystallized in a project that had long been germinating in my mind. It involved the creation of an institute that would devote itself to exploration of the scientific foundations of management, would contribute to the educational development of business executives, and

[1] "New Perspectives in Management," a series of 15 articles in *The Spectator,* 1943–1945.

> would serve as a world center and clearing house for scholars in the field. These and certain collateral objectives appealed to me as goals of indispensable character in the advancement of the function of management.

The published works of Harry Arthur Hopf are classics of management literature. It is a matter for regret, however, that his practical success and the responsibilities that came with it stood between him and that comprehensive book on management which should have collated his writings for easy access by future students.

A man of exceptional gifts of mind and character, Hopf brought to all his professional work the wisdom and humanity of the truly cultured man. The life he built for himself from the most humble beginnings, and the friends he made, may be judged from the memorial issue of *Net Results,* which contains tributes from the first names in management in half a dozen countries. One of these calls him

> . . . a battler against mediocrity. . . . He demanded high standards of accomplishment of his associates and held himself to even stricter self-disciplines. Difficulty always challenged him; . . . few men found so much stimulation and incentive in day-to-day living as he. . . .
>
> His great contribution to the world in which he lived has been the heightened dignity and prestige which his accomplishments have earned for the profession which he graced. The art and science of management in the United States and in the world are permanently the better because of him.[2]

SELECTED PUBLICATIONS

Books:

1940 — Chapter VII, "Administrative Coordination," in *Public Management in the New Democracy.* Edited by Fritz Morstein Marx. New York: Harper & Bros.

1946 — *People and Books.* With Henry C. Link. New York: Book Industry Committee of the Book Manufacturers Institute.

Papers and Booklets:

1915 — "The Planning Department as a Factor in the Modern Office Organization," Efficiency Society *Journal,* Vol. 4, No. 8, November.

1917 — "Home Office Organization," *Proceedings,* 12th Annual Meeting, American Life Convention, Grand Rapids, Mich.

1921 — "Salary Standardization as an Aid to Industrial Stability," *Proceedings,* Society of Industrial Engineers, Fall Convention, Springfield, Mass.

[2] Erwin H. Schell, in *Net Results* (periodical published by Hopf Institute of Management), October 1949, p. 49.

1923	"Physical Factors in Office Planning." Series of eight articles in the *Office Economist,* published by Art Metal Company, Jamestown, N.Y.
1927	"Problems of Bank Organization." Presented at joint meeting of the Taylor Society and American Society of Mechanical Engineers. In *Bulletin* of the Taylor Society, Vol. XII, No. 2, April.
1930	"Housing Business Organizations for Efficient Operation," *Architectural Forum,* April and May. Also in *Proceedings,* Chicago Chapter, American Institute of Architects, February.
1931	"Whither Management?" *Proceedings,* American Life Convention, Pittsburgh, Pa., 26th Annual Meeting.
1932	"The Evolution of Organization," *Proceedings,* Annual Convention, National Association of Cost Accountants, Detroit, Mich.
1933	"The Present Status, Responsibilities, and Future of the Management Engineer," *Proceedings,* Society of Industrial Engineers, 19th National Convention, Chicago, Ill.
1935	"Management and the Optimum," *Proceedings,* VI International Congress, Comité International de l'Organisation Scientifique, London.
1937	"Business Management and the Scientific Point of View," presented to joint meeting of Montreal Branch of Engineering Institute of Canada and four other societies. In *Engineering Journal* (Canada), Vol. XX, No. 12, December.
1943, 1944, 1945	"New Perspectives in Management." Series of 15 articles in *The Spectator* (published by the Chilton Co., Philadelphia).
1944	"Organization, Executive Capacity and Progress," *Proceedings,* Annual Conference, Life Office Management Association, Boston, Mass.
1945	"Executive Compensation and Accomplishment," American Management Association Financial Management Series No. 78.
——	"Soundings in the Literature of Management: Fifty Books the Educated Practitioner Should Know," Hopf Institute of Management Publication No. 6. Also in *Advanced Management,* Vol. X, No. 3, September 1945, and incorporated in G. T. Coman, *Sources of Business Information,* Ch. 9, "Management," published by Prentice-Hall, New York, in 1949.
1946	"Adapting the Industrial Organization to Changing Conditions." New Brunswick, N.J.: Rutgers University.
1947	"Evolution in Organization During the Past Decade," *Proceedings,* VIII International Congress, Comité International de l'Organisation Scientifique, Stockholm. Also published as Hopf Institute of Management Publication No. 10.
——	"Historical Perspectives in Management," *Management Review,* January, February, and March. Also published as Hopf Institute of Management Publication No. 7.
——	"Incentives for Executives," *Proceedings,* 40th Annual Meeting,

American Pharmaceutical Manufacturers Association, Boca Raton, Fla. Also published as Hopf Institute of Management Publication No. 9.

Curriculum Vitae

1882	Born on April 3rd, in London, England. Hopf's parents were naturalized British citizens, his father being of German and his mother of French-German parentage. He attended school in London and subsequently in Kassel, Germany.
1898	Emigrated to the United States as a penniless youth. During the next few years, while earning his living, he managed to complete his education at evening classes, attending the following schools: New York University School of Commerce, School of Law, and Graduate School of Business Administration; Columbia University School of Business. He obtained the degrees of Bachelor of Commercial Science (1906) (Master 1916) and Master of Business Administration (1922).
1898–1902	Held minor clerical positions, including three years as a junior clerk with the American Sugar Refining Co.
1902–1914	At Germania (now Guardian) Life Insurance Co., New York City, rose from foreign-language stenographer to Assistant to Vice-President and head of underwriting and planning activities.
1914–1917	Employed as Manager, Planning Department, Phoenix Mutual Life Insurance Co., Hartford, Conn.
1917–1918	Employed as Manager, Planning Department, Smokeless Powder Operating Department, E. I. du Pont de Nemours & Co., Wilmington, Del.
1919–1922	Employed as Organization Counsel and Chairman, New Building Planning Committee, Federal Reserve Bank of New York. Also, Adviser, Personnel Committee, and Secretary, Pension Committee, Federal Reserve System.
1922–1949	Headed H. A. Hopf & Co., consulting management engineers, New York City and Ossining, N.Y. In his consulting work Hopf advised on problems of organization, management, compensation, special building, planning, and clerical procedures. He numbered many government agencies among his clients.
1938–1949	Became Founder and President, Hopf Institute of Management, Ossining.
1949	Died on June 3rd, aged 67, at Ossining.

Hopf was elected a Fellow of the National Office Management Association in 1936 and was awarded the Taylor Key of the Society for the Advancement of Management in 1947. He was a knight of the Royal Order of the North Star, Sweden, and an honorary member of the Masaryk Academy, Czechoslovakia. He was a corresponding member of the management societies of Great Britain, France, Germany, and Switzerland. In addition, he held the honorary degrees of M.Sc. (Bryant College) and D.Eng. (Rensselaer Polytechnic Institute).

Alvin Earl Dodd
(1883–1951)
United States

ALVIN Dodd was one of those most responsible for the development of the American Management Association from small beginnings into the front-rank management organization it is today.

The American Management Association was founded in 1923. Its early growth was much set back by the Great Depression, and when Dodd became Executive Vice-President in 1933 it was no more than an obscure institution with some 1,600 members. Dodd was a man of organizing and publicizing genius. He set out to establish high quality in AMA's output and then to bring its activities prominently before the attention of the business community. His success during 14 years was triumphant. He considered that the services AMA offered met a direct need on the part of practical managers, no less urgent than the need of their businesses for an essential product or service. And so he used the same direct-selling methods in promoting AMA as those of the merchandising industry in which he had previously worked. Through this approach, and through his systematic organization of activities, including a method for conference planning unrivaled among its kind, the American Management Association grew steadily. Under Dodd's successors as President—Lawrence A. Appley, James L. Hayes, and Thomas R. Horton—it has come to attract enormous attendances of executives, managers, and specialists annually and to achieve the largest publication circulation of any management body in the world.

Dodd's written work was not extensive, but as a "public relations" man he was outstanding. Recognition of this contribution by his colleagues in the

American management movement brought him the Gantt Medal in 1947 "for his leadership in stimulating greater recognition and acceptance of the social responsibilities of management; and for his success in building the American Management Association* into an authoritative forum for collecting, analyzing, and disseminating management knowledge."

Alvin Dodd had a special talent for knowing and liking people, and his sensitive and intuitive nature caused people to like him in return. To a marked degree, the success of his many undertakings was due to his ability to put himself in the place of others. His friend Harry Arthur Hopf called him a catalyst. John M. Hancock spoke of him as "a man gifted in the ability to integrate into meaningful pattern the random concepts and accomplishments of many specialists in diverse tasks and industries. . . ." He was always interested in the human side of business, and he did a great deal to make management more aware of its social responsibilities.

SELECTED PUBLICATIONS

Books:

1940 *Planning the Package.* With others. New York: American Management Association.

1942 *How to Train Workers for War Industries.* With J. O. Rice. New York: Harper & Bros.

Articles (selected from a much longer list):

1940 "The Ideal Boss in 1940," *Supervision,* February.

1940 "What Management Faces," *Forbes,* August 15th.

1941 "Changing the Course of the Stream," *Dun's Review,* August.

1942 "What to Do About Salesmen with Little or Nothing to Sell," *Printers' Ink,* January 16th.

1945 "Negro Employment Opportunities—During and After the War," *Opportunity,* April–June.

1947 "Nine Critical Problems Facing Management," *Dun's Review,* July.

1948 "Management's Role in Shaping the Future," *Dun's Review,* July.

—— "Productivity—Prices and Markets," *Mechanical Engineering,* February.

Curriculum Vitae

1883 Born on March 11th at Hudson, N.Y.

1905 Graduated from Armour Institute of Technology (now Illinois Institute of Technology), with a B.Sc. degree in engineering.

* The American Management Association, which has continued to grow and expand its operations both nationally and internationally, became the American Management Associations in 1972. It awards the Gantt Medal annually in cooperation with The American Society of Mechanical Engineers.

1905–1906 Began work as Assistant Principal, Fifth Ward Manual Training School, Allegheny, Pa.
1906–1907 Head Manual Arts Department, Massachusetts Normal School, North Adams, Mass.
1907–1908 Served as President, Eastern Arts Association.
1908–1912 Served as Principal, North Bennett Industrial School, Boston, Mass.
1912–1916 Was Director, National Society for Promotion of Industrial Education. Largely through his efforts in this position, the Act was passed which began federally sponsored and financed public vocational education in the United States.
1917 Named to Committee on Classification of Personnel, General Staff, U.S. Army. Here he helped to establish the Army's first program of personnel management, testing, classification, and placement.
1917–1921 Served as Director, Retail Research Association and Associated Merchandising Corp.
1921–1927 Served as Manager of Distribution Department, U.S. Chamber of Commerce.
1927–1929 Lectured on trade and industrial problems at Northwestern University, University of Chicago, University of Washington, and Stanford University. Also was Director General, Wholesale Dry Goods Institute.
1929–1930 Employed as Assistant to President, Sears, Roebuck & Co.
1930–1933 Employed as Vice-President, Kroger Grocery and Baking Co. In charge of merchandising and sales.
1933–1936 With the American Management Association as Executive Vice-President.
1936–1948 Continued with AMA as President.
1949–1951 Managing Director, U.S. International Chamber of Commerce.
1951 Died on June 2nd, aged 68, in New York City.

Dodd was made honorary President of the American Management Association in 1948. In that year, also, he was given an honorary Doctor of Laws degree by Temple University.

Edmond Landauer
(1883–1934)
Belgium

EDMOND Landauer's name is closely linked with the history of CIOS and the international management movement. He was one of the chief founders of CIOS, and later he became its first secretary-general and its vice-chairman. He was also a founder of the International Management Institute and the Belgian Committee of Scientific Management. His work was recognized by CIOS in 1935 by the posthumous award of its Gold Medal.

Landauer was a businessman of conspicuous personal success. For many years director of a Rumanian textile manufacturing firm, he brought about in his own managerial performance an admirable realization of management principles. He wrote several articles on his methods, revealing clearly his understanding of the ideals and methods of F. W. Taylor and the right way to apply them, in practice, to a European concern. Since Landauer was himself wholly European in character and outlook, his assimilation and active dissemination of the best American management thought and practice constituted a valuable contribution to international understanding of the subject.

That Landauer was a sound theorist is evidenced by his concept of rational purchasing policy in the textile industry and his several studies of the science of management in general. As a thinker, as an enthusiastic coordinator of national efforts toward the growth of the international movement, and as an architect of CIOS, he has a permanent place in management history.

Although Landauer could on occasion deliver a brilliant speech and captivate an audience, he usually preferred to remain in the background and even seemed unduly reserved in attitude toward the people with whom he was in frequent contact. Yet he was endowed with much human sympathy. "The well-being of his workers was a constant preoccupation. With what feeling did he speak to me on occasion of the day nurseries of one of his favorite factories. Himself a man without family, he was the protector of children and of the humblest of his employees.*

SELECTED PUBLICATIONS

1935 *L'Organisation scientifique.* Posthumous edition of Landauer's writings in various technical journals in Belgium and elsewhere. Published privately by the Comité National Belge de l'Organisation Scientifique (CNBOS), Brussels. The following are the articles reproduced in this book:

1923	"L'Organisation industrielle et commerciale dans l'industrie textile belge."
1925	"Les Prix de revient industriels."
1926	L'Organisation des économies dans l'administration de l'état."
1927	"L'Avenir de l'organisation scientifique."
——	"Le Contrôle du facteur 'temps' dans la fabrication."
1928	"Formules d'achat et de vente dans l'industrie textile."
——	"L'Organisation scientifique dans l'industrie textile."
——	"Un Exemple vécu de rationalisation industrielle: l'oeuvre de Thomas Bata."
——	"Une loi générale de la production industrielle."
1929	"La Direction à distance."
1931	"La Crise economique et la rationalisation."
1931–1933	"Les Crédits de banque et le contrôle budgétaire."
1932	"Comment j'embauche mon personnel d'après ses aptitudes."
——	"Entre l'anarchie et la dictature économique: l'issue; questionnaire pour servir à l'examen systématique de la valeur économique d'une entreprise industrielle."
——	"Les Principes de la méthode Bedaux."
1933	"Le Problème de la distribution."
——	"Le Tissage à métiers multiples."

Curriculum Vitae

1883 Born on November 19th in Brussels. Took a doctorate of science in Brussels and then spent several years traveling in different countries,

* Francesco Mauro, in *L'Organisation scientifique,* the posthumously published collection of Landauer's writings.

including the United States and Canada. Reorganized a Canadian firm with Belgian connections. Afterward took over management of a textile mill in Rumania, the Tessatoria Romana. Connected with this firm for 20 years, drawing from it most of the material for his writings. Lived for several years in Rumania. In later years acted as textile consultant to firms in Belgium, France, England, and Denmark. Led an energetic life of travel throughout Europe, continuing to manage the Rumanian mill from a distance.

1925 Was principal organizer of the Second International Management Congress, Brussels.

1927 Became Secretary-General of CIOS.

1932 Became Vice-Chairman of CIOS.

1934 Died in July at age of 51.

Landauer was a chevalier of the Order of Leopold and a commander of the Order of the Crown of Rumania.

Sam A. Lewisohn
(1884–1951)
United States

SAM A. Lewisohn was a leader in enlightened human relations in industry in the early 1920s and one of the founders of the American Management Association.

His book *The New Leadership in Industry* (1926) gave a new viewpoint to American business. It was a corrective to the previous burst of enthusiasm among managers for appointing specialized personnel officers whose responsibility it was to maintain good human relations within their organizations. Lewisohn said: "The manager cannot delegate this responsibility, even to a personnel officer; it remains his alone." The book gathered together many of the different views on this, the most controversial industrial subject of the day, and exposed their fallacies. He asked: "What does the worker want?" and answered: "Justice, status, and opportunity." Above all, Lewisohn stressed the need of the worker for the feeling of participation on a team and the need for managers to develop the intangible qualities of leadership capable of bringing this about. His outline of the basis, structure, and functions of a personnel department was 20 years ahead of its time.

Sam A. Lewisohn's philosophy of management found perhaps its most enduring outlet in the part he played in founding the American Management Association. The change of name from "National Personnel Association" which brought AMA into existence in 1923 symbolized the new attitude toward human relations in industry which he was himself advocating at the time. Twenty-five years later AMA acknowledged its special debt to Lewisohn for his role in its foundation and development. He was the first elected president, and he gave AMA considerable material help at a time when its existence was financially threatened. His was one of the earliest visions of AMA's potentialities as an educative body or, as he termed it, "an extension university for management groups." To him, therefore, belongs part of the credit for the contributions to management made by this prominent American organization.

The name of Lewisohn in New York, moreover, is indissolubly associated with the arts, for Sam A. Lewisohn followed in the tradition of his father as a renowned connoisseur and patron of music and painting. It was his conviction that life in this century was overcompartmentalized, and he sought in his own way of living what he believed to be a better ideal—the balance of interests among business activity, public work (he was a pioneer of prison reform), and enjoyment of the arts. The many friends who remember him attest to the fact that he achieved this ideal with integrity and generosity.

SELECTED PUBLICATIONS

Books:

1925 *Can Business Prevent Unemployment?* Co-author. New York: Alfred A. Knopf.

1926 *The New Leadership in Industry.* New York: E. P. Dutton & Co. 234 pp.

1945 *Human Leadership in Industry: The Challenge of Tomorrow.* New York: Harper & Bros. 112 pp.

Curriculum Vitae

1884 Born on March 21st in New York City. Educated at Columbia Grammar School, Princeton University, and Columbia Law School.

1907–1910 With law firm of Simpson, Thacher and Bartlett.

1910 Joined his father's business, Adolph Lewisohn & Sons, a Stock Exchange firm.

1921 Served on Economic Advisory Commission, President's Conference on Unemployment.

1923 Elected first president of the American Management Association, having been one of its founders.

1926–1936 Served as Chairman of the Board, American Management Association.

1938 Held office as President, Miami Copper Co.; Chairman of the Board, Tennessee Corp.; President, South American Gold & Platinum Co.; President, General Development Co.; President, Kerr Lake Mines and Kerr Lake Mining Co.; and President, Adolph Lewisohn & Sons, Inc.

1941 Became President, Castle Dome Copper Co.

1942 Served as Consultant, Division of Industry Operations, U.S. War Production Board.
1949 President, Copper Cities Mining Co.
1951 Died on March 13th, at age of 67, in Santa Barbara, Calif.

Lewisohn represented the American Management Association on the Council of the International Management Institute and the Employers of the United States at the International Labor Conference, Geneva (1935).

Francesco Mauro
(1887–1952)
Italy

FRANCESCO Mauro was the pioneer of modern management in Italy and one of the founders of the international management movement. Like many of the other pioneers, he was a man of diverse activities: a distinguished engineer and refrigeration expert, a company director, a management consultant, a deputy of the Italian National Assembly, and an international negotiator for his country.

Mauro emerged as a personality in Italian industry soon after the First World War. He early became known for his advocacy of the new principles and techniques of management and, in particular, of the value of international exchange of information and experience as a means to progress. Through his work as a technician, executive, and consultant, he was able significantly to influence the modernization of many Italian industrial concerns. In 1923 he founded the Italian Institute of Scientific Management (ENIOS), one of the earliest to be created, and served as its first president (1923–1927). In 1927 his international standing brought him the honor of being Founder-President (1927–1929) of the International Committee of Scientific Management (CIOS) and, from 1929 to 1938, Vice-President. Meanwhile, from 1927 to 1933, he served as Vice-President of the International Management Institute. Thus he associated Italy with him in the front ranks of the international management movement.

The Second World War brought a setback to the Italian management movement, but after its close Mauro reconstituted the Institute as ENIOL and worked hard to restore its former international recognition. His labors were rewarded in 1951 when he became President of the Italian Representative Committee for the Organization of Work (CIRIOL) and when, in the same year, he was named an honorary president of CIOS. He also was a pioneer of management education: The business management course which he founded and directed at Milan Polytechnic was the first of its kind in Italy.

Finally, Mauro was a significant contributor to the literature of management. Among his many publications from 1910 on, some described applications of management techniques which he originated in organizations within his own control. Others stressed the advantages of plentiful exchange of information between firms, between industries, and between countries for the progress of management knowledge. Most important of all were his contributions to the philosophy of management. Mauro constantly stressed the fact that the science and techniques of management must be used as a tool for achieving its social objectives and its ultimate goal, the satisfaction of the individual human being within the working group. His last book, published in 1952 and entitled *Organizzazione come civiltà* (Management as Civilization), was devoted to expounding this conviction.

In addition to his innumerable offices, presidencies, platform speaking, and other business and public activities, in addition to the many hours consecrated to the publications of which he was the author, Mauro still found time for fruitful leisure pursuits. He was a keen mountaineer, president of several clubs and author of a book on the subject; President of the Italian Football Club of Milan; and President of the Italian Olympic Committee. He also took a keen interest in cinematography. It has been said that his outstanding personal quality, perhaps grounded in his firm religious faith, was a capacity for synthesis. He could be at the same time a technician, an executive, a teacher, an organizer, and a statesman—yet he remained a simple and harmonious person.

SELECTED PUBLICATIONS

Mauro was a prolific writer of articles, studies, and books on many subjects. The following are the most important of his writings on management:

1927 *L'Organizzazione scientifica nei suoi aspetti italiani ed internazionali* (Scientific Management in Its Italian and International Aspects). Rome: ENIOS.

1928 *L'Automatismo nell'elettrotrazione* (Automatic Control in Electric Traction). With Fiorentini. Milan: Bertieri.

——— *Le Osservazioni di un ingegnere negli S.U.A.* (Impressions of an Engineer in the United States). Rome: ENIOS.

1930 *Esperienze di organizzazione giapponese* (Experience of Japanese Management). Rome: ENIOS.

1933 *L'Uomo e la macchina* (Man and the Machine). Rome: ENIOS.

1934 *L'Ubicazione degli impianti industriali* (The Location of Industrial Factories). Rome: ENIOS.

1938 *La Programmazione degli impianti industriali* (Planning in Industrial Factories). Rome: ENIOS.

1941 *Il Capo nell' azienda industriale* (The Manager of an Industrial Firm). Milan: Hoepli.

1942 *Teratismi dell'industria* (Anomalies in Industry). Milan: Hoepli.

1944–1945 *Industrie ed ubicazioni* (Industries and Locations). 2 vols. Milan: Hoepli.

1945 *Gli S.U.A. visti da un ingegnere* (The United States Seen by an Engineer). Milan: Hoepli.

1948 *Impianti industriali* (Industrial Plants). Milan: Hoepli.

1950 *F. W. Taylor: la vita, le opere, gli epiloghi* (F. W. Taylor: Life, Works, Epilogues). Milan: La Cultura.

—— *Scienza ed industria* (Science and Industry). Milan: Barbier.

1952 *Organizzazione come civiltà* (Management as Civilization). Edited by Dr. A. Giuffre. Milan.

Curriculum Vitae

1887 Born at Domodossola.

1909 Graduated as an electrotechnical engineer from Milan Polytechnic.

1911–1912 Graduated as a refrigeration engineer from the Ecole Superieure (Paris) and Milan Polytechnic.

1912–1925 Active as Secretary, Italian Refrigeration Association, and Assistant Lecturer in Refrigeration Technology, Milan Polytechnic.

1920–1924 Founded and directed Experimental Refrigeration Station, Milan University Faculty of Agriculture.

1920–1925 Served as Vice-President, International Institute of Refrigeration.

1921 Deputy for Milan to the National Assembly.

1922–1926 Served as Elected delegate to the Financial Commission, League of Nations Disarmament Conference.

1924–1927 Active as member of the Higher Council for National Economy.

1928–1937 Served as Professor of Mineralogy and Petrography, then of General Technology, at Milan Polytechnic.

1938–1943 Held office as President, National Commission of Refrigeration Studies, National Research Council.

1952 Died at age of 65.

Mauro was President of the Milan College of Engineers and Architects (1920–1922) and the National Association of Engineers and Architects (1922); Honorary President of the Italian Association of Management Consultants (AICO), Turin (1951); and president or member of numerous economic and technical committees and commissions, both international and national.

As planning engineer, Mauro during his earlier career superintended the construction of many important refrigerating and other mechanical engineering installations and assisted in the reorganization or expansion of many others, including railway installations. He was also a director of several industrial and financial concerns.

Bernard Muscio
(1887–1926)
Australia/Great Britain

BERNARD Muscio provided an early Australian contribution to the advancement of management. He came from Australia to be one of the first research workers in Great Britain to take up the study of the human factor in industry.

In 1917 he had published, in Australia, a book entitled *Lectures in Industrial Psychology*. C. S. Myers, the pioneer of industrial psychology in Great Britain, went on record as saying that he first perceived the possibilities of this field of work on reading Muscio's newly published book* in 1917. The lectures of which it consists achieved much popular success in Australia, where they were delivered to working-class audiences. In England, also, they gained acceptance as a textbook when they were republished in 1920.

In 1919 Muscio was associated with Myers in organizing the Cambridge Summer School of Industrial Administration, whose curriculum was "the study of certain industrial management problems, chiefly from the psychological point of view." Muscio edited the book of lectures given at the School and published them in 1920 as *Lectures in Industrial Administration*. This was the first British book since Elbourne's of 1914 which could be described as a texbook on management. Its novelty was the importance given to the human factor.

* See Myers's autobiographical sketch in Vol. III of *History of Psychology in Autobiography*, edited by Carl Muschison (London: Oxford University Press), 1936, p. 224.

In those early days of industrial psychology in Great Britain, the work of the Health of Munition Workers Committee (formed in 1915) and later the Industrial Fatigue (now Health) Research Board (formed in 1919) was crucial in elaborating the new concepts. Muscio was one of the latter organization's first investigators and contributed, from 1919 to 1922, original research in the form of articles and reports on vocational guidance tests, fatigue measurement, motion study, and other subjects.

The early industrial psychologists, of whom Muscio was one, were pioneers in pointing out that although time-and-motion study and other management techniques were improving the output of machines in industry, no comparable study was being made of the human being, whose contribution to output was obviously no less important. These psychologists were therefore the first to ask the question: Under what conditions will the human being in industry give his or her best? We now know that the subjects they chose for research were not always those calculated to provide the right answer, for they concentrated on physical considerations which we have since learned are less significant than psychological ones. But, without the groundwork of original research which they contributed, we should not have been able to develop the better understanding of human beings at work which we have today.

Bernard Muscio had a quality of extreme judiciousness. Sometimes this appeared to entail perhaps a certain lack, or at least restraint, of enthusiasm. He nevertheless possessed a kindly and warm nature.

SELECTED PUBLICATIONS

Books:

1917 *Lectures in Industrial Psychology*. Sydney: Angus & Robertson. Second edition, London: Routledge; New York: Button, 1920.

1920 *Lectures in Industrial Administration*. Editor. London: Pitman. 276 pp.

Articles:

1920 "Fluctuations in Mental Efficiency," *British Journal of Psychology*, Vol. 10, No. 4.

1921 "Is a Fatigue Test Possible?" and "Feeling Tone in Industry," *British Journal of Psychology*, Vol. 12, Nos. 1, 2.

—— "Vocational Guidance: a Review of the Literature," Industrial Fatigue (now Health) Research Board Report No. 12.

1922 "Motor Capacity with Special Reference to Vocational Guidance," *British Journal of Psychology*, Vol. 13, No. 2.

—— "The Psycho-Physiological Capacities Required by the Hand Compositor," "Three Studies in Vocational Selection" (with E. Farmer), and "The Measurement of Physical Strength with Reference to Vocational Guidance," Industrial Fatigue (now Health) Research Board Report No. 16.

—— "On the Relations of Fatigue and Accuracy to Speed and Duration of Work" and "Two Contributions to the Study of Accident Causation" (with E. E. Osborne and H. M. Vernon), Industrial Fatigue (now Health) Research Board Report No. 19.

—— "Investigation into the Packing of Chocolates" (with R. St. C. Brooke), *Journal* of the National Institute of Industrial Psychology, Vol. 1.

1923 "Vocational Tests and Typewriting" (with S. M. Sowton), *British Journal of Psychology*, Vol. 13, No. 4.

Curriculum Vitae

1887 Born at Purfleet in New South Wales.

1912 Received M.A. in philosophy at University of Sydney. Awarded Woolley Traveling Scholarship.

1913 Received B.A. from Gonville and Caius College, Cambridge, in philosophy.

1914–1916 As demonstrator in experimental psychology, Cambridge, assisted C. S. Myers. In charge of University Psychological Laboratory during absence of Myers on war service in France.

1916–1919 Lectured on psychology and philosophy in Sydney. Gave his "Lectures in Industrial Psychology" at University, first under auspices of the Workers Educational Association and then, in 1917, under auspices of University Extension Board.

1919–1922 Senior Investigator for Industrial Fatigue Research Board in Great Britain. Position entailed lectures at Cambridge.

1920 Lent by Industrial Fatigue Research Board to new National Institute of Industrial Psychology as a special investigator.

1922–1926 Served as Challis Professor of Philosophy at Sydney.

1926 Died at age of 39 in Sydney.

Armando Salles Oliveira
(1887–1945)
Brazil

ARMANDO Salles Oliveira was a distinguished Brazilian statesman and the founder of the Brazilian management movement.

An engineer of wide industrial experience, he came into prominence during the world economic crisis of 1929. About this time he undertook in São Paulo, with the collaboration of others, the creation of the Institute for the Rational Organization of Work which in 1931 became IDORT, the national Brazilian Institute of Scientific Management recognized by CIOS. The economic crisis had shaken the Brazilian economy profoundly, helping to bring about the revolution of 1930. Oliveira participated in the movement to obtain a democratic constitution and, together with his colleagues in IDORT, led a movement for the "rational" and "scientific" organization of the government of Brazil.

In 1934 Oliveira was elected Governor of the State of São Paulo. From then until the Constitutionalist movement lost power in 1937, a situation developed which must surely be unique in the history of national management movements: IDORT became the official adviser of Oliveira's government, and scientific management became the platform on which the State's entire economic and social policy was based. The actions of Oliveira's government were characterized by their fidelity to the principles of good management. IDORT served as official consultant for the reorganization of the public services; it led the government through a turning point in the administrative history of Brazil. The administrative and fiscal structure of the public services was reorganized, technological research was provided for, social reforms were introduced, the University of São Paulo was founded, technical education was extended, and the management of the State's electric-power system was overhauled. In addition, the State Transport System was given a Center for Vocational Selection and Training.

The year 1937 brought exile for Oliveira, which was to last for eight years. However, he had become an idol of the people, and in their eyes he represented the high ideals that prevailed during the period of Constitutionalist government. His release from exile was finally obtained by a petition in which hundreds of Brazilian lawyers joined. His return to São Paulo, and his death and funeral not long thereafter, were occasions for exceptional demonstrations of public esteem.

Oliveira's work in establishing IDORT was, fortunately, a permanent achievement. The Institute prospered, and in 1954 it achieved new international standing when it became the host, for the Tenth International Management Congress, to the management institutions of the Free World.

SELECTED PUBLICATIONS

1935 *Speeches.* São Paulo: Tipografia Siqueira.
1937 *Day of Democracy.* Rio de Janeiro: Livraria Jose Olimpio.
—— *For the Future of Brazil.* Rio de Janeiro: Livraria Jose Olimpio.
1945 *Diagram of a Political Situation.* São Paulo: Editora Renascença.

Messages of the State Governor of São Paulo to the Legislative Assembly exist from the period 1914–1938 when Oliveira was Director of the journal *State of São Paulo.*

Curriculum Vitae

1887 Born in the city of São Paulo. Studied engineering at the Polytechnic School of São Paulo. As a student, Oliveira was responsible for the construction of several parts of the railway line of the Mogiana Co., of which he later became Vice-Chairman, and of the present electric-power station of Marimbondo.

1923–1928 Made study tour of Europe, where he visited the great engineering centers specializing in metallurgy, electricity, railways, and chemical-fertilizer production.

1932 Participated in the movement for obtaining a Brazilian constitution and in the following year was appointed Federal Intervener of São Paulo by the President of the Republic.

1934 When the State of São Paulo recognized the Institute for the Rational Organization of Work as a body of public importance, charged with administrative reorganization of that government. Elected Governor of the State of São Paulo.

1935 Named Honorary President of the Institute for the Rational Organization of Work.

1936 Took up office as Governor. Gave his patronage to the Scientific Management Day for Public Administration, a conference organized by IDORT for the municipalities of São Paulo. Resigned the governorship of the State and took up leadership of the Constitutionalist Party and, later, of the National Democratic Union, by which he was nominated as a candidate for the presidency of the Republic.

1937 After the coup d'état which abolished democratic elections, protesting this violation of the Constitution, wrote a letter of appeal to the military chiefs of Brazil. Arrested and exiled.

1937–1945 Lived in New York, Paris, and finally Buenos Aires.

1945 Freed from exile. Returning to Brazil, again entered politics in São Paulo but handicapped by impaired health.

—— Died at age of 58, in São Paulo.

Oliveira held the Grand Cross of the Order of Christ of Portugal and the Grand Cross of Reunited Poland. He was a grand officer of both the French Legion of Honor and the Crown of Italy, received an honorary doctorate from São Paulo University, and was a member of the Council of the Nationalist League.

James Alexander Bowie
(1888–1949)
Great Britain

JAMES Bowie was an educationalist who did much to convert industry in Great Britain to the belief that management should be taught in educational institutions.

He was the first British writer of importance on education for management. His book *Education for Business Management* (1931) crystallized his own experience as perhaps the earliest full-time teacher of management in Britain, for he had been called to the Manchester College of Technology to teach in the Department of Industrial Administration—Britain's earliest management teaching establishment—in the year following its foundation in 1918. He also drew early attention in Britain to the work of the university business schools in America and urged, in his 1932 series of articles on "American Schools of Business."[1] that British universities should take heed of the attitude to business adopted by their American counterparts. The books and articles which he published on other aspects of management also establish his right to be regarded as an author in advance of his time.

[1] Later quoted in L. Urwick, *The Development of Scientific Management in Great Britain*, a report issued to members of the Seventh International Management Congress, 1938 (London: Reprinted from *British Management Review*, Vol. III, No. 4, as separate 85-page booklet).

During his 12 years at Manchester, Bowie laid a sound basis for the present high prestige of the Manchester diploma. The syllabus was imaginatively framed, since Bowie was usually ahead of current thinking as to the subjects it should contain. At the same time it was kept practical. Bowie early drew attention to the possibilities of the case-study method of teaching management in the form developed by the American business schools. His book *Education for Business Management* described the method in general terms, and the method was actually used in the industrial-relations class at Manchester in the academic session of 1930–1931, the same year in which T. H. Burnham, the pioneer of British management teaching by case study, began building up the regular use of this method with G. A. Robinson at the South-East London Technical College. Bowie was also watchful of the department's external relations: He maintained close contact with the business world and secured promotion for the department to university status.

After 1931, as Founder-Principal of the School of Economics and Commerce, Dundee, Bowie again established a full-time postgraduate course in business administration. This was for some years one of Great Britain's four leading courses in that subject, the other three being those at the Regent Street Polytechnic in London, the Manchester College of Technology, and the London School of Economics.

In his later years, Bowie's interests turned to the wider activities of his college as a whole and to the economic problems of his native Scotland. He continued, nevertheless, to give much time to management propaganda in speeches and writings, although it was not till after the Second World War that his activities bore much visible fruit. The branch of the Institute of Industrial Administration which he founded in Dundee is now active and flourishing, and some of the social and business movements which he sponsored there have, with the help of later supporters, finally justified his good judgment.

In 1954 the Institute of Industrial Administration established the Bowie Medal, to be awarded annually to a member of the Institute for a noteworthy contribution to management. Bowie's name was thus linked with the first award for services to management to be established by the British management movement.

Bowie is described as having been a

> . . . gifted and versatile speaker, who made full use of that characteristic pawkiness which is the birthright of the Aberdonian. He had a wealth of experience and a great flair for translating that experience into an anecdote fitting to the occasion. He was always genial, and even when illness overtook him his spirit remained undaunted and he continued to show great fortitude.
>
> He was much in demand far and near to lecture on the wide field of economics and industrial topics, and he had the rare ability of making the most obscure and profound subjects of interest to the ordinary man in the street.

Dr. Bowie was a strong believer in descending from the purely academic and coming to grips with the practical side of life's problems, and his contacts with everyday life greatly enriched his talks and discussions.

The deep sincerity of the man, his happy friendliness, his ready desire always to help and his dynamic personality will be long remembered by all who came in contact with him.[2]

SELECTED PUBLICATIONS

Books:

1922 *Sharing Profits with Employees.* London: Pitman. 230 pp.

1930 *Education for Business Management.* London: Oxford University Press. 200 pp.

1931 *Rationalization.* London: Pitman. Reprinted from the *Times Trade and Engineering Supplement,* July–September 1930. 36 pp.

1939 *The Future of Scotland.* London: W. & R. Chambers, Ltd. 272 pp.

Articles:

1920 "The Need for a Science of Industrial Administration." Chapter in *Lectures on Industrial Administration* edited by B. Muscio. London: Pitman.

1922 "Profit-Sharing—and Co-Partnership," *The Economic Journal,* Vol. 32, pp. 466–476.

1927 "A New Method of Wage Adjustment in the Light of the Recent History of Wage Methods in the Coal Industry," *Economic Journal,* Vol. 37, pp. 384–394.

1928 Articles on co-partnership, periodic bonus payments, etc., in Pitman's *Dictionary of Business Administration.*

1931 "Preparation for Management: The Manchester Experiment," *Business & Science.* Papers read at the centenary meeting of the British Association for the Advancement of Science. London: Sylvan Press.

1932 "American Schools of Business." Reprint of a series of articles in *The Manchester Guardian* from September 8, 1931 on.

1943 "Management—Today and Tomorrow," *Journal* of the Institute of Industrial Administration, Vol. IV, No. 6, March.

—— "American Developments in Education for Industrial Management," *Proceedings* of the Conference on Training for Industrial Management held in March by the Institute of Industrial Administration, London.

1945 "The Making of Scientific Management." Book review in *Industry Illustrated,* June.

[2] Extract from an obituary in the *Courier & Advertiser,* Dundee, September 3, 1949.

Curriculum Vitae

1888	Born in Aberdeen. Took double honors in economics and philosophy at Aberdeen University. Received M.A. and won Hutton Prize.
1908–1914	Concurrently with university studies, was partner and manager in small family firm of Bowie & Son, builders and contractors.
1914–1918	Saw service in Royal Artillery in Egypt, Palestine, Greece, and Bulgaria.
1919	Joined Faculty of Technology, Manchester University, in the newly established Department of Industrial Administration.
1924	Awarded D.Litt. by Aberdeen University.
1926	Became head of Department of Industrial Administration, Manchester University.
1931	Served as Special Lecturer, Wharton Business School, University of Pennsylvania, Philadelphia, U.S.A. Appointed Founder-Principal of School of Economics and Commerce in Dundee.
1936–1939	Served on staff of London County Council Management Summer Schools.
1940–1943	Was Honorary Food Executive Officer and Honorary Local Registration Officer for Dundee.
1943–1946	On staff of Personnel Administration, Ltd., management consultants in London.
1946	Returned to School of Economics, Dundee. (The School had gradually changed the emphasis of its teaching to concentrate on economics courses.)
1947–1948	Served on staff of Institute of Industrial Administration Management Summer Schools in Oxford.
1949	Died on September 1st, aged 61, in Dundee.

Bowie was a Fellow of the Institute of Industrial Administration and a member of its Council and Education Committee; Secretary of the Economics Section, British Association for the Advancement of Science; a member of the Council, British Association for Commercial and Industrial Education; and a founder-member of the British Institute of Management.

Alfred Carrard
(1889–1948)
Switzerland

ALFRED Carrard was the pioneer, in Switzerland, of vocational guidance and training in industry. He came to this work, not from the world of psychology, but from that of engineering. Ten years in a great Swiss engineering concern convinced him of the need, in the interests of industrial progress, to improve the human relationships among those who work in industry, to bridge the mental gap between managers and workers, and to find means by which the workers could better adapt themselves to their jobs.

In 1924 Carrard abandoned his engineering career to take up the study of "psychotechnics"* and to develop the facilities available in Switzerland for vocational selection, guidance, and training in industry. He became the leader of a powerful movement and gained the collaboration both of the psychologists and of industry. He coordinated the different institutes of applied psychology. He published books and papers which were read in Switzerland and in many other parts of Europe. He did much original research; and, from 1937 on, engineering firms from many different countries sent representatives to him to learn his methods.

Because Carrard was not a psychologist but an engineer, his methods were more empirical than those used by psychotechnical institutes in other countries. His particular contribution was to stress the moral, psychological,

* "Psychotechnics" may be defined as "the application of psychological knowledge to practical problems, especially in industry and other economic activity."

and physical considerations which should prevail in vocational training. "The man who is put on trust to complete a particular task," he said, "has an output and a vigor lacking in anyone who works mechanically, without responsibility and without feeling that he is enjoying the confidence of those for whom he works." Thus his aim was, for example, to improve the training of apprentices by arousing their interest in the ultimate results of their work. Again because of his empirical approach, he was as ready to improve the practices of managers as those of workers, and his publications include several on the subject of industrial leadership.

Carrard has been called "the founder of vocational guidance" in Switzerland. What his work lacked in psychological refinement it more than gained in practical effect. It is a tribute to his zeal and vision that other countries have also adopted the methods which bear his name and have acknowledged him internationally as a pioneer.

Carrard was undoubtedly a man with a sense of dedication. The distinguishing mark of his school has been described as respect for the individual human being. It was that which Carrard had found lacking in industry and which he made it his life work to develop. He liked to say that all people have their own place in society and that it is sufficient to show it to them and teach them how to hold it. His tests were devised, not to submit anyone to an inquisitional examination about his or her job, but to enable individuals to discover for themselves their greatest natural aptitudes. He was kindly, sensitive, and modest.

SELECTED PUBLICATIONS

Books:

1932 *Le Chef: Sa formation et sa tache* (The Chief Executive: His Training and Task). Neuchâtel: Editions Delachaux & Niestlé.

1935 *Die Erziehung zum Führer* (Development for Leadership). Zurich: Polygraphischer Verlag.

1941 *La Jeunesse de demain. Reform scolaire* (The Youth of Tomorrow. Educational Reform). Neuchâtel: Editions Delachaux & Niestlé. Translated into German in 1942 by Editions Emil Oesch, Thalwil-Zurich.

1942 *La Personne dans la vie économique et sociale* (The Individual in Economic and Social Life). in *La Suisse forge son destin*, Editions la Baconnière. Translated into German by Editions Emil Oesch, Thalwil-Zurich, 1944.

1944 *La Formation de la personne* (Training of the Individual). Thalwil-Zurich: Editions Emil Oesch. Translated into German in 1944 by the same publisher.

1948 *Praktische Einführung in die Probleme det Arbeitspsychologie* (Practical Introduction to the Problems of Industrial Psychology). With others. Zurich: Rascher Verlag. Translated into French as *La Psychologie de l'homme au travail*. Neuchâtel: Editions Delachaux & Niestlé, 1953.

Articles:

1927 "Zur Psychologie des Anlernens und Einübens im Wirtschaftsleben" (The Psychology of Teaching and Practice in Economic and Industrial Life), *Schweizer Schriften für rationelles Wirtschaften No. 1.*

—— "Zur Psychologie der Arbeit—zur Psychologie der Führung" (The Psychology of Work—The Psychology of Leadership), *Schweizer Schriften für rationelles Wirtschaften No. 3.*

1928 "Le Développement de la psychotechnique en Suisse' (The Development of Psychotechnics in Switzerland), *Schweizer Schriften für rationelles Wirtschaften No. 8.*

Carrard also contributed various articles to the *Journal des associations patronales* and other periodicals.

Curriculum Vitae

1889	Born on January 26th at Montreux.
1899–1908	Studied at Montreux College and Bern Grammar School.
1908–1912	Studied for an engineering degree at Federal Polytechnic School, Zurich.
1912–1914	Studied for Doctor of Physics degree.
1914–1924	Worked as engineer with Brown Boveri & Co., Baden.
1924	Took up studies with Jules Suter and Hans Spreng at Institute of Applied Psychology, Zurich.
1925	Became Director, Psychotechnical Institute of Zurich.
1927	Founded and became first president, Psychotechnical Foundation of Switzerland, Zurich.
1936 on	Was Director, Institute of Applied Psychology, Lausanne.
1944	Became Special Professor, Federal Polytechnic School for Psychotechnics and Social and Applied Psychology, Zurich.
1948	Died on September 5th, at age of 59, in Lausanne.

Courtesy McKinsey & Co., Inc.

James Oscar McKinsey
(1889–1937)
United States

JAMES O. McKinsey had a short life, but his influence on the art and science of management was significant. The key to that influence was the unusual degree to which he combined intellectual interest in the theory of business with practical capacity for applying, and inducing others to apply, theoretically valid criteria to actual situations.

Starting his business career as a certified public accountant, McKinsey was quick to appreciate a point which some professional accountants fail to realize—that accountancy can never be an end in itself. It is as a tool of good management that figures achieve importance and significance. Having grasped this unifying principle, McKinsey had one intellectual advantage over the majority of his contemporaries in management who had been trained as engineers: His basic education in law and accountancy had taught him to look at a business as a whole. From this appreciation of every business as a unity, coupled with his practical experience as a management consultant, flowed his special contributions to management thought and practice.

First, McKinsey focused attention on the importance of budgeting as a major instrument of management. Budgeting and budgetary control are now accepted practice in all well-managed business enterprises, but McKinsey wrote the first standard book on the subject in 1922. He was unable to attend the International Conference on Budgetary Control held in Geneva in 1931 under the auspices of the International Management Institute; however, his thought and his influence permeated almost every contribution to its proceedings.

He always insisted that the structure of a budget must reflect, not an arbitrary grouping of the figures designed to accord with accounting conventions or convenience, but the actual responsibilities resting on individuals. Thus his interest in budgeting quickly led him to advocate sound organization planning as a basic element in the effectiveness of administration. He had a special facility for persuading top management that the study of organization is not an academic amusement but a real factor in the economy of day-to-day operations. Thus he brought many leading corporations to appreciate that executives and supervisors can perform more effectively when they know what their responsibilities are, have authority commensurate with those responsibilities, and understand clearly their relationships with those who are responsible for other functions.

McKinsey also was particularly sensitive to the interrelationships of business problems. He saw clearly that the solution to many difficulties has its roots, not in the area in which the difficulty becomes manifest, but in some unexpected and apparently unrelated aspect of the business. A marketing defect may be cured through changes in manufacturing procedure and so on.

McKinsey was successful in making these new concepts of influence known through many channels—in particular, through his teaching at the University of Chicago and through his considerable service to the American Management Association, of which he was Chairman of the Board at the time of his death.

SELECTED PUBLICATIONS

Books:

1920 *Bookkeeping and Accounting.* Cincinnati: South-Western Publishing Co. Revised in 1939 by Edwin B. Piper. 2 vols.

—— *Principles of Accounting.* With A. C. Hodge. Chicago: University of Chicago Press.

1922 *Budgetary Control.* New York: Ronald Press.

—— *Budgeting.* In the "Business Administration" series of which McKinsey was also general editor. New York: Ronald Press.

—— *Organization.* In the "Business Administration" series. New York: Ronald Press.

—— *Organization and Methods of the Walworth Manufacturing Company—Cases and Problems No. 3.* Chicago: University of Chicago Press.

—— *Financial Management.* Chicago: American Technical Society.

1923 *Controlling the Finances of a Business.* With Stuart P. Meech. New York: Ronald Press.

1924 *Business Administration.* Cincinnati: South-Western Publishing Co.

—— *Managerial Accounting.* Chicago: University of Chicago Press.

1931 Chapters in *Handbook of Business Administration* (edited by W. J. Donald). New York: McGraw-Hill, for the American Management Association.

1935 *Accounting Principles*. With Howard S. Noble. Cincinnati: South-Western Publishing Co.

Articles:
McKinsey contributed many articles to management journals and publications, particularly those of the American Management Association.

Curriculum Vitae

1889	Born on a farm in Gamma, Mo.
1912	Awarded Ph.B. by State Teachers College, Warrensburg, Mo.
1913	Awarded LL.B. by University of Arkansas.
1916	Awarded Ph.B. by University of Chicago.
1917	Joined University of Chicago faculty, eventually obtaining professorship in accounting.
1917–1919	Enlisted as private in Ordnance Department of U.S. Army.
1919	Received M.A. from University of Chicago. Became Certified Public Accountant, Illinois.
1920–1921	Lectured on accounting at Columbia University, New York City.
c. 1921–1924	Served as Chairman of the Board, Hamilton Bond and Mortgage Co. Also was member of firm of Frazer and Torbet, Certified Public Accountants.
1925–1935	Was Senior Partner, McKinsey & Co.
1926–1935	Taught at University of Chicago as Professor of Business Policies.
1935–1937	Served as Chairman of the Board, Marshall Field & Co.
1936–1937	Served as Chairman of the Board, American Management Association.
1937	Died, aged 48, in Chicago.

Roberto Cochrane Simonsen
(1889–1948)
Brazil

ROBERTO Cochrane Simonsen, an outstanding Brazilian industrialist and public figure, was his country's earliest practitioner of modern principles of management. In 1912 he founded and directed the Cia. Constructora de Santos, a construction company which expanded rapidly and became entrusted with many government contracts in different Brazilian states. From 1916 on, Simonsen was putting the ideas of scientific management into practice in this company, a decade before the beginning of the movement which led to the foundation of the Brazilian Institute of Management (IDORT) in 1931. His report to his shareholders in 1917 listed five principles on which the company's operation methods had been, and would continue to be, based.

1. Careful preliminary analysis of the task.
2. Preliminary planning of the best method, shortest time, and lowest price.
3. Securing the best machinery, facilities, and men.
4. Establishing friendly cooperation between management and employees in the effort to achieve low-cost production.
5. Control by observation of the cost of the work, with a breakdown permitting rapid calculation of detailed costs.

It was not surprising that with this approach to management, closely resembling that of F. W. Taylor, Simonsen built the Cia. Constructora de

Santos into a uniquely successful concern. Many years later (giving a lecture to IDORT in 1938), Simonsen said:

> I see with special pleasure the evolution of the various activities of IDORT because I have been, since the beginning of my professional life, a battler and a "doer" in this field. It was the Cia. Constructora de Santos which, for the first time in the country, openly preached the tenets of scientific management. . . . We have also had the opportunity of applying these principles in a practical way in many engineering and industrial undertakings that have been entrusted to us. I can also observe, with great satisfaction, that several engineers who took their first professional steps in that company are today working for the advancement of IDORT and applying in IDORT the same principles instilled into them at the outset of their careers. . . .

By 1918 he was leading Brazilian industry to realize the importance of the human factor in management. He described the situation in this way:

> The greatest problem that we have before us, the engineers and administrators of the present day, is undoubtedly the economic utilization of work. . . . The industrialists of today must abandon the old-fashioned patterns to consider, as a new force that indisputably exists, the discontent of the working man. We must give him without fear a just remuneration for his work if we do not wish to see production held up by our seeking to solve this problem wrongly, by political paths, when it could be solved rightly, by economic paths.

And later:

> Only the scientific way of administering and rewarding work, in which the two classes equally benefit, will avoid the impasse created by the inevitable reactions of the old systems, placing both parties on a footing of intimate cooperation, in favor of their legitimate interests.

Influenced by the writings of H. L. Gantt, Simonsen gave much attention to methods of remunerating workers. He was convinced that the bad methods in operation were the greatest, if not the only, cause of strikes; and, as a means of mitigating industrial disputes and developing more scientific systems of payment, he set up in Santos the first "board of conciliation and appeal" in Brazil, a precursor of the government-established Boards of Labor Relations. He planned and organized the National Workers Training Service (Serviço Nacional de Aprendizagem Industrial, or SENAI) and the Social Service of Industry (Serviço Social da Industria, or SESI). SENAI ensures that youths in industry are vocationally trained at the employer's expense. It has brought a great improvement in the skill of Brazilian workers. SESI is sponsored and financed by employers to provide welfare services for workers, including balanced nutrition. Both these institutions are considered models in Brazil today.

It was natural that Simonsen should be prominent in the founding of

IDORT in 1931, and in the final phase of his career he was able to bring his national prestige as a statesman and a professor to the support of the movement. His pioneering work over many years was a great and original contribution to the development of management in Brazil.

Dr. Simonsen was indeed outstanding in the breadth and depth of his interests. There were few aspects of the social and economic life of Brazil in which he did not play a part, and it was for this reason that he was so often called upon to represent Brazil abroad. He nevertheless found time for important teaching work and for participation in the work of cultural institutes both at home and abroad. Finally, he achieved distinction in the world of literature when he was admitted in 1946 to membership of the São Paulo Academy of Letters.

SELECTED PUBLICATIONS

1911 *O Municipio de Santos* (The Municipality of Santos).
1912 *Os Melhores aumentos municipais de Santos* (Major Municipal Advances in Santos).
1919 *O Trabalho moderno* (Modern Industry).
1923 *O Calçamento de São Paulo* (The Paving of Sao Paulo).
1928 *A Orientacão industrial brasileira* (The Trend of Brazilian Industry).
1931 *A Construcão de quarteis para a exercito* (Building Barracks for the Army).
—— *As Finanças e a industria* (The Finances of Industry).
1933 *A Margem da Profissão* (Approach to Professionalism).
—— *Rumo e verdade* (Trend and Truth).
1934 *Ordem economica e padrão de vida* (Economic Order and the Standard of Living).
1935 *Aspectos da economica nacional* (Aspects of the National Economy).
1937 *Historia economica do Brasil* (Economic History of Brazil). This book was the first important study of the economic aspects of Brazilian history.
1938 *Aspectos da historia economica do cafe* (Aspects of the Economic History of Coffee).
—— *A Industria em face da economica de cafe nacional* (The Coffee Industry and its Place in the National Economy).
1939 *Evolução industrial do Brasil* (Industrial Evolution of Brazil).
—— *Objectivos da engenharia nacional* (Objectives of National Engineering).
1940 *Niveis de vida e a economia nacional* (Living Standards and the National Economy).
—— *Recursos economicos e movimentos de população* (Economic Resources and Population Movements).

Curriculum Vitae

1889 Born on February 18th in Santos. Trained as civil engineer at São Paulo Polytechnic.

1909–1910 Was engineer with Southern Brazil Railway.
1911–1912 Served as Chief Director of the Prefecture of Santos and Chief Engineer on the Committee for Municipal Improvements in Santos.
1912–1919 Served as President, Cia. Frigorifica de Santos.
1912–1946 Founded and was Director of Cia. Constructora de Santos.
1919 Represented São Paulo on the Brazilian Commercial Committee's delegation to England. Was sole representative of Brazil at the International Congress of Cotton Industrialists, Paris, responsible for the appointment of the Arno-Pearce Commission which helped Brazil to develop her cotton industry.
1919–1924 Was Director, Cia. Frigorifica e Pastoril de Barretos.
1923–1928 Was President, Sindicato Nacional de Combustiveis Liquidos.
1926–1929 Was Director, Cia. Nacional de Artefactos de Cobre.
1926–1927 Was President, Cia. Nacional de Borracha.
1934–1937 Active as Federal Deputy, during which time he served on several committees of the Federal Congress on social and economic matters.
1935–1936 Served as President, Confederação Industrial do Brasil.
1938–1941 Served on Council for the Economic Expansion of the State of São Paulo.
1946 Elected Federal Senator for the State of São Paulo.
1948 Died on May 25th, aged 59, in São Paulo.

At his death Simonsen was President of Cia. Constructora de Santos; Ceramica São Caetano, S.A.; Cia. Santista de Habitaçoẽs Economicas; and Fabrica de Tecidos Santa Helena, S.A. He was also Director of Cia. Brasileira de Credito Hipotecario and Partner in Murray, Simonsen & Co. and Soc. Constructora Brasileira Ltda. In addition, he was Professor of Brazilian Economic History at the São Paulo Free School of Sociology and Politics and Technical Adviser to the Brazilian Institute of Geography and Statistics.

Simonsen was active as well in the following public and professional bodies: São Paulo Engineering Institute (President), Federation of Industries of State of São Paulo (President), Federation of Industries of City of São Paulo (President), Industrial Confederation of Brazil (Vice-President), National Confederation of Industry (Vice-President), Brazilian Economic Society (member of council), Rio de Janeiro Engineers Club, and American Society of Civil Engineers. Simonsen was named as commander of the Order of Orange-Nassau of the Netherlands.

Clovis Ribeiro
(1891–1942)
Brazil

CLOVIS Ribeiro was the right-hand man of Armando Salles Oliveira, and shares with him credit for the achievements of IDORT.

Whereas Oliveira was an engineer, Ribeiro was by training a lawyer and an economist. In the years before the promulgation of the Brazilian constitution in 1932, Ribeiro was Secretary of the Commercial Association of São Paulo; and from this influential position he worked actively, in collaboration with Oliveira, for political and economic reform. Ribeiro was also a founder of IDORT, becoming its first secretary. Like Oliveira he realized the extent of the contribution which the work of IDORT could make toward administrative reform in the public sector. His opportunity came with the election of Oliveira as governor of the State of São Paulo, at which time Ribeiro became Secretary of Finance. His reforms were decisive and outstanding in the fiscal and financial system, in the administrative structure of the civil service, in government economy of expenditure, and in several other economic fields. For the first time, the State's administrative system took on characteristics based on the principles of good management. In this great progress Ribeiro's influence is recognized by the Paulistas to have been decisive.

Ribeiro was one of the most enthusiastic founders of IDORT and one of its most devoted supporters throughout his life. In the later years of his career he continued to be a director of IDORT and Secretary of the Commercial Association. CIOS honors Ribeiro with Oliveira as one who improved the business of government by applying the principles of the effective government of business. A man in whom any kind of ostentation was absent, he is remembered with affection by his colleagues in the Brazilian management movement.

SELECTED PUBLICATIONS

1924 "On the Nonpayment of Bills of Exchange."
1925 "The Crisis of the Port of Santos." Administrative studies.
1927 "The Solution of the Crisis of the Port of Santos." Conclusion.

Ribeiro published juridical, economic, and financial studies on several national problems; among them, the collection of land duties and duties on commercial and industrial profits, the readjustment of the customs tariff, and the collection of the 2 percent gold tax. In addition, he was a director of the *Commercial and Industrial Review.*

Curriculum Vitae

1891 Born in São Paulo or elsewhere in Brazil.
1900 At preparatory school.
1910 Earned Bachelor of Science and Letters degree.
1915 Awarded Bachelor of Juridical and Social Science degree by Faculty of Law of São Paulo University.
1916 Did agricultural work at Casa Branca and Paraibuna.
1920 Founded and was director of a publishing firm.
1925 With others, founded journal *Diario da Noite* of São Paulo; became one of its directors.
1926 Became a founder of the Nationalist League and of the Democratic League which played the leading part in the struggle for the secret ballot. As Legal Adviser and Secretary of the Commercial Association and an Economic and Financial Editor of the journal *State of São Paulo,* achieved a noteworthy orientation of opinion among the conservative classes on all questions of agriculture, industry, and commerce.
1931 Elected a director of IDORT at its foundation. Retained post till his death.
1932 Participated in the Constitutionalist movement.
1934 Drafted and promulgated the "great letter" of July 16th. After the Constituent Assembly of Brazil was installed, became Economic Adviser to the Deputies of São Paulo, particularly with regard to the distribution of income, which had many repercussions on the tax organization of the State in the Brazilian Federation.
1935 Became Technical Adviser to the Federal Council for External Trade, carrying out, among other projects, noteworthy studies for the reorganization of the merchant navy.

1936 Under the government of Oliveira in the State of São Paulo, headed the Secretariat of Finance, where he: (1) regularized the collection of State duties and taxes; (2) reorganized the Secretariat for greater effectiveness; (3) created the Duties and Tax Tribunal, which enabled those who paid taxes to have a voice in fiscal matters which concerned them; (4) created an advanced course of study for Secretariat employees; (5) created the Customs Expedition Section; and (6) created the Office for Economic and Financial Studies and other services of a general nature concerned with State economy and with assistance to civil servants. All these measures gave a new impetus to the efficient collection of taxes, with increased returns to the State, and this enabled the government to undertake a much more extensive administrative program.

1940 Once the University College had been organized, was appointed Professor of Political Economy while continuing to act as Legal Adviser and Secretary of the Commercial Association of São Paulo.

1942 Died at age of 51.

Oliver Sheldon
(1894–1951)
Great Britain

OLIVER Sheldon wrote a management classic: *The Philosophy of Management.* Published in 1923, it at once became an authoritative textbook in both Britain and America.

Sheldon spent all his working career in the service of Rowntree & Co., in York, and there he was closely associated with the great advances in managerial practice being made under B. S. Rowntree's direction. In 1921 Sheldon emerged as one of the founders of the Institute of Industrial Administration and a contributor to its *Journal.* And in 1922 an article of his became the basis for a paper, "The Case for the Institute", which was an important document in the British management movement—one of the earliest cases made for the establishment of professional standards in management.

The Philosophy of Management was original in two ways. First, it put the arguments for the scientific method in management with a cogency not yet achieved by any British writer on this subject. Secondly, it expounded the social responsibilities of management as a major partner in the community alongside capital and labor. In the words of B. S. Rowntree's foreword, "the author recognizes that business has a soul." There were not many articulate defenders of such a concept in industrial Britain in 1923, and so the scope and novelty of the book earned it great influence. In particular, it discussed the application of the functional principle to the higher organization of industrial enterprises. The author's distinction between administration and management has been widely quoted. Of special interest, also, is the unified code of management principles with which the book concludes and which gave philosophical expression to the aims of the newly founded Institute of Industrial Administration. Written in a practical vein for practicing managers, it also had an imaginative appeal, drawing the manifold activities of management into a single pattern around the two themes of scientific method and social responsibility.

Sheldon made further contributions to management literature in later years. These are notable for their clear analysis and precise definition of terms. Finally, he was prominent as B. S. Rowntree's colleague in organizing, in the 1920s, the Rowntree Lecture Conferences, the forerunners of the management conferences of today.

Oliver Sheldon was essentially a quiet thinker, a man who preferred to state a case and leave it to time and the gradual infiltration of truth to carry conviction to others. He hoarded his restricted capital of energy carefully, spending it as sparingly as he could on those things which came highest on his scale of values.

First on his list was his home. To sustain its deep personal satisfactions, he had to win and retain his place in a large and competitive business undertaking. This he did quickly. And here again he selected a function which placed him a little outside the daily struggle of the parent organization. First as Assistant to the Director and subsequently as Representative Director working with Rowntree's large circle of associated and subsidiary companies, he was the ideal personality to do all that could be done by gentle persuasion to integrate their activities and encourage them to assimilate what the parent company had to teach. It was an exacting task and one which would only be trusted to a man whose devotion to his duty was uninterrupted by too many outside interests.

Sheldon may have thought that he was unsuited for the role of propagandist. It is a strange fact that, having written one of the most distinguished books on management produced by an Englishman, he made little further public contribution to the field. His daily work, however, was a constant if gentle sermon on management to a wide circle of directors. This and his home, with some public service, were the things that seemed to him of greatest importance.

SELECTED PUBLICATIONS

Books:

1923 *The Philosophy of Management.* London: Pitman. 296 pp.

1928 *Factory Organization.* With Northcott, Wardropper, and Urwick. London: Pitman. Reprinted in 1937.

Articles:

1923 "The Elimination of Waste in Industry." Address to 16th Rowntree Lecture Conference, Oxford.

1925 "Management as a Profession." Address to 21st Rowntree Lecture Conference, Oxford.

1928 "Function of Administration and Organization," "Industrial Organization," and "Distribution of Responsibility." Articles contributed to the *Dictionary of Industrial Administration.* London: Pitman.

Curriculum Vitae

1894	Born on July 13th at Congleton, Cheshire. Sheldon's father was the Town Clerk successively of Burnley and Wimbledon. The son was educated at Burnley Grammar School; King's College School, Wimbledon; and Merton College, Oxford (B.A.)
1914–1918	Commissioned in the East Surrey Regiment.
1919	Became personal assistant to B. S. Rowntree at Rowntree & Co., York. Later became Representative Director, working with the Associated Companies.
1931	Appointed to the general Board of Directors.
1951	Died on August 7th at age of 57.

Outside his business interests, Sheldon was deeply concerned with the welfare of York and held several important public offices in that city. He was a member and at one time Governor of the Merchant Adventurers, founder and Chairman of the York Georgian Society, and one of the founders of the York Civic Trust, of which he was Joint Secretary with the Dean of York.

Henry (Hrant) Pasdermadjian
(1904–1954)
Switzerland

DR. Henry Pasdermadjian was an internationally recognized author and speaker on the general subject of organization and on the particular subject of retail management.

By birth Armenian, at the age of three a refugee in Western Europe, Pasdermadjian had a brilliant international career. His earliest writings on management were published when he was on the staff of the International Management Institute, Geneva. By the time of the Sixth CIOS Congress in 1935, to which he presented a paper, he had published articles in Swiss and French journals covering a wide range of management principles and practice. The list of his writings from then on, published in several languages and in several different countries, indicates the breadth of his contribution to the management field.

It was also a contribution in depth; his books are accepted as authoritative. In writing on the philosophy of management, he stressed the impossibility of achieving results by using scientific techniques unless they are adapted to the economic and social situation within which they must operate. He expounded the value of the scientific method and of long-term policy thinking.

The world of large-scale retail management was fortunate in having the outlook of Pasdermadjian—engineer, economist, and thinker on organization—brought to bear on its problems. As General Secretary for 18 years of the International Association of Department Stores, founded in 1928 as a society for management research, he used to say: "My role consists in giving to department store management a new dimension. I am like the manager of an extra function—the function in charge of the future." His contribution may best be judged by reading his internationally known books, *Management Research in Retailing* (1950) and *The Department Store* (1954). Of the first, Henry S. Dennison wrote in his foreword:

> This is much more than a lucid and eminently usable description of the adoption of the principle of Scientific Management by seven to ten European Stores. . . . It is the most illuminating practical and readable description of the principles of Scientific Management and of their many varieties of application which I remember ever to have read.

Because of the nature of the Association, with its strictly limited membership, much of Pasdermadjian's work has never been made available to a wider public. He was, for example, the author of the handbooks of the Association, seven in number, which remain probably the most comprehensive guides to various aspects of department-store management ever compiled. There is virtually no retailing problem on which he has not written for the benefit of the Association's members. His talent for synthesis enabled him to set out clearly and forcibly a large number of apparently contradictory ideas from various sources, particularly in the United States, and blend them into a whole in which certain fundamental principles became at once apparent. Much of the credit for the introduction and adaptation of American management ideas and techniques into European stores goes to Dr. Henry Pasdermadjian.

He was happiest, and had most influence, when working at the level of top management and dealing with such questions as policy determination and control or problems of organization structure. His paper on American department-store organization, written in 1938, remains a model of its kind, and his work on such topics as the separation of buying and selling, the organization of the sales function, the job of the buyer, and the position of the personnel function, will not easily be superseded. The experience Pasdermadjian gained in retail management, on the other hand, no doubt illuminated his thinking on the general issues of management and society. The book on which he was engaged at his death was to be called *The Second Industrial Revolution,* appraising the impact of the science of management on industrial development.

> Although he passed the greater part of his life in Europe and was an enthusiastic visitor to the United States, Pasdermadjian remained essentially oriental. His intuition for foreign languages, his tact in negotiations, his liberal outlook in history and geography, his courage in the continuous sufferings of the last years, the careful management of his personal affairs, his patience and generosity towards others (to the chance visitor in particular), all indicated a man born and bred in

the traditions of the East. At the same time, he owed much to France and French culture, which symbolized for him everything of the best that the western world possessed. He was at ease in all the cities of Europe, preferring especially Paris and Copenhagen, but he retained everywhere, towards men and things, the perspicacious and unbiassed outlook of the penetrating observer and the insatiable reader.*

SELECTED PUBLICATIONS

1932 *L'Organisation scientifique du travail* (Scientific Management). Geneva: Georg. 157 pp.

1936 *Le Memento de l'organisateur. 300 suggestions pour augmenter le rendement d'une entreprise* (The Organizer's Manual. 300 Suggestions for Increasing the Productivity of an Enterprise). Brussels: Comité National Belge de l'Organisation Scientifique. 91 pp.

1938 *Developments and Trends in Administrative Management.* Papers of the Seventh International Management Congress, Washington, D.C.

—— *Le Gouvernement des grandes organisations* (The Management of Large Businesses). Paris: Presses Universitaires de France. 225 pp.

1947 *Principes de comptabilité industrielle* (Principles of Industrial Accounting). Neuchâtel: Delachaux & Niestlé. 76 pp.

—— *Rationel Driftsorganisation* (Rational Business Organization). Danish translation by T. Bak-Jensen. Copenhagen: Schulz Forlag. 179 pp.

1949 *Le Grand Magasin. Son origine, son evolution, son avenir* (The Large Store. Its Origin, Its Evolution, Its Future). Paris: Dunod. 166 pp.

1950 *Management Research in Retailing.* London: Newman Books. 177 pp.

1951 *Les Frais généraux. Leur traitement comptable et leur signification* (Overhead Expenses. Their Costing and Their Economic Importance). Geneva: Librairie de l'Université. 42 pp.

1954 *The Department Store. Its Origins, Evolution, and Economics.* London: Newman Books. 217 pp. Published in German by Westdeutscher Verlag Köln-Opladen, 1954. 216 pp.

—— *Les Caractéristiques économiques des grandes entreprises de distribution* (The Economic Characteristics of Large-Scale Distributive Enterprises). Basel: *Revue Suisse d'Economie Politique et de Statistique.* 20 pp.

1955 *Quelques aspects de l'organisation des entreprises* (Some Aspects of Business Organisation). Paris: *Revue d'Economie Politique.* Published posthumously. 29 pp.

In addition, Pasdermadjian published from 1930 on a large number of articles, reports, and studies in the journals of several countries. He was the historian of Armenia, his book having gained the Brémond Prize from the Paris School of Oriental Studies in 1954.

* From the obituary by D. Knee circulated by the Secretary-General of CIOS.

Curriculum Vitae

1904	Born at Tiflis, in Georgia (Russia), on April 17th; son of an Armenian engineer. His parents led the Armenian resistance.
1907	Emigrated with his family to Geneva, which remained his real home throughout his life. Educated in Switzerland, France, and the United States. Received civil engineer's diploma at Zurich Polytechnic (1928); studied commercial economics at Columbia University, New York; awarded LL.D. in economics at Grenoble University (1932).
1929–1933	Served as assistant at the International Management Institute, Geneva.
1933–1936	Worked as an engineer with Aluminium Ltd.
1936	Became General Secretary, International Association of Department Stores. Worked in Paris, then Copenhagen, then (from 1950 on) Geneva.
1937	Was a member of the Distribution Commission of the International Chamber of Commerce.
1952	Became special professor at Geneva University in industrial organization and industrial accounting.
1954	Died in Geneva, aged 50, after a severe and protracted illness.

Pasdermadjian gave support for many years to the Swiss National Management Council.

Appendix I

Key Management Books and Papers Mentioned
(arranged by year of publication)

DATE	TITLE	AUTHOR OR EDITOR
1826	*A Comparative View of the Various Institutions for the Assurance of Lives*	Babbage
1832	*On the Economy of Machinery and Manufactures*	"
1881	"The Nomenclature of Machine Details"	Smith
1885	*The Cost of Manufactures and the Administration of Workshops, Public and Private*	Metcalfe
1886	"The Engineer as Economist"	Towne
1889	"Gainsharing"	"
1891	"The Premium Plan of Paying for Labor"	Halsey
1895	"A Piece-Rate System"	Taylor
1896	*The Commercial Organization of Factories*	Lewis
1901	"A Bonus System of Remunerating Labor"	Rowan
	"A Premium System of Rewarding Labor"	Gantt
	"The Proper Distribution of Establishment Charges"	Church
1903	"Principles of Collective Work"	Adamiecki
	Shop Management	Taylor

In addition, the Editor has access to a number of obituaries, other papers, and similar materials.

1905	*Concrete, Plain and Reinforced*	Thompson
1910	*Factory Organization and Administration*	Diemer
1911	*Principles of Scientific Management*	Taylor
1912	*Construction Costs*	Thompson
1913	"Engineering Workshop Organization"	Renold
	Principles of Industrial Organization	Kimball
	Psychology and Industrial Efficiency	Münsterberg
1914	*The Science and Practice of Management*	Church
	Factory Organization and Accounts	Elbourne
1915	"The Progressive Relationship of Efficiency and Consent"	Valentine
	Scientific Management and Labor	Hoxie
1916	*Administration industrielle et genérale*	Fayol
	Industrial Leadership	Gantt
1917	*In Days to Come*	Rathenau
	Lectures in Industrial Psychology	Muscio
	Scientific Office Management	Leffingwell
	The Taylor System in Franklin Management	Babcock
1918	*The New Economy*	Rathenau
	Present-Day Applications of Psychology	Myers
1920	*Advice to Students of the National Colleges Wishing to Familiarize Themselves with the Methods of Scientific Management in Industry*	Le Chatelier
	Graphic Production Control	Knoeppel
	Lectures in Industrial Administration	Muscio
1921	*The Human Factor in Business: Experiments in Industrial Democracy*	Rowntree
1922	*Budgetary Control*	McKinsey
	"Ten Years' Progress in Management"	Alford
1923	*The Philosophy of Management*	Sheldon
1924	*Management's Handbook*	Alford

	Manual of Standard Processing Times	Hegner
1925	*Office Management Principles and Practice*	Leffingwell
1926	*The New Leadership in Industry*	Lewisohn
	Profit Sharing and Stock Ownership for Employees	Dennison
1927	"Ten Years of Standardization in Germany"	Hellmich
1928	*Dictionary of Industrial Administration*	Lee
1928 on	*Prospérité*	Michelin Brothers
1929	*The Art of Management*	Gérard
1930	*The Model Stock Plan*	Filene
	Education for Business Management	Bowie
1931	*Organization Engineering*	Dennison
	Rationalization and the World Economic System	Streeruwitz
1932	"American Schools of Business"	Bowie
	The Chief Executive: His Training and Task	Carrard
1933	*The Human Problems of an Industrial Civilization*	Mayo
	Profit Engineering	Knoeppel
	Psychotechnics	Sollier
	The Second REFA Book	Meyenberg
1934	*Cost and Production Handbook*	Alford
	The Flexible Budget	Williams
1935	"Management and the Optimum"	Hopf
	Scientific Management	Landauer
1937	*Economic History of Brazil*	Simonsen
	A Man's Profession	Dautry
1942	"Twenty-five Years of Standardization in Germany"	Hellmich
1943–1945	"New Perspectives in Management"	Hopf
1944	*Production Handbook*	Alford and Clark
1945	*The Social Problems of an Industrial Civilization*	Mayo
1946	"Adapting the Industrial Organization to Changing Conditions"	Hopf

1947	"Evolution in Organization During the Past Decade"	"
1949	"The Cultural Mission of the Engineer"	Hellmich
1950	*Management Research in Retailing*	Pasdermadjian
1952	*Organization as Civilization*	Mauro
1954	*The Department Store*	Pasdermadjian

Appendix II

Select Bibliography
(publications dealing wholly or in part with the history of management, used in preparing this volume)

	Name of pioneer or subject about which information is given or references are made
ALFORD, Leon P., *Henry Laurence Gantt, Leader in Industry*. Memorial volume published by The American Society of Mechanical Engineers. New York: Harper, 1934. 310 pp.	*Gantt*
AMERICAN MANAGEMENT ASSOCIATION, *25 Years of Management Progress*. New York: AMA, 1948. 16 pp.	*Dodd, Lewisohn, McKinsey*
AMERICAN SOCIETY OF MECHANICAL ENGINEERS, *History of Scientific Management in America*. Prepared for 1938 International Management Congress by H. S. Dennison, H. P. Dutton, H. P. Kendall, H. S. Person, and S. E. Thompson. New York: *Mechanical Engineering*, September 1939. 10 pp.	*History of management in the United States*
BABBAGE, Charles, *Passages from the Life of a Philosopher*. London: Longmans, Green, 1864. 496 pp.	*Babbage*

	Name of pioneer or subject about which information is given or references are made
CANNONS, H. G. T., *Bibliography of Industrial Efficiency and Factory Management.* London: Routledge, 1920. 167 pp.	*Bibliography of management publications in English*
CHEVALIER, J., and PEHUET, Louis, *L'Organisation du travail en France depuis cent ans.* Paris: Comité National de l'Organisation Française, 1949. 58 pp.	*History of management in France*
CIOS (Comité International de l'Organisation Scientifique), *Manual.* Second edition, 1952–1953. Geneva: CIOS. 80 pp. See historical chapter, pp. 23–30.	*History of international management movement*
CITE UNIVERSITAIRE, *Hommage à Raoul Dautry.* Paris: 1952. 35 pp.	*Dautry*
CLARK, Pearl Franklin (Mrs. Wallace), *The Challenge of American Know-How.* New York: Harper, 1948. 172 pp.	*Clark*
COLE, Margaret, *Robert Owen of New Lanark.* London: Batchworth Press, 1953. 231 pp.	*Owen*
COMITE NATIONAL DE L'ORGANISATION FRANÇAISE, *Promotion les Frères Michelin.* Paris: 1951. 26 pp.	*Michelin Brothers*
COPLEY, Frank Barkley, *Frederick W. Taylor.* New York and London: Harper, for the Taylor Society, 1923. 2 vols., 472 and 467 pp.	*Taylor and history of management in United States, with mention of many other pioneers*
DENNISON MANUFACTURING CO., *Henry S. Dennison.* Memorial booklet. Framingham, Mass.: 1952.	*Dennison*

	Name of pioneer or subject about which information is given or references are made
DICTIONARY OF AMERICAN BIOGRAPHY. New York: Scribner, 1928–1937. 20 vols.	*Follett, Gantt, Halsey, Hoxie, Münsterberg, Taylor, Towne, Valentine*
DICTIONARY OF NATIONAL BIOGRAPHY. London: Oxford University Press, 1908–1909. 22 vols. and supplement.	*Babbage, Lee, Owen*
DRURY, Horace Bookwalter, *Scientific Management: A History and Criticism.* New York: Longmans, Green, for Columbia University, 1915. Second edition, 1918.	*History of management in the United States*
DUPONT, J. B., "Outline of the Present Position of Applied Psychology in Switzerland," *Bulletin* of the Association Internationale de Psychotechnique (Psychologie Appliquée), Paris, Vol. 3, No. 2, July–December 1954.	*Carrard*
DUTTON, Henry P., "A History of Scientific Management in the United States of America," in *Advanced Management.* Society for the Advancement of Management (New York), October 1953.	*History of management in United States*
FORTUNE (New York), *The Fruitful Errors of Elton Mayo . . . Who Proposes to Management and Labor a Social Basis for Industrial Peace,* November 1946.	*Mayo*
FREMINVILLE, Charles de, "Evolution de l'organisation scientifique du travail," *Revue de métallurgie* (Paris), April–May 1926.	*History of management in France*
GILBRETH, Frank B., and Ernestine CAREY, *Cheaper by the Dozen.* London, Melbourne, Toronto: Heinemann, 1949. 247 pp. Also *Belles on Their Toes,* Heinemann, 1950.	*Gilbreth*

	Name of pioneer or subject about which information is given or references are made
GILBRETH, Lillian Moller (Mrs. Frank B.), *The Quest of the One Best Way*. Chicago: Society of Industrial Engineers, 1924. Published privately. 64 pp.	*Gilbreth*
HAYES, E. P., and Charlotte HEATH, *History of The Dennison Manufacturing Company*. Cambridge, Mass.: Harvard University Press, for the Business Historical Society and the Harvard Graduate School of Business Administration, 1930. 202 pp.	*Dennison*
HOPF, Harry Arthur, "Historical Perspectives in Management." Ossining, N.Y.: Hopf Institute of Management Publication No. 7, 1947. 38 pp.	*International history of management*
——————, "Soundings in the Literature of Management—Fifty Books the Educated Practioner Should Know." Ossining, N.Y.: Hopf Institute of Management, Publication No. 9, 1949.	*Bibliography of management publications in English*
——————, "The Management Movement at the Crossroads." Ossining, N.Y.: Hopf Institute of Management, 1933. 28 pp.	*History of international management movement*
HOPF INSTITUTE OF MANAGEMENT, *Net Results*, periodical published at Ossining, N.Y. See Vol. 23, Nos. 9 and 10, September–October 1948, and Vol. 24, No. 5, October 1949 (biographical and obituary issues).	*Hopf*
HUNT, Edward Eyre (editor), *Scientific Management Since Taylor*. New York: McGraw-Hill, 1924. 263 pp.	*History of management in United States*

	Name of pioneer or subject about which information is given or references are made
INDUSTRIFORBUNDETS RATIONALISERINGSKONTOR AS, *Rationalization in Denmark, Finland, Norway, and Sweden.* Oslo: 1954. 30 pp.	*History of management in Scandinavia*
INSTITUT DES HAUTES ETUDES DE BELGIQUE, *Discours prononcés à la mémoire du Docteur Paul Sollier.* Brussels: February 8, 1934.	*Sollier*
JOHNSON, Gerald W., *Liberal's Progress.* New York: Coward-McCann, 1948. 268 pp.	*Filene*
KESSLER, Harry Graf, *Walther Rathenau. Sein Leben und sein Werk.* London: Gerald Howe, 1929.	*Rathenau*
KIMBALL, Dexter S., *I Remember.* New York: McGraw-Hill, 1953. 259 pp.	*Kimball*
LADAME, Mary, *The Filene Store.* New York: Russell Sage Foundation, 1930. 541 pp.	*Filene*
LEENER, de, *Un Grand Belge—Ernest Solvay.* Brussels: Office de Publicité, 1942.	*Solvay*
LEWISOHN, Sam A. Memorial booklet published by family and friends. Stamford, Conn: Overbrook Press, September 1951. 50 pp.	*Lewisohn*
MASON, Alpheus Thomas, *Brandeis: A Free Man's Life.* New York: Viking, 1946. 714 pp.	*Brandeis*
METCALFE, H. C., and URWICK, L. (editors), *Dynamic Administration,* by Mary Parker Follett. London: Pitman, 1949. 320 pp.	*Introductory chapter summarizing life and work of Mary Parker Follett*
MICHELIN & CIE, *Edouard Michelin.* Memorial booklet (privately printed), 1940. 20 pp.	*Michelin*

	Name of pioneer or subject about which information is given or references are made
MÜNSTERBERG, Margaret, *Hugo Münsterberg. His Life and Work.* New York: Appleton, 1922. 462 pp.	*Münsterberg*
MURCHISON, Carl, (editor), *A History of Psychology in Autobiography* (including a 15-page biographical sketch by C. S. Myers). Worcester, Mass.: Clark University Press, 1936. London: Oxford University Press, 1936.	*Myers*
NATIONAL CYCLOPAEDIA OF AMERICAN BIOGRAPHY. New York: James T. White & Co., 1932. 35 vols.	*Alford, Brandeis, Clark, Dodge, Filene, Kimball, Münsterberg, Smith, Taylor, Towne*
NATIONAL MANAGEMENT COUNCIL OF THE U.S.A., *Harry Arthur Hopf, Fifth CIOS Gold Medalist.* New York: 1940. 48 pp.	*Hopf*
OWEN, Robert, *The Life of Robert Owen.* Autobiography. London: Effingham & Wilson, 1857–1878. 2 vols.	*Owen*
PEHUET, Louis, "Un Chef qui était un homme—M. Raoul Dautry," *Journal* of the Comité National de l'Organisation Française, November 1951.	*Dautry*
PODMORE, Frank, *Robert Owen.* London: Allen & Unwin, 1924, 667 pp.	*Owen*
REICHSKURATORIUM FÜR WIRTSCHAFTLICHKEIT, *Handbuch der Rationalisierung,* Berlin: 1930.	*International history of management*
REVUE DE METALLURGIE, memorial issue devoted to Henry Le Chatelier, Vol. 35, January 1937.	*Le Chatelier*

	Name of pioneer or subject about which information is given or references are made
ROBACK, A. A., *History of American Psychology.* New York: Library Publishers, 1952, 425 pp.	*Münsterberg*
ROLL, Erich, *An Early Experiment in Industrial Organization.* London: Longmans, Green, 1930. 320 pp.	*Boulton, Jr. and Watt, Jr.*
ROSE, T. G., *A History of the Institute of Industrial Administration.* London: Pitman, 1954. 204 pp.	*Bowie, Elbourne, and history of management movement in Britain since 1920*
ROWNTREE & CO., *B. Seebohm Rowntree, 1871–1954. In memoriam.* York: 1954. 36 pp.	*Rowntree*
SALES APPEAL (London), November–December 1953.	*Michelin*
SHAW, Anne G., *The Purpose and Practice of Motion Study.* Manchester, Eng.: Harlequin Press, 1952. 311 pp.	*Gilbreth*
SIMPSON, Robert G., *Case Studies in Management Development.* New York: American Management Association, 1954. 140 pp. See Chapter IX, "The Dennison Manufacturing Company."	*Dennison*
SOLOMONS, David, *Studies in Costing,* London: Sweet & Maxwell, 1952, 643 pp.	*Church, Emerson*
STEVENS INSTITUTE OF TECHNOLOGY. *Classified Guide to the Taylor Collection.* New York: The American Society of Mechanical Engineers, 1951	*Taylor*
TAYLOR SOCIETY (now Society for the Advancement of Management), *Frederick Winslow Taylor: A Memorial Volume.* New York: 1920. 108 pp.	*Taylor*

	Name of pioneer or subject about which information is given or references are made
THOMPSON, C. Bertrand, *Scientific Management.* Cambridge, Mass.: Harvard University Press, 1914. London: Oxford University Press, 1914. 878 pp.	*Early history of scientific management in United States and selected articles by early pioneers*
TORRENCE, George P., *James Mapes Dodge: Mechanical Engineer, Pioneer in Industry.* New York, San Francisco, Montreal: Newcomen Society in North America, 1950. 24 pp.	*Dodge*
URWICK, L., *Management's Debt to the Engineer.* Calvin W. Rice Lecture, September 1952. New York: The American Society of Mechanical Engineers. Reprinted from *Mechanical Engineering,* May 1953. 7 pp.	*History of management in the United States*
———, *The Development of Scientific Management in Great Britain.* Report distributed to members of the Seventh International Management Congress, 1938. London: *British Management Review,* Vol III, No 4 (reprinted as separate booklet). 85 pp.	*British pioneers including appendix devoted to Hans Renold*
———, and BRECH, E. F. L., *The Making of Scientific Management:* Vol. I, *Thirteen Pioneers,* 196 pp. (latest edition, 1951); Vol. II, *Management in British Industry,* 242 pp. (latest edition, 1953); and Vol. III, *The Hawthorne Investigations,* 226 pp. (latest edition, 1949). London: Pitman.	*International history of management; mention of Babbage, Dennison, Elbourne, Fayol, Follett, Fréminville, Gantt, Gilbreth, Le Chatelier, Rathenau, Rowntree, Taylor (Vol. I); Boulton and Watt, Lewis, Mayo (Vol. III), Owen and Renold (Vol. II)*

	Name of pioneer or subject about which information is given or references are made
VERNEY, Henry, *Un Grand Ingenieur—Henri Fayol.* Paris: Société Armicale des Anciens Elèves de l'Ecole Nationale des Mines de St. Etienne, 1925. Circular No. 188, recording speeches at testimonial dinner. 51 pp.	*Fayol*
VITELES, Morris S., *Industrial Psychology.* New York: W. W. Norton, 1932. 652 pp.	*Münsterberg*
WHO WAS WHO IN AMERICA: Vol. I, 1897–1942; Vol. II, 1943–1950. Chicago: A. N. Marquis, 1942 and 1950.	*Alford, Barth, Clark, Diemer, Emerson, Filene, Gilbreth, Halsey, Hathaway, Hopf, Hoxie, Leffingwell, McKinsey, Münsterberg, Smith, Taylor, Thompson, Towne, Valentine, Williams*
WHO'S WHO IN ENGINEERING. New York: Lewis Historical Publishing Co., 1942–1948.	*Barth, Clark, Diemer, Hathaway, Hopf, Kimball, Thompson*
YOST, Edna, *Frank and Lillian Gilbreth; Partners for Life.* New York: The American Society of Mechanical Engineers, 1949. New Brunswick, N.J.: Rutgers University Press, 1949.	*Gilbreth*

Part Two

William B. Wolf, Editor

Preface to Part Two

IN 1956, the first version of *The Golden Book of Management* was published. Now, almost 30 years later, a second, expanded version is being presented.

As conceived by Lt. Col. Lyndall F. Urwick, the *Golden Book* is an honor roll of the "greats" in the field of management. To be selected for inclusion in this book, a person must (1) have made a significant contribution to management, (2) have given tangible evidence of that contribution in the form of published work, and (3) no longer be living. The overriding goal has been to catalog significant contributors and to suggest, as nearly as possible, the essence of their respective contributions. These were the guidelines set up by Col. Urwick in developing and compiling the first *Golden Book*. His success in adhering to them is evident in the usefulness of the volume, the regard in which it is held, and the numerous references to it in the literature.

In this second *Golden Book*, I have attempted to be faithful to Col. Urwick's editorial policies. It has been my goal, in expanding the original honor roll of the world's greats in the field of management, to apply the same criteria for inclusion in the new, larger volume.

The process for obtaining nominees was as follows: CIOS chapters throughout the world were canvassed; I wrote personally to each organization requesting nominees. This appeal was later reinforced by a request from Alfred Lederer, Managing Director of CIOS. Furthermore, a committee consisting of David Moore, Alfred Lederer, the late Harold F. Smiddy, and James L. Hayes suggested additional nominees and gave me valuable editorial advice.

As names were received, a preliminary screening took place. Usually a data sheet was written up for each nominee, and this was sent to the International Academy of Management *Golden Book* Committee. A special committee, established in 1976 by Harold Koontz, Chancellor of the International Academy of Management, selected those persons who would be added to Col. Urwick's list. The Chairman of the International Committee was Dr. John F. Mee, distinguished American Professor Emeritus of Indiana University's Graduate School of Business. The other members were Dr. Kalyan S. Basu, Dr. Ernest Dale, Dr. Paul M. Haenni, Dr. Harold Koontz (ex officio), Dr. Peter Kuin, Dr. John Marsh, Dr. Anton E. Rupert, Dr. Flavio P. Sampaio, the late Dr. Harold F. Smiddy, Dr. Susumu Takamiya, and Col. Urwick himself.

Sir Walter Scott, former Chancellor of the International Academy of Management, paid me the compliment of appointing me Editor of the new *Golden Book.* This gave impetus to the project. As the work proceeded, Harold Koontz provided important backup and support. James L. Hayes has at all times been available, not only for general guidance and editorial help, but for the emotional kind of backing that is necessary to so large a task. Harold Smiddy, until his untimely death, had been an invaluable adviser and supporter, as have David Moore, Alfred Lederer, Ernest Dale, Kisou Tasugi, Arthur Bedeian, Ronald Greenwood, Charles Wrege, Terry Schuster, and many others.

Early in the project it was decided that the expanded *Golden Book of Management* should consist of a single two-part volume. Part One would present the original *Golden Book* essentially as Col. Urwick planned and wrote it. Part Two would embody additional entries approved by the International *Golden Book* Committee. This decision reflected the desire of all those concerned to preserve the Colonel's work as a distinct, recognizable entity, and every effort has been made in designing the combined volume to achieve that end.

There have been numerous successful entrepreneurs in the decades since 1956. However, the International Committee has sought consciously to live up to the strict criteria for selection which Col. Urwick set himself. As a result, eminent industrialists who were doers but who did not publish significant works are not included.

I wish to express my appreciation for the inspiration and help given by Lt. Col. Lyndall F. Urwick. He himself is one of the true pioneers of the management movement. He, more than any other person, has been responsible for bringing to the fore the significant contributions to management. The world of management is indebted to him for his own books and for his efforts in bringing to universal attention the work of Follett, Fayol, Graicunas, Mooney, and others—and for the *Golden Book* in both its first and this, its second, appearance.

WILLIAM B. WOLF
Laguna Beach, California

Editor's Acknowledgments

INEVITABLY, given a project with the dimensions of a new and expanded *Golden Book*, the Editor has to call on numerous individuals and groups for help. I am grateful to all those organizations, executives both active and retired, librarians, management historians and consultants, and friends, relatives, and colleagues of the pioneers themselves to whom we appealed.

First of all I wish to cite the members of the History of Management Division of the Academy of Management who participated in the actual work of writing: Arthur C. Bedeian, of Auburn University; Ronald G. Greenwood, of the University of Wisconsin at La Crosse; Harold Koontz, of the University of California at Los Angeles and Chancellor of the International Academy of Management; Charles D. Wrege, of Rutgers University; and George F. F. Lombard, of Harvard. Each of them wrote one or more of the biographical sketches on the basis of special knowledge of the individual in question.

In addition, there were numerous other people who contributed necessary information on our selected group of management "greats." Ernest Dale was helpful with material on Clarence Bertrand Thompson. Peter Drucker provided valuable information about Donaldson Brown, Harold F. Smiddy, and Ralph J. Cordiner. Mrs. Douglas McGregor, Ms. Patricia McPherson, and Professor Charles Myers supplied valuable data on Douglas McGregor. Mrs. Diana Tead Michaelis was helpful with information on her father, and Mrs. Gertrude Weiss Lewin provided materials on her late husband. Harold Smiddy, who is himself included as a *Golden Book* "great," before his death shared with Ron Greenwood his thoughts, impressions, and reminiscences of General Electric's Ralph Cordiner.

In Japan, Dr. Susumu Takamiya, Dr. Kisou Tasugi, and Osamu Mano not only supplied information on Keiji Baba, Yasutaro Hirai, Yojiro Masuchi, Fukumatsu Muramoto, Torao Nakanishi, Teijiro Ueda, and Yoichi Ueno, but also wrote several of the profiles.

In Brussels, Michael A. Johnson, Director of Corporate Affairs for Management Centre Europe, undertook the job of encouraging added nominations from both Britain and the Continent. Later he made efforts far beyond the call of duty to supply leads and actual information on those candidates who were finally selected. We particularly thank M. Jacques Baruzy, of the Association de Management Française, for the material on Louis Armand sent us through Mr. Johnson; Myrna Bustani, of London, for extensive information on her father, Emile Bustani; G. Delalande, of the Secrétariat of the Comité Hyacinthe Dubreuil, Paris, for personal impressions of Dubreuil especially written by M. Max Richard of the Comité and greatly appreciated; Eivind Hellern, of Oslo, for abundant information on his father, Bernhard Hellern; Jacqueline Lusseyran, Chef de la Biblioteque, Institut Européen d'Administration des Affaires, Fontainebleau, for supplementary facts on Armand, Dubreuil, and Rolf Nordling; the Olivetti Company, Ivrea, Italy, for a specially prepared biography of Adriano Olivetti; Gerhard Stoltz, Rector of the Norges Handelshøyskole, in Bergen, for information on Bernhard Hellern; and Dr. Sigfrid von Weiher, of the Siemens Museum in Munich, for biographical data and a complete bibliography, with actual copies, of publications by Carl Friedrich von Siemens.

Obtaining usable photographs was difficult; so we are doubly grateful to the family members and others who made them available to us. Ron Greenwood, at the University of Wisconsin (La Crosse), has literally made himself responsible for finding as many photos as possible; we cannot thank him enough for his interest and assistance. Among the many individuals and organizations that also have lent or contributed photographs are Myrna Bustani (Emile Bustani), Comité Hyacinthe Dubreuil (Dubreuil), Mrs. Richard Feiss (Horace King Hathaway and Harlow Stafford Person), Eivind Hellern (Bernhard Hellern), John P. Kendall (Henry Plimpton Kendall), Professor Masuchi, Japan (Yojiro Masuchi), Ann B. Michaels, Chief Librarian of the Johns-Manville Corporate Information Center (Alvin McCreary Brown), the Olivetti Company (Adriano Olivetti), Mrs. Harold F. Smiddy (Harold F. Smiddy), and Dr. Sigfrid von Weiher of the Siemens Museum (Carl Friedrich von Siemens).

We are indebted to Anne Skagen, of the AMACOM editorial staff, for translating the material on Bernhard Hellern from the original Norwegian. And we owe very special thanks to Elizabeth T. Massey, who responded nobly to our last-minute need for Japanese translation and not only translated the crucial materials but supplemented them with her own research and presented the results in the required form within barely a week.

Finally, I wish to thank Elizabeth Marting, AMACOM Vice-President Emerita and now a publishing and editorial consultant and writer, for the work she did in bringing the manuscript to completion. She labored diligently with everyone involved in the project to ensure that the manuscript would be as correct as care could make it, well written and edited, and assembled with a view to maximum usefulness and attractiveness yet with all due respect for Lyn Urwick's original inspiration. Not only did she personally translate the materials received from Europe in French, German, and Italian, but she wrote or edited all the European profiles.

Most of all, however, I must express my thanks and appreciation to Lyn Urwick himself, Editor (with a capital "E") of the first *Golden Book*. Through the long years of planning and compiling this new version, he has been an active supporter of all our efforts. Without his interest, his cooperation, and his dedication to management, this book could never have been published.

W. B. W.

Authorship of Individual Entries (in order of listing)

ALFRED WEBER (Elizabeth Marting); FRIEDRICH EDLER VON GOTTL-OTTLILIENFELD (Elizabeth Marting); WALTER DILL SCOTT (William B. Wolf); MORRIS LLEWELLYN COOKE (C. D. Wrege); CARL FRIEDRICH VON SIEMENS (Elizabeth Marting); EUGEN SCHMALENBACH (Elizabeth Marting); HARLOW STAFFORD PERSON (William B. Wolf); ALFRED PRITCHARD SLOAN, JR. (William B. Wolf); HENRY PLIMPTON KENDALL (Arthur C. Bedeian); LILLIAN MOLLER GILBRETH (William B. Wolf and Harold Koontz); TEIJIRO UEDA (Kisou Tasugi and Elizabeth T. Massey); CLARENCE BERTRAND THOMPSON (Ronald G. Greenwood); HYACINTHE JOSEPH DUBREUIL (Elizabeth Marting); YOICHI UENO (Ichiro Ueno and Susumu Takamiya); JAMES DAVID MOONEY (William B. Wolf); F. DONALDSON BROWN (William B. Wolf); CHESTER IRVING BARNARD (William B. Wolf); ERWIN HASKELL SCHELL (William B. Wolf); FUKUMATSU MURAMOTO (Elizabeth T. Massey); KURT LEWIN (William B. Wolf); ORDWAY TEAD (Arthur C. Bedeian); ROLF NORDLING (Elizabeth Marting); ALVIN McCREARY BROWN (John F. Mee); TORAO NAKANISHI (Tatsu Nabeshima and Susumu Takamiya); BERNHARD HELLERN (Elizabeth Marting); CHARLES PERRY McCORMICK (William B. Wolf); YASUTARO HIRAI (Kisou Tasugi and Elizabeth T. Massey); YOJIRO MASUCHI (Kisou Tasugi); KEIJI BABA (Susumu Takamiya); FRITZ J. ROETHLISBERGER (George F. F. Lombard); RALPH JARRON CORDINER (Ronald G. Greenwood); HAROLD FRANCIS SMIDDY (Ronald G. Greenwood); ADRIANO OLIVETTI (Olivetti Company); RENSIS LIKERT (David G. Bowers); LOUIS-FRANÇOIS ARMAND (Elizabeth Marting); DOUGLAS McGREGOR (William B. Wolf); EMILE BUSTANI (Elizabeth Marting); BARRY M. RICHMAN (Harold Koontz and William B. Wolf).

Contents

(Part Two)

Names are arranged chronologically by date of birth. For an alphabetical listing, see Master Contents, pp. v–vii, for Parts One and Two combined.

Alfred Weber
(1868–1958)
Germany

EARLY in this century, Alfred Weber developed and published his *Reine Theorie des Standorts*; that is, the famous theory of industry location to which he attributed the movement of large numbers of people into certain geographic areas, particularly since the Industrial Revolution in the second half of the 1800s and certainly in modern times. It is a theory basic to a sound understanding of the problems involved in managing today's great monolithic, often international institutions. It is Alfred Weber's important contribution to the thinking that underlies management practice as we know and practic it today.

Alfred Weber, political economist and sociologist, was the second son of Max Weber, liberal politician and a member of the Prussian provincial diet and the Berlin city council. Alfred's mother, Frau Helene Weber, came from a prominent liberal family and, in Berlin, was active in social-welfare work. Then there was brother Max, four years older than Alfred. Both had noteworthy academic careers and shared much the same interests: chiefly the social sciences and, with passionate conviction, politics.

After lecturing in turn at the University of Berlin and at Charles University in Prague, Alfred Weber was offered an appointment by Heidelberg. Here, in 1909, he unveiled his theory of industry location. He used as his basis the work of an earlier scholar, Johann Heinrich von Thünen, on factors that influenced the location of agriculture. Recasting von Thünen's ideas in an industrial context, Weber proceeded to apply them to an analysis of location factors in the development and legal status of various industries. The book *Über den Standort der Industrien* (On Industry Location) is in fact the product of research on German centers of industry from 1860 on.

Weber begins by differentiating in abstract terms among location factors generally. Next he discusses transportation and the nature of the work as specific factors of importance in attracting industry. In this way he arrives at a consideration of the laws affecting the agglomeration of people in given locations—together with the economic and social conditions that bring them there. Thus the resulting theory—which he calls *reine*, meaning "pure," "unadulterable," or "absolute"—comes close to being a model of historical reality. Weber explores the interrelationships of all these factors—transportation, work, agglomeration, and the rest—so as to identify stages in the growth of manufacturing. In the process, he achieves not only a theory concerning the location of industry but also a tenable theory of economic growth.

Alfred Weber himself believed that knowledge of the factors in industry location was a key to the universal sociological phenomenon of today's aggregations of people as well as a whole array of other social and cultural forces of our time. He therefore used hypotheses built about these forces to make economic and political judgments concerning the dynamics of world economy. He further believed that the study he had made of the increasing tendency of people in our modern-day culture to gravitate into the great industrial centers, thereby aggravating and augmenting the world's social ills, proved that this and other such problems could be explained by economic theory and dealt with accordingly. He also saw his research thus far as a bridge between the theoretical and the historical aspects of political economy. In any case, he made it a point of departure for his later explorations of historical sociology.

A glance at the titles of some of Weber's publications suggests the breadth of his thinking: for example, *Religion und Kultur* (Religion and Culture) in 1912 and, much later, the article "Über die moderne Kunst und ihr Publikum" (On Modern Art and Its Public). But Weber also, in his *Einführung in die Soziologie* (Introduction to Sociology), developed principles and methods of cultural sociology for use in explaining both historical and contemporary phenomena.

By the 1920s, however, much of Weber's output mirrors his political concerns and his fears for the future of not only his own country but all Europe. He writes, now, on *Deutschland und die europäische Kulturkrise* (Germany and the European Cultural Crisis) and *Die Krise des modernen Staatsgedanken in Europa* (The Crisis of Modern Political Thought in Europe). After 1933, of course, no German publisher could have touched such subject matter—at least not openly. Weber, who was retired prematurely by the University of Heidelberg soon after Hitler came to power, suspended all academic activity while the National Socialists tightened their grip on the German people, World War II was launched and very nearly won before it was lost, and Germany herself was occupied while the Führer committed suicide in his bunker under Berlin. At least one Weber book seems to have been published during this period in the Netherlands, secretly or not, and reissued 15 years later in Munich, but for the most part the writer was silent.

He was hopeful even so. He could scarcely have foreseen the full horror of the Hitler years, but he had followed closely the political events that paved the way for the Third Reich and he had sensed the conflict between economic growth and politics on the one hand and between human rights and nationalism on the other. In his eyes, the catastrophe he lived through was far from exclusively German but, rather, European. The war that brought about the total loss of political strength in Europe was likewise responsible for the collapse of its intellectual tradition. Communism and fascism were the aftermath of Europe's one-time political thinking, now disintegrated. Final victory over both these antidemocratic forces therefore lay in reviving a political consciousness that would be not just national but European—indeed, universal.

Meanwhile, in 1945, Weber went back to his teaching. It had been 12 years since he "retired"; he was approaching his late seventies when, assisted by some of his students, he wrote the introductory text that would be his last important contribution to the field of sociology.

Perhaps his theory of industry location, Weber's significant contribution to management, will become all the more meaningful as more and more people continue to crowd into the world's large centers of population and the resulting problems—personal, social, economic, and political—become unsolvable to a degree that Alfred Weber in the year 1909 would never have dreamed possible.—ELIZABETH MARTING

SELECTED PUBLICATIONS

Books and Pamphlets:

1909 *Über den Standort der Industrien. I: Reine Theorie des Standorts* (On Industry Location. I: Absolute Theory of Location). Tübingen. Reprinted in 1922.

1911 *Die Standortlehre und die Handelspolitik* (Location Theory and Business Politics). Tübingen.

1924 *Deutschland und die europäische Kulturkrise* (Germany and the European Cultural Crisis). Berlin.

1925 *Die Krise des modernen Staatsgedanken in Europa* (The Crisis of Modern Political Thought in Europe). Stuttgart, Berlin, and Leipzig.

1927 *Ideen zur Staats- und Kultursoziologie* (Ideas on Political and Cultural Sociology). Karlsruhe.

1931 *Kultursoziologie* (Cultural Sociology). Stuttgart. Reprinted in 1959.

1935 *Kulturgeschichte als Kultursoziologie* (Cultural History as Cultural Scoiology). Leiden (Netherlands). Reissued as of 1950 in Munich; reprinted in 1960.

1943 *Das Tragische und die Geschichte* (Tragedy and History). Hamburg. Reprinted in 1959.

1946 *Abschied von der bisherigen Geschichte. Überwindung des Nihilismus?* (Farewell to History So far. The Victory of Nihilism?). Bern and Hamburg.

1953 *Der dritte oder der vierte Mensch. Vom Sinn des geschichtlichen Daseins* (The Third or the Fourth Man. On the Meaning of Historical Existence). Munich.

1955 *Einführung in die Soziologie* (Introduction to Sociology). Written in collaboration with students. Munich.

Speeches and Articles:

1912 *Religion und Kultur* (Religion and Culture). A speech. Jena.

1920–1921 *Prinzipielles zur Kultursoziologie* (Principles of Cultural Sociology). Tübingen.

1931 *Das Ende der Demokratie? Ein Vortrag* (The End of Democracy? A Lecture). Berlin.

1955 "Über die moderne Kunst und ihr Publikum" (On Modern Art and Its Public), in Gottfried Eisermann, ed., *Wirtschaft und Kultursystem* (Economics and Cultural System). Erlenbach-Zurich and Stuttgart.

1960 "Soziologie" (Sociology), in Golo Mann, ed., *Propyläen-Weltgeschichte, IX: Das 20. Jahrhundert* (Propylaea World History, Vol. IX, The Twentieth Century). Berlin.

Curriculum Vitae

1868 Born on July 30th in Erfurt.

1899 Qualified to lecture on political economics at University of Berlin.

1904 Became Professor, Charles University, Prague.

1907 Moved to University of Heidelberg.

1933 Retired prematurely from University because of conflict with National Socialist Party when it came to power.

1945 Resumed academic activities.

1958 Died on May 2nd, aged 89, in Heidelberg.

Friedrich Edler von Gottl-Ottlilienfeld
(1868–1958)
Austria/Germany

PROFESSOR Friedrich von Gottl-Ottlilienfeld, in the context of the German rationalization movement, is remembered for his lifelong efforts to move dogmatic philosophy in the direction of its pragmatic application. He strove consistently to do away with scientific management's somewhat "sterile" image and present it as a reasonable—even a valuable—tool.

Son of an Austrian general, von Gottl-Ottlilienfeld was born in Vienna. During his school years he showed great mathematical and technical abilities along with a marked feeling for history. At the universities of Vienna, Berlin, and Heidelberg, this unusual combination of scientific interests with studies in political economy and history soon led to his unique field of specialization—the boundary area between economics and technology. His early studies; his doctoral dissertation at Heidelberg, in which he calls the value concept "an obscure dogma of political economy"; his founding of the first German engineering/economics institute at the Technische Hochschule in Munich; his later academic work—all these centered about the link between economics and technology that von Gottl-Ottlilienfeld believed it was his scientific duty to demonstrate.

Prevailing doctrine held that technological and production-oriented concerns lay completely outside the realm of economics. "Yet," wrote von Gottl-Ottlilienfeld,

> . . . economics is linked to technology in two ways. It is indebted to technology and to the engineers who provide it with information on existing possibilities and on ways and means of production, but it also is dependent on them for a realistic view of the final return on goods manufactured and sold. Moreover, engineering is indebted to economics, and is influenced by it, in a double sense. It owes to economics—in the form of problems—not only the basis for its development but a direct line to the realization of that development. For economics does not simply set problems for engineers, it also governs their solution.

Von Gottl-Ottlilienfeld's academic career took him from Heidelberg to Brünn—Brno in present-day Czechoslovakia—and eventually to Munich. Here, in addition to teaching at the Technische Hochschule and founding his engineering/economics institute, he advised the Bavarian government on industrial matters. With this highly desirable mixture of teaching, research, and consultation on the practical problems of encouraging industrial activity, von Gottl-Ottlilienfeld's theoretical knowledge expanded greatly. He understood more fully the relationship of technology, as embodied in engineering, to a dynamic industrial economy. The result was his *Grundriss der Sozialökonomik* (Groundplan of Social Economics), which first appeared in published form in 1914.

In this work, the author's grasp of the essentials of rationalization is fully apparent, along with his maturing analysis of man's basic independence of spirit throughout history. Thus von Gottl-Ottlilienfeld is able to integrate the pioneering achievements of Taylor and his disciples into a serious, severely critical clarification of work and its management in the early twentieth century. He offers no collection or catalog of principles; rather, *Grundriss der Sozialökonomik* is remarkable for its systematization of methodically correct procedures for increasing the level of worker performance and its impact on overall effectiveness. Productive, profitable work therefore supplies the basis for a consistent theory of rationalization. At the same time, von Gottl-Ottlilienfeld acknowledges in complete scientific honesty the never-ceasing demand, on the part of management, that operations be speeded up. This sort of rationalization, he declares, too often produces a mere approximation of the hoped-for optimum results, and the true values to be gained from meeting rational goals are realized only marginally.

After the First World War, it was von Gottl-Ottlilienfeld's fate to find himself doing battle against the currents of the day, standing firm, in answer to his innermost convictions, against the forces of national and international disintegration. In his own country, he supported completely the efforts of the new Reichskuratorium für Wirtschaftlichkeit (National Trusteeship for Economic Affairs) to do away with the prejudices of German industrial leaders against scientific management, in particular by writing up the experiences of companies in other Western countries that were using its principles to good advantage. The RFW publication entitled *Vom Sinn der Rationalisierung* (Of the Common Sense of Rationalization) includes a representative selection of the lectures and essays in which von Gottl-Ottlilienfeld pleaded passionately for even a moderate, reasonable broadening of German rationalization.

Meanwhile, von Gottl-Ottlilienfeld's career continued. In 1919 he went to the University of Hamburg as Professor of Political Economy. From there he moved to Kiel and finally, in 1926, to Berlin, where he was simultaneously Professor of the Theory of Political Economy at the University and Honorary Professor at the Technische Hochschule of Charlottenburg until his retirement in 1938. Also, he was for 20 years a member of the Unterkommission für Universitäten (University Subcommission) in the Völkerbundskommission für Geistige Zusammenarbeit (League of Nations Commission for Intellectual Cooperation), and he participated in the Paris conferences organized to set up an international bibliography of the economic sciences.

Friedrich von Gottl-Ottlilienfeld died at Frankfurt am Main on October 19, 1958. He was then nearly 90 years old and had lived through the Second World War and the occupation of Germany by the Allied powers. Although his had been a minority view of the application of science to management, his intense convictions and the scholarly way in which he sought to advance his theories won him many supporters and national prominence.—ELIZABETH MARTING

SELECTED PUBLICATIONS

Books and Collections of Essays:

1897 *Der Wertgedanke, ein verhülltes Dogma der Nationalökonomie* (The Concept of Value, an Obscure Dogma of Political Economy). Doctoral dissertation. Jena.

1901 *Die Herrschaft des Wortes* (The Supremacy of Words). Jena.

1904 *Die Grenzen der Geschichte* (The Limits of History). Leipzig.

1914 *Wirtschaft und Technik* (Economics and Technology). Two volumes. Tübingen. Revised edition published in 1923. The famous *Grundriss der Sozialökonomik* (Groundplan of Social Economics) is Part II of Volume II.

1923 *Die wirkschaftliche Dimension* (The Economic Dimension). Jena.

1925 *Wirtschaft als Leben* (Economics as Life). Jena.

—— *Volksvermögen und Volkseinkommen* (National Capital and National Income). Jena.

1928 *Bedarf und Deckung* (Need and Its Fulfillment). Jena.

1929 *Vom Sinn der Rationalisierung* (Of the Common Sense of Rationalization). Jena: Reichskuratorium für Wirtschaftlichkeit.

1931 *Wirtschaft und Wissenschaft* (Economics and Science). Two volumes. Jena.

1932 *Der Mythus der Planwirtschaft* (The Myth of Economic Planning). Jena. Translated into Japanese in 1942.

1934 *Die Läuterung des nationalökonomischen Denkens als deutsche Aufgabe* (The

Clarification of Thinking on Political Economy as a German Duty). Berlin.

—— *Zeitfragen der Wirtschaft* (Economic Issues of the Times). Berlin.

1935 *Wesen und Grundbegriffe der Wirtschaft* (Essence and Basic Concepts of Economics). Leipzig. Translated into Japanese in 1938.

1936 *Volk, Staat, Wirtschaft und Recht* (People, State, Economics, and Law). Berlin. Translated into Japanese in 1939.

1937 *Vom Ringen nach Wirtschaftswissenschaft* (From Economic Struggle to Economic Science). Berlin.

—— *Wirtschaft* (Economics). Collected essays. Jena.

1939 *Theorie blickt in die Zeit* (Theory Looks into the Times). Four essays. Jena.

—— *Volkswirtschaftslehre* (Lessons in Political Economy). Berlin

—— *Wirtschaftspolitik und Theorie* (Politics and Theory of Economics). Berlin. Translated into Japanese in 1945.

1940 *Wirtschaft als Wissen, Tat, und Wehr* (Economics as Knowledge, Action, and Defense). Berlin.

1943 *Ewige Wirtschaft* (Enduring Economics). The basics. Two volumes. Berlin.

Articles and Lectures:

1910 "Der wirtschaftliche Charakter des technischen Arbeit" (The Economic Nature of Technological Work). Berlin.

1923 "Freiheit vom Worte" (Freedom from Words), in *Hauptprobleme der Soziologie* (Chief Problems of Sociology). Munich and Leipzig: M. Palyi.

1924 "Fordismus: Über Industrie und technische Vernunft" ("Fordism": On Industry and Technological Sense). Jena. Expanded edition published in 1926 by Kieler Vorträge.

—— "Technischer Fortschritt und Wirtschaftleben" (Technological Progress and Economic Life). Hamburg: *Hamburger Jahrbuch.*

Curriculum Vitae

1868 Born on November 13th in Vienna.

1897 Awarded Ph.D., University of Heidelberg.

1900 Appointed Lecturer at University of Heidelberg.

1902 Called to Technische Hochschule (School of Advanced Technology) in Brünn (then in Austria-Hungary; now Brno, Czechoslovakia) as a Special Professor.

1904 Became a regular professor at Brünn.

1908 Called to Technische Hochschule of Munich. While teaching there, consulted with Bavarian government on industrial matters.

1909 Founded engineering/economics institute at Technische Hochschule of Munich.

1919 Moved to University of Hamburg as Professor of Political Economy.

1924 Moved to University of Kiel.
1926 Became Professor of the Theory of Political Economy at the University of Berlin and Honorary Professor at the Technische Hochschule of Charlottenburg.
1938 Retired from teaching.
1958 Died on October 19th, aged almost 90, in Frankfurt am Main.

Courtesy Northwestern University Archives.

Walter Dill Scott
(1869–1955)
United States

WALTER Dill Scott was among those Americans who led the way in the application of psychology to industry. In 1901 he wrote one of the earliest-known series of articles on the psychology of advertising and, in so doing, became one of America's first industrial psychologists.

During 1917 Scott served as Director of the Bureau of Salesmanship Research at the Carnegie Institute of Technology. There he pioneered the development of tools to improve personnel management practices. He made notable contributions to the techniques of selecting employees and rating individuals for promotion. Later he adapted and refined these techniques for use by the U.S. Army during the First World War. Scott's selection and rating techniques, along with his system of classifying personnel, aided the war effort and were the forerunners of more general applications in American industry. Through his teaching, writing, and consulting, he was a central force in the use of psychology by business managers. The book *Personnel Management*, which he wrote in 1923, was one of the most comprehensive treatments of advanced personnel management in its day. It helped educate numerous students and practitioners.

Walter Dill Scott was raised on a farm and early in his life learned to accept responsibility. His father was an invalid, and from the time he was six years old Walter helped with the chores. When he was 14, he took over practically the whole job of managing the family farm. His sister Louise tutored him and thus provided him with a rudimentary education, but his formal education did not begin until 1888, when he undertook a high-school-level course at Illinois State Normal. Three years later, at age 22, he had earned his diploma.

Walter then went to Northwestern University on a scholarship of $15 per term. There he had a classic education—Latin, Greek, English literature, German, French, chemistry, Bible theology, ethics, and philosophy. At Northwestern, too, he was active in campus affairs. He was a guard on the varsity football team, a member of the editorial board of *Syllabus*, vice-president of the student literary society, president of the university YMCA, a member of the Settlement Committee, and president of his senior class. In addition, he found time to act in campus plays and win election to Phi Beta Kappa.

After graduating from Northwestern, Walter Dill Scott attended McCormick Theological Seminary. He was preparing himself to become a teacher and missionary in the American College in China. However, when he finished his studies at McCormick, he decided to become a psychologist. He was 29 years old when he went to Germany to study. He first attended the University of Leipzig to study under Professor Wilhelm Wundt, the father of modern psychology. Scott wrote his doctoral thesis under Professor Wundt and, in 1900, was awarded his Ph.D. Afterward, from 1900 to 1916, he taught psychology at Northwestern University.

As a professor, Scott wrote extensively; he was extremely productive. As early as 1915 his publications numbered 107 items! Of these, 67 were directly related to problems of business.

Scott's first book was *The Theory and Practice of Advertising*.[1] This was a simple exposition of the principles of psychology from the standpoint of their relation to successful advertising. Later he turned to more general applications of psychology in business, writing 11 articles for *System*, all published in 1910 and 1911, on "The Psychology of Business." In these articles Scott emphasized the unutilized capabilities of individuals, the development of habits that promote individual efficiency and reduce wasted effort, and the use of precept and example to establish a climate of efficient work. In addition, he stressed the development of an atmosphere in which employees would spontaneously refer to their organization as "we," and he took the position that "love of the game" was an important factor in success as head of a business. The result of this series of articles was the book *Increasing Human Efficiency in Business*[2] and another, closely related, which he called *Influencing Men in Business: The Psychology of Agreement and Suggestion*.[3]

In 1916 Scott left Northwestern University to become Professor of Applied Psychology at the Carnegie Institute of Technology and, also, Director of the newly established Bureau of Salesmanship Research. With assistance

[1] Boston: Small, Maynard & Co., 1903.
[2] New York: Macmillan, 1911.
[3] New York: Ronald Press, 1911.

from students, Scott promptly turned out the 36-page *Aids in the Selection of Salesmen*.[4] It contained (1) a model application blank; (2) a standardized letter to former employees; (3) a set of interview guides and record blanks; and (4) a series of tests designed to measure an applicant's intelligence, alertness, carefulness, imagination, resourcefulness, and verbal facility. It should be noted, incidentally, that Scott was the first academic in the United States to have the title "Professor of Applied Psychology."

When the United States entered the war against Germany in 1917, Scott began working on U.S. military problems concerned with the classification and motivation of personnel. At this time he became Chairman of the Committee on Problems of Motivation in Connection with Military Service, which was established by the National Research Council. After the First World War he set up his own consulting business. In 1920, however, he was made President of Northwestern University, a post which he held until his retirement in 1939.

That same year, of course, war again broke out in Europe, and in December 1941 the attack on Pearl Harbor forced the United States into the conflict against both Japan and the European Axis powers. Even though he was by now in his seventies, Scott once more served his country for the duration of the emergency. From 1941 to 1946 he was chairman of the Solid Fuels Advisory War Council.

Walter Dill Scott was a self-made man. Early in life he learned the virtues of hard work and rigorous study. He was widely respected as an academic, a research psychologist, and a college administrator. He wrote on subjects ranging from "the Wundt pendulum complication apparatus as tested by the Dudell oscillograph"[5] to the psychology of public speaking. In the course of his career he had to his credit more than 200 publications. And he could and did teach college courses that included—along with general psychology—the lives of great educators such as Rousseau and Pestalozzi.

Walter Dill Scott was a leader who was personable and had the courage to stand by his convictions. Underlying much of his work was a concern for human behavior and for improving human potential. In applied psychology he saw the possibility of meeting the needs of workers for a feeling of responsibility, of offering a needed social service, and of social approval and cooperation from fellow workers.[6,7] —WILLIAM B. WOLF

[4] Pittsburgh: Carnegie Institute of Technology, 1916.

[5] *Psychological Bulletin*, 1905, Vol. 2, p. 201.

[6] Cf. Walter Dill Scott, "The Psychology of the Twentieth Century American," in *The Edison Round Table* (1913), Vol. 5, No. 6, pp. 176–179; "Modern Motives to Action," *The Caxton* (1914), Vol. 4, No. 7, pp. 33–42; "Putting America First, The Road to National Efficiency," *Cosmopolitan* (1915), Vol. 59, pp. 165–168.

[7] For a summary of the contributions of Walter Dill Scott, see Leonard W. Ferguson, *The Heritage of Industrial Psychology* (privately printed by the author, 1962). See also Edmund C. Lynch, *Walter Dill Scott, Pioneer in Personnel Management* (Austin: Bureau of Business Research, University of Texas, 1968) and J. Z. Jacobsen, *Scott of Northwestern: The Life Story of a Pioneer in Psychology and Education*, Studies in Personnel and Management No. 20 (Chicago: Louis Mariano Press, 1951).

SELECTED PUBLICATIONS

Books:

1903 *The Theory and Practice of Advertising*. Boston: Small, Maynard & Co. 240 pp.

1907 *The Psychology of Public Speaking*. Philadelphia: Pearson Bros. 222 pp.

1908 *The Psychology of Advertising*. Boston: Small, Maynard & Co. 269 pp.

1911 *Increasing Human Efficiency in Business*. New York: Macmillan. 339 pp.

——— *Influencing Men in Business*. New York: Ronald Press. 168 pp.

1916 *Aids in the Selection of Salesmen*. Pittsburgh: Carnegie Institute of Technology. 36 pp.

1921 *Psychology of Advertising in Theory and Practice*. Boston: Small, Maynard & Co. 437 pp.

——— *Science and Common Sense in Working with Men*. With Mary H. S. Hayes. New York: Ronald Press. 154 pp.

1923 *Personnel Management: Principles, Practices, and a Point of View*. With Robert C. Clothier. New York: A. W. Shaw. 643 pp.

Articles:

1902 "The Psychology of Involuntary Attention as Applied to Advertising," *Agricultural Advertising,* Vol. 9, January, pp. 10, 31, 32, 34, 36, 38, 39.

1904 "Psychology of Advertising," *Atlantic Monthly*, Vol. 93, January, pp. 29–36.

1910 "The Psychology of Business" (series in *System*):
  "Increasing Human Efficiency," Vol. 17, March, pp. 252–258.
  "Imitation: Spur to Efficiency," Vol. 17, April, pp. 368–373.
  "More Manpower Through Competition," Vol. 17, May, pp. 469–475.
  "Making Employees Say 'We'," Vol. 17, June, pp. 605–611.
  "Focusing on the Day's Work," Vol. 18, July, pp. 41–47.
  "Putting Men in the Mood to Work," Vol. 18, August, pp. 155–160.
  "Wages: Part I," Vol. 18, November, pp. 492–496.
  "Wages: Part II," Vol. 18, December, pp. 608–611.

1911 "The Psychology of Business" (continued series in *System*):
  "The Love of the Game," Vol. 19, January, pp. 26–30.
  "The Rate of Improvement in Efficiency," Vol. 20, August, pp. 155–162.
  "Making Experience an Asset," Vol. 20, October, pp. 364–369.

1915 "The Scientific Selection of Salesmen," *Advertising and Selling,* Vol. 25, October (Part I), pp. 5, 6, 94, 96; November (Part II); and December (Part III).

1916 "Experiments in Vocational Selection," *Psychological Bulletin,* Vol. 13, February, pp. 87–88.

1917 "An Experiment in Vocational Selection," *Psychological Bulletin,* Vol. 14, February, pp. 61–62.

——— "A Fourth Method of Checking Results in Vocational Selection," *Journal of Applied Psychology*, Vol. 1, March, pp. 61–66.

—— "Vocational Selection at the Carnegie Institute of Technology," *U.S. Bureau of Labor Statistics Bulletin No. 227*, October, pp. 114–119.

1919 "Measurements of Trade Skill and Intelligence," in *Proceedings,* First Annual Convention of Employment Managers, Cleveland, Ohio. Newark: Wolber Co., pp. 63–67.

1920 "Changes in Some of Our Conceptions and Practices of Personnel," *Psychological Review,* Vol. 27, March, pp. 81–94.

Curriculum Vitae

1869	Born on May 1st in Cookesville, Ill.
1880	Owing to father's illness, took over almost complete management, with brother John, of family's 120-acre farm.
1883	John having left to attend Northwestern University, managed farm single-handedly.
1891	Graduated from Illinois State Normal University.
1891–1895	Attended Northwestern University, studying Latin, Greek, English literature, and theology. Active in student affairs; played guard on varsity football team; elected to Phi Beta Kappa. Awarded A.B. in 1895.
1895–1898	Studied at McCormick Theological Seminary, Chicago. Completed training but decided to study psychology instead of being a missionary.
1898–1899	Attended University of Halle.
1899–1900	Attended University of Leipzig. Studied under Wundt, father of modern psychology. Awarded Ph.D. by Leipzig in 1900.
1900–1916	Taught at Northwestern University as Associate Professor of Psychology and Education and as Director of the Psychological Laboratory.
1916	Took position at Carnegie Institute of Technology, becoming first person in United States to hold title "Professor of Applied Psychology."
1916–1917	Served as Director, Bureau of Salesmanship Research.
1917	Under Psychology Committee of National Research Council, contributed to war effort as Chairman, Committee on Problems of Motivation in Connection with Military Service. Elected Executive Secretary, Committee on Classification of Personnel of National Research Council. Later elected Director, Commission on Classification in the Army.
1918–1919	Commissioned a colonel in the U.S. Army and assigned to Personnel Branch of Operations Division.
1919–1921	Served as President, Scott Co., consultants and engineers in industrial personnel.
1919–1955	Served as Chairman of the Board, Scott Co.
1920–1939	Held office of President, Northwestern University.

1941–1946 Served as Chairman, Solid Fuels Advisory War Council.
1955 Died on September 23rd at the age of 86.

Over the years, Walter Dill Scott held office in various professional groups. In 1915, for example, he was President of the Association of Teachers of Advertising; in 1927, Chairman of the American Council on Education; and, in 1933–1934, a member of the Board of Trustees for the "Century of Progress" exposition in Chicago. In 1948, he was Chairman of the Editorial Board for the *American People's Encyclopedia*. His honorary degrees included: Ph.D., Northwestern (1920); LL.D., Cornell College (1921); and LL.D., University of Southern California (1932). Scott, in 1933, received a Distinguished Service Medal for "devising, installing, and supervising the personnel system in the U.S. Army" and was awarded the Legion of Honor.

Morris Llewellyn Cooke
(1872–1960)
United States

MORRIS Llewellyn Cooke played a significant role in the development and the dissemination of scientific management. More than that, he applied the principles of scientific management to government and educational institutions, and in the process he himself gained a reputation as an outstanding practitioner.

Morris Cooke's contact with scientific management began in the late 1800s when, as a young graduate engineer, he became an apprentice at Cramp's Shipyard in Philadelphia. This was just after Frederick Winslow Taylor, the "father of scientific management," had worked there as a consultant. The shipyard experience helped Cooke understand Taylor's approach to management. Later, in 1896, Cooke was employed as a journeyman machinist at the Southwork Foundry in Philadelphia. There his formal interest in scientific management began, and he started a movement in the shop to eliminate inefficient practices. Thus, in 1905, when Taylor became President of The American Society of Mechanical Engineers, he employed Cooke to reorganize the group. A close friendship developed between Taylor and Cooke. In fact, until Cooke's death he still wore a watch chain that had belonged to Taylor.

In the spring of 1907, working with Taylor, Cooke developed a four-phase plan for propagating the Taylor system. This included the following steps:

1. Cooke wrote a book, *Industrial Management*, which—though never actually published—popularized the Taylor system of scientific management.
2. Cooke applied scientific management to university administration.
3. Cooke helped Taylor write the classic *Principles of Scientific Management*.
4. Cooke became instrumental in applying scientific management to municipal government.

In November 1909 Cooke wrote Taylor to say that Chapter 2 of his own book was in reality based on Taylor's "Boxly" talk. The chapter does in fact use 31 pages of Taylor's 62-page talk. However, because Cooke greatly modified Taylor's talk, he created an entirely new piece of work. The importance of Cooke's chapter in the development of scientific management is indicated by Taylor's later use of it to write his own *Principles of Scientific Management*. At the time, Taylor was having difficulty in preparing what he believed would be an acceptable paper for presentation to The American Society of Mechanical Engineers. He called upon his friend Cooke for help, and in this way Chapter 2 of Cooke's book became an important part of the framework of Taylor's book.[1] Moreover, Cooke helped Taylor rewrite his material. As a reward, Taylor agreed to turn over all the profits from the sale of *Principles of Scientific Management* to Cooke.[2]

In 1910, the Carnegie Foundation for the Advancement of Teaching decided to study the cost as compared with the output of leading universities. Both Cooke and Taylor saw this as a way of extending the scope of Taylor's concepts; so it was arranged that Cooke conduct the investigation. From his study Cooke determined that there was a need to apply Taylor's techniques to universities by specialization on the part of professors, better utilization of rooms, and, finally, the adaption of functional management to the administration universities.

In 1911, Taylor rewarded Cooke further by securing for him the position of Director of Public Works in Philadelphia under the reform administration of Mayor Rudolph Blankenburg. Cooke saw this as an opportunity to apply Taylor's ideas of routing, time study, and planning to municipal government. One result was the utilization of experts to study city problems. The most outstanding example was the study made by Taylor and Sanford Thompson of the construction at League Island Park, in which they uncovered a great deal of fraud. Their disclosures eventually led to changes in Pennsylvania law regarding municipal contracts.

During his tenure as Philadelphia's Director of Public Works, Cooke struggled to obtain fair rates from utilities for municipalities. To do so, he

[1] Charles D. Wrege and A. M. Stotka, "Cooke Creates a Classic, The Story Behind F. W. Taylor's Principles of Scientific Management," The Academy of Management *Review*, Vol. 3, No. 4, October 1978, pp. 741–743.

[2] Letter from Taylor to Cooke, dated December 10, 1910, in Folder 114A, F. W. Taylor Collection, Stevens Institute of Technology.

took the unheard-of step of bringing the Philadelphia Electric Co. into court and utilizing experts to challenge its rate structure.

Cooke's revolutionary book *Our Cities Awake* grew out of his work in municipal government.

For not only was Morris Cooke active in disseminating scientific management to the world but he was also a social pioneer. He was one of President Franklin Delano Roosevelt's closest advisers, a diplomat and an envoy extraordinary, a leading arbitrator between labor and industry, and one of the nation's most effective conservationists—all in addition to being a foremost exponent of scientific management. There is, however, an important difference between Cooke's scientific management and that of Taylor. Cooke saw individuals as ends in themselves. He believed that there should be a working experience between labor and management which would transcend organization, and he believed that it would be facilitated if workers were allowed to participate in field-type decisions. In short, he put his emphasis on the psychological factors in production.

Morris Cooke had a number of eccentricities which puzzled his associates. In Washington, he was noted for a kind of personal "trademark"—a battered black notebook containing an alphabetical list, more than 5,000 names in all, of his friends and acquaintances. He used it as an address finder for the little personal gifts and mementoes he mailed out every day and as a source of potential experts and researchers to help him solve problems that arose in his work.

In Washington, also, Cooke preferred to be known by the simple "consulting engineer." He avoided politics; and he seldom, if ever, went to cocktail parties. His modus operandi was to avoid publicity and work as a freelance, usually on ad hoc assignments—which he received, more often than not, directly from the President. Despite Cooke's tremendous accomplishments, he is not widely known to students of management.

Probably Cooke's most outstanding personal characteristic was his great interest in people. He inspired trust in individuals from all walks of life; he was an independent thinker with his own personal style of democracy. In Washington, his skill as administrator of the Rural Electrical Administration gave him the reputation of being one of the most effective managers in government service. Here he cultivated the friendship of each of his employees, adopted the practice of setting aside one evening each month during which they might bring their personal troubles to him, encouraged open communications, and introduced innovations in pensions and other employee benefits and services.

Another outstanding characteristic of Morris Cooke was his ability to keep an independent and optimistic outlook. In 1907, for example, he criticized Taylor's way of speaking and presenting materials, and this led to Cooke's helping Taylor improve his public talks. And in 1915 he questioned the real powers behind the activities of the Federated American Engineering Societies and pointed to the important role played by large companies in the policies of the societies associated with the group. It was Cooke who worked to make engineers aware of their social responsibilities and encouraged them to question the engineer's code of ethics, who challenged the Philadelphia Electric Co. and won, who pioneered conservation and rural electrification in the United States.

Morris Llewellyn Cooke always seemed younger than his actual years. Even when he was in his 70s, he appeared to be about 50. He was 5′ 9″ tall and kept his weight around 170 pounds. Throughout most of his life he enjoyed rigorous sports, particularly tennis and squash, and he also liked camping in the deep woods. Although, on first contact, he might seem stern and aloof, this impression soon vanished as he began to talk about the many subjects that interested him. —C. D. WREGE

SELECTED PUBLICATIONS

Books:

1910 *Academic and Industrial Efficiency*, a report to the Carnegie Foundation. New York: Carnegie Foundation.

1918 *Our Cities Awake*. Garden City, N.Y.: Doubleday, Page.

1919 *Modern Manufacturing: a Partnership of Idealism and Common Sense*. Editor. Philadelphia: The American Academy of Political and Social Science.

—— *An All-American Basis for Industry; Democracy in Industry Can Only Be Reached Through Collective Action and Collective Responsibility*. Philadelphia: Published privately.

1924 *Public Utility Regulation*. Editor. New York: Ronald Press.

1925 *Giant Power, Large Scale Electrical Development as a Social Factor*. Editor. Philadelphia: American Academy of Political and Social Science.

1933 *What Electricity Costs in the Home and on the Farm*; a Symposium. Editor. New York: *New Republic*.

1934 *Report of the Mississippi Valley Committee of the Public Works Administration*. Submitted October 1, 1934, to Harold L. Ickes, Administrator, Federal Emergency Administration of Public Works. Washington, D.C.: U.S. Government Printing Office.

1936 *The Future of the Great Plains*. Report of the Great Plains Committee. Washington, D.C.: U.S. Government Printing Office.

1940 *Organized Labor and Production: Next Step in Industrial Democracy*. With Philip Murray. New York, London: Harper.

1944 *Brazil on the March, A Study in International Cooperation: Reflections on the Report of the American Technical Mission to Brazil*. New York, London: Whittlesey House, McGraw-Hill.

1946 *Professional Ethics and Social Change*. New York: American Ethical Union.

1947 *The Early Days of the Rural Electrification Idea 1914–1936; A Memorandum Written for the Library of Congress*. Washington, D.C.: U.S. Government Printing Office.

1950 *Groundwork for Action*. With Calvin J. Nichols, Dorothy Detzer, and Peter G. Franck. Washington, D.C.: Public Affairs Institute.

Articles:

1915 "Casual and Chronic Unemployment," *Annals of American Academy of Political and Social Science*, Vol. 59, No. 148, May, pp. 194–199.

1921 "Committee on Eliminating of Waste in Industry," in *The Men's Ready-made Clothing Industry*. Washington, D.C., New York: Federated American Engineering Societies, pp. 95–130.

—— "Unemployment Within Employment," *International Labor Review*, Vol. 4, December, pp. 469–479.

1924 "Giant Power and Coal," *Annals* of the American Academy of Political and Social Science, Vol. 111, January, pp. 212–218.

1925 "Labor's Ideals Concerning Management," discussion by John A. Fitch, Royal Meeker, Morris L. Cooke, and others, *Bulletin* of the Taylor Society, Vol. 10, December, pp. 241–253.

—— "Giant Power: Large Scale Electrical Development as a Social Factor," *Annals* of the American Academy of Political and Social Science, Vol. 118.

1926 "Giant Power: An Interpretation," *Atlantic Monthly*, Vol. 138, December, pp. 813–822.

—— "Power Supplement," *New Republic*, Vol. 47, May 26, pp. 18–36.

1929 "Some Observations on Workers' Organizations." *American Federationist*, Vol. 36, January, pp. 23–35.

1935 "What Electricity Should Cost," *New Republic*, Vol. 82, May 1, pp. 330–332.

—— "Twenty Years of Grace," *Survey Graphic*, Vol. 24, June, pp. 277–282.

1936 "Bringing Electricity to the Farm," *Labor Information Bulletin*, Vol. 3, No. 8, August, pp. 1–3.

—— "An Engineer Looks at Rural America," *The Journal of Land and Public Utility Economics*, Vol. 12, February, pp. 1–18.

1938 "Some Advice to Labor Unions," Society for the Advancement of Management *Journal*, Vol. 3, January, pp. 2–4, 39.

1940 "Modern Collective Bargaining and the New Technology," *American Labor Legislation Review*, Vol. 30, June, pp. 81–84.

1941 "Calling All Employers," *Survey Graphic*, Vol. 30, November, pp. 606–609.

Curriculum Vitae

1872 Born on May 11th in Carlisle, Pa.

1889 Graduated from Ulrick's (a private secondary school) in Bethlehem, Pa.

1889–1890 Studied mechanical engineering at Lehigh University.

1890 Worked as reporter for *Philadelphia Press*.

1891–1895 Returned to Lehigh University. In middle of junior year, funds depleted; worked as reporter for *Denver News* and later as Financial Editor for *New York Evening Telegram*. In 1895 awarded degree in mechanical engineering.

1895–1898 Served as apprentice at Cramp's Shipyard, Philadelphia. Within several months employed as journeyman machinist in Southwork Foundry, Philadelphia, becoming interested in elimination of inefficient factory practices and thus in scientific management. Moved from Southwork Foundry to Acetylene Co., Washington, D.C.

1897–1901 Engaged in engineering work for commercial organizations.

1898–1899 Served as assistant engineer in U.S. Navy during Spanish-American War.

1901–1905 Employed as executive in a book-publishing company.

1905–1911 Worked as consulting engineer. In 1910 made special study of college administration for Carnegie Foundation for the Advancement of Teaching.

1911–1916 Served as Director of Department of Public Works, Philadelphia. Through court action, forced substantial reduction in rates charged by Philadelphia Electric Co.

1917 Named Chairman, Storage Section, War Industries Board of the Council for National Defense. Later in First World War, was Executive Assistant to Chairman of U.S. Shipping Board.

1923–1925 Helped pave way for federal rural-electrification program by heading "Giant Power" survey in Pennsylvania. Report proposed a central authority similar to TVA.

1927 Elected President of the Taylor Society.

1928–1933 Served as a trustee of Power Authority, State of New York.

1932 Appointed Chairman of Mississippi Valley Committee by President Franklin Delano Roosevelt. Report dealt with flood control, power development, agriculture, navigation, reforestation, and elimination of pollution.

1934 Served as Director, Water Resources Committee of National Resources Board.

1935–1937 Was first administrator of Rural Electrification Administration.

1940–1941 Served as technical consultant to Labor Division, Office of Production Management.

1942 Represented the United States in negotiating with Mexico on claims of U.S. companies arising from expropriation of oil properties. Headed American Technical Mission to Brazil, seeking ways of increasing Brazil's contribution to hemisphere defense effort.

1943 Headed War Labor Board panel that mediated anthracite coal miners' strike.

1946–1947 Member of committee appointed to study U.S. patent system.

1950	Appointed Chairman of Water Resources Policy Commission by President Truman.
1960	Died on March 5th, aged 87, in Philadelphia.

Morris Cooke was a Fellow of the American Association for the Advancement of Science and a Fellow of The American Society of Mechanical Engineers. He received an honorary D.Sc. degree from Lehigh University and was awarded the Czechoslovak Order of the White Lion and the Mexican Order of the Aztec Eagle.

Courtesy Siemans Aktiengesellschaft.

Carl Friedrich von Siemens
(1872–1941)
Germany

THE House of Siemens was beyond a doubt one of the largest and most prominent German industrial firms to be influenced, under Carl Friedrich von Siemens, by the rationalization movement. And its increasingly international scope provided full opportunity for the interest that Carl Friedrich early developed in organizational form. But he discovered almost immediately that neither rationalization nor sound organization structure was enough. His importance in the context of German management lay in his understanding of the need to take seriously every thought, feeling, and action of each individual employee. "The organization," he said, "can do no more than create opportunities for cooperation; these can be realized only by the human spirit—which must be awakened, nurtured, and encouraged." There must be a social climate that favors productivity.

Carl Friedrich von Siemens was the youngest child of Werner, the eldest of the famous four Siemens brothers, and the one who, with the mechanic Johann Georg Halske, founded the Berlin telegraph factory that grew to become the gigantic House of Siemens.

Siemens & Halske had flourished after its establishment in 1847. Soon it had subsidiaries in London, St. Petersburg, Vienna, and Paris; it laid cables across the Mediterranean, from Europe to India, and even from Rio de Janeiro to Montevideo in South America; but—thanks to Werner's talents as engineer and inventor—it was a steady stream of readily marketable new products, especially in the electrical field, which ensured the firm's success in that rapidly developing industry and in steel as well.

Karl Wilhelm, the second of the four brothers, became the "English" Siemens and in time "Sir William." He first visited London in 1843, returned to settle there in 1844, did some business for the family firm, but in 1858 became managing director of what seems to have been an entirely separate organization. Later on, however, the family took over its management. Then, still later, the firm's name was changed from Siemens & Halske to Siemens Brothers. Sir William died in 1883, leaving his interest in the company to his brothers. It was this Siemens enterprise that Carl Friedrich, aged 30, was sent to manage in April 1901. He remained there through 1908.

Carl Friedrich had entered Siemens & Halske, according to his father's plans for him, three years earlier and had since been "learning the business." And he applied himself seriously, even though his school record had been unimpressive and he appears to have previously been the typical playboy son of a wealthy family. London was the first big test of his abilities. Not only were there disagreements between the Siemens group and the other interests, German and English, represented on the Board of Directors, but Werner Siemens's determination to build a new high-voltage power plant at Stafford in Lancastershire, halfway between London and Manchester, had created many problems—particularly in an anti-German atmosphere provoked by the war in South Africa. Carl Friedrich plunged in boldly; he smiled in later years at the brashness of his inexperience. And there were severe difficulties—technical, political, organizational, interpersonal—not just with the advanced technology of the prospective new plant but with day-to-day operations. Carl Friedrich certainly learned respect for the art of management: part knowledge, part intuition. Apart from bringing the Stafford installation on stream in mid-1903 through crisis after crisis, he made many changes in Siemens Brothers' London organization.

Carl Friedrich had frequently declared back at headquarters that in modern industry there was more to ascertaining a company's financial position than counting unsold garments like an old-clothes dealer. Now he would not tolerate premature decisions based on only a superficial knowledge of the circumstances. Instead, he had information quickly consolidated and distributed in the form of operating statistics which he used skillfully to control costs and measure performance. At the same time he gained considerable skill in dealing with people—who, he learned, should be judged not simply "by the numbers" but as individuals. He learned, too, that he who presumes to judge others must make the effort to know and judge himself. Naturally open and frank, he generally was able to sum up his associates correctly and, for the most part, win their confidence.

By 1906, Carl Friedrich was anxious to get back to Berlin. In particular, he hoped to take charge of the Siemens-Schuckertwerke, a firm set up a few years earlier when Siemens had come to the rescue of an ailing competitor and bought an interest in it. But Stafford continued to be a problem in itself and the new man appointed to manage it lost his life en route to England when the Harwich-Hoek van Holland night boat went down in a storm. And within another year Siemens & Halske's foreign business had increased to such an extent that Wilhelm assigned his young brother the job of managing the firm's overseas operations, beginning with an exploratory trip to India and the Far East. Again Carl Friedrich threw himself into the work conscientiously, so that over a four-year span the overseas business continued to grow at a gratifying rate, particularly in Central and South America and in the Orient.

Meanwhile, a drama was unfolding that made it impossible to go on limiting Carl Friedrich's authority to the overseas area. The chief characters in this drama were Wilhelm and Carl Friedrich von Siemens; Dr. Alfred Berliner of the Siemens-Schuckertwerke; and Sigmund Bergmann, founder and head of the Bergmann Elektrizitätswerke AG. Bergmann proposed a merger of his company—AEG, as it was called—with Siemens-Schuckert, which Berliner opposed violently; he thought Bergmann was a fool and not to be trusted. Carl Friedrich went along with Berliner, but Wilhelm rather leaned toward the venture. Negotiations dragged on for months, till, at the turn of the year 1911–1912, Bergmann justified Berliner's suspicions by failing.

Wilhelm, in poor health, was spending that winter in Meran, then in the South Tirol of Austria. Berliner and Carl Friedrich, with whom the Deutsche Bank—obligated to both sides—had worked out an alternative merger plan which would help Bergmann but still offer some protection to Siemens, traveled down in February to obtain Wilhelm's approval of yet another arrangement. This they presented, on their return, to Bergmann and the bank. It was April, however, before agreement was finally reached. Then, since there must be a representative of the Siemens group in the overall management of AEG, Berliner proposed that Carl Friedrich be that person. He eventually consented to serve if Wilhelm would agree, but Wilhelm stood firm on his earlier rejection of the whole plan.

Carl Friedrich promptly dropped the matter; and when he next wrote his brother, on April 29, 1912, it was to announce that Alfred Berliner had had a nervous breakdown. Contributing to this was the fact that the old Schuckert group, with which he had never been popular, had at last risen against him. Wilhelm had no choice, upon returning from his long sick leave, but to replace Berliner with Carl Friedrich as head of Siemens-Schuckert.

To all intents and purposes, then, Carl Friedrich von Siemens managed the entire, far-flung Siemens empire from that time on. When war broke out two years later, he at first served on the Western front as a driver in the Reichsautomobilkorps (Imperial Automobile Corps), but he was placed on indefinite leave after only a few months and by Christmas he was home in Berlin. Here he spent the next years coping with the many problems of converting the Siemens facilities to the production of war materiel in the face of a diminishing workforce, iron and steel shortages, lack of food, and in the end military defeat, revolution, the flight of the Kaiser, and the brith of the new Weimar Republic.

With Wilhelm's death on October 14, 1919, Carl Friedrich reached the high point of his career, but it could have made little difference that he now headed the House of Siemens officially as well as in simple fact. The problems continued, what with the doubts and uncertainties of the German people, a country that had shrunk geographically and lost all its colonies, reparations to be paid, inflation out of control, a worldwide depression, and always the dangers of social unrest. As he extended his command over the Siemens organization, Carl Friedrich deliberately made himself visible to his employees as a means of encouraging them. Realizing that the well-being of the individual presupposed the recovery of the national economy through increased productivity, he freed some of his best associates in Siemens—for example, Carl Köttgen,[1] who was Managing Director—to work in the common interest. Also, he became a prominent and articulate spokesman for the rationalization movement in which Dr. Köttgen was involved.

Von Siemens had been exposed to the principles of rationization—that is to say, scientific management—while he was taking courses at the Technische Hochschule in Berlin, back before the turn of the century. Now he arranged for men like Waldemar Hellmich, a strong advocate of rationalization who had been trying to tighten work standards in the public sector, to get a fair hearing—this in a day when many people suspected that scientific management with its standards was merely a way of speeding up work processes and achieving greater efficiency at the expense of the workers.

Simultaneously, von Siemens was broadening his concern for excellence in management beyond his own company. In the fall of 1924, he was elected to head the governing board of the Deutsche Reichsbahnverwaltung (German National Railways Administration). Here he faced a rationalization task of special importance: how to improve the economic status of a mammoth government enterprise, with more than a million employees, and still not burden it with the tremendous costs and social responsibilities of mass retirements. The German railways, during this postwar period, of course employed many disabled veterans. Carl Friedrich devoted himself daily to this and other railroad problems, whether they had to do with management matters, bookkeeping methods, the compiling of statistics, the modernization of the railroad yards, or just human politicking.

Von Siemens proved that when economic growth is accelerating, the action of management in providing a social climate favorable to increased productivity is quite as significant as scientific and technological progress. And so a report by the International Labor Office in Geneva on "The Siemens Plants in Siemensstadt" closes with these words:

> The organization of social relations in Siemens firms was guided to a very high degree by what is effective. The social policies of the

[1] See Part One for a profile of Karl Köttgen.

> companies are fully centralized in the Social Policies Department, and these policies are carried out loyally and effectively in the plants, where every detail is handled by highly qualified managers. . . . It would be possible for such a system, however admirable, to be merely a formality and show no tangible results in terms of improved behavior and closer working relationships. Every danger of this type seems in Siemensstadt to have been successfully overcome thanks to the deep personal interest that the head of the companies, Dr. Carl Friedrich von Siemens, has manifested in social relations and thanks to his personal example. Siemens is without a doubt a noteworthy example of the maintenance of immediate personal relations between management and the workers in an organization of the greatest size. . . . [2]

Another goal dear to von Siemens's heart was the systematic furtherance in Germany of scientific and technological processes, which, during the war, had lagged behind the efforts of other countries. He was one of a group that in 1921, through the Reichsverband der Deutschen Industrie (National Association of German Industry), founded an emergency group for the purpose of uniting industry and science in a common cause. For 13 years von Siemens himself served as chairman of the group's administrative council.

Carl Friedrich von Siemens was called to serve his organization in the highest post it offered between two devastating wars. Before the German economy and the spirit of the German people could recover from the first catastrophe, they were overcome by another, even more shattering. Von Siemens had to shoulder the near-impossible task of preserving Siemens through eight years of the Hitler regime. Beginning in 1933, he guided it through the burning of the Reichstag, the establishment of a police state, the pressure on everyone of any prominence to support the Party, the petty officials placed in every office and factory, and—worse—the progressive anti-Semitism, which von Siemens countered to the extent possible by pensioning off all the firm's Jewish employees. Finally, Carl Friedrich for the second time had to place his plants, equipment, and technology on a wartime basis.

He was not deceived by the easy military successes of 1939 and 1940. His comment was "This is the end of Germany!" when Hitler, who'd signed a treaty with the Soviet Union and joined it in overrunning Poland in 1939, suddenly executed a complete aboutface and declared war on the Soviet Union in June 1941. He did not live to see how close his prophecy came to being realized, much less participate in the "miracle" of German industry's recovery after the end of hostilities. He died in his sleep on July 9, 1941.

"I must keep thinking," were his last words. "Is there anything else I've forgotten?"—ELIZABETH MARTING

[2] In *Studien und Berichten* (Studies and Reports), Series A, No. 33, 1930.

SELECTED PUBLICATIONS

Papers and speeches:

1917 "Die Bedeutung der Wohungsfrage für die Industrie" (The Significance of the Housing Question for Industry). Address to the Gross-Berliner Verein für Kleinwohnungswesen (Greater Berlin Association for Popular Housing). February 6th. 20 pp.

1921 "Veredelte Umsatzsteuer" (An Improved Value-Added Tax). Berlin-Siemensstadt.

1931 "The Electrical Industry and the Present Economic Situation" (Die elektrische Industrie und die gegenwärtige wirtschaftliche Lage). Address to the Eighth Conference of Major Industries under the auspices of Columbia University and the Institute of American Meat Packers with the cooperation of The Chamber of Commerce of the State of New York and The Merchants' Association of New York. October 21st. 12 pp. (English); 13 pp. (German).

—— "The Present German Situation" (Die gegenwärtige Lage Deutschlands). Address to a breakfast meeting of the Bond Club in New York City. October 30th. 12 pp. (English); 13 pp. (German).

1933 "Rede des Herr Dr. Carl Friedrich von Siemens in der Generalversammlung der Siemens & Halske AG. am 28. Februar 1933" (Speech by Herr Dr. Carl Friedrich von Siemens at the General Meeting of Siemens & Halske AG on February 28, 1933). 8 pp.

1937 "90 Jahre Haus Siemens—90 Jahre Elektrotechnik" (90 Years in the House of Siemens—90 Years of Electrotechnology). Read at Berlin-Siemensstadt, October 12th.

In 1972, on the 100th anniversary of von Siemens's birth, the Werner von Siemens Institute in Munich published a 19-page brochure of quotations from Carl Friedrich von Siemens's speeches and other publications.

Curriculum Vitae

1872 Born on September 5th in Charlottenburg (Berlin).

1893 Spent some months at Siemens Brothers in London to begin learning family business. Accompanied brother Arnold on business trip to Chicago; sat in on conferences, later discussed, as form of training. Saw Chicago Exposition; visited West.
In fall went to Strasbourg to begin year's military service in cavalry; also attended lectures at University of Strasbourg.

1894–1899 Studied at University of Munich and later in Berlin.

1899 On August 21st, at age of 27, began career, as planned by father, at Siemens & Halske headquarters.

1901 Returned to London in April to manage Siemens Brothers there.

1904 With brother Wilhelm, made second trip to United States.

1908 In December, left for trip to India and the Far East, exploring prospects for Siemens business and returning by Transsiberian Railway.

1909 Now back at Berlin headquarters, took on management of overseas operations (Zentralverwaltung Übersees).

1912 In effect, as head of Siemens-Schuckertwerke, assumed management of entire Siemens empire during illness of brother Wilhelm.

1914 At age 42, served in Kaiserliches Automobilkorps on Western front after outbreak of war; placed on indefinite leave and then released by end of year.

1915–1918 Managed Siemens operations on war-emergency basis; some experimentation with building of Zeppelins. Increasing problems with shortages, especially of iron and steel. Labor troubles developed as war continued, food became scarce, and workers lost first enthusiasm.

1919 Became head of Siemens in actual fact upon Wilhelm's death on October 14th.

1921–1934 Instrumental in formation of group to promote working relationships between research and industry; for 13 years served as President, Stiftverband der deutschen Forschungsgemeinschaft (League of German Research Personnel), the resulting organization.

1924 Elected President, Verwaltungsrat der Deutschen Reichsbahnverwaltung (Board of Directors, National German Railways).

1941 Died on July 9th, aged 68, in Heindendorf.

Eugen Schmalenbach
(1873–1955)
Germany

EUGEN Schmalenbach belonged to the old school of business economists. However, even though he is primarily remembered for his work in the area of accounting and never lost an opportunity to stress the need for efficiency, he did not consider it his principal responsibility to show business how to make a profit. Others might accuse him of being a materialist simply because he tended to occupy himself with material problems, yet he saw business as a group that was entrusted with the management of economic affairs.

Schmalenbach favored precise, efficient control of capital, and by "capital" he meant the resources that a company must have at its disposal in adequate supply to fulfill its goals. The purpose of capital, he said, was the constant creation of sufficient new capital, whether it was a question of company, state, or individual ownership, and this capital must be used wherever its productivity would be greatest and therefore would not be wasted. Some of his words have a decidedly modern ring:

> I belong [we read in his book *Dynamic Accounting*, as it is known in English] to the supporters of the *principle of decentralized administration* who are convinced that the administrators of all sections of the company right down to foreman level have been chosen sensibly and have a mind of their own and can use it and that from them it can be expected that they are more familiar with the problems of their particular section of the company than the general director.

True, Schmalenbach believed that accounting was an instrument for measuring management's efficiency, but he reacted strongly whenever—as happened too frequently—accounting methods threatened to become formalized. Above all, he believed the company accounting system was an instrument for management itself to use—and *at all levels.*

His career as lecturer and writer gathered momentum in 1906 with his move from the Leipzig Handelshochschule (Business College) to its counterpart in Cologne. Here, in 1909, he started his *Zeitschrift für handelswissenschaftliche Forschung* (Journal for Research in the Science of Business), which has survived him by many years. He also was a pioneer in chartered accountancy, or certified public accounting, and in the German trusteeship movement, founding his own trusteeship company—Treuhand-Aktiengesellschaft—in Cologne. At the same time he found time and energy to write a number of books in addition to his journal articles; and in many cases these books—on such topics as financial planning, accounting systems, and pricing policy—have been issued in successive editions and remained standard works.

Schmalenbach made frequent use of the inductive method in his analysis of financial or accounting problems; that is, he reasoned from the part to the whole, from the particular to the general, from the individual to the universal. Nevertheless, he was an astute theoretician as well, able to isolate the significant factor in each problem by systematically eliminating all the others. And he could present even the most abstract ideas in clear, lively, interesting language—a gift that undoubtedly had much to do with his popularity as a lecturer and the invitations he received to address audiences in cities as different as Stockholm, Bern, and Istanbul. He himself, though, attributed the success of his lectures to his fondness for the Socratic method of asking a series of questions designed expressly to guide his hearers to the answer he was after.

In 1933, when the National Socialists came into power in Germany, Schmalenbach voluntarily withdrew from academic life, although he did continue to lecture abroad prior to the outbreak of war in 1939. He produced numerous manuscripts during the war years in spite of the fact that the Nazis would not allow them to be published, and some of them circulated among the Schmalenbach Society "work circles" which existed at this time. Such were his professional standing and reputation that not only did these groups exist but he was able to resist the Party and bring his wife, who was Jewish, safely through the Hitler period.

Particularly while he was out of the Handelshochschule, Schmalenbach did a great deal of thinking about organization and its problems. In 1941 he wrote a treatise on organization in large companies. It was printed surreptitiously and sold under the counter as "Schmalenbach's forbidden book." After the author's death, it reappeared, formally published in 1959 by Westdeutscher Verlag (Cologne-Opladen).

Obviously, Schmalenbach's research was not limited to the responsibilities and the organizational position of accounting and finance. He made detailed studies of such functions as warehouse management and personnel administration. It may, in fact, have been the breadth of his own activities that demonstrated to him the proper scope of business economics. After resuming his work at the Handelshochschule in 1945, he declared that within the overall framework of general economics the various aspects of business economics should be organized functionally: purchasing and sales and distribution as *external functions*; personnel, production, traffic within the company, and the like as *internal functions*; and finance, accounting, and organization as *general functions*. In other words, Schmalenbach was now speaking in terms not so much of accounting and financial responsibilities and procedures as of the overall task of managing the company.

Eugen Schmalenbach was not a typical academic. He had no great liking for intensive research or study of the literature of a given field; what he did have was his gift for creative thinking. And so his influence on his profession, and on corporate finance and accounting practice, was marked. In his preface of June 1953 to the eleventh edition of *Dynamic Accounting*, he recalled how businesses had originally gauged their end-of-year position by the extent to which capital had increased or decreased; how he had fought for his view that the results of business operations ought to be figured into the annual profit-and-loss statement; how he had preached the concept of depreciation as an expense to be allocated over the useful life of fixed assets. He decried the "idea that although overvaluation of assets is always forbidden, undervaluation can be indulged in at will" and reiterated his conviction that "the ascertainment of operating results by means of annual accounts is important for both the national and business economies and that its object is to show in which direction a business is moving, and thus to act as its compass."

More than two years later, when the twelfth edition of the book appeared, the publisher wrote tersely:

> At this moment there is no reason to make any changes in its contents, as they conform with the latest ideas of business economists and also the current state of accounting.

Nor is that all. With his speical way of seeing things and coming to grips with practical problems—plus his ability to express himself aptly, always with a spice of humor—Eugen Schmalenbach contributed extensively to the development of management theory in Germany.—ELIZABETH MARTING

SELECTED PUBLICATIONS

Book:

1919 *Dynamische Bilanzlehre* (Dynamic Accounting). See also "Schmalenbach's forbidden book" on the organization of large companies, published posthumously in 1959 by Westdeutscher Verlag, Cologne-Obladen.

Articles:

1910 "Über den Zweck der Bilanz" (On the Purpose of the Balance Sheet).
1915 "Theorie der Erfolgsbilanz" (Theory of Successful Accounting).
1919 "Grundlagen dynamischer Bilanzlehre" (Fundamentals of Dynamic Accounting).

Most of Schmalenbach's articles appeared in *Zeitschrift für handelswissenschaftliche Forschung* (Journal for Research in the Science of Business), the periodical which he himself founded in 1909. "Grundlagen dynamischer Bilanzalehre," upon its reprinting, became the first edition of the book *Dynamische Bilanzlehre*.

Curriculum Vitae

1873 Born on August 20th at Schmalenbach near Halver, Westphalia.
1891 Graduated from Gymnasium (high school) in Elberfeld. Began seven years' apprenticeship in father's ironware factory, first as mechanic and later on business side.
1898–1900 Began studies at new Handelshochschule (Business College) in Leipzig. Awarded Diplom-Kaufmann, equivalent of bachelor's degree in business.
1901 Became assistant to Karl Bücher, former teacher.
1906 Moved to Cologne. Qualified as Lecturer at Handelshochschule there.
1906–1933 Pursued academic career at Handelshochschule in Cologne.
1909 Invited to lecture in Stockholm. Founded *Zeitschrift für handelswissenschaftliche Forschung* (Journal for Research in the Science of Business). Founded own trusteeship company (Treuhand-Aktiengesellschaft).
1933 Voluntarily withdrew from academic life when National Socialists came to power in Germany.
1937 Lectured in Istanbul.
1939 Invited to lecture in Bern.
1945 Resumed academic career at end of Second World War.
1950 Retired as of end of summer semester.
1955 Died on February 21st, aged 81, in Cologne.

In 1953, two years before his death, Eugen Schmalenbach was awarded the Grosses Bundesverdienstkreuz (Grand Federal Cross of Merit).

Courtesy The National Cyclopaedia of American Biography.

Harlow Stafford Person
(1875–1955)
United States

HARLOW Stafford Person was a central figure in organizing and promoting the scientific management movement in the United States. It was he who, in October 1911, as Dean of the Tuck School at Dartmouth College, initiated and played host to the first scientific management conference. This meeting did much to give academic recognition to the work of Frederick W. Taylor and to the burgeoning new movement.

Person's contribution to management is most readily understood against the backdrop of the period 1900–1934 in the history of scientific management. In 1910 Louis D. Brandeis,[1] a lawyer for shippers, successfully argued that the Interstate Commerce Commission should not approve railroad-rate increases on the East Coast of the United States. One of Brandeis's arguments held that the railroads could save a million dollars a day if they used scientific management. The "Eastern rates case" was widely publicized, and scientific management was hailed as a significant breakthrough. As one expert said, scientific management was "almost on a plane with the discovery of fire."

In this zeitgeist, management became a topic worthy of investigation. However, The American Society of Mechanical Engineers—which was the organizational home for those interested in scientific management—was not enthusiastic. From 1886 through 1910 it accepted only 19 papers on

[1] See Part One for a profile of Louis D. Brandeis and his handling of this case with its implications for scientific management.

management. It even dragged its heels on publishing Taylor's book, *The Principles of Scientific Management*; in 1911, after an unsuccessful attempt to get ASME to sponsor his work, Taylor published it privately.

During this period new societies came into being. A society of business managers was formed in 1907, and the Efficiency Society was organized in 1912. Probably, however, the most significant and enduring of these new groups was the Society to Promote the Science of Management, organized on December 4, 1911. The founders and charter members all came from ASME. The first president was James M. Dodge, Chairman of the Link-Belt Co. in Philadelphia.

Then in 1913, Harlow Stafford Person became President of SPSM. Whereas Dodge had a narrow view of scientific management, which he saw as focusing essentially on the Taylor system of scientific management, Person took a broad view and encouraged discussion on the widest possible basis. He brought in the views of social scientists, working people, and social philosophers. His leadership established that scientific management was not simply another term for the work of efficiency experts or the exploitation of workers.

In 1915, Taylor died and SPSM honored him by changing its name to the Taylor Society. In 1934, the Taylor Society merged with the Society of Industrial Engineers to become the Society for the Advancement of Management. Finally, in 1934, SAM joined the National Management Council, which in 1964 represented the United States in the federation of world management organizations—the International Committee of Scientific Management, or Comité International de l'Organisation Scientifique, now known familiarly as CIOS. And it was Harlow Person who, as managing director, guided the Taylor Society from 1918 to 1933, contributing to its development as an economist and a philosopher rather than as a technician or an engineer. Under his leadership, meetings ranged over a wide variety of topics. His leadership, along with his editing of the Society's *Bulletin*, did much to establish the scientific approach to management in American industry.

Harlow Person was, in fact, one of the principal missionaries and philosophers for the scientific management movement. He defined its terms carefully and, in a disciplined manner, set forth its potential benefits. He identified scientific management as characterizing the form of organization and of procedures in purposive collective effort.[2] His point was that scientific management provided laws and principles derived by the process of scientific investigation and analysis. To prevent misunderstanding, Person separated *management* from *administration*. To him, administration involved values, goals, and judgments; although it might encompass the scientific method, it also involved social, political, and philosophical considerations. In contrast, Person identified management as concerned with the activities necessary to

[2] For the material covered in this and the following two paragraphs, see Edward Eyre Hunt, ed., *Scientific Management Since Taylor* (New York: McGraw-Hill, 1924), especially pp. 5, 6, 33, and 56.

achieve the goals set by administration. He saw management as being more or less mechanistic in its nature. Thus management was able to utilize principles and laws determined by the scientific method of investigation.

The scientific management movement first was concerned primarily with shop management. It was Person who emphasized that it was applicable to the enterprise as a whole. In fact, it was his conclusion that "the Taylor philosophy of management first gave logical and coherent expression to the idea that business should be an aggregate of processing enterprisers instead of an aggregate of speculative enterprises." He believed that this would lead to increased comfort and promote the happiness of all concerned.

One of Harlow Person's central interests was planning. To him, it was the critical factor for institutional survival. "He observed that the problems of institutional development and co-ordination lay beyond the capacity of any one individual. . . . There must be developed for an enterprise an 'institutional mind,' independent of individuals who come and go, which possesses its institutional power of perception (research), memory (records), capacity for reasoning (group analysis) and power to direct the application of conclusions through a period longer than the life of an individual (institutional administration)."[3] Harlow Person identified this process as planning. It encompassed defining goals, arranging ways and means of attaining them, and pursuing them in a consistent manner yet with sufficient flexibility to permit adjustment to changing conditions. Moreover, Person saw responsibility, authority, and control as inherent parts of the planning process. These he believed must be used in accordance with the "laws of the situation." In planning, the design must be such that in execution the control and authority reflected the forces inherent in the situation.[4]

According to Person, the planning process and its proper implementation should and could be extended to the American economy. He recognized the danger that planning could lead to dictatorship, but he believed that the "laws of the situation" and American democratic traditions would alleviate this threat. Moreover, his ideal for the U.S. economy needs to be examined in the context of his times. It was a period when the United States was suffering from a severe depression. Thus, to Person, *national planning* was the means of moving from a "confused to an orderly democracy."—WILLIAM B. WOLF

SELECTED PUBLICATIONS

Books:

1907 *Industrial Education,* A System of Training for Men Entering upon Trade and Commerce. . . . Boston and New York: Houghton, Mifflin.

[3] See "On the Technique of Planning," *Bulletin* of the Taylor Society and of the Society of Industrial Engineers, Vol. 1, No. 1, November 1934, p. 29.

[4] *Idem.*

1929 *Scientific Management in American Industry*, by the Taylor Society, H. S. Person, ed. New York and London: Harper.

1936 *Little Waters*, A Study of Headwater Streams and Other Little Waters, Their Use and Relation to the Land. Washington, D.C.: U.S. Government Printing Office.

1942 *Mexican Oil*, Symbol of Recent Trends in International Relations. New York: Harper.

Articles:

1906 "Education for Business," *Annals* of the American Academy of Political and Social Science, July.

1924 "Scientific Management: A Brief Statement of Its Nature"; "The Contribution of Scientific Management to Industrial Problems"; "Shaping Your Management to Meet Developing Industrial Conditions"; and "Scientific Management and the Reduction of Unemployment," in *Scientific Management Since Taylor* (first edition), a collection of authoritative papers edited by Edward Eyre Hunt. New York: McGraw-Hill.

1926 "Basic Principles of Administration and of Management," in *Scientific Foundations of Business Administration*. Baltimore: Williams & Wilkins.

1927 "The Reaction of Workers to Machine Work and Working Conditions"; "The Worker's Reaction to Supervision and the Procedures of Supervision"; and "Reaction to Rewards," in *The Psychological Foundations of Management*, Henry C. Metcalf, ed. Chicago: A. W. Shaw.

1928 "Scientific Management: An Analysis with Particular Emphasis on Its Attitude Toward Human Relations in Industry," *Bulletin* of the Taylor Society, Vol. 13, October, pp. 199–205.

—— "The Work-Week or the Work-Life?" *Bulletin* of the Taylor Society, Vol. 13, December, pp. 230–248.

1929 "Inspection of Performance," in *Scientific Management in American Industry*. New York: Taylor Society, pp. 385–397.

—— "Inspection of Physical Standards," in *Scientific Management in American Industry*. New York: Taylor Society, pp. 377–383.

—— "A New Way of Looking at the Five-Day Week," *Survey*, Vol. 61, January, pp. 505–507.

—— "What Management Can Do to Relieve Unemployment," in *Trade Unions Study Unemployment*. . . . Washington, D.C.: American Federation of Labor, p. 167.

1932 "The Approach of Scientific Management to the Problem of National Planning," *Annals* of the American Academy of Political and Social Science, July, pp. 19–26.

—— "Scientific Management as a Philosophy and Technique of Progressive Industrial Stabilization," *Bulletin* of the Taylor Society, Vol. 17, December, pp. 204–228.

——— "Stabilization Through Regulation of Investment," *Bulletin* of the Taylor Society, Vol. 17, June, pp. 113–124.

1933 "Economics Makes the Front Page," *Survey Graphic*, Vol. 22, March, pp. 156–159.

1934 "On the Technique of Planning," *Bulletin* of the Taylor Society and of the Society of Industrial Engineers, Vol. 1, No. 1, November, pp. 29–34.

1936 "On Planning; With Especial Reference to Social-Economic Planning," *Journal* of the Society for the Advancement of Management, November.

——— "Planning and Free Enterprise," *Survey Graphic*, Vol. 25, No. 4, April.

1937 "The Bedaux System," *New Republic*, Vol. 93, November, p. 24.

1939 "Carl Georg Lange Barth, February 28, 1860–October 28, 1939," *Advanced Management*, Vol. 4, Fall, p. 114.

——— "Influences of Environmental Changes on Distribution Problems," *Advanced Management*, Vol. 4, Fall, pp. 137–140.

1945 "Planned Execution: The Issue of Scientific Management," *Advanced Management*, December, pp. 131–138.

Curriculum Vitae

1875 Born on February 16th in Republican City, Nebr.

1899 Awarded Ph.B., University of Michigan.

1900 Awarded M.A., University of Michigan.

1902 Awarded Ph.D., University of Michigan.

1902–1919 Associated with Amos Tuck School of Administration and Finance at Dartmouth College:

- 1902–1904 Instructor of Commerce and Industry.
- 1904–1905 Assistant Professor of Commerce and Industry.
- 1905–1908 Director and Assistant Professor of Commerce and Industry.
- 1908–1919 Dean and Professor of Business and Organization.

1913–1917 Served as President of the Society to Promote the Science of Management, which, in 1915, became the Taylor Society.

1917 Served on War Industries Board.

1918 With U.S. Army Ordinance Corps.

1918–1933 Became Managing Director of the Taylor Society, New York.

1921–1942 Lectured on business administration at Columbia University.

1933–1953 Active as management consultant.

1934 Appointed member of Mississippi Valley Committee, Public Works Administration.

1935–1953 Served as Consulting Economist and Special Assistant to the Administrator of the Rural Electrification Administration, Washington, D.C.

1942 Served as Consulting Economist and Chief of Staff to the U.S. Mexican Oil Committee.

1955 Died on November 7th, aged 80, in Dobbs Ferry, N.Y.

Harlow Stafford Person was named a knight in the Order of the White Lion by the government of Czechoslovakia (1924); made an honorary member of the Masaryk Academy for helping to organize the First World Congress of Scientific Management, held in Prague (1924); and received the Taylor Key of the Society for the Advance of Management (1943) and the gold medal of CIOS (Comité International de l'Organisation Scientifique) (1947). He was a member of the American Economic Association, American Statistical Association, American Society for Public Administration, American Association for Labor Legislation, National Management Council, National Economic and Social Planning Association, International Industrial Relations Institute, Society for the Advancement of Management, National Planning Association, American Society of Mechanical Engineers, and American Association of University Professors.

Photo by Fabian Bachrach.

Alfred Pritchard Sloan, Jr.
(1875–1966)
United States

ALFRED P. Sloan Jr.—industrialist, philanthropist, and author—did much to shape the General Motors Corp. into one of the largest and most effective manufacturing enterprises in the world. In the process, he made significant contributions to management. His innovations at General Motors have been adopted by a considerable number of large firms, and his ideas provide a guideline for understanding the structure and strategy of administration.

Sloan's association with General Motors came about through William C. Durant, who, in 1916, purchased the Hyatt Roller Bearing Co. Through the purchase he obtained the services of Alfred P. Sloan, Jr. Durant soon arranged for Sloan to become President of United Motors, a company providing accessories for General Motors. In 1918, when United Motors was merged with General Motors, Sloan became Vice-President, in which capacity he was in charge of a group of accessory divisions. Shortly thereafter he became a member of the GM Executive Committee and a director of the corporation.

Sloan's philosophy of management centered upon the concept of an executive team which functioned in the interest of the company as a whole. Essential to such a team were the concepts of well-defined job responsibilities,

See the profiles of F. Donaldson Brown and James David Mooney in Part Two for further light on General Motors during the Sloan era.

fair promotion policy, performance incentives, and the use of persuasion rather than arbitrary authority. Furthermore, Sloan, as a director, believed that he represented the general body of stockholders rather than any special-interest group. He pioneered in developing a well-planned stockholder relations program, which he backed with detailed, professional-level annual reports.

A good way to appreciate Sloan's contribution to management is to review his plan for the reorganization of General Motors. In 1920 GM faced a crisis. The market for GM cars had suddenly evaporated. From July to August sales had dropped by 25 percent from their previous peak. In October they dropped by 60 percent and in November by 75 percent. Moreover, productive capacity at GM had been overexpanded, inventories were too high, and working capital was nearly exhausted. To save the situation, the du Pont and Morgan interests raised a large sum of money and arranged for Pierre S. du Pont to come out of retirement and assume the GM presidency. The arrangement was that he would retire as soon as a qualified man could be found to head GM.

As Ernest Dale reports the situation, Sloan had in May 1920 prepared a thorough plan for the reorganization of GM. He had given this plan to the then president, Will Durant, but no action was forthcoming.[1] Later he submitted his plan to Pierre du Pont, who, in December 1920, presented it to the GM Board of Directors. It was accepted. Sloan, still Vice-President, was placed in charge of the advisory staff and, within a short time, became Operating Vice-President. In April 1922, Sloan's responsibilities were further increased when he was appointed to GM'S Finance Committee; also, during that same month, he joined the du Pont Board of Directors. Then, on May 10, 1923, he was made President of General Motors.

Sloan's plan for the reorganization of GM is considered by many authorities to be a landmark in the history of management thought. It is tightly written, clear, and concise and takes up only 28 pages. The two basic concepts underlying it are these: (1) Operations should be *decentralized* in the sense that the chief executive for each major operating unit should have reporting to him every function necessary to enable his organization to achieve its logical development and exercise its full initiative. (2) Staff functions should be *centralized*, as should the measurement of results. Centralization of these functions is essential to proper coordination of the corporation's activities.

It should be noted that Sloan's plan was specifically designed to deal with problems at GM. However, its more general applicability is illustrated by the four specific goals Sloan aimed to achieve. These were:

1. To establish a clear division of work so that the functions of the various groups would be definitely determined both in relation to one another and in relation to the central organization of the company.

[1] Ernest Dale, *The Great Organizers* (New York: McGraw-Hill, 1960), pp. 84–85. The writer is indebted to Dale for much of this material on Alfred Sloan, Jr. See *The Great Organizers*, pp. 71–111.

2. To establish the status of the central organization and to coordinate its operations with those of the corporation as a whole.
3. To centralize in the President, as chief executive officer, control of all the executive functions of the organization.
4. To concentrate the chief executive's work on innovation and representation by delegating all operating functions and by coordinating the planning of general advisory staffs.

In his plan Sloan differentiated between *major control* and *executive control.* Major control ran from stockholders to directors to two major groups: (1) the Finance Committee and (2) the Executive Committee. The Finance Committee was to pass on the major capital investments recommended by the Executive Committee, and it was to formulate the corporation's financial policy. Executive control was to rest with the President, acting within the framework laid down by major control.

According to Sloan's design for the new formal structure of GM, operations reported to the President. His guides for grouping operations were common characteristics and common geographical bases. General managers of operational units had as great administrative control over sales, finance, and engineering as the chief executive of an independent corporation. Related operations of lesser importance were consolidated under a single executive. The divisions of GM were encouraged to compete. The transfer of products from one division to another was to be treated in the same way as purchases from outside suppliers.

Sloan's plan called for an *Operations Committee* made up of the heads of the operating divisions. One of its jobs was to ensure coordination of the company's overall activities. Sloan also provided for a *general advisory staff* which was to be of help to the decentralized divisions. However, Sloan was explicit in calling attention to the fact that these staffs only gave "advice"; divisions were free to accept or reject that advice. Sloan's plan also required the development of a general financial and accounting staff under the direction of the Chairman of the Finance Committee. And, finally, the plan assigned to the President a "personal staff" consisting of a number of "assistants to."

Probably one of Sloan's greatest achievements at GM was his development of a systemized government for the corporation. Wherever possible, it was a government based on facts and a systematic approach. He and his executives inaugurated mechanisms for communication and decision making which allowed control of the total corporation and rapid adjustment to changing conditions. The key aspects of this systemized government follow:

1. An accurate system of inventory control and capital budgets based upon careful forecasting of the demand for cars.
2. Production plans to accommodate different segments of the market.
3. Pricing policies to provide an optimum return on investment.

4. Structuring of the chief executive's job so that he could spend a significant portion of his time working personally with executives and with GM automobile dealers. Sloan saw that the GM sales organization was central to the corporation's success. He frequently traveled at night so that he could interview dealers during the day. Each year he personally talked to thousands of dealers, constantly helping them to apply his systematic approach to business. He wanted them to have the facts, maintain good accounting records, and be able to handle business problems intelligently.
5. Professional performance by all executives along with contribution to the corporation as a whole (as contrasted with personal loyalty and "politics"). Sloan encouraged participation in policy making. To him, his principal associates were partners in the management of the enterprise. He developed the GM executive bonus plan which reaffirmed this concept of partnership and, by its ingenious design, discouraged GM executives from moving to other firms.
6. What might be called the "administrative ideology"[2] developed by Sloan and his associates. Executives at General Motors shared a system of beliefs and values which Sloan and those who were close to him preached and taught by precept and example. They believed in the individual and in the applicability of basic concepts of "federal decentralization" to a large, complex organization such as GM. To them, decentralization was a policy closely "akin to atomistic competition"[3]—each self-sufficient activity of the corporation would operate on its own within the overall framework of rules and policies. This would lead to each decentralized unit's contributing to the maximum of its ability. Within the same framework, moreover, a coordinated control system operated which provided for the accountability of all executives and also gave higher-level executives veto power.

This, in essence, was the General Motors theme put forth in memos, speeches, and articles and stressed in committee meetings. The system of beliefs it represented was spread directly by Sloan. He participated in group meetings at all levels, where, by both statements and example, he gave meaning to his philosophy of management. The meetings usually took on the characteristics of a seminar; Sloan encouraged debate and discussion and tended to delay final decisions until the underlying concepts had been accepted by those who were responsible for their implementation.[4]

The GM ideology also was disseminated by the training program originated under Sloan's administration. One of his great satisfactions was the General Motors Technical Institute in Flint, Mich. Because he was deeply

[2] Dale, *op. cit.*, p. 101.
[3] *Idem.*
[4] Dale, *ibid*, p. 103.

concerned with higher education, he considered "GM Tech" one of his most important achievements.[5] However, he chose not to publicize the Institute even though it was an effective force in training GM engineers and managers.

Above all, Alfred Pritchard Sloan, Jr., was a professional manager. He built one of the worlds largest organizations run by professional managers. To him, a professional was one who acts in accordance with well-understood guidelines based on personal goals, ethics, and understanding of facts. Decisions are reached only after systematic and careful deliberation. Most of all, a professional serves the organization, divorcing the "personal" from the "professional." Thus, in his book *My Years with General Motors*, the hero and central focus is General Motors, not Sloan.[6]

As a professional manager, Sloan objected to personal pomp and ceremony. The only ornament in his austere office was the framed announcement of his election as Chairman of the Board of Trustees of GM Tech. When Sloan stayed overnight in Detroit, he slept in a bare cubicle in the dormitory on the top floor of the GM building. Despite the fact that he spent about three nights a week in the city, he had no hotel suite or apartment.[7]

As a professional manager, Sloan maintained personal distance. He isolated himself from his fellow executives. Around General Motors he was addressed as "Mr. Sloan"; moreover, he did not call anyone by his or her first name. Peter Drucker describes this characteristic:

> Whenever he noticed a new elevator man at the GM building, he'd ask: "And what is your name, sir?" "I am Jack," the black "boy" would say. Sloan would turn crimson with rage, would say, "I asked for your *name*, sir," and would thereafter always say, "Good morning, Mr. Jones," when he encountered the man. The only exceptions he made were women secretaries young enough to be his daughters. "I've always wanted to have daughters," he said, "but Mrs. Sloan and I haven't been able to have children." And so "Sadie" and "Rosie" and "Cathie"—all outrageously spoiled by the old man—were his "substitute daughters."[8]

As a professional manager, also, Sloan carefully attempted to separate his personal feelings from his corporate decisions. This is illustrated by another vignette from Drucker: A young marketing man had aroused the antagonism of the elder executives by challenging their policy. They urged that he be fired. "'No' said Mr. Sloan. 'We don't penalize people for their opinions—we want them to have opinions.' And he gave the man a very big promotion, appointing him General Manager of the Electro-Motive Division

[5] Peter F. Drucker, *Adventures of a Bystander* (New York: Harper & Row, 1978), p. 290.

[6] This is a point made by Peter Drucker in *Adventures of a Bystander*. In fact, most of the comments about Sloan's personal characteristics have been drawn from Drucker's excellent characterization. *Op. cit.*, pp. 256–294.

[7] *Ibid.*, p. 285.

[8] *Ibid.*, pp. 284–285.

in Chicago. . . . 'This way,' Sloan said, 'he'll make as much money through his bonuses as if he had reached a top position at GM, or more. Yet he'll be out of Detroit, where he can't really function with all the enemies he's made, including myself.'"[9]

In another case an executive seriously annoyed Sloan to the point of anger. Someone asked, "Mr. Sloan, why don't you let him go?" "Let him go?" Sloan replied. "What an absurd idea; he *performs*."[10]

Sloan had a characteristic way of making decisions. He would generally hear all parties and then summarize their positions. Next he would focus upon the assumptions implicit in the various positions and ask for data to test them. He rarely made a decision by vote. His philosophy was to make it by creating understanding. Furthermore, after each meeting he wrote a memorandum in which he identified the key question and asked: "Is this what the decision is all about?"[11]

Sloan's professionalism was manifest in his human relations. His insight and kindness had directly touched most of his key executives. One story concerns a newly appointed general manager who panicked in a meeting and under cross-examination began making outrageous speculations. He was in the process of destroying himself when Sloan jumped in and made common cause with the distraught man. When asked why, Sloan responded: "As chairman of this company, it is my responsibility to preserve income-earning assets, and we have twenty years of heavy investment in this young man."[12]

To Alfred P. Sloan, Jr., managing General Motors was his hobby, his love, and his lifework. He dedicated himself to the organization; and, although he built a mythology in GM to the effect that the key executives were invariably men who rose from the school of hard knocks, he himself had a strong belief in the value of college education. He left a fortune to education; and, in addition to the General Motors Technical Institute, his impact is felt through his financing of the Sloan School of Administration at M.I.T., the Sloan School of Hospital Administration at Cornell University, and his contributions to the Sloan-Kettering Institute for Cancer Research.—WILLIAM B. WOLF.

SELECTED PUBLICATIONS

Books:

1941 *Adventures of a White-Collar Man.* In collaboration with Boyden Sparkes. New York: Doubleday, Doran. 208 pp.

1963 *My Years with General Motors.* Edited by John McDonald with Catherine Stevens. New York: Doubleday. 467 pp.

[9] *Ibid.*, p. 283.
[10] *Ibid.*, p. 282.
[11] *Ibid.*, p. 287.
[12] *Ibid.*, p. 282.

Reports and Articles:

1920 The General Motors Reorganization Plan, Defendant's Exhibit No. 300, in Civil Action No. 49 C-1071, United States of America v. E. I. duPont de Nemours and Company, General Motors Corporation, et al., U.S. District Court for the Northern District of Illinois, Eastern Division, Chicago 1953.

1924 "The Most Important Thing I Ever Learned About Management," *System,* August.

1946 "Importance of Management," reprinted from *General Motors Corporation Annual Report.*

Curriculum Vitae

1875 Born on May 23rd in New Haven, Conn.

1895 Received B.S. in Sciences, Massachusetts Institute of Technology.

1895 Employed as a draftsman, Hyatt Roller Bearing Co.

1895–1898 Worked for Hygienic Refrigerator Co.

1898–1916 Became Partner in Hyatt Roller Bearing Co., serving as President and General Manager.

1916 Became President, United Motors Corp.

1918 With United Motors absorbed into General Motors, became GM Vice-President. In charge of group of accessory divisions.

1918–1966 Employed by General Motors.

- 1919 Made a director and member of Executive Committee.
- 1920 Had plan for reorganization of GM accepted by Board of Directors. Still Vice-President, placed in charge of advisory staff.
- 1921 Named Operating Vice-President.
- 1922 Became member of GM's Finance Committee.
- 1923 Became President of GM and member of du Pont Board of Directors.
- 1937–1956 Served as Chairman of GM Board of Directors.
- 1956–1966 Continued as Honorary Chairman of GM Board of Directors.

1966 Died on February 17th, aged 90, in New York City.

Alfred P. Sloan, Jr., was Chairman of the Board of Trustees of GM Tech, Trustee of the Sloan-Kettering Institute for Cancer Research, Trustee of the Institute of Social Research of the University of Michigan, and Governor and Chairman of the Alfred P. Sloan Foundation. He was awarded the following honorary degrees: LL.D., Princeton University (1947); LL.D., Syracuse University (1955); LL.D., Wabash College (1957); LL.D., Columbia University (1957); LL.D., Dartmouth College (1957); D.C.S., New York University (1962); D.Sc., Duke University (1962), and D.Sc., Colgate College (1962).

Photo by Fabian Bachrach.

Henry Plimpton Kendall
(1878–1959)
United States

HENRY P. Kendall is remembered for his innovative applications in the area of scientific management, to which he was first introduced by Frederick W. Taylor's classic *Shop Management.*

Kendall went to work with his uncle at Plimpton Press in Norwood, Mass., after his graduation from Amherst College in 1899. Profoundly influenced by Taylor, he proceeded to transform Plimpton into a showcase for the Taylor system. Kendall, however, carried his ideas about sound management even beyond those of Taylor. Demonstrating his understanding of the importance of the human factor in industry, he discarded the "traditional" system of hiring and firing employees indiscriminately. Kendall firmly believed that workers could find satisfaction in their jobs; he was responsible for the formation of one of the earliest "employees' departments." A leader in labor relations as well, he expressed the opinion that one of management's duties was to work with unions so that they would better understand that "prosperity for industry meant prosperity for workers."

In 1903, Kendall became associated with Lewis Batting Co., a small and virtually insolvent gauze-manufacturing firm. With Taylor's aid, Kendall again followed what was to become a well-established pattern of organization improvement. By 1912, thanks to the methods of scientific management that were installed, plus the development of a new process of bleaching cotton, Lewis Batting was paying cash dividends. Kendall then purchased the company and extended its operations by acquiring a series of additional mills that were incorporated in 1924 as Kendall Mills. Characteristically, Kendall was one of the first employers in the New England textile industry to cut working hours from 60 to 48 a week with no reduction in pay and to end the employment of women and minors on evening shifts.

Henry Kendall was a keen and perceptive student of business who clearly foresaw the role sound management would play in the next generation. Commenting on the evolution and future of industry, in a 1922 address before the Taylor Society, he stated:

> I believe industry passes through cycles of change. We have had the cycle of the development of labor-saving machinery; the cycle of the growth of the corporate form of industry and of big combinations; the cycle of the distribution of securities and of the borrowing of capital from wealthy countries of the world; we have seen centralized and cooperative selling and purchasing. What next? From my observation I will hazard the guess that we are about to see a cycle of refinements in management.

As an industrial leader, Kendall fully recognized the problems and responsibilities of being a chief executive. The evolution of the Kendall Co. from its beginnings in 1912 until Henry Kendall's death in 1959 is a success story of American enterprise and resourcefulness. Originally a simple supplier of hospital gauze, it became a major producer of diversified hospital products. Under Kendall's direction, it grew from one mill with 75 employees into an international corporation employing more than 5,000 people. During this same period, its annual sales increased from $200,000 in 1912 to $110,733,408 in 1959. And, unquestionably, an integral part of the company's success was due to Kendall's early adoption of scientific management and his strong emphasis on product research. Kendall was the first textile operation in the United States to institute a research program, and many Kendall-developed products—such as Curity diapers and infants' wear and Curad plastic bandages—have become standard consumer items around the world.

Avidly interested in education, Kendall lectured for many years at the Harvard Business School, the Tuck School of Dartmouth College, and the Wharton School of the University of Pennsylvania. He served on the boards of Mt. Holyoke College and Deerfield Academy; and both institutions as well as Amherst College and Andover-Newton Theological School, were million-dollar beneficiaries in his will.

Henry P. Kendall was a man of great initiative and integrity. Intuitively, he sought to improve continuously the operation of any venture in which he was involved. He was dedicated, enthusiastic, and persistent, and his curiosity was boundless. Moreover,

> . . . he had the courage to put his convictions into action: the growth of the Kendall Company was built on his willingness to venture boldly. Friendship through respect was part of him: his friends spanned

completely the top echelons of American business, and the camaraderie within the Kendall Company was important to its development.*

—ARTHUR C. BEDEIAN

SELECTED PUBLICATIONS

Books:

1918 *Profit Sharing, Its Principles and Practices.* With Arthur W. Burritt, Henry S. Dennison, Edwin F. Gay, and Ralph E. Heilmen. New York: Harper.

1926 *Profit Sharing and Stock Ownership for Employees.* With Gorton James, Henry S. Dennison, Edwin F. Gay, and Arthur W. Burritt. New York: Harper.

Articles:

1913 "Prerequisites to Scientific Management," *Industrial Engineering and Engineering Digest*, Vol. 13, pp. 201–202.

—— "Systematized and Scientific Management," *Journal of Political Economy*, Vol. 21, pp. 593–617.

1922 "The Problem of the Chief Executive," *Bulletin* of the Taylor Society, Vol. 7, (April), pp. 39–46.

1923 "Unsystematized, Systematized and Scientific Management," *Bulletin* of the Taylor Society, Vol. 8, October, pp. 189–200.

1924 "A Decade's Development in Management," *Bulletin* of the Taylor Society, Vol. 9, April, pp. 54–65.

1927 "Scientific Management in a Textile Business," *Bulletin* of the Taylor Society, Vol. 12, December, pp. 519–525.

Monographs:

1939 *The Administrator Looks at Research.* Proceedings No. 4, Industrial Research Conference. Columbus, Ohio: Ohio State University.

1953 *The Kendall Company, 50 Years of Yankee Enterprise.* New York: Newcomen Society in North America.

Curriculum Vitae

1878 Born on January 15th in Charlestown, Mass.

1899 Received A.B. from Amherst College.

1899–1925 Employed at Plimpton Press, Norwood, Mass. Rose to General Manager and Treasurer (1910) and finally became part owner (1913).

* Marjorie W. Young, ed., *Textile Leaders of the South* (Anderson, S. C.: James R. Young, 1963), p. 773.

1903	Elected Treasurer of Lewis Batting Co., Walpole, Mass. Introduced Taylor system of management.
1912	Purchased Lewis Batting Co. (later Lewis Manufacturing Co.).
1917	Became member, War Industries Board, Council of National Defense.
1918–1919	Served as Chairman, Commission on Industrial Relations of the Chamber of Commerce of the United States.
1924	Incorporated mills owned as Kendall Mills.
1928	Changed name of Kendall Mills to the Kendall Co.
1931–1933	Served as member, Massachusetts Commission on Stabilization of Employment.
1933–1934	Served as member, Federal Advisory Council of the U.S. Department of Labor.
1933–1959	Served as member, Business Advisory Council of the U.S. Department of Commerce. Was Chairman, 1934–1935.
1939–1940	Served as member, Division of Engineering and Industrial Research, National Research Council.
1942–1946	Served as Regional Chairman, First Federal Reserve District Commission for Economic Development.
1942–1956	Served as member, New England Committee on Economic Development (was Chairman, 1946–1956). Served as Trustee, Committee for Economic Development (later Honorary Chairman).
1959	Died on November 3rd, aged 81, in Sharon, Mass.

Henry Plimpton Kendall was a member of the Taylor Society. In 1928 he was elected President of the Society, and in 1944 he received its Taylor Key for the Advancement of Management. In addition, he was a Fellow of the American Academy of Arts and Sciences.

Courtesy R. Greenwood.

Lillian Moller Gilbreth
(1878–1972)
United States

LILLIAN Moller Gilbreth was a pioneer of scientific management. In 1914 she published *The Pyschology of Management*, one of the earliest U.S. books focusing on industrial psychology. But, more important, she worked closely with her husband, Frank Bunker Gilbreth, in the development of motion study. Not only did she collaborate with him on consulting assignments and in writing books, but when, in 1924, he died suddenly of a heart attack, she presented his papers and took his place generally at the London Power Conference, at the World Congress of Scientific Management held in Prague that year, and at Prague's Masaryk Academy.

Lillian Gilbreth represented scientific management and, more particularly, motion study to the entire world. She was both an intellectual and a teacher, thereby adding status, dignity, and academic acceptability to the field. She lectured on technology and the human relations problems of management in Asia, Australia, Canada, Europe, Mexico, and the United States. Furthermore, she taught industrial engineering in Taiwan. And, in addition to contributing significantly to the scientific management movement, Lillian Gilbreth—still a relatively young woman—also raised a family of 12 children single-handedly after her husband suffered his fatal heart seizure. Because she herself was one of the few qualified industrial psychologists of the mid-1920s and because she had shared her husband's interest in the actual practice—the "nuts and bolts"—of management, she picked up the Gilbreth firm's consulting and lecturing work quickly and smoothly. Moreover, the publicity received from the books* written by two of the children—*Cheaper by the Dozen* and *Belles on Their Toes*, to name the most popular of the series—has done much to familiarize a wide audience with the names of both parents.

And Lillian Gilbreth did far more than just contribute a feminine note to the early scientific management movement. She was a moving force in it—first through her understanding and support of her husband, then through her own activities. The substance, not simply the folklore, of management is the richer for her work. Especially in her later years, feeling that the principles of scientific management applied to a home as well as to a business, she developed a high degree of expertise in the specialty of household management. Her lectures on this subject, before college and executive audiences over the United States and abroad, were exceptionally well received, particularly by the wives of managers who knew at first hand all the challenges and problems of managing a home.

Lillian Gilbreth was a gracious lady. She had charm and dignity as well as the intellectual acumen that most people immediately recognized and respected. A humanistic concern underlay much of her work. Her first book was directed at relieving waste, fatigue, and drudgery in industry; her last dealt with helping the disabled.

She was a relatively tall woman with piercing blue eyes and a presence that indicated maturity and understanding. In the field of industrial engineering she was respected as a woman who carried the responsibilities of an active consultant in addition to heading a large family. She successfully combined the two roles of professional industrial engineer and single parent, performing each with distinction.

Lillian was for years known in managerial circles as the "first lady of management." And indeed she was a "first." Her book on managerial psychology was one of the first in its field. She was probably the first woman to head a prominent management consulting firm. Then, when the International Academy of Management was founded in 1954, she was the first and, for years, the only woman Fellow.

As an interesting aside, Lillian greatly enjoyed remembering each of her children, grandchildren, and great-grandchildren with a Christmas gift and a note every year. There being something like 50 of them in all, this was a tremendous task. She solved it by planning in advance, starting each January with her list and a program for personally buying the appropriate gifts, wrapping them herself, and enclosing eagerly anticipated notes. By December, she had these personalized remembrances ready to go.

All those who knew Lillian Gilbreth counted it an enormous privilege and a great pleasure to be able to sit at her feet over the years. She was

* Frank B. Gilbreth, Jr., and Ernestine Gilbreth Carey, *Cheaper by the Dozen* (New York: T. Y. Crowell, 1949), and *Belles on Their Toes* (New York: T. Y. Crowell, 1950). Published in other English-speaking countries by Heinemann.

always stimulating, not a bit pompous—on the contrary, rather humble about her ideas and achievements. To meet her was a gratifying experience.—WILLIAM B. WOLF AND HAROLD KOONTZ.

SELECTED PUBLICATIONS

Books:

1912 *Primer of Scientific Management.* With Frank B. Gilbreth. New York: D. Van Nostrand. Mrs. Gilbreth's name does not appear in this book because the publisher did not wish it known that there was a woman co-author.

1914 *The Psychology of Management.* New York: Sturgis & Walton.

1916 *Fatigue Study.* With Frank B. Gilbreth. New York: Sturgis & Walton.

1917 *Applied Motion Study.* With Frank B. Gilbreth. New York: Sturgis & Walton.

1920 *Motion Study for the Handicapped.* With Frank B. Gilbreth. New York: Macmillan; London: Routledge.

1924 *The Quest of the One Best Way, A Sketch of the Life of Frank Bunker Gilbreth.* Chicago: Society of Industrial Engineers (published privately).

1927 *The Homemaker and Her Job.* New York: Appleton-Century.

1928 *Living with Our Children.* New York: W. W. Norton.

1945 *Normal Lives for the Disabled.* With Edna Yost. New York: Macmillan.

1947 *The Foreman in Manpower Management.* With Alice Rice Cook. New York: McGraw-Hill.

1954 *Management in the Home.* With Orpha Mae Thomas and Eleanor Clymer. New York: Dodd, Mead.

Curriculum Vitae

1878 Born on May 24th in Oakland, Calif.

1900 Awarded B. Litt., University of California at Berkeley.

1902 Awarded M. Litt., University of California at Berkeley.

1904 Married Frank Bunker Gilbreth on October 19th.

1915 Received Ph.D. from Brown University.

1921 Made honorary member, Society of Industrial Engineers.

1924 When husband died suddenly, leaving 12 children to support, became President of Gilbreth Inc., consulting engineering firm in management.

1929–1933 Served as member of New Jersey State Board of Regents.

1930 Headed Womens' Work for the President's Emergency Committee for Unemployment. Also served on President's Organization on Unemployment Relief.

1935–1948 Served as Professor of Management at Purdue University. Also Lecturer at Bryn Mawr and Professor of Management at Rutgers.

1941–1943	Headed Personnel Relations Department, Newark College of Engineering.
1944–1954	On Board of Trustees, Montcalir (N.J.) Library.
1950	Served as consultant to Institute of Rehabilitation Medicine, New York University Medical Center.
1951–1953	Served as member of Civil Defense Advisory Council.
1953–1954	Did university teaching in Philippine Islands and Taiwan.
1955	Served as Professor of Management, University of Wisconsin.
1972	Died on January 1st at the age of 93.

Lillian Gilbreth held the following honorary degrees: M. Engr., University of Michigan, 1928; D.E., Rutgers College, 1929; Sc.D., Brown University, 1931; Sc.D., Russell Sage College, 1931; LL.D., University of California, 1933; LL.D., Smith College, 1945; D. Industrial Psychology, Purdue University, 1948; L.H.D., Alfred University, 1948; L.H.D., Temple University, 1949; Sc.D., Colby College, 1951; Sc.D., Lafayette College, 1952; LL.D., Mills College, 1952; D.E., Syracuse University, 1952. She was similarly honored by Milwaukee Downer College, Washington University, Princeton, Skidmore College, University of Wisconsin, Pratt University, University of Massachusetts, Western College for Women, Arizona State University.

In 1944, Dr. Gilbreth was awarded the Henry Laurence Gantt Medal; in 1948, the American Woman's Association Award for Eminent Achievement; in 1951, the Wallace Clark Award, the Gold Medal of the Comité International de l'Organisation Scientifique, and the Washington Award; in 1959, the Allan R. Cullimore Medal; and, in 1966, the Hoover Medal of the American Society of Civil Engineers.

Teijiro Ueda
(1879–1940)
Japan

TEIJIRO Ueda was Japan's first scholar of business administration and a superb teacher under whom virtually all Japan's professionals in the field of management studied at one time or another. Abroad, he was known as an articulate spokesman for Japan's interests in the many important international meetings he attended as adviser to the Japanese government.

Ueda was born in Tokyo in 1879 within the compound of the Kishu branch of the Tokugawa family; his connections with the Tokugawas were to continue throughout most of his life. He graduated from the Tokyo Commercial High School (now Hitotsubashi University) in 1900 and from the school's Special Studies program in 1902. Immediately he was appointed Instructor, and in 1905 he was promoted to Professor. Meanwhile, he managed to teach courses at several other high schools and to begin a prolific writing career.

In 1905 Ueda made the first of two study trips to Europe, spending two years in England and two in Germany. He studied business administration under Professor William Ashley at the University of Birmingham and under Professor Meredith at the University of Manchester, after which he attended a series of lectures at the Universities of Bonn and Berlin. Upon his return to Japan in 1909, he threw himself into the task of introducing the new discipline, giving lectures on the scientific study of business administration at Tokyo Commercial High School as well as at Meiji and Nihon Universities.

His second study trip to England, begun in late 1913, was cut short by the outbreak of the First World War.

Ueda's students remember with affection the enthusiasm with which he lectured, often scarcely bothering to glance at his notes. They remember, too, the rigor with which he insisted they have a critical appreciation for the written word and to write themselves with a firm grasp of the relevant facts. His own writing bears witness to his dislike for pure theory and academicism. Ranging widely over the crucial questions of each decade, a number of his works still stand as classics in his chosen field of business administration: the 1928 *Kabushiki kaisha keizairon* (Economic Theory of the Corporation), the 1930 *Shoko keiei* (Business Administration), and the 1937 *Keiei keizaigaku soron* (Science of Business Administration). These books may seem dated today, yet each was a seminal work stimulating other specialists to refine the concepts and methods presented.

Ueda himself saw his work as progressing through three stages. He was the first in Japan to undertake the study of business administration and to do so through description and analysis of the structure of enterprises in the context of the national economy. Later, he was the first to analyze in detail the relationship between the corporation and its manifestation in the productive enterprise. And, finally, he was among the first to treat the subject of population, relating it to size and quality of the labor force and to the need for economic growth.

Ueda's concerns were always pragmatic. In studying the enterprise and its management, he asserted that in the long run it is the manager and not the capitalist/financier whose function is of major importance to the productivity of the firm. He argued the need for a class of managers—"enterprise men"—who would amass the capital to promote foreign trade, outlining his position in the 1928 *Shinjiyushugi to jiyu tsusho* (New Liberalism and Foreign Trade). At the 1927 International Economic Convention in Geneva and elsewhere, he stressed Japan's reliance upon foreign trade for her very survival; he called not only for a reduction in trade barriers but also for recognition of a new breed of manager who, accountable to both the enterprise and to society, would plan the growth of production and of foreign trade. He was opposed to the Manchester school of profit-oriented management, believing instead that labor and management resemble a set of meshed gears, both necessary for the health of the national economy.

Population research was the other area in which Ueda's work was especially valued. He declared that only by expanding production to meet growth in foreign trade would the problem of a growing population be solved. His particular contribution to discussions of this problem lay in devising a scientific method for calculating age-adjusted population projections. The formula which he proposed gave more accurate estimates of the size of the labor force.

Ueda was a man of leadership who, in addition to his teaching, writing, and consulting activities, served on the boards of many distinguished professional associations. Where he encouraged thoughtful consideration of the many problems of business administration, especially those faced by small and medium-size enterprises.—KISOU TASUGI AND ELIZABETH T. MASSEY

SELECTED PUBLICATIONS

Books:

1903 *Gaikoku boeki genron* (Principles of Foreign Trade). Fukkyusha.

1915 *Senji keizai kowa* (Lectures on the Wartime Economy). Toyamabo.

1923 *Eikoku sangyo kakumei shiron* (A History of the English Industrial Revolution). Toyko: Dobun-kan.

1928 *Kabushiki kaisha keizairon* (Economic Theory of the Corporation). Tokyo: Nihon Hyuron-sha.

—— *Shinjiyushugi to jiyu tsusho* (The New Liberalism and Foreign Trade). Tokyo: Dobun-kan.

1930 *Shoko keiei* (Business Administration), Vol. 5 in *Shogaku zenshu* (The Study of Commerce: The Complete Reader). Tokyo: Chikura Shobo.

1933 *Saikin shogyo seisaku* (Recent Industrial Policy). Tokyo: Nihon Hyuron-sha.

1937 *Keiei keizaigaku soron* (The Science of Business Administration), Vol. 1 in *Keieigaku zenshu* (Business Administration: The Complete Reader). Tokyo: Toyo Shuppan-sha.

Edited Works:

1927 *Kokusai keizai kaigi to sono mondai* (The Problems of International Economic Conferences). Tokyo: Dobun-kan.

1933 *Nihon jinko mondai kenkyu* (Research on Japan's Population Problem). Kyochokai.

1934 *Nihon jinko mondai kenkyu* (Research on Japan's Population Problem), Part 2. Kyochokai.

Textbooks:

1905 *Shogyoshi kyokasho: nihon no bu* (Textbook on the History of Commerce: Japan). Tokyo: Sanseido. Revised editions published in 1919 and 1924.

—— *Shogyoshi kyokasho: gaikoku no bu* (Textbook on the History of Commerce: Foreign Countries). Tokyo: Sanseido. Revised editions published in 1909 and 1924.

Curriculum Vitae

1879 Born on May 3rd in Tokyo.

1900 Graduated from Tokyo Commercial High School. Immediately entered Foreign Trade Section of Special Studies program.

1902 Graduated from Special Studies program. Appointed Instructor at Tokyo Commercial High School.
1905 Promoted to Professor, Toyko Commercial High School. In October, sailed via Suez for a four-year residence in England and Germany to study management and administration. Entered University of Birmingham, then transferred to University of Manchester.
1907 Moved to Bonn in July, where he spent a month learning German. Entered University of Bonn.
1908 On to Berlin. Attended lectures at Berlin College of Commerce and University of Berlin. Began return trip to Japan by way of United States and Canada.
1909 Returned to Japan. Resumed teaching at Tokyo Commercial High School as well as lecturing at Meiji and Nihon Universities.
1913 Left for second study trip to England.
1914 Entered King's College, Cambridge, with G. H. Dickenson as his mentor. Recalled to Tokyo when war broke out.
1915 Resumed teaching.
1919 Received Doctor of Law degree. Named delegate to First International Labor Convention, Washington.
1925 Became an adviser to Tokugawa family.
1926 Helped found Japan Management Association, becoming a director.
1929 Traveled extensively throughout Russia and Europe as a consultant to the Japanese government.
1930 Established Japan Economic Research Association.
1931 Resigned as financial adviser to Tokugawa family.
1933 Began lecturing at Tokyo Imperial University, Faculty of Economics. Became a member of the Economics Division, Japan Society for the Promotion of Science.
1936 Appointed President, Tokyo College of Commerce.
1939 Died, at age 62, after brief hospitalization.

Teijiro Ueda played an important role in the Japan Management Association, the Japan Economic Research Association, the Japan Society for the Promotion of Science, the Committee on Small and Medium Enterprises, the Population Research Association, the Population Research Institute, the Pacific Basin Study Group, the Japan Statistics Association, and the Japan Economic Policy Association.

Courtesy R. Greenwood

Clarence Bertrand Thompson
(1882–1969)
United States/France/Switzerland/Uruguay

C. BERTRAND Thompson's contribution to the development of scientific management grew out of his association with Frederick W. Taylor and his work in spreading the Taylor system to many parts of the world.

In 1911 Thompson was called to the newly founded Harvard Graduate School of Business Administration, where he remained as Instructor and later Lecturer in Business Management until 1917. At the same time he worked under the direction of Taylor, and in association with Morris Llewellyn Cooke, Horace Hathaway, and Carl Barth, in various enterprises in which the Taylor system was being developed. His relationship with Taylor was close, but his relationship with Barth was not friendly.

In 1917, declining a full-time appointment as Assistant Professor at Harvard, Thompson decided to devote all his time to practice as a consulting management engineer. His first major job was a reorganization of three enterprises of the Pacific Commercial Co. in the Philippine Islands. Next, in late 1917, he was engaged by the British Embassy in China to organize the recruitment of its Chinese Labor Corps, then under way in China. Thereafter, between 1917 and 1941, Thompson was a management consultant with many important private and government organizations in the United States, France, Germany, Italy, North Africa, England, and Spain. He made his home during these years in France, where he worked with Le Chatelier and Henri Fayol's son.

In 1918, Thompson was asked by the French Munitions Ministry to organize some of its plants, and with the consent of the American authorities he accepted the proposal, which had originally been suggested by Le Chatelier. In the course of this work he developed contacts with many concerns which he later accepted as clients. In 1919 he was given the medal of the Conservatoire des Arts et Métiers for a series of lectures presided over by President Millérand. Later he gave a course in business organization at the Haute Ecole de Commerce in Strasbourg. In 1934 he was made Chevalier de la Légion d'Honneur for the whole of his work toward improving French industry and developing French engineers to that end.

Thompson was also responsible for the spread of scientific management in languages other than English. The publisher Payot asked him to supervise the selection and translation of a number of important American works and to write introductions for them. In this bibliotèque or library, he introduced Gantt, *Travail, salaries et beneficies*; Going, *Principles d'organisation industrielle*; Tarbell, *La Règle d'or des affaires*; and Clark, *Le Graphique Gantt*. In addition, he was able to publish his own books, *Méthodes américaines d'établissement des prix de revient en usines* and *The Taylor System of Scientific Management*, in both French and Polish.

Thompson made unique contributions to the Taylor system. He strongly advocated cooperation with the labor unions and, in his reorganizations in France, always worked with union delegates. For, despite the criticism and pessimism with which Taylor responded to such cooperation, Thompson never encountered difficulties with labor in his entire career. Also, it was he who suggested to Frank Gilbreth the inclusion of a large clock as the background of his motion pictures. In theory, Thompson believed that the most important single contribution made by scientific management was Taylor's "exception principle," which held that, to avoid becoming enmeshed in details, a manager should concentrate on the study of exceptionally good or bad cases in order to discover possibilities for improvement.

In 1934, Thompson retired after 18 years of intensive work, leaving a well-trained group to carry on. He was, however, recalled by the French Air Ministry at the beginning of the Second World War in 1939. Escaping from France as the German army invaded the country, he then went to the United States to take up the serious study of biochemistry, in which, ever since taking a course in 1912, he had been greatly interested. In 1945, after three years as a student at the University of California, he was appointed Assistant in Biochemistry there.

Two years later, in 1947, Thompson went to Switzerland to devote himself to research on arginase as a possible aid in the treatment of cancer. He spent a year at the Policlinique Universitaire in Lausanne before going to Montevideo, Uruguay, where he was offered a laboratory in the Department of Physiology as "colaborador honorario." His research here led to the publication of work in biochemistry which reached the practical clinical test stage before his death in 1969.

Although Thompson published six books and some 50 articles on management, his reputation today is centered on two books. The first is a collection of articles published in 1914: *Scientific Management: A Collection of the More Significant Articles Describing the Taylor System of Management.*[1] The second book, dating from 1917, is one of the earliest and most concise statements of its subject—*Theory and Practice of Scientific Management.*[2]

C. Bertrand Thompson is best remembered in France as a man who dominated those around him physically and intellectually. He was more than six feet tall and considered his ideal weight to be 230 pounds. Fluent—and humorous—in many languages, he was a prodigious reader who spent more than four hours a day reading nontechnical books on literature, history, and philosophy.

His demeanor was both shocking and attractive to those with whom he worked. He declared that "life is too short" for concession and discretion and preferred a direct approach at all times. Yet, say his co-workers, he "outclassed all by the force of his intellect allied with prodigious realism." Preeminently, he was an ideal teacher—he gave his associates the direction needed to develop lucid, experienced, and imaginative management.

His wife has suggested that he is best described by his 50th-anniversary report to his Harvard class of 1908. In it he wrote:

> Among my deepest satisfactions, which spring from my deep convictions and philosophy of life, I may mention the following: the opportunity to satisfy a wide-ranging curiosity by study, experience and travel; the feeling of constructive achievement in the reform of important business affairs and the consequent amelioration in the well-being of their employees; the stimulation of younger minds in business and scientific research; the possibility of seeing at first hand some of the world's finest art and hearing the best music, drama, and ballet in their most perfect interpretations; and finally in the conviction that life is all-pervading and everlasting and that our little individual shares in it are not entirely without significance.

—RONALD G. GREENWOOD

SELECTED PUBLICATIONS

Books:

1909 *The Churches and the Wage Earners.* New York: Scribner's.

1914 *Scientific Management: A Collection of the More Significant Articles Describing the Taylor System of Management.* Cambridge, Mass.: Harvard University Press.

1917 *How to Find Factory Costs.* Chicago: Shaw.

—— *The Taylor System of Scientific Management: A Report in Manual Form.* Chicago: Shaw.

—— *Theory and Practice of Scientific Management.* Boston: Houghton, Mifflin.

[1] Cambridge, Mass.: Harvard University Press.
[2] Boston: Houghton, Mifflin.

1920 *Méthodes américaines d'établissement des prix de revient en usines*. Paris: Payto.

—— *Le System Taylor*. Paris: Payto.

1925 *System Taylora*. Warsaw: Liga, Pracy.

1926 *La réorganisation des usines*, Vols. I and II. Paris: Ed. Langlois et Cie.

Articles and Pamphlets:

1915 "Collection des memoires les plus importants relatifs au système Taylor," *Revue de métallurgie*, Vol. 12, p. 233 et seq.

1916 "Has Scientific Management Made Good?" Boston: Thompson & Charrington.

1918 "Les Résultats de l'organisation scientifique du travail." Paris: Soc. Ing. Civ.

1923 "Signification de la préparation du travail comme facteur de l'organisation rationnelle en l'organisation scientifique," Paris: Conference de l'Organisation Scientifique Ravisse.

1927 "Impressions of Current American Economic Life," *Annalen der Betriebswirtschaft*, Vol. 1, p. 311 et seq.

—— "What You Want to Know About France," *System*, November.

1930 "La rationalisation en agriculture." Paris: Com. Nat. d'Etudes.

1932 "Reorganization of the Commercial and Bookkeeping Departments of Messrs. Thibaud Gibbs & Cie." Geneva: International Management Institute (Cyril Kerr). Also in French and German.

1933 "The Taylor System in the Colle Factories." Geneva: International Management Institute (Cyril Kerr). Also in French.

1934 "L'organizzazione dell'impresa l'organizzazione del lavoro." *Enrios* (Rome), October.

1935 "Il Problema della filatura della seda," *Organizzazione aziendale*, March.

1936 "Classificazione e simbolizazione: l'organizzazione scientifica del lavoro," *Enrios*, March, April, May, September.

1940 "The Taylor System in Europe," *Advanced Management* (Society for the Advancement of Management, New York), Vol. 5, p. 171 et seq.

Curriculum Vitae

1882 Born on April 12th in Denver, Colo.

1888 Moved to Los Angeles; at 15 entered Law School of University of Southern California.

1900 Received LL.B. degree.

1903 Admitted to practice law in California.

1905–1909 Studied at Harvard University, taking A.B. in 1908 and M.A. in 1909.

1909 Published *The Churches and the Wage Earners*; served as Secretary, Committee of Industrial Relations, Boston Chamber of Commerce; met Taylor and read his work for first time.

1910–1917	Taught manufacturing in newly founded Harvard Graduate School of Business; worked under Taylor's direction on a number of reorganization projects.
1917	Declined full-time Harvard appointment to devote self fully to management consultation; reorganized groups in Philippine Islands for Pacific Commercial Co. and in China for British Embassy.
1918–1934	Undertook private consulting work in France as "management engineer"; introduced Taylor system and scientific organization to France; taught business course at the Haute Ecole de Commerce in Strasbourg.
1919	Awarded medal of Conservatoire des Arts et Métiers for series of lectures.
1934	Made Chevalier de la Légion d'Honneur for efforts toward betterment of French industry and development of French engineers.
1934–1939	Traveled throughout Europe, North Africa, and Near East.
1939–1940	Returned as consultant to French Air Ministry; had adventurous escape from occupied France to United States.
1942–1945	Studied biochemistry at University of California.
1945–1947	Served as assistant in biochemistry until mandatory retirement age.
1948	Worked in cancer research at Policlinique Universitaire, Lausanne, Switzerland.
1948–1969	Continued cancer research at University in Montevideo, Uruguay; "colaborador honorario" in Faculty of Medicine.
1969	Died on January 12th at the age of 86.

Courtesy Comité Hyacinthe Dubreuil.

Hyacinthe Joseph Dubreuil
(1883–1971)
France

IF, in Hyacinthe Dubreuil's early years, anyone had predicted that he would be included in a roster of men and women distinguished for having contributed to management knowledge and practice, the idea would have seemed ludicrous. The fact is that his highly successful and unusual career—from factory worker through labor leader to writer on management and management consultant—proves that scientific management, even with its emphasis on standards and improved productivity, need by no means be inimical to the interests of either the individual worker or the cause of unionism.

Dubreuil's father was a manual laborer. The son apparently had no more than a primary school education. In 1897, at the age of 14, he went to work for a factory; then, three years later, he found himself a job in Paris as a mechanic in the new but growing French automobile industry.

At first, Dubreuil's interest in management practices and attitudes was that of a worker concerned about fair treatment for himself and his colleagues. He naturally joined the union. His obvious intelligence and ambition made him recognized by his fellow workers as a potential leader. In 1912, he became Secretary of the Mechanics Union in the Department of the Seine, and in 1919 he moved to the Union des Syndicats de la Seine (Union of Seine Syndicates) in the same capacity.

Dubreuil's great opportunity, which turned out to be the watershed of his life, came in 1927 and 1928—months which he spent working as a mechanic in the United States in order to study American methods of management. He published the results of his research in 1929 under the title *Standards: le travail américain vu par un ouvrier français*. This book on American labor as seen through the eyes of a French worker was a huge success; 30,000 copies eventually were printed, and the volume was translated into a variety of languages, including Czech. It also won a gold medal for its author.

From then on, it was clear that Hyacinthe Dubreuil's true metier was writing; he is listed as "écrivain" in French biographical dictionaries and encyclopedias. Book followed book, all addressed to such issues as the worker's right to be treated well on the job and the need for improved management methods and working conditions. Self-educated he might be, but Dubreuil's credentials were impressive enough by now that men as disparate as Aldous Huxley and Louis Armand[1] willingly supplied prefaces for Dubreuil books.

The period 1930–1938 Hyacinthe Dubreuil spent with the Bureau International du Travail (International Labor Office) in Geneva. After the Second World War, however, he lectured frequently, both in France and abroad, on employee training and development. More particularly, he specialized in the study of psychological factors in worker productivity, company change, and management methods in manufacturing plants. And, as a direct result of his writings, he was brought into companies, in cooperation with an engineering society, to set up autonomous work teams on an experimental basis. The experiments, it should be added, were usually successful in terms of both increased output and improved morale.

In 1956, Hyacinthe Dubreuil published *Des Robots ou des hommes*? (Robots or Men?). Its subject was the life and work of Frederick W. Taylor. Without in the least forgetting his own origins and his concern for the worker, the former union member and official had evolved into a management consultant and an admirer of the father of scientific management itself.

Hyacinthe Dubreuil was an exceptional man, says Max Richard,[2] a disciple and friend who first met him in 1935. Dubreuil was then 52; Richard was 21, and he "devoured" the newly published *A chacun sa chance* and later discovered the still debated *Standards*. Dubreuil "pretended with a straight face—he who was tenacity itself—that he'd had a great deal of luck when, reaching the age of military service, he worked out his time with a regiment of sappers and firefighters." Here he received a kind of solid training and development which no ignorant boy who'd left school at 13 could otherwise have had. "That is how, at 20, he discovered the values he never ceased to extol for the rest of his life: work, through which one achieves self-fulfillment; the trade or profession thanks to which one participates in the great work of Creation." And—as a result of this discovery—humility of spirit, accept-

[1] See the profile of Louis Armand in Part Two.

[2] Max Richard, "Hyacinthe Dubreuil—mon maître et mon ami," specially written reminiscences communicated through the Comité Hyacinthe Dubreuil, Paris.

ance of reality, the nobility of putting one's hand to the task ('You don't make a blacksmith out of a clod!'), and the natural urge of the worker to become an artisan and of the artisan to achieve the level of the artist.

Dubreuil's "American adventure" made a profound impression on him. He came to the United States alone—without any sort of support, letters of introduction, or sponsorship. He worked for almost a year and a half in four separate Ford plants in the Detroit area; and everywhere he watched, made notes, and asked questions. In spite of his lack of schooling, he was able to grasp the significance of what he was seeing and make precise observations in simple, direct language. He went as far as it was possible to go into the psychology and philosophy of work, but not, of course, in any academic way. Instead, he drew from his own life those encounters and experiences which, after long and careful thought, he found to be the best. Nor was his approach at all ideological. Dubreuil had no patience, later on, with European anti-Americanism. "Over there," he declared, meaning in America, "they don't know what condescension is."

Dubreuil "neither spoke nor wrote unless he had something to communicate." His conversation was magnificent, particularly in the years after his adoring wife died and he turned to a few friends for companionship. He never tried to be brilliant; he never sought for effect. Rather, the words came out pell-mell: crackling and sparkling and full of a humor in which the comical always verged on the serious. He had seen and heard so much, and retained so much of it, that even when he was in his eighties his memory was inexhaustible. A solitary octogenarian might have been excused for feeling misunderstood or neglected by the world, but Dubreuil was never bitter. He knew that he had built up for himself capital in a unique form: a sense of freedom with order, a strong belief in the efficacy of creative effort, the certainty of release through work, and the exhilaration that comes of being linked solidly with others in doing an important job.

A Comité Hyacinthe Dubreuil still exists in Paris. Founded by friends and other fervent followers, it has brought together managers, chief executives, labor leaders, and specialists in the training and development of human beings—all of them inspired by the Dubreuil philosophy and example.—ELIZABETH MARTING

SELECTED PUBLICATIONS

1929 *Standards: le travail américain vu par un ouvrier français* (Standards: American Labor as Seen by a French Worker). With a preface by H. Le Chatelier. Paris: Grasset. Also translated into English, German, Italian, Spanish, Czech, and Swedish.

1931 *Nouveaux standards* (New Standards). Paris: Grasset. Also translated into Dutch.

1935 *A chacun sa chance* (To Everyone His Chance). Paris: Grasset. Also translated into English with a preface by Aldous Huxley.

1936 *L'Exemple de Bata* (The Bata Example). Paris: Grasset.

1939 *Deux hommes parlent du travail* (Two Men Talk About Work). In collaboration with Colonel Rimailho. Paris: Grasset.
1953 *Le Travail et la civilisation* (Work and Civilization). Paris: Plon.
1956 *Des Robots ou des hommes?* (Robots or Men?). About the life and work of Frederick W. Taylor. Paris: Grasset.
1962 *Si tu aimes la liberté* (If You Love Freedom). Paris: Nouvelles Editions Latines.
1963 *Promotion.* With a preface by Louis Armand. Paris: Editions de l'Entreprise Moderne.
1971 *J'ai fini ma journée* (I've Finished My Day). Paris: Editions de l'Entreprise Moderne.

Curriculum Vitae

1883 Born on May 3rd at Béroux-la-Mulotière (Eure et Loir).
1897 At age 14, became a factory worker.
1900 Began work as mechanic in Paris automobile industry.
1912 Named Secretary, Union des Mecaniciens de la Seine (Mechanics Union, Seine).
1919 Became Secretary, Union des Syndicats de la Seine (Union of Seine Syndicates).
1927–1928 Worked as a mechanic in the United States.
1929 Published *Standards* on basis of observation during stay in the United States.
1930–1938 With Bureau International du Travail (International Labor Office) in Geneva, Switzerland.
1945 on Gave numerous lectures, in France and abroad, on employee training and development; later, brought into companies to organize autonomous work teams on an experimental basis.
1971 Died on March 7th, aged 87, in Paris.

In 1930, the book *Standards* won Hyacinthe Dubreuil the gold medal of the Societé d'Encouragement pour l'Industrie Nationale (Society for the Encouragement of National Industry). He was a member of the Comité National de l'Organisation Française (National Committee for French Management), a member of the Académie Internationale de l'Organisation Scientifique du Travail (International Academy of Scientific Management), and a chevalier of the Légion d'Honneur. Also, the Académie des Sciences Morales et Politiques made him a member at the age of 84.

Courtesy R. Greenwood.

Yoichi Ueno
(1883–1957)
Japan

YOICHI Uneo's contributions to industrial management in Japan can be divided into six broad areas. He

1. Initiated the study of industrial psychology by combining psychology and management in the early twentieth century.
2. Was Japan's first management consultant.
3. Worked, as a university professor, toward the introduction and diffusion of modern management concepts and techniques through his writings, his lectures, and the seminars which he conducted. His 1939 *Nohritsu Handbook* (Management Handbook)—literally, according to its Japanese title, concerned with "efficiency" but actually a true "management guide"—was a milestone in the history of Japanese industry.
4. Opened the way for the exchange of information and experience with Western management experts through his participation in various international meetings, his activity in the Japan chapter of the Taylor Society, and so on.
5. Introduced modern management concepts and techniques into various government and public offices as one of the three commissioners for the National Personnel Authority in postwar Japan.
6. Laid the foundations of what is now the Sanno Institute of Business Administration (SIBA) in Tokyo, a complex of management colleges,

research/consulting/seminar organizations, and a publishing house dealing exclusively in management-related materials.

While studying psychology, which was a new academic subject in the early twentieth century, Ueno wrote *Shinrigaku tsugi* (Introduction to Psychology). This sold well and made him a well-known psychologist. Then, around 1910, he came across an article by F. B. Gilbreth in an American magazine on experimental psychology; and through it his professional interest started to drift in the direction of management. During this period he introduced many noteworthy Western writings to Japanese readers: for example, *A Method of Measuring the Development of the Intelligence of Young Children*, by A. Binet and T. Simon; *La Logique des sentiments*, by T. Ribot; and *On the Employment Test for the Job of Streetcar Operator*, by H. Münsterberg.

But the most interesting studies that Ueno introduced during the early 1900s were Frank B. Gilbreth's work on bricklaying, Frederick W. Taylor's on pig-iron handling, and S. E. Thompson's on the inspection of bicycle bearings. Also, as the psychologist who laid the basis for industrial psychology in Japan, Ueno was responsible in 1914 for introducing Sigmund Freud to the country.

Ueno became Japan's first management consultant when he conducted research on operations at a Lyons toothpowder-manufacturing plant in Tokyo. Here the object of his study was the work of packing the powder, which was done by girls. Previously, they had maintained a steady rate of 62.2 dozen per day—a level of productivity which had been constant regardless of either encouragement or nonintervention on the part of plant management. Ueno's recommendations included a new plant layout, improvements in work methods, a change in the girls' work schedule, and the establishment of time standards through the use of stopwatches. Once implemented, his efforts paid off. Total daily production jumped to 79 dozen, 60 square meters of working space were saved, and there was even a reduction in the work schedule of one hour a day.

In addition, Ueno's early consulting work produced remarkable results at cosmetic, textile, and other manufacturing plants in the country. As his achievements became widely known, he was invited to head the Efficiency* Research Institute, which was a part of the government-endorsed employer-union association named Kyochokai. Kyochokai, as backed by the government, was formed to serve as a go-between in management-labor problems, which were then increasing in number. It worked especially on the equitable sharing of benefits, concentrating its efforts on higher productivity so that each side could receive a bigger share. Two years after Ueno's appointment, the Research Institute became independent of Kyochokai. Ueno continued to head the organization until 1941, when he opened a private school of

* In prewar days, the term "efficiency," as used by Harrington Emerson, was more common in Japanese industrial circles than the term "management."

management which he called Nihon Nohritsu Gakko (Japan Efficiency School).

During these years, Ueno was engaged in consulting, lecturing, and writing on a variety of subjects relating to management. Among his important contributions to Japanese management literature were translations of *The Principles of Scientific Management* (Kagakuteki kanri-ho) by F. W. Taylor, as well as articles by Taylor and books by other Western writers. Moreover, the editing and publication of the best-selling *Nohritsu Handbook* (Management Handbook) date from this same period. There were few Japanese publications dealing with the management of business and industry at the time; so this manual—comprehensively covering such subjects as production, sales, finance, personnel, and office administration—was enthusiastically received by Japanese industry. In each of the book's sections Ueno attempted to include all the relevant theories and approaches, ready for application. This book virtually was the "bible" of every Japanese manager from the time of its publication up through the 1950s, adding immensely to the advancement of management philosophy in Japan.

Ueno's professional activity kept expanding gradually. He taught management at several universities and extended his research efforts into the areas of advertising, marketing, personnel, and executive development. He headed the Taylor Society in Tokyo and, always, continued teaching people in industry.

A substantial part of Ueno's contribution to management was the result of his personal enthusiasm about exchanging knowledge and experience with Western experts on an international basis. He made his first overseas tour in 1921, and in 1925 he attended the fourth Comité International de l'Organisation Scientifique conference, held in Paris. On these travels abroad, he became closely acquainted with many of the pioneers of scientific management: the Gilbreths, Harrington Emerson, King Hathaway, Wallace Clark, Morris Cooke, and many more. Later, he in turn was visited in Tokyo by Mrs. Gilbreth, Emerson, and Hathaway.

One item in the Taylor Collection of the Stevens Institute of Technology in Hoboken, New Jersey, is a unique "map of management history" which Ueno had developed for his presentation at the Paris conference. It traces the development of scientific management graphically from 1856 through 1929, using unique symbols to represent major management schools and pioneers throughout the world. Those who saw the map at the conference admired it tremendously.

At about the time the Second World War broke out, Ueno became deeply concerned over the education of younger specialists in management. This marked a step forward from devotion to personal attainment to the desire to pass professional knowledge on to a new generation. Ueno was by no means exempt from wartime hardships; like all Japanese in the 1940s, he suffered many privations and was more or less hindered from carrying out his life plans. During the 12 years after the war, however, he threw all his energies into building and strengthening his school of management, which, he fully expected, would grow into the complex of integrated management development organizations that now exists as SIBA.

Throughout his life, Ueno never ceased to study, speak, write, and consult with people in business and industry. The books he wrote—some 100 of them—are treasured by the SIBA library. In 1955, when he was already past 70, he was assigned to India as a consultant by the Economic Commission for Asia and the Far East (ECAFE) of the United Nations.

With his family background of pioneer Japanese scientists, Yoichi Ueno had an inborn curiosity in many scientific areas. His grandfather Shunnojo, an early chemist, was known as the "father of photography" because he imported the daguerreotype camera into Japan for the first time. His uncle Hikoma later became the first professional photographer in the country, having for his subjects such noted men as U.S. President Ulysses S. Grant and novelist Pierre Loti. It was in Ueno's blood to introduce and develop something that would be useful to Japan—and that turned out to be, first and foremost, management.

Ueno, in short, was an accomplished writer and lecturer; however, he derived the greatest pleasure from teaching students. His interaction with them, and the skill of his teaching, attracted a small army of followers. He might be outspoken and stubborn in his beliefs, but his followers knew him best as the witty, kind-hearted "good old professor."

As a father, Ueno was affectionate. He loved his children and seldom showed his temper toward them. He made no secret of his wish for his son to succeed him in the same profession, yet he never explicitly urged the boy to do so. Whether his psychologist's expertise was responsible or not, the fact remains that the son did take over all that the father left behind when he died.

Ueno's curiosity and thirst for knowledge led him not only through the sciences but also into the personal and spiritual discipline of Zen Buddhism. Several of his written works deal with Zen thought, and he was constantly seeking to improve his way of life. Racial and cultural differences meant nothing to him, and he was dedicated to maintaining good relations between the United States and Japan. One of his close American friends, King Hathaway, wrote him just before the eruption of hostilities in the Pacific that if Ueno and he had been the rulers of their respective countries, such bitterness between the two nations would never have been possible. Without being an emotional man, Ueno had a gentle heart and often took the deaths of friends like the Gilbreths, Emerson, and Hathaway very hard. Perhaps this gentleness led to his befriending so many people from both East and West.

Above all, Ueno's dedication to work was tremendous. He showed little interest in sports and entertainment, and his death early in the morning of October 15, 1957, followed a routine evening of teaching management to his devoted students.—ICHIRO UENO and SUSUMU TAKAMIYA

SELECTED PUBLICATIONS

Translations:

1903 *The School and Society*, by John Dewey (Gakko to shakai). Tokyo: Matsumura Sanshodo.

1910 *Functional Psychology*, by J. R. Angell (Kinoshugi shirigaku). Tokyo: Dobun-kan.

1919 *Experimental Pedagogy*, by E. Neumann (Jikken kyoiku-gaku gaiyo). Co-translated. Tokyo: Dainippon Tosho.

1932 *The Principles of Scientific Management*, by F. W. Taylor (Kagakuteki kanri-ho). Tokyo: Dobun-kan.

—— *Shop Management*, by F. W. Taylor (Kojo kanri-ho). Tokyo: Dobun-kan.

—— *A Piece Rate System*, by F. W. Taylor (translated under same title). Tokyo: Dobun-kan. *Note*: This 1932 series also included some of Taylor's articles and letters.

Books written or edited:

1914 *Shinrigaku tsugi*. (Introduction to Psychology). Tokyo: Dainippon Tosho.

1919 *Hito Oyobi jigyo nohritsu no shinri* (Psychology of People and Business). Tokyo: Dobun-kan.

1928 *Jigyo tosei-ron* (Control of Enterprise). Tokyo: Dobun-kan.

1929 *Sangyo nohritsu-ron* (Industrial Management). Tokyo: Chikura Shobo.

1936 *Jimu hikkei* (Office Worker's Manual). Edited. Tokyo: Dobun-kan.

1939 *Nohritsu Handbook* (Management Handbook). Edited. Tokyo: Dobun-kan.

1948 *Nohritsu-gaku genron* (Principles of Management). Tokyo: Nihon Nohritsu Gakko.

Curriculum Vitae

1883 Born on October 28th in Tokyo.

1886–1900 Completed elementary school; moved with family to Nagasaki after father's death. Studied at a Nagasaki mission school.

1900 Returned to Tokyo alone to further studies. Doing part-time work, graduated from junior high school.

1904 Selected as special student by Tokyo University. Later became regular student by passing high school equivalency test.

1908 Graduated from Department of Literature, Tokyo University, with degree in psychology. Wrote and translated works dealing with experimental psychology, pedagogy, etc.

1912–1925 Edited and published *Shinri kenkyu*, a monthly psychological journal. Featured article by noted psychologist H. Münsterberg in early issue.

1913 Wrote article in journal on "How to Improve Efficiency," describing accomplishments by Western management pioneers (Taylor, Gilbreth, and Thompson).

1914 Introduced, for first time in Japan, ideas of psychologist Sigmund Freud. Published best-selling *Shinrigaku tsugi* (Introduction to Psychology).

1919 Lectured on advertising at Waseda University.

1920 As Japan's first management consultant, examined work methods at a Lyons toothpowder plant in Tokyo. By improving powder-packing process used by girls, improved work flow in plant.

1921 Sponsored by Kyochokai (private, government-sponsored organization set up to coordinate union/employer efforts), toured United States and Europe. Visited many plants and institutions; met numerous leaders of scientific management movement.

1922–1925 As head of Efficiency Research Institute (Kyochokai affiliate), engaged in consulting and teaching.

1925 Took over Efficiency Research Institute (renamed Japan Management Research Institute); concentrated on improving operations of light industries and sales activities. Also participated in fourth CIOS world conference in Paris.

1926 Traveled to Manchuria on consulting project in productivity improvement for Manchurian Railway Co.

1934 Became Professor, Kanagawa College (later Kanagawa University).

1939 Organized industrial mission to visit United States, covering some 100 stops in two months.

1941 Founded Nihon Nohritsu Gakko (Japan Efficiency School).

1943 Forced to close school down because of war. Became Professor, St. Paul University, Tokyo.

1947 Upon request of allied occupation forces, acted as commissioner in creation of National Personnel Authority and Civil Service personnel structure for government.

1951 Stepping down as commissioner, became President of Nihon Nohritsu Gakko, now Sanno Institute of Business Administration, Tokyo.

1954 Attended tenth CIOS world conference in São Paulo.

1955 Went to India on consulting project, sponsored by ECAFE of United Nations, having to do with flood prevention and power-source development.

1957 Died on October 15th, aged 73, of a heart attack.

Yoichi Ueno was posthumously awarded the Second Order of the Sacred Medal for his services to Japan.

Courtesy General Motors.

James David Mooney
(1884–1957)
United States

IN 1931, James Mooney published a book which, through several revisions, became a landmark in the development of management thought. At that time Mooney was President of General Motors Overseas Corp., and to complete this book he had a professional writer, Alan C. Reiley, collaborate with him. It was entitled *Onward Industry: The Principles of Organization and Their Significance to Modern Industry*. A revised edition, published in 1939, was called simply *Principles of Organization*; and in 1947 still another version appeared under the title *The Principles of Organization*. James Mooney was the sole author of the 1947 edition. The book consists of both a historical and an interpretive study of the principles that govern the organized efforts of man. It traces organization structure from primitive forms to modern practices. Its main value, however, lies in its identification and illustration of sound principles for application in various forms of organized activity.

Mooney's contribution to management thought and to management in general is best understood against the background of his own experience. He was the eldest son in a third-generation Irish family. Early in life he was forced to accept responsibility; as a boy, he sold newspapers, and he dropped out of high school to become a sailor. He completed high school by correspondence. Later, earning his own way, he obtained a Bachelor of

See the profiles of Alfred P. Sloan, Jr. and F. Donaldson Brown in Part Two for more on GM during Sloan's tenure as President.

Science degree from New York University and a degree in mining engineering from Case Institute of Technology. After graduation, his first job was as a field engineer in the copper mines of northern Mexico. He worked in mining for two years and then became a "first reader" of technical books for the Hill Publishing Co.; he was an associate editor when he left in 1911 for a sales job with Hyatt Roller Bearing. There he became associated with Alfred P. Sloan, Jr., who was President and General Manager. This was to be a key relationship in Mooney's professional career.

In 1916 William C. Durant and Sloan merged Hyatt Roller Bearing into a new company: United Motors. Sloan became President and Chief Operating Officer of United Motors. Then, in 1918, United Motors was acquired by General Motors and Jim Mooney became President of Remy Electric Co., an affiliate. Through these changes, he moved from Hyatt to General Motors. In 1921 he was named General Manager of General Motors Export Division, and in 1923 he became President of General Motors Overseas Corp. and Vice-President and Director of GM itself.

Mooney's writing shows the influence of his years with General Motors. Many of his concepts can be related to Alfred P. Sloan, Jr.'s philosophy of management. Although Mooney's thesis is that basic principles of organization span the ages, the substantive content of what he writes adheres closely to the General Motors model of his day. But—more important—he captures the essence of the "classical" approach to the theory of organization. To Mooney, organization relates specific duties or functions in a coordinated whole. He differentiates it from administration, which he describes as "the art of directing and inspiring people."[1] He sees the techniques of organization as preceding the issues of administration, and his book focuses on deriving the principles of sound organization so that the techniques can be readily developed and applied.

Mooney's first principle of organization is *coordination,* "the orderly arrangement of group effort, to provide unity of action in the pursuit of a common purpose."[2] According to his thinking, all other principles are contained in this first one. His remaining principles are simply those through which effective coordination operates. Thus he develops the idea that in every organization there must be a supreme coordinating power—what Mooney calls "authority" and identifies as the source of all coordination. Authority is a right which inheres legitimately in the structure of the organization. Moreover, there is a moral aspect to the principle of coordination: the obligation to mutual service by participants. Other principles implicit in Mooney's concept of the principle of coordination are *doctrine*—definition of the objective and the procedures for its attainment which are internalized as values by the participants in an organization—and *discipline,* in which, to Mooney, the key concept is self-discipline at the top level. Those who hold positions of command in an organization must impose discipline

[1] James D. Mooney, *The Principles of Organization.* New York: Harper, 1947, p. 3.
[2] *Ibid.,* p. 5.

on themselves as well as on their subordinates. This is discipline by example, not just command.

The two major concepts which Mooney develops in addition to coordination are (1) the scalar principle and (2) the functional principle. As Mooney sees it, the scalar principle involves a scaling of duties according to degrees of authority and corresponding responsibility; the functional principle has to do with differentiating between the kinds of duties performed.

To sum up—Mooney's book emphasizes that efficient organization must have formalism, and this formalism must be based on principles. To derive these principles, he traverses the recorded history of church, state, and industry from the ecclesia and boule of Athens, through the comita of Rome, to the growth of the monastic orders and the feudal system up to modern times.

Part of Mooney's influence arose from his position as President of General Motors Overseas Corp. and his subsequent position as President and Chairman of the Board of Directors of Willys-Overland Motors. From his London headquarters he developed an international network of General Motors affiliations; moreover, his General Motors Overseas Corp. always operated at a large profit. It was said of him that, outside Detroit, he was the biggest man in General Motors; outside the United States, he *was* General Motors.

James D. Mooney was a genial man who looked more like a film star than a hard-driving executive. He was skilled in diplomacy and negotiation. As President of General Motors Overseas Corp., he had direct contact with leaders in most of the countries of the world. His background and abilities led President Franklin D. Roosevelt to send him to Hitler as a secret emissary in order to determine whether the 1939–1940 hostilities in Europe could be stopped before they became the Second World War and involved America. Much later, in 1957, secret documents were released which revealed that from 1937 up until the outbreak of that war Mooney had been reporting to the U.S. Office of Naval Intelligence on European aviation and other developments.

Not only was Mooney a big man at General Motors, where he was the fourth-highest-paid executive, but he was physically a large person. He was 6 feet 2 inches tall and weighed more than 200 pounds. He also had the reputation of being a doer—a man who got things done and solved difficult problems. In his years with GM, he built General Motors Overseas Corp. up to the point where it was second only to the Chevrolet Division in terms of sales volume.

Mooney had an interest in history. He was familiar with figures from Alexander the Great to Aristotle and from Augustus Caesar to William of Normandy. He had the habit of quoting St. Thomas Aquinas. And his circle of friends ranged as widely as his historical knowledge. Among them he included John Watson, the eminent psychologist; Theodore Dreiser, the novelist; European heads of state; and Mexican peons.

Most of all, Mooney was a pragmatic and dynamic businessman. He practiced what he preached. He was the great delegator. He believed in the principle of indoctrination through personal example and precept. He infused his organization with a mental set which carried the distinctive mark of his character and its underlying philosophy, methods, and morals. It was this ability to spread distinctive doctrines growing out of his own personality that enabled him to attract, stimulate, and motivate the best possible subordinates.—WILLIAM B. WOLF

SELECTED PUBLICATIONS

Books:

1920 *Advertising the Technical Product*. With Clifford A. Sloan. New York: McGraw-Hill.

1931 *Onward Industry: The Principles of Organization and Their Significance to Modern Industry*. With Alan C. Reiley. New York: Harper. Revised edition, entitled *Principles of Organization*, issued in 1939.

—— *Wages and the Road Ahead*. London and New York: Longmans, Green.

1933 *Toil and the New Capitalism*.

1947 *The Principles of Organization*. New York: Harper.

Article:

1933 "Organizing the Executive Group," *Personnel*, Vol. 10, No. 1, August.

Curriculum Vitae

1884 Born on February 18th in Cleveland, Ohio.

1906 Awarded B.S. by New York University.

1906–1909 Earned B.S. in mining engineering and master's degree in Engineering at Case Institute of Technology.

1909–1910 Employed as field engineer in mining operations in California and northern Mexico.

1910–1911 Worked as First Reader, Technical Books, and Associated Editor, Hill Publishing Co.

1911–1918 Employed by Hyatt Roller Bearing Co., of which Alfred P. Sloan, Jr., was half-owner and President. Sloan, working with William C. Durant, merged this firm into United Motors. Mooney became President of Remy Electric Co., a subsidiary.

1921 Named General Manager of General Motors Export Division.

1923 Became President, General Motors Overseas Corp. (United Motors had been acquired by GM in 1918.)

1923–1942 Served as Vice-President and member of GM Board of Directors.

1942–1945 As Captain, U.S. Navy (Reserve), on active duty as Commander in Bureau of Aeronautics, with Advanced Base Division of 11th Amphibious Force in Europe, and on staff of Chief of Naval Operations.

1946–1949 Held office as President and Chairman of the Board of Directors, Willys-Overland Motors.

1949–1957 In consulting as Principal, J. D. Mooney and Associates.
1957 Died on September 21st, aged 73, in Tucson, Ariz.

In 1951 and 1952 James D. Mooney was Chairman of the United Hospital Fund campaign in New York City. He later was Chairman of the Central Committee of the New York University Bellevue Medical Center campaign, and he also worked with the Hoover Commission on its study of the organization of the executive branch of the U.S. government. He was a member of the Council of New York University and a Trustee of Case Institute of Technology.

Courtesy General Motors.

F. Donaldson Brown
(1885–1965)
United States

F. Donaldson Brown spent most of his career working for the du Ponts. First he was with E. I. du Pont de Nemours; later, when the du Ponts bought a controlling interest in the General Motors Corporation, he moved to that firm.

Brown was trained as an electrical engineer, and it was his engineering perspective that shaped most of his contributions to management. Underlying his work was a major interest in bringing a scientific approach to top-level management. At du Pont he recommended the use of the rate-of-return-on-investment formula and chart—and indeed originated the famous du Pont chart system of financial control that was later adopted by General Motors.

One of Brown's contributions to management everywhere developed in relation to his role at General Motors. In 1921 GM was caught with a severe shortage of working capital. It was Brown's job to ensure that such a crisis did not recur. His solution involved careful forecasting of product demand, establishing pricing policies based upon analysis of incremental costs and revenues, and developing a system of financial controls based upon centralized policy and decentralized administration.

Probably the best way to state F. Donaldson Brown's contributions to management thinking and practice is to quote Alfred Sloan, Jr.'s comment

See also the profiles of Alfred P. Sloan, Jr. and James David Mooney in Part Two.

at the time of Brown's death:

> Donaldson Brown's contributions to financial thought have long been recognized, and his papers on the subject are still considered classics. Mr. Brown's concepts have helped American business rise to the world leadership it enjoys today.[1]

Donaldson Brown also had an indirect but important role in the development of modern management as a distinct discipline. He was always interested in synthesizing and defining the role of the modern business corporation, and his interest led him to read *The Future of Industrial Man,* by Peter Drucker.[2] This book dealt with problems and issues which directly concerned Brown in his work at General Motors—for example, the governance of large organizations, the place of the large corporation in society, and the principles of industrial order in a free society. Brown felt that in relation to these issues General Motors had been doing pioneering work. Because of this work, and also because of the important role General Motors had played in the Second World War, he engaged Peter Drucker to prepare an analysis of General Motors and its wartime experience. He wanted this study to preserve for future generations a record of how General Motors under the guidance of Alfred Sloan, Jr., and Donaldson Brown had dealt with these central issues of corporate management. According to Drucker, it was to be strictly an internal study in the sense that it would be used only within GM. At the time both Sloan and Brown were contemplating retirement.

The result of Drucker's study was a classic book. *The Concept of the Corporation*[3] helped set off the management boom of the 1950s and 1960s and was instrumental in helping gain recognition for the discipline of management.

Brown's central role in this chain of events was due not only to his interest in the management of large corporations but also to his own basic character. Drucker, who started his study by interviewing in the General Motors organization, tells how the book came to be written and published.

> I took a quick trip round the circuit and came back and reported to Donaldson Brown, who was Vice-Chairman, that this [interviewing] could not be done because his management people were not really willing to have a stranger come in and do it. I said, "There is only one way in which this can be done. I have to pretend that I am writing a book. Because in America, if you say you are writing a book, everything goes." Mr. Brown, who was a Quaker and absolutely the soul of honesty, refused to have anything to do with a transparent lie. And so it was a stand-off for about three weeks. He finally, most reluctantly, gave in; and although he never allowed it officially, it was the understanding that I could say (and my liaison man could say) that I

[1] *New York Herald-Tribune,* October 3, 1965.
[2] Peter F. Drucker, *The Future of Industrial Man.* New York: John Day, 1942.
[3] Peter F. Drucker, *The Concept of the Corporation.* New York: John Day, 1946.

was contemplating writing a book. But the idea was that this was to be an internal report.

Mr. Brown was so bothered by this white lie that after I had handed the report in, he bulldozed a resolution through the executive committee to release the manuscript to me to have it published. I changed it somewhat—it had to be changed because there were things in there that were much too specific. This was not intended for publication, and if Mr. Brown hadn't suffered from so delicate a conscience it would never have been published.[4]

The Concept of the Corporation takes a pivotal position in the development of modern management. It pioneers in bringing together and analyzing many of the concerns of management: social responsibility, the relations between individuals and the organization, decision processes, community relations, customer relations, top management functions, and the like. This book established Drucker as an authority on management and so marked the start of a career which has made Drucker a central figure in modern management thought. By insisting that the book be published, Donaldson Brown inadvertently played a significant role in influencing current thinking about management.

At General Motors Donaldson Brown was one of the main "idea" men. Many referred to him as "the brains of General Motors." However, even though he was a very wise man, he was handicapped by his manner of communicating. To many General Motors executives he appeared aloof and difficult. He had a habit of presenting ideas by first discussing all the fine points in the language of mathematics and the jargon of social science. Only after a lengthy introduction of assumptions, conceptions, and qualifications did he come to the point. True, after these preliminaries he did state himself clearly and concisely.[5]

On the job at General Motors, Donaldson Brown was reserved and formal. He generally wore a conservative business suit and a high-collar shirt. Few called him anything but "Mr. Brown." Yet, if encountered on his Maryland farm, he often would be wearing a lumberman's shirt, sloppy tweeds, and a battered fisherman's hat with trout flies in the band. He was devoted to his wife and family as well as his work.

Donaldson Brown was a very intelligent and complicated individual. By some he is judged as having been probably the most brilliant of the group that reorganized General Motors.—WILLIAM B. WOLF

SELECTED PUBLICATIONS

Book:

1958 *Some Reminiscences of an Industrialist.* New York: Hive Publishing.

[4] Interview with Peter Drucker by William B. Wolf, March 16, 1966.

[5] See Peter F. Drucker, *Adventures of a Bystander.* New York: Harper & Row, 1978, p. 264.

Articles:

1924 "Pricing Policy in Relation to Financial Control," *Management and Administration,* Vol. 7, No. 2, February, pp. 3–15.

1927 "Decentralized Operations and Responsibilities with Coordinated Control," American Management Association, Annual Convention Series, February.

1929 "Forecasting and Planning as a Factor in Stabilizing Industry," Part I, *Sales Management,* Vol. 17, No. 4, January, pp. 181–183; 236–237; Part II, Vol. 17, No. 5, February, pp. 258–259, 300.

1942 "Readjustments Required Within Industry Because of the Defense Program," *Vital Speeches,* February 4.

1943 "Industrial Management as a National Resource," *The Conference Board Management Record,* Vol. V, No. 4, April, pp. 142–148.

Curriculum Vitae

1885 Born on February 1st in Baltimore, Md.

1902 At 17, graduated with a B.S. in electrical engineering from Virginia Polytechnic Institute.

1903 Undertook postgraduate study at Cornell University.

1903–1904 Worked in Electrical Department of B & O Railroad.

1904–1908 Employed as General Manager, Baltimore Sales Office of Sprague Electrical.

1908–1912 Employed in Sales Department, E. I. du Pont de Nemours & Co.

1914–1918 Employed as Assistant Treasurer, du Pont.

1918–1921 Served as Treasurer, member of Executive Committee, and member of Board of Directors at du Pont.

1921–1937 Employed in Detroit as Vice-President of Finance, General Motors Corp.

1921–1959 Served as member of Board of Directors and Finance Committee, General Motors.

1937–1946 Served as Chairman of Finance Committee and Vice-Chairman of Board of Directors, General Motors.

1946 Retired, remaining on Board of Directors.

1959 Resigned from GM Board of Directors after court order forcing du Pont to sell GM holdings and ruling out interlocking directorships.

1965 Resigned from du Pont Finance Committee in June, again remaining on Board of Directors.

—— Died on October 2nd, aged 80, at Port Deposit, Md.

Donaldson Brown was a trustee of Johns Hopkins University, a director of Gulf Oil Co., a director of the Mercantile Safe Deposit and Trust Co. of Baltimore, a director of the Federal Reserve Bank of New York, and a member of the American Ordnance Association.

Courtesy R. Greenwood.

Chester Irving Barnard
(1886–1961)
United States

CHESTER I. Barnard was a practicing manager who had a rare bent for rigorous study and abstract writing. His contribution to management is found primarily in his classic book *The Functions of the Executive.* Here Barnard presents a system of ideas describing the nature of formal organizations and the functions of the executive. The book is a fundamental conceptualization that has stimulated much of the current research in the field, and Barnard's contributions center around this conceptualization. For example, he was among the first to emphasize the "open systems" nature of organizations, the role of informal organization, the functional and dysfunctional aspects of status systems, the role of the executive as a center of communication, decision processes as significant aspects of formal organization, the acceptance theory of authority, the moral aspects of leadership, and the essential conditions of business ethics.

Barnard's contribution to management thinking placed the functions of the executive directly in the area of social science. His book in many ways was one of the early sociologies of organization.

The significance of Barnard's impact on management is evidenced by the fact that his book has been translated throughout the world. Furthermore, it is selling as well now as it did when it was first published in 1938. Many academics have been inspired by Barnard. For example, the eminent economist Kenneth Boulding states that one of the writers on management who has most influenced him is Chester I. Barnard,[1] and still other distinguished

[1] Kenneth Boulding, "The Pioneer Work of Chester I. Barnard," in *The Image* (Ann Arbor: University of Michigan Press, 1956).

academics who publicly acknowledge their indebtedness to Barnard include Professors Philip Selznick, Robert Tannenbaum, Herbert Simon, and Melvin Dalton.

It cannot be emphasized too strongly that Barnard was essentially a practitioner. He was one of the founders of the New Jersey Bell Telephone Co. and became its President. He also was President of the Rockefeller Foundation. He reorganized the United Service Organization (USO) and administered it during the Second World War. He was frequently sought out by government officials for help with pressing problems. For example, he was a member of the Atcheson-Lilienthal Committee on the Control of Atomic Energy, he was Assistant to the Secretary of the Treasury of the United States, he was a member of the Hoover Committee on the Reorganization of the Executive Branch of the Federal Government, and he served on the Task Force in Personnel and Civil Service—the Second Hoover Commission. Finally, he was Chairman of the National Science Board of the National Science Foundation.

In summary, Chester I. Barnard was an active man of affairs who contributed both to the literature and to the practice of management. His ideas were precursors to much of the current theoretical work in the field.

Chester I. Barnard represents an American ideal in that he overcame adversity to become a successful man. He started life with physical, social, and economic handicaps. His mother died when he was five years old. He had problems with his eyesight, and his family never had much money. He was self-supporting from the time he was 12 years old.

However, Barnard was endowed with a superb mind, and early in life he developed the habit of rigorous study—he would generally read a book five to seven times. He was a thoughtful person who simultaneously lived in the world of the mind and that of practical business. On the one side he was a warm, considerate, effective business executive with a wry sense of humor; on the other, he was a serious student of a wide variety of subjects. He was self-taught in Greek, German, and French. He was an excellent pianist and made a careful analysis of the subtleties of the piano as a musical instrument.

Barnard wrote scholarly essays on subjects ranging over such topics as economic theory, world peace, business ethics, control of atomic energy, medical education, the concept of equilibrium in organization theory, the meaning of loyalty, and nonlogical thought processes. His intellectual brilliance caused one professor at Harvard University to observe that Chester I. Barnard had "a power of analysis and synthesis so sweeping that I class his gift with that of St. Thomas and da Vinci." Certainly his accomplishments support the statement that Chester I. Barnard "possibly" possessed "the most capacious intellect of any business executive in the U.S."[2]

Probably most important of all, Chester I. Barnard sought neither publicity nor power for himself. He served the public well.—WILLIAM B. WOLF

[2] *Fortune,* June 1948, p. 188.

SELECTED PUBLICATIONS[3]

Books:

1938 *The Functions of the Executive.* Cambridge, Mass.: Harvard University Press.

1946 *A Report on the International Control of Atomic Energy.* With J. R. Oppenheimer, C. A. Thomas, H. A. Winne, and D. E. Lilienthal. Washington, D.C.: U.S. Government Printing Office.

1948 *Organization and Management.* A collection of nine articles. Cambridge, Mass.: Harvard University Press.

Articles:

1922 "Business Principles in Organization Practice," *Bell Telephone Quarterly,* Vol. 1, July, pp. 44–48.

1947 "Some Aspects of Organization Relevant to Industrial Research." Address upon the occasion of the 25th anniversary of the Wharton School of Finance and Commerce, University of Pennsylvania, January 10, 1947. Reprinted in *The Conditions of Industrial Progress* (Philadelphia: Wharton School of Finance and Commerce, University of Pennsylvania), pp. 62–72.

1948 "Social Factors in the Medical Career." Address to the graduate classes, Medical Divisions, University of Pennsylvania, March 15, 1947. Reprinted in *The General Magazine and Historical Chronicle* (University of Pennsylvania General Alumni Society), Vol. 50, No. 2, Winter, pp. 114–120.

1949 "Arms Race v. Control," *Scientific American,* Vol. 181, No. 5, November, pp. 11–13.

1951 "Science and Organization," in *Proceedings* of the annual conference of The Philosophical Society, Philadelphia, November 8th and 9th.

1952 "Social Science: Illusion and Reality," *The American Scholar,* Vol. 21, No. 3, Summer.

1957 "A National Science Policy," *Scientific American,* Vol. 197, No. 5, November, pp. 45–49.

1958 "Elementary Conditions of Business Morals." Barbara Weinstock Lecture at the University of California, Berkeley, May 25, 1955. Reprinted in *California Management Review,* Vol. 1, No. 1, Fall, pp. 1–13.

Curriculum Vitae

1886 Born on November 7th in Malden, Mass.

1889 Left school at 12 to support self as piano tuner and farm laborer.

[3] For a synthesis of Barnard's writings and a complete bibliography of his published and unpublished works, see William B. Wolf, *The Basic Barnard: An Introduction to Chester I. Barnard and His Theories of Organization and Management* (Ithaca, N.Y.: New York State School of Industrial and Labor Relations, Cornell University, 1974).

1891	Entered Mt. Hermon School, Northfield, Mass., at 14.
1906	Entered Harvard University. Completed studies in three years except for laboratory work in chemistry. Entirely self-supporting.
1909–1948	Left Harvard without degree. Went to work as statistician for American Telephone & Telegraph Co. Progressed rapidly. By 1922 was Assistant Vice-President and General Manager, Bell Telephone Co. of Pennsylvania. In 1926 became Vice-President of the Pennsylvania company and in 1927 was made President, New Jersey Bell Telephone Co.
1942–1945	Served as President of USO.
1946	Served as member of Atcheson-Lilienthal Committee on the Control of Atomic Energy.
1948–1951	Served as President of Rockefeller Foundation.
1951–1956	Served as Chairman of National Science Board of National Science Foundation.
1961	Died on June 7th, aged 74, in New York City.

Barnard was active in numerous civic, cultural, and educational activities. He was a founder and President of the Bach Society of New Jersey, a founding member of the Newark Arts Theatre, a charter member of the Newark Music Foundation, a founder and member of the Advisory Board of the New Jersey Musical Foundation, a director and member of the Executive Committee of the Newark Institute of Arts and Sciences, and a member of the Board of the Rachmaninoff Fund Finance Committee.

In the area of education, Barnard served on visiting committees for the Division of Sociology and the Division of Mathematics at Harvard University. He was a trustee of Mt. Hermon School, of Rutgers University, and of Newark University. He held honorary degrees from Rutgers University, Newark University, Brown University, Bloomfield College, Princeton University, and the University of Pennsylvania.

Among the many honors bestowed upon Chester I. Barnard were the United States of America's Medal for Meritorious Service, a certificate of commendation from the President of the United States, a certificate of appreciation from the U.S. Navy, election to the presidency of the Telephone Pioneers of America, and the American Political Science Association award as a member of the Board of Consultants to the U.S. Department of State.

Courtesy M.I.T. Press.

Erwin Haskell Schell
(1889–1965)
United States

PROFESSOR Erwin Haskell Schell was among the best-known American experts on business administration. His role as a teacher and author once led the magazine *Business Week* to call him the "grand old man of American management." At the time of his retirement in 1955, he numbered among his former students 130 corporation presidents, 115 vice-presidents, 30 treasurers, and 30 owners of businesses.

Schell joined the Massachusetts Institute of Technology in 1917 as Assistant Professor. In 1929 he became Professor, and in 1931 he was named head of the Business and Engineering Administration Department. His lectures were notable events. He was able to relate theory and practice in such a way that he imparted managerial knowledge with a minimum of painful trial-and-error learning. One of Schell's presentations described the attributes of success as an executive. Because so many graduates used its precepts effectively, it became known as "The Million Dollar Lecture."

Management is indebted to Erwin Schell for the development of university-conducted programs for executives. He was among the first to organize courses which brought executives to the campus for six to eight weeks of intensive education.

Erwin Schell wrote numerous books and articles. Underlying most of them were two main concerns. The first had to do with synthesizing theory and practice to provide an integrated overview of management. The second was Schell's concern for the manager's basic moral character and adjustment to life. His *Techniques of Executive Control,* together with the collection of his writings entitled *Management Thought and Action,* illustrates these concerns and highlights Schell's desire to bring into clear perspective the totality of the executive's responsibility and human experience. He emphasized the dignity and obligations associated with the profession of management.

Erwin Schell was a highly creative, dedicated individual. He kept in close contact with most of his students and with many alumni, and his personal warmth and sociability made him a welcome member of the management circles of his day. He was, in fact, extremely active in the management movement. He knew the Gilbreths, Mary Parker Follett, Harrington Emerson, and many more of the principal figures of the early years, not to mention many of the leading industrialists. He was active in most of the management societies in the United States and abroad, particularly the Society for the Advancement of Management and the Council for International Progress in Management (U.S.A.). Schell was quiet but astute. He had a delightful sense of humor and an appropriately witty story for every occasion. Most of all, Schell was an enthusiastic person with a creative mind. He instilled in those with whom he had contact a desire to learn and to seek new knowledge. His was a personality of exceptional force and warmth.—WILLIAM B. WOLF

SELECTED PUBLICATIONS

Books:

1923 *The Million Dollar Lecture.* Boston: Privately printed.

1927 *Problems in Industrial Management.* With H. H. Thurlby. Chicago: A. W. Shaw.

1932 *Scientific Management in Production: Readings and Cases.* Cambridge, Mass.: Privately printed.

1935 *The Scope of the Purchasing Function.* New York: National Association of Purchasing Agents Pamphlet No. 22.

1936 *Administrative Proficiency in Business* (first edition). New York: McGraw-Hill.

1939 *Manual for Executives and Foremen* (first edition). With Frank Forester Gilmore. New York: McGraw-Hill.

1942 *New Strength for New Leadership.* New York: Harper.

1951 *Technique of Administration* (second, retitled edition of *Administrative Proficiency in Business*). New York: McGraw-Hill.

1952 *The Million Dollar Lecture and Letters to Former Students.* New York: McGraw-Hill.

1957 *Techniques of Executive Control.* First edition, 1924, 133 pp.; second edition, 1926, 143 pp.; third edition, 1930, 171 pp.; fourth edition, 1934, 231 pp.; fifth edition, 1942, 252 pp.; sixth edition, 1946, 270 pp.; seventh edition, 1950, 296 pp.; eighth edition, 1957, 357 pp. Eighth edition also in paperback. New York: McGraw-Hill.

Articles:

1929 "Trends in the Functions and Composition of Boards of Directors" (Contribution from The Department of Economics, Serial No. 2, January 1929). *Publications from the Massachusetts Institute of Technology,* Vol. 64, No. 74, Pub. Serial No. 614.

1930 "The Future of Production," *Annals* of the American Academy of Political and Social Science, No. 149, May, p. 28 et seq.

1933 "Managerial Centralization vs. Decentralization Under Present Conditions," *Management Review,* Vol. 22, August, p. 227.

1934 "New Practices in the Technique of Executive Control," in American Management Association Office Management Series, No. 62.

1935 "Education and Training of Personnel Suitable for High Administrative Positions," Taylor Society *Bulletin,* October.

1937 "A Conversation with Presidents," *Nation's Business,* January. Also in *Review of Reviews,* February.

—— "Current Industrial Problems," *Journal* of the Society for the Advancement of Management, November.

1938 "Discussion of Annual Wage Plans" (with D. W. Weed and others), in American Management Association Production Series, No. 111.

1942 "Product Development—The Ugly Duckling of Business," *Dun's Review,* February.

1943 "Management Attitudes" (article in the "Ten Years' Progress in Management" series), American Society of Mechanical Engineers *Transactions,* April.

—— "Tools for Management Diagnosis," *Advanced Management,* January–March.

1945 "Observations on Top Policy Determination," in American Management Association General Management Series, No. 133.

1947 "Current Changes in Management Operating Policy," in American Management Association Production Series, No. 171.

—— "Formal Education in Scientific Management," in *Papers* of the Eighth International Management Congress (Stockholm).

1953 "Dealing with Difficult Personalities," *Advanced Management,* January.

1954 "Spiritual and Moral Values in Business," in *Responsibilities of Business Leadership* (talks at General Electric leadership conferences, Association Island).

1955 "The Importance of Attitudes," *Supervisory Management,* December.

1958 "The Changing Philosophy of Management," *Advanced Management,* December.

Curriculum Vitae

1889 Born on September 29th in Kalamazoo, Mich.

1912 Received B.S. from M.I.T.

1912–1913 Worked as operations engineer for the American Locomotive Co., Providence, R.I.

1913	Became Resident Engineer for H. C. Raynes, Inc., industrial engineers, Boston, Mass.
1915	Became Industrial Engineer and Labor Manager, U.S. Cartridge Co., Lowell, Mass.
1916	Became Treasurer, Henry F. Miller and Sons Piano Co.
1917	Became Assistant Professor of Business Management, M.I.T.
1917–1919	Employed as Industrial Engineer, Assistant to the Vice-President, and Treasurer, American International Shipbuilding Corp.
1921–1923	Served on Management Council, American International Corp.
1924	Joined Harvard Graduate School of Business Administration, on part-time basis, as Assistant Professor of Industrial Management.
1929	Became Professor of Business Management, M.I.T.
1931	Placed in charge of Department of Business and Engineering Administration at M.I.T.
1944	Served U.S. Department of State as consultant on administration.
1952	Consulted with Mutual Security Agency.
1955	Retired.
1958	Was a Founding Fellow of the International Academy of Management. Became its first Chancellor.
1965	Died on January 4th, aged 75, in Norwich, Vt.

Schell was awarded the Gilbreth Medal of the Society for the Advancement of Management in 1938. He served as President of the Academy of Management and as Vice-President of the National Management Council, and he was a director of Keystone Custodian Funds, Inc., and the American Management Association. In addition, he held membership in The American Academy of Arts and Sciences, The American Society of Mechanical Engineers, Theta Delta Chi, and The Executive Club of Boston.

Fukumatsu Muramoto
(1890–1973)
Japan

FUKUMATSU Muramoto was one of the many young Japanese who were attracted to the new field of management, went abroad to further their studies, and returned home to a long and distinguished career of teaching, research, and consultation, influencing whole new generations of Japanese managers. His principal contributions to management thinking lay in the area of business administration.

Muramoto was born in Osaka in March 1890. After graduating from the Osaka Commercial High School, he went to the United States, where he studied American business administration, focusing on Taylor's scientific methods of management. In 1919 he was the first Japanese ever to receive the Master's degree from Harvard's School of Business Administration. He went on to specialize in the study of administration with Professor William Ashley at the University of Birmingham, returning home to Japan in 1920. Eight years later he became Professor at the Osaka College of Commerce, where he remained for the rest of his teaching career; at his death, he was Professor Emeritus.

Shortly after he returned to Japan, Professor Muramoto published an article on "The Theory of Business Administration" in the *Proceedings* of the Society of the Tokyo Commercial High School. This article appears to have been the first publication in Japan on the subject of business administration. His major works followed during the next two decades.

While at Osaka College of Commerce Muramato edited two journals:

Keikan mondai (Problems in Administration) and *Kigyo keikan* (The Administration of Enterprises). He expressed his convictions in nearly every issue.

At first, Muramoto was greatly attracted by the American method of studying administration, especially the Taylor system. Later, he embraced the German method; and, finally, he abandoned both these approahes and strove to establish in Japan a systematic means of looking at business administration as pure psychology.

In his own individual work Muramoto advocated research on the appropriate limits of administration. He voluntarily carried on such work in his capacity as Chairman of the 109th Study Committee of Nihon Gakujutsu Shinkokai (Japan Society for the Promotion of Science). Here he was concerned with overall research on the rational scale of administration for enterprises. He also was a member of committees on problems of retail enterprises, problems of small- and medium-scale enterprises, and general problems of administration.

Besides these academically oriented activities, Muramoto worked as a consultant, advising the Osaka Prefectural Office of Statistics on its operations. In addition, he took on lecture appearances at the new Kobe College of Commerce, wrote an introductory text on administration, and developed a theory of productive management.—ELIZABETH T. MASSEY

SELECTED PUBLICATIONS

Books and Articles:

1929 *Shoko keiken keizairon* (Theory of Economics and Business Administration). Bungado.

1934 "Keikan Genron" (Principles of Administration), in *Shogaku zenshu* (Complete Reader on Commerce).

1937 *Hyakkaten keikan to sono mondai* (Problems in the Management of Department Stores). Bungado.

1942 "Keikangaku gairon" (General Introduction to the Study of Administration), in *Keikangaku taikei* (Systematic Study of Administration).

Curriculum Vitae

1890 Born in March in Osaka.

1919 Was first Japanese to receive M.A. from Harvard School of Business Administration.

1919–1920 Studied with Professor William Ashley at University of Birmingham (England).

1920 Returned to Japan.

1928 Became Professor, Osaka College of Commerce, remaining for rest of his teaching career.

1973 Died in June at age 83, as Professor Emeritus, Osaka College of Commerce.

Kurt Lewin
(1890–1947)
Germany/United States

ALTHOUGH Kurt Lewin is relatively unknown to most of the profession, he probably ranks close to Taylor and Gilbreth for his contributions to modern management. It is from his work and that of his students that the modern group-dynamics movement springs. Moreover, his research has significantly influenced concepts relating to leadership style, decision processes, motivation, communication, conflict management, and the management of change.

Lewin was trained as a psychologist. However, he had an interest in both the theoretical and the practical worlds. One of his favorite sayings was: "There is nothing so practical as a good theory." In modern human relations and personnel management many of his concepts are commonplace. For example, we hear of "force-field analysis," "action research," "laboratory training," and "democratic vs. autocratic" leadership styles. And these are only a few of the reminders we have of Kurt Lewin's contributions.

Lewin, in fact, was responsible for the classic studies of leadership style. Working with his graduate students at the University of Iowa, he conducted carefully designed experiments proving that leadership style was an important cause of group behavior.[1] In these experiments, individuals in leadership

[1] K. Lewin, R. Lippitt, and R. White, "Patterns of Aggressive Behavior in Experimentally Created 'Social Climates,'" *Journal of Social Psychology*, Vol. 10, 1939, pp. 271–299. Also R. Lippitt and R. White, *Autocracy and Democracy: An Experimental Inquiry* (New York: Harper, 1960).

roles changed their style as they moved from group to group. The results indicated that under the democratic leadership style subordinates tended to support each other, to keep working when the leader was out of the work area, and to develop loyalty to the group and its projects. In contrast, under authoritarian or autocratic leadership the groups appeared to have little capacity for initiating action, showed more discontent and aggression toward their leader, expressed more feelings of irritability and aggression toward the group, and practically ceased working when the leader left the room.

During the Second World War Lewin conducted experiments on changing food habits among Americans. The goal of the project was to get Americans to eat types of meat which they normally would reject. In his usual manner Lewin tried to determine the most efficacious procedure for bringing about change. The results indicated that where people were lectured to there was little change; however, where there was active participation in group discussion, the participants did modify their behavior.

From 1937 to 1947 Lewin had a close relationship with the Harwood Manufacturing Co. There he and his students conducted a number of experiments that dealt with training, overcoming resistance to change, altering perceptions of stereotypes, and reducing conflict. One of these experiments, conducted by students John French and Lester Coch, showed that motivation, morale, and productivity were highest where work groups had participated fully in a change in working conditions.[2] Alex Bavelas, another student of Lewin's, carried out a project which, in modern jargon, would be identified as "organization development" work. Lewin reported it as "the solution of a chronic conflict in industry."[3] In this case Bavelas functioned as a third-party consultant who helped sewing-machine operators and maintenance workers define the problem causing their conflict and then jointly work out an action plan for correcting the situation.

In the United States, Lewin founded the Center for Group Dynamics. It still is important in advancing our knowledge and skills in human relations. Lewin's influence is also evident at Tavistock Institute in London. It is probably significant that the first volume of the Tavistock journal *Human Relations* carries two papers by Lewin on "frontiers in group dynamics."

Although he would probably object to the strong focus upon the individual in modern "sensitivity training" programs, it was Kurt Lewin who pioneered their development. In 1946 he helped organize and design a program for the State of Connecticut Interracial Commission which was designed to train leaders in the most effective means of combating community prejudice. As usual, Lewin set up a research project within the program, employing a

[2] John R. P. French and Lester Coch, "Overcoming Resistance to Change," *Human Relations*, Vol. 1, 1948, pp. 512–532.

[3] *Proceedings* of Second Brief Psychotherapy Council (Chicago: Institute for Psychoanalysis, 1944), pp. 36–46. Included in Kurt Lewin, *Resolving Social Conflicts*, Gertrude Weiss Lewin and Gordon W. Allport, eds., New York: Harper, 1948, pp. 125–141.

number of observers who were to report back to the program leaders at separate night sessions. The participants soon became involved in this feedback, and from their involvement Lewin formalized the concept of using small groups for training where the group itself was the training laboratory. Thus he pioneered in starting so-called "T-groups," the "T" standing for training. The T-group was unique in that the group's own behavior in the immediate environment was the central focus of the learning experience. With Lewin's help a summer workshop to be held in Bethel, Maine, was organized. Lewin died before the workshop took place, but his concepts and charisma influenced the results, and many years later, summer meetings of the same type were still being held. They have been modified, and their names have gone through a succession of changes from group dynamics to sensitivity training to human relations laboratories; however, underlying them all are many of Kurt Lewin's theories and approaches to learning about human behavior.

In summary, Lewin has contributed significantly to the management of human resources. His work has helped us to understand communication, participation, motivation, training, and change. Most important, his students have applied his concepts to the management of organizations, so that we see modern managers deeply concerned with communication networks, leadership style, socio-technical systems, group dynamics, organization development, force-field analyses, and committee decision processes. However, it should be recognized that the contribution Lewin made during his lifetime had an impact that is in no way limited to management; rather, it is significant in the historical development of the scientific study of human beings in society as a whole. Lewin's philosophy of science, his penetrating conceptual insights, and his pioneering experiments continue to permeate and influence current research. Moreover, Lewin made original and strategically influential contributions to a wide area of social science—especially in terms of child development, anti-Semitism, the integration of minorities, leadership behavior, food-consumption patterns, social change, and other aspects of the human condition.

Lewin grew up in Germany during the Weimar Republic. Serving in the German army during the First World War, he rose from the rank of private to that of lieutenant and was awarded the Iron Cross. He was, of course, educated at German universities, where he studied with a number of the intellectual giants of his time: Ernst Cassirer, Carl Stumpf, Wolfgang Koehler, Kurt Koffka, and Max Wertheimer. When Hitler came to power, however, Lewin recognized that Nazi Germany was no place for him or anyone else who was interested in freedom and scientific inquiry. He therefore decided to remain permanently in the United States, where he had been working for some years. However, the only available position he could find was that of Professor of Child Psychology at the University of Iowa's Child Welfare Research Station, now the Institute of Child Behavior and Research. Thus he was only on the periphery of the community of professional psychology during his most productive period. It was not until the year before his death that he was awarded a position at the Massachusetts Institute of Technology and could focus upon his central interests.

When we consider, in brief, not only that Kurt Lewin was uprooted by the Nazi movement in his native country but that his life was cut short by his untimely death at the age of 56, his impact on management and on the social sciences in general is remarkable.

Kurt Lewin was a "practical theorist." He had a love of life and a concern for the development of a "practical social science" anchored in a rigorous and solid theory of behavior. He was sincerely interested in his students and possessed a charisma that attracted people to his ideas. He had, however, no desire to develop a school of thinking; rather, he worked to encourage thinking and research related to the practical aspects of human behavior. He was always the psychologist. With him, even the choice of a salad in the university cafeteria was an experiment in psychology. His research and his methodology supplied the underpinning for much of modern social psychology, and a large share of current human relations theory has been developed by his students.

Lewin himself thrived on discussion, and he found it a means of inspiring others. Perhaps his greatest attribute as a psychologist and teacher was that he encouraged his students to develop their own talents; in so doing, they matured and carried their legacy into human relations and group dynamics as these fields exist today.—WILLIAM B. WOLF.

SELECTED PUBLICATIONS

Books:

1935 *Dynamic Theory of Personality*. New York: McGraw-Hill. Selected papers edited by Donald K. Adams and Karl F. Zener.

1936 *Principles of Topological Psychology*. New York: McGraw-Hill. Edited by Fritz Heider and Grace M. Heider.

1948 *Resolving Social Conflicts*. New York: Harper. Selected papers on group dynamics, 1935–1946, edited by Gertrude Weiss Lewin and Gordon W. Allport.

1951 *Field Theory in Social Science*. New York: Harper. Selected theoretical papers edited by Dorwin Cartwright.

Articles:

1935 "Some Social Psychological Differences between the United States and Germany," *Character and Personality*, Vol. 4, pp. 265–293.

1936 "Psychology of Success and Failure," *Occupations*, Vol. 14, pp. 926–930.

1938 "An Experimental Approach to the Study of Autocracy and Democracy: A Preliminary Note," *Sociometry*, Vol. 1, pp. 292–300. With R. Lippitt.

—— "Experiments on Autocratic and Democratic Atmospheres," *The Social Frontier*, Vol. 4, No. 37, pp. 316–319.

1939 "Patterns of Aggressive Behavior in Experimentally Created 'Social Climates,'" *Journal of Social Psychology*, Vol. 10, pp. 271–299. With R. Lippitt and R. White.

1942 "Training in Democratic Leadership," *Journal of Abnormal and Social Psychology*, Vol. 37, pp. 115–119. With A. Barelas.

—— "The Relative Effectiveness of a Lecture Method and a Method of Group Decision for Changing Food Habits," Committee on Food Habits, National Research Council, Washington, D.C. Mimeographed.

1943 "Forces Behind Food Habits and Methods of Change," National Research Council *Bulletin*, No. 108, pp. 35–65.

1944 "The Solution of a Chronic Conflict in Industry," *Proceedings* of the Second Brief Psychotherapy Council. Chicago: Institute for Psychoanalysis, pp. 36–46.

—— "Dynamics of Group Action," *Educational Leadership*, Vol. 1, pp. 195–200.

—— "A Research Approach to Leadership Problems," *Journal of Educational Sociology*, Vol. 17, pp. 392–398.

1946 "Action Research and Minority Problems," *Journal of Social Psychology*, Vol. 2, pp. 34–46.

—— "Research on Minority Problems," *The Technology Review*, Vol. 48, No. 3, January, pp. 163, 164, 182.

—— "Problems of Group Dynamics and the Integration of the Social Sciences: I. Social Equilibria," *Human Relations*, Vol. I, pp. 5–41.

1947 "Frontiers in Group Dynamics: II. Channels of Group Life: Social Planning and Action Research," *Human Relations*, Vol. I, pp. 143–153.

—— "Group Decision and Social Change," in T. H. Newcomb and E. L. Hartley, eds., *Readings in Social Psychology*. New York: Henry Holt, first edition, pp. 330–344.

Curriculum Vitae

1890 Born on September 9th, in Germany.
1903–1908 Attended Kaiserin Augusta Gymnasium.
1908 At University of Freiburg.
1909 At University of Munich.
1909–1914 At University of Berlin, receiving Ph.D.
1914–1918 Saw service as private in German army.
1921 Employed as assistant at Psychological Institute in Berlin.
1921–1926 Held position of Professor of Philosophy at University of Berlin.
1926–1932 Active at Stanford University, Palo Alto, Calif., as Visiting Professor of Psychology.
1933–1935 Served as Acting Professor of Psychology at Cornell University.

1935–1944	Served as Professor of Child Psychology, Child Welfare Research Station, University of Iowa.
1944–1947	Directed, Research Center for Group Dynamics, Massachusetts Institute of Technology.
1942–1947	Served as Counselor, U.S. Department of Agriculture.
1944–1945	Served as Counselor, Office of Strategic Services.
1947	Died on February 12th, aged 56, at Newtonville, Mass.

Kurt Lewin was a member of the American Psychological Association, the Society for Psychology, AAAS, Phi Epsilon Pi, and Sigma Xi. He also served as Chairman, Study of Special Issues, Psychometric Society.

Courtesy Diana Tead Michaelis.

Ordway Tead
(1891–1973)
United States

A man of many facets, Ordway Tead was recognized as an expert in numerous fields. By some he is remembered as a member of the New York City Board of Higher Education; others recall him as an editor of social and economic books; while still others think of him as an author and pioneer in the field of personnel and industrial relations.

Until the middle of his senior year at Amherst College, Tead was planning to follow his father into the Congregational ministry. His several reasons for abandoning this idea were to influence his entire life. He was particularly bothered by the "hypocrisy" of so-called "Christians" in regard to race and economic relations. He was sure that a great difference existed between the "Christian" statements of industrial owners and managers and their true relations with the rank and file of workers. Problems of poverty, unemployment, racial discrimination, exploitation, and inequalities of income were much in his thoughts. He was particularly influenced by the writings of authors like H. G. Wells, John Galsworthy, George Bernard Shaw, Henrik Ibsen, G. Lowes Dickinson, Ralph W. Emerson, Beatrice and Sidney Webb, Graham Wallas, William James, and John Dewey. Later in his life, he was greatly stirred by W. MacNeill Dixon's *The Human Situation* and the writings of Alfred North Whitehead.

After graduation from Amherst College in 1912, Tead accepted an appointment as an Amherst Fellow in Boston's South End House. This settlement-house experience, combined with his work with the voluntary

Massachusetts Committee on Unemployment in 1914 and 1915, led to his association and later partnership with Robert G. Valentine in Valentine, Tead and Gregg, industrial counselors. He was particularly impressed at this time, not only by what he learned at South End and from Valentine, but by the psychological approach in Thompson J. Hudson's *Law of Psychic Phenomena*.

During the First World War, Tead served as a member of the New York City Bureau of Industrial Research. At the same time, he joined with Henry C. Metcalf to present a series of War Emergency Employment management courses for the U.S. War Department at Columbia University. He had published his first book, *Instincts in Industry*, in 1918. Two years later, in 1920, he and Metcalf expanded the material they had developed for their Columbia courses into the book entitled *Personnel Administration: Its Principles and Practices*. It was one of the first university texts in its area.

Also in 1920, Tead joined the staff of McGraw-Hill Book Co. as Editor of Business Publications. Then, in 1925, he accepted the expanded position of Editor of Social and Economic Books at Harper & Bros. Here he continued "the extraordinary consistency of purpose that governed each of his careers." Under Tead's direction, Harper led the way in publishing books on a variety of social issues—race relations, public housing, the cooperative movement, labor relations, group dynamics, and trends in higher education.

Tead was an early advocate of what was to become known as "human relations" and much later as "participative management." Pursuing his academic interests, he himself taught labor relations part-time at the New York School of Social Work from 1920 to 1930. In addition, beginning in 1920 and continuing up to 1956, he was Lecturer and later Adjunct Professor at the Columbia University Graduate School of Business, where he taught a course each year on personnel administration.

In 1937, Tead was appointed by Mayor Fiorello LaGuardia to the New York City Board of Higher Education, which then had jurisdiction over a total of four city colleges. He served as Chairman of the Board during some of its most trying days.

Ordway Tead saw as his responsibility the need "to help build a society in which every man, woman and child would have an opportunity to realize their full potential—and that meant to him a truly democratic society. He assumed a great capacity to produce on the part of those who worked with him, and they usually responded in kind. He was generous with encouragement and appreciation to assist, as he put it, 'the onward and upward.' He could be moved to anger or the edge of tears by situations of suffering and injustice, but he never used an angry word with his associates." His motto was "Moveo et proficio—I move and I get things done."*—ARTHUR C. BEDEIAN

* Richard McAdoo (Senior Editor, Houghton, Mifflin), remarks in "Memoriam of Ordway Tead," January 9, 1974. Unpublished.

SELECTED PUBLICATIONS

Books and Pamphlets:

1918 *Instincts in Industry: A Study of Working-Class Psychology*. Boston: Houghton, Mifflin. 221 pp.

—— *The People's Part in Peace*. New York: Henry Holt. 156 pp.

1920 *The Labor Audit: A Method of Industrial Investigation*. U. S. Federal Board for Vocational Education *Bulletin* No. 43 (*Employment Management Series* No. 8). Washington, D.C.: Government Printing Office. 48 pp.

—— *Personnel Administration: Its Principles and Practices*. With Henry C. Metcalf. New York: McGraw-Hill. 538 pp. Revised 1926, 1933.

1923 *A Course in Personnel Administration*. New York: Columbia University Press. 246 pp.

1928 *The Problem of Terminology in Management Research*. New York: American Management Association. 12 pp.

1929 *Human Nature and Management*. New York: McGraw-Hill. 312 pp. Revised 1933.

1931 *Theories and Proposals for Stabilizing the Wage Earner's Income*. New York: American Management Association. 16 pp.

1933 *Labor Relations Under the Recovery Act*. With Henry C. Metcalf. New York: Whittlesey House, McGraw-Hill. 259 pp.

1935 *The Art of Leadership*. New York: Whittlesey House, McGraw-Hill. 308 pp.

—— *Creative Management*. New York: Association Press. 59 pp.

1938 *The Case for Democracy and Its Meaning for Modern Life*. New York: Association Press. 120 pp.

1939 *New Adventures in Democracy*. New York: Whittlesey House, McGraw-Hill. 229 pp.

1945 *Democratic Administration*. New York: Association Press. 78 pp.

—— "The Importance of Administration in International Action," in *The Permanent Court of International Justice, Its Continuance Advocated by Forty-Four Prominent Members of the Legal Profession*. New York: Carnegie Endowment for International Peace, Division of Intercourse and Education, International Conciliation No. 45. 51 pp.

Articles:

1917 "Work and Pay: A Suggestion for Representative Government in Industry." With Robert G. Valentine. *Quarterly Journal of Economics*, Vol. 31, February, pp. 241–258.

1921 "Building Guilds in Great Britain," *Journal* of the American Institute of Architects, Vol. 8, February, pp. 33–38.

1927 "The Nature and Uses of Creative Leadership," *Bulletin* of the Taylor Society, Vol. 12, June.

1929 "Personnel Research" and "The Maintenance of Labor Standards," in *Scientific Management in American Industry*, edited by Harlow S.

Person for the Taylor Society. New York: Harper, pp. 94–109 and 398–411.

1931 "The Leader as Coordinator," in *Business Leadership*, edited by Henry C. Metcalf. New York: Pitman.

Curriculum Vitae

1891	Born on September 10th in Somerville, Mass.
1912	Graduated from Amherst College with a B.A. degree.
1912–1915	Accepted appointment as Amherst Fellow and worked as Assistant Head Resident at South End House, Boston.
1914–1915	Served on Massachusetts Committee on Unemployment.
1915–1917	Served as associate and then partner, Valentine, Tead and Gregg, industrial counselors.
1917–1919	Served as member, New York City Bureau of Industrial Research.
1917–1918	Taught War Emergency Employment courses for U.S. War Department at Columbia University.
1920–1930	Taught labor relations part-time at New York School of Social Work.
1920–1950	Employed as Lecturer in Personnel Administration at Columbia University.
1920–1925	Employed as Editor, Business Publications, McGraw-Hill Book Co.
1925–1961	Served Harper & Bros. as Editor, Social and Economic Books.
1937–1964	Served as member, New York City Board of Higher Education. Was Chairman, 1938–1953.
1950–1956	Continued teaching at Columbia University as Adjunct Professor.
1973	Died on November 15th, aged 82, in Westport, Conn.

During his career, Tead was the recipient of numerous honors. He was an early member of the Taylor Society and was elected first president of the Society for the Advancement of Management after its birth in 1936 through a merger of the Taylor Society, the Society of Industrial Engineers, and the Industrial Methods Society. He was awarded the Gilbreth Medal by SAM in 1937.

Tead served on the National Commission for UNESCO (1952–1954), the President's Commission on Higher Education (1946–1947), and the Board of Trustees of Briarcliff College. In addition, he was a member of the American Economics Association, the American Management Association, the American Association for Labor Legislation, the Society for the Advancement of Management, the American Psychological Association, the American Academy of Political and Social Sciences, Alpha Delta Phi, Beta Gamma Sigma, and Phi Beta Kappa.

Rolf Nordling
(1893–1974)
Sweden/France

HIMSELF a concerned chief executive, Rolf Nordling set an example of what is required to achieve sound relationships between management and its employees. During the post-World War years, however, he became convinced that training was not just for workers; managers too must "go back to school" and learn to be better managers. His success, despite initial apathy, is undoubtedly his greatest contribution to the quality of management in his adopted country.

Rolf Nordling was the son of a Swedish father and a French mother; his father was consul general in Paris for both Sweden and Norway. When the son came of age, he decided to become a French citizen, but he maintained close ties with his father's country, particularly since, in 1920, he married a young Swedish teacher of French.

Rolf studied at the Lycée Janson de Sailly and later earned the degree of Bachelier des Lettres at the University of Paris. He went to Sweden to learn the lumber business, but he returned to France in 1914, the year in which the First World War broke out and disrupted every young Frenchman's plans.

It was not until 1924 that Rolf's real career in industry may be said to have begun. In that year, with his brother Raoul, he founded a company known as Solitaire to develop and manufacture a cleaning product which the brothers called Solitaire Universel. It turned out to be highly successful; today it would undoubtedly be advertised as a "miracle" cleanser. In fact, the other products that the Nordlings added to their line by merger or acquisition were successes as well: Saponite, Mayola, Lion Noir, and PPZ.

In the years between the wars, Sweden's experiment with socialism was attracting worldwide attention. Influenced by this example, which he knew well and admired, Rolf Nordling—as President of Solitaire—from the start introduced into the company a new spirit and a variety of new methods of dealing with employees. He was convinced that in the work organization cooperation at all levels was a key factor in success, and he set himself the task of promoting his new principles not only among the managers of his own company but in industrial circles generally. During these years, too, he participated actively in the well-known "Décades de Pontigny"—discussions or conversations which sought to explore in depth the contradictions of an industrial society.

The Second World War gave Nordling a chance to demonstrate both his courage and his generosity. In August 1944, when the Allies had landed on the Normandy beaches and were slowly forcing the Germans inland, he undertook the dangerous mission of crossing the enemy lines to ask that General Omar Bradley, the American in charge of the Allied troops, speed up his march on Paris. This Bradley did, entering the city two days ahead of schedule and thereby saving it from destruction. And Nordling was equally successful, the following December, in getting food and medicines to the besieged populace of La Rochelle, who expressed their appreciation by making him an honorary citizen of their city.

After the war, Rolf Nordling renewed his relationship with CNOF—the Comité National de l'Organisation Française (National Committee for French Management). Early in his career he had found its Ecole d'Organisation Scientifique du Travail (School of Scientific Management) most helpful. Now he organized a series of international conferences on "Aspects sociaux de l'Organisation du Travail" (Social Aspects of Management). Held at the Cercle Culturel de Royaumont, this series was so well attended that it was repeated for 13 consecutive years. Nordling himself was President of CNOF from 1950 to 1952, during which time he restored much of its prewar status.

As was then fashionable, the French sent a "mission de productivité"—called in English a "productivity team"—to the United States in 1952 to study American industry's methods of developing middle management and in this way increasing productivity. The team consisted almost solely of consulting engineers or management consultants. Nordling, who headed it, was neither; yet it was he who presided over the writing and editing of the team's report—and this report had one dominant theme. In the United States. management development took place at all levels. Furthermore, the development of middle managers would make no sense unless it were accompanied—or even preceded by—the development of higher-level managers and even chief executives. In France, efforts were being made currently to train and develop middle and first-line managers, but almost nothing was being done for their superiors.

From all this, Nordling drew a conclusion which, for him, became a duty:

to promote training and development for top management throughout France. It was not a popular idea, even among those who were handicapped by having to serve under executives who were most in need of help. But Nordling persisted, and finally an additional group of three "missionnaires" spent nine weeks studying American practices in greater detail. Then, under the Marshall Plan, four Americans—professors and industrialists—came to Paris and for four months worked with a small team of French recruits to plan and conduct five days of talks, illustrated by visual aids (relatively new in France) and followed by practical discussions. Afterward, these conferences became mobile, circulating around Paris and beyond in order to reach as many people as possible.

There were—or would soon be—several French groups interested in the training and development of organization heads and other high-level managers. Nordling's own CNOF was, of course, one of them. During this period, however, Nordling founded L'Institut Français pour la Formation et le Perfectionnement des Chefs dans L'Entreprise (French Institute for the Training and Development of Chief Executives); and, together with a CNOF subgroup, it became the point of departure for the so-called Groupement des Animateurs et Responsables de Formation d'Entreprises (Association of Company Sponsors and Directors of Management Development). Then, too, there was the Centre de Recherches et d'Etudes des Chefs d'Entreprise (Research and Study Center for Chief Executives), one of whose most earnest supporters was Rolf Nordling himself.

It was the Center that in April 1954 held its first session in temporary quarters at Annet-sur-Marne, moving the next year to its permanent home in the "grand château" of Jouy-en-Josas. Rolf Nordling's idea was at last materializing. In 1969, moreover, he would have the satisfaction of seeing a new wing of the château solemnly named the Aile Rolf Nordling.

Unsurprisingly, Nordling continued to be productive during the third and last decade of his 30 years as President of Solitaire, SA. In 1966, for example, he founded PRODEF, the group in which he brought together, for the first time in France, the most powerful manufacturers of maintenance products. This, he said, was the crowning achievement of his career in industry, fulfilling his ambition to create an organization on a truly European scale. His modesty was so genuine, however, that none of his successes could alter it in the slightest degree. He wove a network of solid friendships for himself around the world. At CNOF he set an example of diligence and discreet effectiveness for his younger associates. He rarely intervened in a discussion; but when he did, something would happen: The problem being debated would suddenly appear in a new light, the group would unexpectedly hit upon a principal idea that had heretofore eluded the members, or a proposal made would receive the kind of support which, up to that moment, no one had dared to hope for.

Especially in the early days of CNOF, when Nordling was still fully active in his own company, he often participated in CNOF training and development sessions—without any dramatic exaggerations but always with a piquant and very personal touch. Furthermore, this was true of all his public appearances. Once in Paris, for instance, when asked to speak on a topic about which—as usual—he pretended to know very little, he began in this way: "During the dark days of the Occupation, I read on the front of a butcher shop this inscription: 'No meat, no fat, nothing but bones.' Gentlemen, here are *my* 'bones.'"

On another occasion, this one in New York, he was receiving the Wallace Clark Award from CIOS along with Lillian Gilbreth,* mother of the 12 children of that famous dozen. Impulsively he decided to dedicate his speech of thanks to her. "Madame," he said:

> I am very honored to have the distinction which your country is according me. But perhaps I am even more honored to have it at the same time as you, because you are not an ordinary person. In the United States there is one chance in several million that a woman may be a remarkable engineer and management consultant. In this same country, there is even less of a chance that a woman may be the mother of 13 [*sic*] children. If we combine these two probabilities, there is no chance at all, Madame, of your being a human being who can be explained by the laws of statistics. You are an angel, and you understand how honored I am to receive this medal beside you.

To quote Père Lacordaire, the brilliant nineteenth-century orator and preacher, "It is characteristic of great minds that they discover the principal need of the time in which they live and then dedicate themselves to it." That is what Rolf Nordling did. Having discovered the need for management development on a continuing basis, he asked only to serve that need.

Rolf Nordling was French, but he was also Swedish. And, with his two halves so obviously in equilibrium, he may have had the best each nation has to offer. He was a man of spirit—said one of his associates in CNOF—a man of thought, and a man of action. Blessed with inexhaustible perseverance in the search for improvement of the social climate, he dedicated the last years of his life to convincing his colleagues in industry of the need to make the great mass of French men and women understand more clearly the economic principles which govern their lives. In brief, he made his influence felt by a whole generation of business people through his participation in the creation and the encouragement of organizations devoted to his—and their—cause.—ELIZABETH MARTING

SELECTED PUBLICATIONS

Book:

1970 *Suède socialiste et libre entreprise* (Socialist Sweden and Free Enterprise). Written in collaboration with Anne Hutchings-Giessecke. Paris: Fayard-Mame.

* See Dr. Gilbreth's profile in Part Two.

Rolf Nordling was also the author of other publications of varying lengths. Among the topics he discussed were "Six points de Fayol sur l'organisation scientifique du travail" (Fayol's Six Points on Scientific Management), "L'Organisation scientifique, facteur d'harmonie sociale" (Scientific Management—Factor in Social Peace), "Le Rôle de l'ingénieur psychologue dans l'industrie américaine (The Role of the Engineer/Psychologist in American Industry), "Comment réaliser la solidarité dans l'entreprise" (How to Build Solidarity in the Organization), "Enquête sociologique dans deux entreprises françaises (Inquest into Two French Companies), "Comment réaliser une communauté de vues et d'interêts entre le personnel et la direction des entreprises" (How to Achieve Commonality of Views Among Company Employees and Managers), and "La Formation des cadres aux Etats-Unis" (The Development of Management Teams in the United States).

In addition, Nordling collaborated with the other members in preparing the 1952 report of the French "mission de productivité" which visited the United States to study methods of training and developing middle managers. It is entitled "Cadres et maitrise" (Management and Control).

Curriculum Vitae

1893	Born on October 12th, in Neuilly-sur-Seine, of a French mother and Swedish father (Consul General of Sweden and Norway in Paris). As a youth, went to Sweden to familiarize self with lumber business.
1914	Returned to France at start of the First World War. At age of 21, chose French citizenship.
1914–1918	War delayed serious business career.
1918–1939	Participated actively in "Decades de Pontigny"—explorations of contemporary thinking on contradictions of an industrial society.
1924	Career began in earnest. With brother Raoul Nordling, founded Solitaire, a company which developed and made a success of Solitaire Universel, a "miracle" cleaning product.
1924–1974	Served as President and General Director of Solitaire, SA. During his 30-year tenure, company grew and acquired subsidiaries (Saponite, Mayola, Lion Noir, PPZ) that were exceptionally successful.
1944	In August, after Allies' landings in Normandy, crossed enemy lines to urge General Omar Bradley (U.S.A.) to speed march on Paris. Troops entered two days ahead of schedule, thereby saving city from destruction. In December, got medicines and food to La Rochelle, then under siege, in name of Swedish Red Cross. Made honorary citizen by inhabitants.
1945	With Comité National de l'Organisation Française (National Committee for French Management), set up series of international conferences on "Aspects sociaux de l'Organisation du

Travail" (Social Aspects of Management), held foı 13 successive years at Cercle Culturel de Royaumont.

1950–1952 Served as President of CNOF, restoring it to prewar status Founded Institut Français pour la Formation et le Perfectionnement des Chefs dans L'Entreprise (French Institute for the Training and Development of Chief Executives), which, with a CNOF group, produced the Groupement des Animateurs et Responsables de Formation d'Entreprises (Association of Sponsors and Directors of Management Development). In addition, promoted work of Centre de Recherches et d'Etudes des Chefs d'Entreprise (Research and Study Center for Chief Executives).

1952 Headed "mission de productivité" on visit to United States, following up trip with program to popularize management development, particularly for top executives, in France. With other members of mission, wrote and edited report for publication.

1954 Saw hopes for continuing development of chief executives realized with first CRC session at Annet-sur-Marne (April).

1966 Founded PRODEF, bringing together in one group, for the first time in France, the most powerful manufacturers of maintenance products.

1968 Shocked by events of May (touched off by student rioting in Paris), established the Fondation pour la Diffusion des Connaissances Economiques (Foundation for a Broader Knowledge of Economics).

1974 Died on October 9th, three days short of 81st birthday.

Nordling, as Honorary President of CNOF, saw the new wing of its headquarters in the Grand Chateau de Jouy-en-Josas named the Aile Rolf Nordling after him. In 1951 he received the Wallace Clark Award from CIOS in New York.

Courtesy News Pictorial.

Alvin McCreary Brown
(1893–1972)
United States

ALVIN Brown proved himself a perceptive manager in both government and industry before he published the ideas that make up his contribution to the development, principally, of organization as a management area. During his era, he was somewhat of a maverick among the practitioners and professors of management. His observations, his research, and his publications were devoted almost exclusively to the concept that organization is a separate branch of management. He likened it to the writing of a play as opposed to the casting of the actors for that play, which, he declared, was another function altogether.

In his 1949 address to the Academy of Management, Brown presented his concept of organization in the following words:

> I think industrial enterprise—or any human enterprise for that matter—has three concerns. One, certainly, is personnel. Another is administration, by which I mean all things that have to be done to carry out the purpose of the enterprise. The third is organization. In the sense in which I have defined it . . . it is a subject, an activity, a science, separate and apart from both personnel and administration.

Brown went on to to state that his only concern was to convince managers that "organization is a separate and unique subject." He commented that "most managers practice organization by intuition, not by principle." And, by way of concluding his address, he told the Academy, "My hope is to see schools teach organization—as such."

For the purpose of advancing the concept that organization is a separate and unique subject in terms of both practice and teaching, Brown published three authoritative books over a span of eight years. All three influenced scholars and practicing managers alike. The first book, published in 1945, was *Organization: A Formulation of Principles.*[1] It advocated principles of organization that would be applicable to any kind of concerted human endeavor. However, it was his second effort, in 1947, that proved to be his most successful and influential publication. In *Organization of Industry,*[2] Brown not only advocated principles of organization, he formulated them. This second book starts by listing 96 distinct principles of organization and is aimed throughout at the application of these 96 principles to the organization of industrial enterprise. Brown emphasizes his belief that organization is both an art and a science. The *science*, he says, involves the development of principles, whereas the *art* deals with their application.

The interest in organization theory that emerged in many schools of business during the decade of the 1960s was foreshadowed by many of Brown's ideas. No one ever listed any more than his 96 principles, which were known to the academic community by number if not by content. And Brown was a purist in the treatment of organization. In *Organization of Industry*, he deliberately avoided the terms "management," "functional," and "staff." He considered them too often misused, too broad, and too frequently misunderstood. For the terms which he did use to demonstrate the application of his principles—"responsibility," "obligation," "authority," "delegation," and "coordination"—he provided his own definitions.

Brown's enumeration of the 96 principles and their application marked the zenith of what might be called the "principles" era. The postwar years involved college professors in greater concern with theory and research than with learning from the experiences of practicing managers.

Organization of Industry also presents an interesting conceptual framework or model that shows three aspects of industrial management as a flow arrangement. First there is *purpose*, which is the objective of the enterprise; second, purpose demands *administration*, which is the sum of the endeavors of all members of the enterprise directed toward the accomplishment of its purpose. Administration consists of (*a*) planning activities, (*b*) seeing that the activities are performed, and (*c*) performing or directing the performance of the activities to achieve the purpose of the organization. And, third, administration demands *organization* that prescribes individual tasks or endeavors and the relations among them.

In his third authoritative book, published in 1953, Alvin Brown moved into a nonindustrial area: the Armed Forces of the United States. *The Armor*

[1] New York: Hibbert Printing Co.
[2] New York: Prentice-Hall.

of Organization[3] is an unusual book. After tracing the historical development of military organization and the growth of the staff concept, he offers an analysis of military organization. In it he finds two errors: (1) neglect to differentiate functions and (2) failure to delegate responsibility. He concludes that the nation can no longer afford the neglect "the armor of organization." And he explains how his principles of organization could be applied to devise an effective organization for the Armed Forces.

By formalizing his observations on organization, Brown built a conceptual framework and a system of principles that could serve as a guide for any operating manager. This made him one of the influential authorities of his time. His thinking won popular acceptance in both college courses and executive development programs for practicing managers.

Brown was a quiet man with both the intellectual capacity for the formulation of fundamentals and principles from analytical observation and the skills needed to administer the finance function in a large industrial corporation. His personality was pleasing, with overtones of dry wit and drollery. He is remembered for his ability to cool heated discussions with an appropriate classical allusion or poetic quotation, often from the works of Rudyard Kipling. His diction was always faultless and his sartorial taste impeccable.

Although Brown studied law and graduated from a school of law, he preferred the challenging environment of government and industry—with, however, periodic interludes for joining in the academic and professional activities of the college professors who accepted and acclaimed him. He was one of the very few top managers in business who was ever elected President of the Academy of Management. He had many friends among university faculty members. A prolific letter writer, he maintained contact with them through correspondence and kept a chronological file of his communications with each of them. Alvin Brown was a man for all seasons: versatile, competent, and admired.—JOHN F. MEE

SELECTED PUBLICATIONS

Books:

1945 *Organization: A Formulation of Principles.* New York: Hibbert Printing Co. 308 pp.

1947 *Organization of Industry.* New York: Prentice-Hall. 370 pp.

1953 *The Armor of Organization.* New York: Hibbert Printing Co. 597 pp.

1957 *Financial Analysis of Johns-Manville.* New York: Johns-Manville Corp. 590 pp.

Articles:

1953 "Is Industry Autocratic?" *Advanced Management Journal*, Vol. 18, May.

[3] New York: Hibbert Printing Co.

1954 "Some Reflections on Organization: Truths, Halftruths, and Delusions," *Personnel*, Vol. 31, July.
1955 "Judging the Effectiveness of Organization," *Advanced Management Journal*, Vol. 20, January.
1956 "The Case (or Bootstrap) Method," *Advanced Management Journal*, Vol. 21, July.
1957 "All Decisions Are Financial," *Financial Approach to Industrial Operations*. New York: Society for the Advancement of Management pamphlet, pp. 6–10.

Paper:
1949 "Organization as a Separate Branch of Management." Presented at annual meeting of the Academy of Management at the Columbia University Club, New York City, December 30th.

Curriculum Vitae

1893 Born on December 17th in Washington, D.C.
1914 Received A.B. from George Washington University.
1916 Received LL.B. from George Washington University.
1925–1929 Employed as Vice-President and Treasurer, Moline Implement Co.
1933 Named Assistant to Director of the Budget (U.S.A.).
1933–1935 Served as Assistant Administrator for National Recovery Act.
1937–1939 Employed as Vice-President, West Virginia Coal and Coke Corp.
1940 Employed as Assistant to Vice-President of Finance, Johns-Manville Corp.
1946 Employed as Vice-President for Finance and Director, Johns-Manville Corp.
1946–1951 Lectured at Massachusetts Institute of Technology.
1957 Elected President, Academy of Management.
1972 Died at age 78.

Alvin Brown, besides serving a term as President, contributed greatly to the development of the Academy of Management and to the formation of its Fellows group, to which he himself was elected. In addition, he held membership in the Society for the Advancement of Management. In short, Brown was a man of the industrial world who had many interests and associations in the academic community.

Torao Nakanishi
(1896–1975)
Japan

IN the half-century between his return to Japan from study in Germany in 1926 and his death in 1975, Torao Nakanishi was one of the outstanding Japanese leaders in the field of business economics, a discipline which comprises both accounting and business administration as these are thought of in the United States. His major works, *Keiei keizaigaku* (Business Economics) and *Keiei hiyoron* (The Theory of Management Costs) are classics; they represent a monumental achievement that has lost none of its significance with time.

Keiei keizaigaku (Business Economics) dealt with its subject, at that time poorly defined in scientific terms, by studying the nature of individual movements of capital as independent units. This book laid a foundation for business economics by defining it as a branch of theoretical economics in its own right.

In *Keiei hiyoron* (The Theory of Management Costs), Nakanishi treated the circulation of capital in the enterprise as a process that relates costs, gains, and profits. He clarified the nature of costs, taking as his point of departure the assumption that the problem of costs constitutes the essence of business economic theory. He developed a profit-and-loss theory, a cost-accounting theory, and a management-comparison theory all based on this theory of costs.

The integrated accounting system that Nakanishi devised in his later years focuses on cost accounting and links profit-and-loss accounting, funds accounting, and budget accounting. This concept can be seen in embryonic form in *Keiei hiyoron* (The Theory of Management Costs). It was eventually set forth fully and clearly in *Chusho-kigyo no tame no genka keisan* (Cost Accounting for Smaller Businesses), which was published in 1959 in the name of the Japan Productivity Center but, in reality, is Nakanishi's work. This is a unique academic achievement worthy of the highest praise.

Nakanishi was an exceptional theorist, but he was not a scholar who spent all his time in his study. He was at the same time a superb practical leader. Beginning in 1948, when the Business Accounting Research Board was established by the Japanese government, he was an important member. In this capacity, he strove to improve postwar Japan's business accounting system through the establishment and diffusion of general principles of business accounting and cost-accounting standards. With the enactment, in that same year, of the Certified Public Accountant Act, he also became a member of the Certified Public Accountant Administration Commission. Thus he contributed to the establishment and development, for the first time in Japan, of certified public accountancy.

In 1962 Nakanishi became Managing Director of the Japan Productivity Center and head of the Productivity Research Institute, through which he provided both theoretical and practical guidance for campaigns designed to increase productivity in Japanese industry. He gave special attention and enthusiasm to analytical research and training in value-added productivity, and he also made a great contribution to the compilation of value-added statistics for major Japanese industries and to practical training in management and accounting.

Torao Nakanishi's attitude toward his academic pursuits was very strict throughout his entire life. He was severe with himself in both his thinking and his writing; he never ceased to reconsider and revise his views. His habit of continually looking ahead inspired respect and deference in his followers, and his personal leadership and guidance were noted for their kindliness and boundless enthusiasm. Many people who knew him from contacts on campus or in their place of work still remember him with great reverence and affection.—TATSU NABESHIMA AND SUSUMU TAKAMIYA

SELECTED PUBLICATIONS

Books:

1931 *Keiei keizaigaku* (Business Economics).Tokyo: Nihon Hyoron-sha.

1936 *Keiei hiyoron* (The Theory of Management Costs). Tokyo: Chikura Shobo.

In addition, the following books were either edited or supervised by Nakanishi:

1938 *Hyakkatenho ni kansuru kenkyu* (Studies in the Department Stores Law). Edited. Tokyo: Dobun-kan.

1950 *Kigyo to zeisei kaikaku* (Businesses and Tax-System Reform). Supervised. Tokyo: Moriyama Shoten.

1952 *Saishin genka keisan* (Up-to-Date Cost Accounting). Edited. Tokyo: Okura Zaimu Kyokai.

1954 *Keiei kanri* (Business Management). Supervised. Tokyo: Chuo Keizai-sha.

1955 *Keiei yosan tosei no jitsurei* (Practical Examples of Operating-Budget Control). Supervised. Tokyo: Diamond-sha.

1958 *Kindai genka keisan* (Modern Cost Accounting). Edited. Tokyo: Dobunkan.

—— *Yosan tosei no riron to jitsurei* (Theory and Practice of Budget Control). Supervised. Tokyo: Diamond-sha.

Curriculum Vitae

1896 Born on March 11th in Wakayama Prefecture, Japan.

1920 Graduated from Faculty of Economics, Tokyo Imperial University.

1921 Appointed Assistant, Tokyo Imperial University.

1923 Appointed Assistant Professor, Tokyo Imperial University.

1923–1926 Studied management of commercial affairs in Germany.

1927–1939 Served as Professor, Tokyo Imperial University, in charge of first and third courses of study in commercial science.

1939–1941 Worked in Finance and Accounting Bureau, Ministry of War.

1939–1942 Worked for Cabinet Planning Board.

1942–1945 Was Managing Director, Central Price Control Cooperation Council.

1948–1952 Headed Tokyo Commerce and Industry Guidance Center.

1948–1975 Served as member and Chairman, Fourth Section, Business Accounting Research Board, Economic Stability Center (later transferred to Ministry of Finance and called Business Accounting Council). Also served as member of Certified Public Accountant Administration Commission in Ministry of Finance and as Chairman of its Certified Public Accountant Examination Board.

1951 Served as Business Accounting Examiner, Securities and Exchange Commission.

1952 Appointed Professor, Faculty of Economics, Osaka University.

1954 Received Ph.D. in economics from University of Tokyo.

1956 Became head of Faculty of Economics, Osaka University.

1959 Retired from Osaka University with title of Professor Emeritus.

1959–1969 Was Professor, Faculty of Commercial Science, Keio University.

1962–1975 Served as Managing Director, Japan Productivity Center.

1969–1975 Was Professor, Takushoku University.

1975 Died on April 25th, aged 79, in Tokyo.

Courtesy Eyvind Hellern.

Bernhard Hellern
(1896–1972)
Norway

ALL his adult life, Bernhard Hellern preached rationalization to Norwegian industry. During his engineering studies in Stavanger and Bergen, he was aware of the developing principles of scientific management—or rationalization, as it had become known in Norway. His early telephone and electrical-works experience convinced him of the new methods' practicality; and by 1929, when he returned to his native country after six years as a student and a Westinghouse production engineer in the United States, he was ready to sell rationalization to every Norwegian factory owner and foreman, not to mention every practicing engineer and every student of engineering.

Hellern first of all promoted rationalization as an *engineer*. At the Brooklyn plant of the Westinghouse Electric & Manufacturing Co. he had been a supervisor in charge of determining time-study rates and controlling costs. He therefore had an opportunity to see how the Taylor theories and procedures worked on the plant or shop floor and, above all, how they affected worker attitudes and worker performance. His subsequent employment as project engineer with National Industri—owned by Westinghouse, incidentally—was equally valuable. But it was his move to Industriforbundets Rasjonaliseringskontor (Federation of Industry's Rationalization Office) that gave his determination to preach the rationalization gospel full scope.

Here was a consulting group that employed 30 engineers and economists. Its clients with their varied operations and problems offered a far greater field in which to demonstrate the importance of rationalization and so make an impact on Norwegian industry in general. Hellern was Chief Engineer for two years, from 1933 to 1935, before he was named Administrative Director, after which both his responsibilities and his opportunities broadened to include those of a true *manager*. As head of the Rationalization Office, he supervised the guidance offered by the group to small Norwegian manufacturing firms, not just in an overall way but in the context of specific industries. At the same time, he undertook studies to determine "normal" output, devise standard models for work of differing types, design a work-evaluation system appropriate to Norway, and the like. Hellern took four years off (1946–1950) to manage E. Sunde & Co., an Oslo concern which employed more than 300 laborers and office personnel, manufactured water and steam equipment, and engaged in a variety of plumbing work. Upon his return to the Rationalization Office, he remained there for 15 more years; essentially, 1965 marked the end of his active career.

Beginning very early in that career, Bernhard Hellern served as a *teacher* to the extent that his other obligations would permit. This too gave him an important audience for his favorite topic: He taught the principles of rationalization from 1933 to 1940 at the Statens Teknologiske Institutt (State Institute of Technology). From 1942 to 1944 he was a judge for oral examinations in production methods at Bergen Tekniske Skole (Bergen School of Technology). Moreover, he was a frequent *lecturer* before technical and industrial societies not only in Norway but in Denmark and Finland.

Hellern further served the cause of better management as a *writer*. He has two textbooks to his credit, both rationalization-oriented. And, in addition to the numerous articles with his by-line in newspapers and periodicals, he broadcast a series of radio presentations which an Oslo publisher collected under the title *Rasjonalisering som ledd i gjenoppbygning* (Rationalization as the Key to Rebuilding).

Hellern traveled extensively for business and study apart from his six-year stay, as a young man just starting his life's work, in the United States. He revisited that country in 1948, and he made trips regularly to Sweden and Denmark and at least once to Germany, England, Scotland, Finland, Italy, and Belgium. Yet, even if he had never left Norway, his consulting work at the Rationalization Office would have given him, not only endless opportunities to share his enthusiasm for scientific management, but also an extraordinary familiarity with a broad range of industries and their special problems. For the paper industry, the Office made a study of spooling—with the emphasis on determining the optimum number of spindles—and others on paper sorting designed to improve work methods and systematize the detection of faults. For the lumber industry, the Office's staff investigated the problem of log transportation from sawing site to log pile. This called for determining the most satisfactory ways of stacking the individual logs and arranging the piles in rows. It also meant gauging the physical exertion required to pile logs. Then, for the Norske Elektrisitetsverkers Forening (Norwegian Electrical Works Association), Hellern and his group studied debt collection and debiting methods and, for the mining industry, maintenance and repair with primary attention to preventive measures.

Problem solving on this scale implies a shrewd *researcher*—one in particular who seizes every opportunity for on-the-spot study and investigations. On his trips abroad, Hellern made it a point, when possible, to visit outstanding research institutes and universities noted for their work in a field that interested him: for example, the Mellon Institute and the University of Pittsburgh, New York University, the British Institute of Management in London, the Production Engineering Research Association in Melton Mowbray, the Instituut voor Onderzoek en Voorlichting (Institute for Research and Investigation) of Amsterdam, and not only the general Industrins Utredningsinstitut (Industrial Research Institute) in Stockholm, but also the Swedish shoe industry's special facility there. On two occasions, Hellern received grants for travel and study: one in 1941 from the Polyteknisk Forening to conduct research on work, especially with regard to the problems of compensatory rest time, and the other in 1948 from the Norges Teknisk-Naturvitenskepelinge Forskingsråd (Norway Advisory Council on Technology and the Natural Sciences) to study production methods in the United States.

In summary, Bernhard Hellern bore witness to the values of rationalization as engineer, manager, teacher, lecturer, and researcher. It may not be too much to say that he was a leader—very possibly the principal leader—in bringing the concepts and techniques of modern management to his country.—ELIZABETH MARTING

SELECTED PUBLICATIONS

1933 *Produksjonteknikk* (Production Technology). Oslo: Norges Industriforbund.

1943 *Rasjonell bedriftsledelse* (Rational Management). Oslo: Norges Industriforbund.

1945 *Rasjonalisering som ledd i gjenoppbygning* (Rationalization as the Key to Rebuilding). Oslo: H. Aschehoug.

1963 *Trekk fra rasjonaliseringens: historie av Industriforbund.* (Road to Rationalization: Story of the Norwegian Federation of Industry). Oslo: Polyteknisk Forening, Rasjoniserungs Gruppe av Norges Industriforbund.

In addition, Hellern contributed many articles to magazines and newspapers on production technology and on rationalization in industry, commerce, and public administration.

Curriculum Vitae

1896 Born in Stavanger on May 7th.

1915 Entered Stavanger Elektrotekniske Dagskole (Stavanger Trade School for Electrical Technology), completing course in 1916.

1917 Entered Bergen Tekniske Skole (Bergen School of Technology), completing course in 1919.

1919–1921 Worked as project engineer for Stavanger Telefonselskap (Stavanger Telephone Company).

1920–1922 Managed Skudesneshavn municipal electrical works.

1923–1929 Came to United States; studied alternating-current technology at College of the City of New York (1923) and in Chicago (1924–1926); worked as production engineer in Brooklyn plant of Westinghouse Electric & Manufacturing Co.

1929–1932 Returning to Norway, was a production engineer with National Industri A/S (Westinghouse-owned manufacturer of cooking and heating appliances), in Drammen.

1932–1940 Taught principles of rationalization at Statens Teknologiske Institutt (State Institute of Technology).

1933–1935 Was Chief Engineer, Industriforbundets Rasjonaliseringskontor A/S, Oslo (Federation of Industry's Rationalization Office). Taught principles of rationalization at Oslo Tekniske Skole (Oslo School of Technology).

1935–1946 Was Administrative Director, Industriforbundets Rasjonaliseringskontor A/S.

1938–1949 Headed committee responsible for initial effort of Polyteknisk Forening (Polytechnic Society) to found its rationalization group; then served as group's chairman.

1939–1940 Headed committee to plan and organize Produksjonsteknikk Forskningsinstitutt (Research Institute for Production Technology), in Oslo.

1942–1944 Served as judge for oral examinations in production technology at Bergen Tekniske Skole (Bergen School of Technology).

1946 Responsible for establishment of Norske Nasjonalkomite for Rasjonell Organisasjon (Norwegian National Committee for Rationalization), becoming chairman in same year.

1946–1950 Managed A/S E. Sunde & Co. Ltd. (makers of water and steam equipment in Oslo).

1948 Visited United States again, under grant from Norges Teknisk-Naturvitenskapelinge Forskingsråd (Norway Advisory Council on Technology and the Natural Sciences) to study status of American research in production technology.

1950–1965 Again served as Administrative Director, Industriforbundets Rasjonaliseringskontor. Concurrently was Administrator, Produksjonsteknikk Forskningsinstitutt (Research Institute for Production Technology), in Bergen.

1972 Died on May 17th, aged 76, in Oslo.

Bernhard Hellern was a member of the Norske Ingeniørforening (Norwegian Engineering Society) and the Polyteknisk Forening (Polytechnic Society) as well as the steering committee responsible for the publication of their *Teknisk ukeblad* (Technology Weekly). He belonged to the Norsk Arbeidsstudieselskap

(Norwegian Society for Work Study) and its Examination Committee, of which he was Chairman; the Norges Standardiserings Forbund (Norway Standardization Association); the board set up by the Statens Teknoliske Institutt (State Institute of Technology) to help various trades and professions solve work problems through rationalization; and the Mekaniske Verksteders Landsforening (National Association of Machine Shop Owners) and its Rationalization Board. In the international area, he held membership in the Collège International pour l'Etude Scientifique des Techniques de Production Mécanique (International College for the Scientific Study of Mechanical Production Methods) and the Comité International de l'Organisation Scientifique (International Committee of Scientific Management). The latter organization, CIOS, he served as a member of the Executive Committee.

The Polyteknisk Forening awarded Bernhard Hellern honorary membership in 1940. He also was a recipient of the King's Gold Medal.

Charles Perry McCormick
(1896–1970)
United States

CHARLES Perry McCormick was a successful business practitioner. His major contribution to management was the creation at McCormick and Co. of "multiple management," a system involving the establishment of several boards—senior, junior, factory, and sales—as a means of obtaining employee participation and developing executives. More than 2,000 firms in the United States and abroad have adopted the basic ideas of this plan.

McCormick's innovation in management was grounded in a number of beliefs. First, he felt that experience was the best teacher. Second, he believed that an individual's contribution to an organization should be recognized objectively and that merit should be rewarded. Third, it seemed to him that one of the basic needs of every individual was to be an active member of a group. Finally, in his opinion a business organization should maintain a firm policy of promotion from within.

To McCormick, business was primarily a matter of people. The primary purpose of management was to build people. If the human factor was placed above profit and the organization was constructed of the right material, then profit would take care of itself.

On the basis of these ideas and principles, McCormick designed multiple management. The plan is designed to tap as much existing knowledge about managing as possible and to develop still greater knowledge and new managers. It operates through a combination of auxiliary management boards, participation, sponsorship, merit rating, and two-way communication among all employees in management. The auxiliary boards are composed of lower-level managers and assistant managers. These supplement a senior board of directors that retains veto power over them. The boards elect their own members on a semiannual basis, they draft their own by-laws, and they have to make all their recommendations unanimously. Furthermore, there are no limitations on the topics which these boards may discuss.

The system is designed to ensure that election to the boards is won on merit rather than on popularity. To help achieve this goal, the plan includes a sponsorship program to identify potential managerial talent among new employees and facilitate compatibility with the organization. Auxiliary board members act as the sponsors of high-potential recruits, rotating these protégés semiannually and rating them on an informal basis.

Charles P. McCormick was a gregarious, energetic, sympathetic, and highly articulate man. He loved sports, having once been President of the Baltimore Colts football team, and he was also an amateur painter and woodcarver. Because he had a talent for friendship, he felt that his 1,600 fellow-workers at McCormick and Co. were his friends. McCormick had strongly held convictions about brotherliness, the importance of teamwork, the need to recognize merit, the individual's duty to be of service to mankind, and the importance of experience in determining truth and skill in managing. His system of multiple management reflects these beliefs, and it is significant that in his later years he annually awarded special "unsung hero" awards to football and lacrosse players in Baltimore-area high schools. These awards went, not to those who were recognized stars, but rather to individuals who exerted the most "doggedness and contribution to the team."

The concept of encouraging and rewarding team performance was, in fact, one of McCormick's major themes in life. It helped guide his management system.—WILLIAM B. WOLF

SELECTED PUBLICATIONS

Books:

1938 *Multiple Management.* New York: Harper.

1949 *The Power of People.* New York: Harper.

Curriculum Vitae

1896	Born on June 9th in Morelia, Mexico.
1912–1917	Attended college; worked summers for McCormick and Co.
1917	Graduated from Johns Hopkins University.
1917–1919	Served in U.S. Navy, including nine months as Athletic Director of 5th Naval District.
1919–1955	Worked for McCormick and Co.
1932	Elected President and Chairman of the Board.
1955	Retired as President, remaining Chairman of the Board.

1969 Retired as Chairman of the Board.
1970 Died June 16th, aged 74.

Charles P. McCormick served as Chairman of the Board, Baltimore Branch, Federal Reserve Bank; Director, Chairman, and Federal Agent, Richmond (Virginia) Federal Reserve Bank; Director, Massachusetts Mutual Life Insurance Company and Equitable Trust Co., Baltimore; Chairman, Maryland Board of Agriculture; Chairman, Civic Center Commission of Baltimore.

He was President, Baltimore Convention Bureau; Director, Chamber of Commerce of the United States; member, Business Council and Import Advisory Commission of the U.S. Department of Commerce; Director, Council, U.S. Association, International Chamber of Commerce; Trustee, Nutrition Foundation; Chairman, Board of Regents, University of Maryland; Director, Boys Club of America, Inc.; Vice-President, Baltimore Commerce Association; President, Better Business Bureau, Baltimore; member, War Savings Commission, Maryland; Chairman, Army & Navy, Inc., 3rd Corps Area; U.S. employer delegate to International Labor Organization; President, International Organization of Employers; adviser to Senate Subcommittee on Relations with International Organizations; Vice-President and Chairman of the Board, Q. M. Association; Director, Baltimore School Commission; member, American Management Association; President, Baltimore Export Managers Club; member, Baltimore Criminal Justice Commission; and Adviser, Council member, and Chairman, Maryland Employment Service. In addition, he was a member of the Memorial Royal Society of Arts (London), the Maryland Historical Society, and the U.S. Academy of Political Science and an honorary life member of the Junior Chamber of Commerce and the American Legion.

McCormick received a citation and medal for human relations from the Society for the Advancement of Management (1946); the Gantt Gold Medal award from the American Management Association and the Society of Mechanical Engineers (1960), and the Distinguished Service award from the U.S. Treasury (1964).

Yasutaro Hirai
(1896–1970)
Japan

IN a career which spanned the 50 years from 1920 to 1970, Yasutaro Hirai showed himself to be an extraordinary teacher, an able college administrator, and an author who made major contributions to the literature on business administration in Japan.

Professor Hirai devoted his whole life to the development, in his country, of the science of business administration. And he indeed influenced it not only in Japan but elsewhere. Professor Karl Hax, a famous German scholar of business administration and a former president of the University of Frankfurt, began his memorial article on Professor Hirai with the following sentence: "In my private library, I have a book from my student days inscribed 'Karl Hax, cond. rer. pol. 24.3.1925' (Karl Hax, Candidate, March 24th, 1925). This volume is *Quellenbuch der Betriebswirtschaftslehre* (Sourcebook of Business Administration), published in 1925. The editors were Yasutaro Hirai, B.A. in Commerce, Professor at Kobe Commercial College . . . and Dr. Alfred Isaac." Both *Quellenbuch der Betriebswirtschaftslehre* and *Neues Betriebswirtschaftsliches Quellenbuch*, the latter edited by Yasutaro Hirai and Dr. Paul Deutsch and published in 1938, were at that time two of the most popular business-administration texts in Germany and in other countries where German is spoken.

Hirai was born on October 15, 1896. After graduating from Kobe Commercial High School in 1918, he went on to complete the Special Studies program at Tokyo Commercial School in 1920. He then returned to Kobe Commercial High School, where he taught for 40 years, retiring in 1960 with the title of Professor Emeritus of Kobe University, as the school had become known by then. He remained active as a teacher, however, taking a position as professor at Rissho University, where he continued to stimulate students with his profound knowledge of business administration until his death in 1970.

Hirai's first specialty was accounting; he had taken for his high school thesis the accounting methods of the fifteenth-century Italian Luca Pacioli. Moreover, both this thesis and his later research on the history of bookkeeping and accounting in the West as well as Korea and Japan were of more than historical interest. Hirai argued that accounting should be an integral part of financial management and a highly important element of business administration.

From the first, Hirai took a comparative approach to his research, one that was sustained and strengthened by his four-year residence in Germany (1921–1925). Here he studied first under H. Nichlisch at the University of Berlin and then under J. A. F. Schmidt at the University of Frankfurt. Immersing himself in the German methodology of business administration, he became acquainted at the same time with many of the leading students of the subject. Soon he began writing articles and then, with Alfred Isaac, edited *Quellenbuch der Betriebswirtschaftslehre*, which came into wide use as a college text.

When Hirai returned to Japan in 1925, his former professor, Teijiro Ueda, was calling for the creation of a new, independent discipline of business administration. It was largely on Hirai's shoulders that this task rested; in addition to the courses he taught at Kobe Commercial High School on all aspects of the subject, he was working slowly and surely within the school to establish a department of business administration. By 1949, when the school was renamed Kobe University, it finally had the first Faculty of Business Administration in Japan. Although Hirai was not to be appointed Dean until 1956, it is well known that his persistence ensured that the department, then a mere "faculty," would be established with the designation of "business administration" rather than "commerce." His appointment as Dean came five years after he was the first to receive a Doctor of Business Administration degree in a degree-granting program which he himself had helped to organize.

Hirai's contributions to the science of business administration can be divided into three categories: The first includes his efforts to systematize the then current knowledge of business administration into a science. The second includes his work in establishing a business-education system in Japanese universities, and the third includes his consulting activities for the business world and for the government.

Hirai's theory of business administration was based on the concept of the noneconomic man who had various kinds of needs and also various intellectual limitations. Hirai believed that business should be a cooperative and open system. He subscribed to the theory that the principal purpose of business as a cooperative activity was one of maintenance and development. This purpose could be distinguished from the more direct goal of satisfying the needs of the individuals concerned. In concrete terms, it might be defined as the pursuit of various goals determined by the particular conditions surrounding each cooperative system.

According to Hirai, each cooperative system evaluates its activities or its assets in light of its immediate objectives. This evaluation differs from market evaluation in that it is carried out by the cooperative system itself and is based on the particular economic needs of the cooperative system. The organizational economy is different from either a political or a social economy; therefore, to understand business activities, it is necessary to use an approach quite different from that used by social economists.

Hirai, then, chose an organizational approach to systematize existing knowledge about business administration. Using this approach, he analyzed many kinds of businesses and business activities: the large-scale enterprise, the relationships between the large-scale enterprise and its subsidiaries or subcontractors, the group-business enterprise, the not-for-profit business, and the regulatory activities of government Hirai offered many unique suggestions for both business and government.

As for Hirai's contributions to the development of the business-education system in Japan, to comprehend its importance fully one must look at Japan's historical approach to business enterprise. Japanese industrial modernization was carried out by the government; therefore, many scholars believed that the study of business activities should logically take place in law schools. It was sufficient, they said, that this subject be covered as a part of political economics. The study of business from a managerial point of view was often thought of as an attempt to pursue self-interest; thus there was strong opposition to teaching such a subject in the universities. In this environment, Hirai had to work very hard to gain acceptance for the idea of business education as a separate discipline.

Despite opposition, however, Hirai made many contributions in this area. He helped establish the Japanese Society for the Study of Business Administration in 1926; and, as Director and President, he worked to promote an understanding of business administration as a science. He also established a Department of Business Administration at Kobe Commercial College in 1944, even before it became Kobe University. Then, in 1949, he succeeded in establishing the Kobe University School of Business Administration. This was Japan's first such school. In contrast, there are now 15 graduate programs of business administration in Japan, 56 departments of business administration within schools of economics or commerce, and 24 independent undergraduate business schools. In 1975, as many as 65,000 students were enrolled in these programs.

In addition to his success in promoting business administration as a legitimate science and furthering its study in Japanese universities, Professor

Hirai made many contributions to management through his consulting activities. He had clients in both national and local governments and the business world. During the 1930s, he advised the government of the need to mechanize business procedures, and in 1944 he established the Institute for the Mechanization of Office Management at Kobe Commercial College. Many early Japanese leaders, especially engineers, in the field of business automation were educated there. Hirai also served on government committees of many kinds and contributed to management education as director or president of various management institutions. Finally, in 1968, he established the Japanese Association of Management Consultants through which he strove to improve the quality of consulting work.

A productive author, Hirai wrote numerous articles and wrote or edited a number of important books on a wide range of topics relating to business administration. The first clear statement of Hirai's understanding of the discipline is set out in the 1932 *Keieigaku nyumon* (Introduction to Business Administration). Twenty years later, he published the important 1952 *Keieigaku jiten* (Handbook of Business Administration). As Editor, Hirai had worked with some 300 contributors to compile this first reference book of its kind in Japan—one which did much to spread the word about the still-emerging discipline among students and faculty. Through his editorship of several journals, moreover, he was instrumental in giving both young and established scholars opportunities to share their research in monographs; for example, those on business administration published periodically by Hyuron-sha were specially noteworthy.

Professor Yasutaro Hirai was a man of vision. His own abilities hardly came into their own prior to the later years of the Second World War and the period immediately following, yet it can be said that he was a missionary of business administration from his youth on. Although his father was not particularly successful in business, Hirai the son grew up surrounded by business; because of his environment and his diligence, he learned a great deal about its activities. For this reason, his opinion was always respected in the business world.

Professor Hirai was strong-willed. When he had finished all the work required for his doctorate, he firmly refused to accept any degree except one in business administration. Finally he succeeded in establishing a school of business administration at the university level, and from it he received the first doctor's degree in business administration in Japan.

Hirai's was an outgoing personality. He was an optimist, and he had a good sense of humor. He enjoyed the theater very much, and he was fond of children and young people—in fact, he wrote a book of children's fairy tales. Often he would have discussions with students in his home until late at night, always taking a great interest in what they had to say. Because of his excellent foresight, he often surprised them—and others—with his ability to predict future events accurately.—KISOU TASUGI AND ELIZABETH T. MASSEY

SELECTED PUBLICATIONS

1925 *Quellenbuch der Betriebswirtschaftslehre* (Sourcebook of Business Administration). With Dr. Alfred Isaac. Berlin: Speath Linde.

1932 *Keiei gorika zuroku* (Chart of Industrial Rationalization). Tokyo: Shunyoda.

—— *Keieigaku nyumon* (Introduction to Business Administration). Tokyo: Chikura Shobo.

1933 *Boki kyokasho* (Bookkeeping). Tokyo: Shunseido.

—— *Keizai zadan* (Essays on Economy). Tokyo: Chikura Shobo.

1935 *Keieigaku truron* (Principles of Business Administration). Tokyo: Chikura Shobo.

1938 *Neues betriebswirtschaftliches Quellenbuch* (New Sourcebook of Business Administration). With Dr. Paul Deutsch. Leipzig: Felix Meiner.

1942 *Toseikeizai to keieikeizai* (Controlled Economy and Business Administration). Tokyo: Nippon Hyuron-sha.

1950 *Keizaitosei no teiryu* (Economic Stabilization and Business Administration). Tokyo: Toyokeizaishinpo-sha.

1952 *Keieigaku jiten* (Handbook of Business Administration). Edited. Tokyo: Daiamondo.

1964 *Keieigaku jiten* (Handbook of Business Administration). Edited. Tokyo: Seirinshoin.

In all, Hirai wrote 30 books, edited 3 handbooks and 21 additional books, translated 3 foreign texts, and wrote several hundred papers.

Curriculum Vitae

1896 Born on October 15th in Kobe.

1918 Graduated from Kobe Commercial High School.

1920 Graduated from Tokyo Commercial High School's Special Studies program, majoring in management and administration and receiving degree in commerce. Appointed Instructor, Kobe Commercial High School.

1921 Traveled extensively in Europe, studying statistics and commerce.

1923 While still in Germany, promoted to Professor at Kobe Commercial High School.

1925 Returned to Japan and resumed teaching.

1926 Helped found the Japanese Society for the Study of Business Administration, of which he was a director for many years.

1931 Remained Professor at Kobe Commercial High School, now renamed Kobe Commercial College (later Kobe University).

1944 Became Director, Research Institute of Business Mechanization.

1949 Instrumental in Kobe University's establishment of first Faculty of Business Administration in Japan.

1951 Received doctorate in business administration from Kobe University.

1956 Appointed Dean, Faculty of Business Administration, Kobe University.
1958 Appointed Director, Kobe University/Kobe College of Economics Research Institute.
1960 Retired at mandatory age of 65.
1961 Was first Japanese to be appointed a Fellow of Academy of Management.
1962 Appointed Professor, Rissho University.
1968 Was first Japanese to be appointed an honorary member of the German Management Association.
1970 Died on July 2nd, aged 73, in Kobe.

Hirai was a director of numerous professional associations and a consultant to many others. He was a Managing Director of the Japan Management Association from its founding until 1968; Managing Director of the Japan Accounting Society, the Japan Society on Research in Commerce, and the Japan Research Institute on Industrial Efficiency. He was Deputy Director of the Japan Society for Diagnostic Management, a director of the Industrial Management Association, and a member of the Science Council of Japan. In 1969, one year before his death, he was awarded the Second Class Order of the Sacred Medal.

The Verband der Hochschullehrer für Betriebswirtschaftslehre (Society of University-Level Teachers of Business Administration) appointed Hirai an honorary member in 1963. Paris made him an "Ami" in 1957, and he was elected a Fellow of the International Academy of Management in 1961.

Yojiro Masuchi
(1896–1945)
Japan

PROFESSOR Yojiro Masuchi was one of Japan's pioneers and most influential theorists in the area of business administration. Born in Kyoto in 1896, he studied at Tokyo Commercial College—later Tokyo Industrial College and now Hitotsubashi University—under Professor Teijiro Ueda.

To begin with, Masuchi was concerned primarily with business forms; he translated books on the subject by Gustav Schmoller and Robert Liefmann into Japanese. From 1923 through 1925, however, he had an opportunity to study in Germany, mainly in Berlin, and here he was greatly influenced by the German theorist Heinrich Nichlisch. His book *Introduction to Business Economy,* which he wrote just after his return home in 1926, very naturally follows the German line of thinking.

Somewhat later, Masuchi became interested in Frederick W. Taylor's scientific management, as well as the special field of financial management. Both of these he introduced into Japan. In addition, he did research on the separation of ownership and control in joint stock companies—an important topic then being discussed in both the United States and Japan. One might therefore say that Masuchi integrated the German and American schools of thought—in other words, he put rich American flesh on German backbone.

Masuchi was a founder of the Japan Society for the Study of Business Administration. Moreover, he wrote many books in the field. He was Editor in Chief of the academic periodical *Review of Business Administration*, and he participated in the work of the Committee on Business Administration.

Modest in behavior, neat and refined in dress, Yojiro Masuchi nevertheless had strong convictions about the validity of his thinking. That is to say, he might have seemed outwardly soft, but inwardly he was hard.

In his day, Tokyo Commercial College was the most important Japanese center for the study of business administration; and because Masuchi was a tolerant and broad-minded person, he fostered many able young scholars who came under his influence and who, at present, are very active in Japan.—KISOU TASUGI

SELECTED PUBLICATIONS

Books:
1926 *Introduction to Business Economy.*
1929 *Theory of Business Administration.*
1930 *Forms of Business.*
1934 *Financial Management.*
1937 *The Joint Stock Company.*
1940 *Management of Industry and Commerce.*

Curriculum Vitae

1896 Born in Kyoto.
1919 Graduated from Tokyo Commercial College (later Tokyo Industrial College; presently Hitotsubashi University).
1923–1925 Studied in Germany, mostly Berlin.
1926 Took up position as Associate Professor, Tokyo Commercial College.
1937 Received doctorate.
1944 Became Professor, Tokyo Industrial College (Tokyo Sangyo Daigaku).
1945 Died, at age 48 or 49, during Tokyo air raid.

Keiji Baba
(1897–1961)
Japan

KEIJI Baba, a forerunner in the field of business administration in Japan, laid the foundations for training and extensive studies in this discipline. During his long years in the Economics Department of what was then Tokyo Imperial University, Dr. Baba gave lectures on the theory of both business administration and factory management and published a great number of relevant books and articles. He therefore played a leading role in the development of the field in Japan; his achievements as a founding figure will stand permanently in its history.

Dr. Baba's first published work was *Sangyo-keiei no shokuno to sono bunka* (Function and Its Specialization in Industrial Management), which appeared in 1926. This work, an analysis and elucidation of American scientific management, was the first theoretical treatment of its subject in Japanese economic literature. Dr. Baba's later studies went on to encompass all aspects of management in industry, culminating in the publication of *Sangyo-keiei riron* (Theory of Industrial Management) in 1927. This work traces trends in management in a modern economy and develops the theory of management in detail.

Keiji Baba's research led him to favor a scientific treatment of the methodology of business administration. This was the period of the 1920s, when business administration in Japan was striving to establish itself as a discipline of science. Dr. Baba met the challenge enthusiastically, immersing himself in the study of philosophy. Laying the base for an extensive philosophical investigation, he developed the scientific methodology of business administration. This resulted in the publication of *Keieigaku hohoron* (The Methodology of Business Administration) in 1931 and *Keieigaku kenkyu* (A Study of Business Administration) in 1932.

In addition, Dr. Baba was keenly interested in technology; in his research, he explored the relationship between technology and business administration. It was just at this time that the pretensions of "technocracy" were receiving significant public attention, and Baba's studies in this area were followed by the publication of three important Baba works: *Gijutsu to keizai* (Technology and the Economy) in 1933, *Gijutsu to shakai* (Technology and Society) in 1936, and *Soshiki to gijutsu no mondai* (The Problem of Organization and Technology) in 1941.

Dr. Baba then turned from the scientific methodology of business administration to its systematization. His findings were first brought together in *Keieigaku no kisoteki shomondai* (Fundamental Problems of Business Administration). In this book, which dates from 1934, he declared that the fundamental problems of business administration were problems of organization and value flow. He then proceeded to develop a theory that integrated the two on an organizational base. In this way the so-called Baba school of business administration came into being.

Keiji Baba had been greatly interested in organizational problems almost from the outset of his career, and he began his studies in this field very early, but it was not until the later stages of his investigations that he came to focus his attention on the question of organization itself. *Soshiki no kihonteki seishitsu* (The Basic Nature of Organization), 1941; *Soshiki no choseiryoku to sono shorinengata* (Fundamentals of Organizational Coordination), 1948; and *Keieigaku to ningensoshiki no mondai* (Business Administration and Problems of Human Organization), 1954, are just a few of the fruits of his work in organization. His studies took on increasing scale and scope; he aspired to establish a theory of organization as a synthetic science, and also made a vigorous attempt to systematize the substance of business administration as the theory of organization.

Dr. Baba's unremitting efforts were cut short by his untimely death in 1961. Two year earlier, however, he had founded the Society for the Study of Organizational Science, which had as its purpose the advancement of interdisciplinary research into organization and has since made great progress as an influential forum for management affairs.

Keiji Baba was extremely strict in his academic pursuits and, in his private life, had a firm foundation of religious belief which made him both strict and gentle at one and the same time. He studied every night until dawn; then, after a little sleep, he made his way to the university for his classes. During his entire career, from assistant professor to full professor, he never once missed a single class.

Dr. Baba was very thorough in training his students. Not only did he hold weekly seminars at his home that lasted until late at night, giving the students just time to catch the last train home, but he also taught them how to study by lending them books in foreign languages that he would require them to comment upon in detail one or two weeks later.

In his studies and in his duties as a teacher, he became so immersed in what he was doing that he would forget everything else. For instance, the story is told that once, while talking on the telephone to an acquaintance, he got so carried away by the conversation that he let the receiver stray from his mouth. When the other person complained, "I can't hear," he retorted, "*I* can hear fine!" and went on talking. Another time, when the person he was speaking to interrupted him by saying, "If you'll excuse me, I have some urgent business I must attend to," he said, "Don't be rude! I'm telling you something very important!" and hung up.

Dr. Baba's wife, too, was a woman of character. It was she who made it possible for him to devote all his time to his studies. She died only a year after his own death.—SUSUMU TAKAMIYA

SELECTED PUBLICATIONS

Books:

1926 *Sangyo-keiei no shokuno to sono bunka* (Function and Its Specialization in Industrial Management). Tokyo: Daito-kaku.

1927 *Sangyo-keiei riron* (Theory of Industrial Management). Tokyo: Nihon Hyoron-sha.

1931 *Keieigaku hohoron* (The Methodology of Business Administration). Tokyo: Nihon Hyoron-sha.

1932 *Keieigaku kenkyu* (A Study of Business Administration). Tokyo: Moriyama Shoten.

1933 *Gijutsu to keizai* (Technology and the Economy). Tokyo: Nihon Hyoron-sha.

1934 *Keieigaku no kisoteki shomondai* (Fundamental Problems of Business Administration). Tokyo: Nihon Hyoron-sha.

1936 *Gijutsu to shakai* (Technology and Society), Vol. 1. Tokyo: Nihon Hyoron-sha.

1938 *Kagaku kogyo keizairon* (The Economics of the Chemical Industry). Tokyo: Kyoritsu-sha.

1941 *Soshiki no kihonteki seishitsu* (The Basic Nature of Organization). Tokyo: Nihon Hyoron-sha.

—— *Soshiki to gitjutsu no mondai* (The Problem of Organization and Technology). Tokyo: Nihon Hyoron-sha.

1948 *Soshiki no choseiryoku to sono shorinengata* (Fundamentals of Organizational Coordination). Tokyo: Nihon Hyoron-sha.

1954 *Keieigaku to ningensoshiki no mondai* (Business Administration and Problems of Human Organization). Tokyo: Yuhi-kaku.

Curriculum Vitae

1897 Born on March 22nd in Osaka.
1920 Graduated from Department of Electrical Engineering, Faculty of Engineering, Tokyo Imperial University.
1923 Graduated from Department of Economics, Faculty of Economics, Tokyo Imperial University.
1925 Appointed Assistant Professor, Faculty of Economics, Tokyo Imperial University.
1931 Promoted to Professor, Tokyo Imperial University, concurrently in charge of third course in commerce, Faculty of Economics, and introductory courses in economics, Faculty of Engineering.
1939 Appointed to University System Study Committee.
1940 Appointed to Third Standing Committee (Economics and Business Administration) of Japan Society for Promotion of Science.
1941 Appointed to Tokyo Imperial University Board of Councilors.
1948 Appointed to Provisional Council for Administrative Reform of Government.
1950 Received Ph.D. in Economics.
1952 In charge concurrently of Tokyo University Graduate School and commerce curriculum.
1957 Resigned from Tokyo University, after reaching retirement age, with title of Professor Emeritus.
1961 Died on August 10th, aged 64.

Courtesy R. Greenwood.

Fritz J. Roethlisberger
(1898–1974)
United States

FRITZ J. Roethlisberger, Wallace Brett Donham Professor Emeritus of Human Relations at the Harvard University Graduate School of Business Administration, is most widely remembered for his association with the pioneering research at the Hawthorne (Ill.) plant of the Western Electric Co. At the time Roethlisberger, who had tried graduate work in such diverse fields as engineering and philosophy, was counseling students at Harvard who were experiencing psychological problems in connection with their studies. He participated actively with Elton Mayo in the interviewing program at Hawthorne and also in the Bank Wiring Room study. When the research was brought to a close, he and William J. Dickson of Western Electric spent three years analyzing and writing up the results. Their book, *Management and the Worker*,[1] published in 1939, became a landmark in the literature of management and the social sciences.

Roethlisberger made his entire professional career at the Harvard Business School, teaching and doing research. His first appointment, in 1927, was as an instructor. He became a full professor in 1946 and was appointed to the Donham Chair in 1950. Five years later he received Harvard University's Ledlie Prize, awarded to a member of the faculty who "made the most valuable contribution to science or in any other way for the benefit of mankind."

[1] Fritz J. Roethlisberger and William J. Dickson, *Management and the Worker* (Cambridge, Mass.: Harvard University Press, 1939).

Roethlisberger's work fell into four periods. During the first of these, from 1927 to 1937, research was his dominant activity and the business organization viewed as a social system was his major topic. This was the period when he developed the clinical method of research, interviewing, and observation. The work at Western Electric and the writing of *Management and the Worker* date from this time.

The second period, from 1937 to 1947, encompassed Roethlisberger's main teaching years. He now focused on communicating the results of the earlier research program to business people and students of business. These activities required much experimentation, the development of course outlines and materials, and the sequencing of topics as well as the training of instructors. His article on "The Foreman: Master and Victim of Double Talk" is a good example of his thinking about the administrator's role, just as "Training Supervisors in Human Relations" is a statement of his views about pedagogy.

During the Second World War, Fritz Roethlisberger taught experienced executives in the Business School's retraining programs. In the postwar period he was a major architect of the course, originally called "Administrative Practices," that was included in the first year of the School's MBA Program. He also was one of the original faculty members to teach in the Management Training Program at Radcliffe College, Harvard's first program in management for women. All these activities were pioneering efforts that affected developments in management development programs around the world.

During the third period, from 1947 to 1957, Roethlisberger gave his major attention to the human relations field. The development of its subject matter became the focus of his work. He developed and taught a "Human Relations" course presented during the second year of the MBA Program at the School and experimented with advanced programs of training and research. *The Motivation, Productivity, and Satisfaction of Workers*,[2] of which he was co-author, reports on this work. He felt at the time that the knowledge component of human relations—that is, the subject matter which would give it legitimacy—was not developing to the extent he believed it should in order to meet the management problems of modern complex organizations.

During the fourth and last period, the ten years immediately preceding his retirement in 1967, Roethlisberger took part in establishing the field of organizational behavior in the Doctoral Program at the School. Reviewing with his students the work done in the social sciences gave him the opportunity to try to understand why there had been few if any developments at the level of knowledge which he thought was necessary. He was convinced that the knowledge needed would not be gained until this problem, which seemed to him a recurring one in the social sciences, was understood.

Though many people in academic life teach and carry out research

[2] Fritz J. Roethisberger, A. Zalesznik, and R. C. Christensen, *The Motivation, Productivity, and Satisfaction of Workers* (Boston: Division of Research, Harvard University Graduate School of Business Administration, 1958).

projects on a variety of topics, not many have the opportunity to participate in the development of a new field of knowledge from the beginning of their careers. This was the dominant theme of Roethlisberger's professional life. He was never satisfied with the culturally accepted definition of professional schools as user-oriented institutions whose role was to communicate to practitioners the knowledge developed by others. If knowledge was to be relevant to practice, he believed, those who worked in professional schools should participate fully in the adventure of creating new fields of knowledge through research. This belief guided the important decisions he made during his life about where to direct his efforts professionally.

Whether Fritz Roethlisberger was designing a program of advanced training and research, working on a study of his own, or teaching doctoral students, what mattered to him was the opportunity to contribute to the development of a field of knowledge relevant to the problems of practicing managers. Even though he felt his past experience gave him few skills for the task, if the opportunity was there, that was where he put his effort, irrespective of the cost to him personally of any feelings of insecurity that he might have as a result of venturing into unfamiliar territory.

In Fritz Roethlisberger, a quiet, self-effacing appearance and a quick sense of humor masked a keen intellect and intense feelings. Though he said of himself that he did not accept leadership responsibility gladly, neither did he avoid it when it was thrust upon him. He himself often found the ordinary routines of modern living perplexing—making a reservation, for example, or buying a ticket—yet he was always ready to listen sympathetically to the problems of others and try to understand their feelings. He gave people freely of his time—to the extent that many sought his help. He had, to a high degree, that rare quality of mind that builds bridges between personal experiences and feelings on the one hand and conceptual insights on the other.—GEORGE F. F. LOMBARD

SELECTED PUBLICATIONS

Books:

1939 *Management and the Worker: An Account of a Research Program Conducted by the Western Electric Company, Hawthorne Works, Chicago*. With William J. Dickson. Cambridge, Mass.: Harvard University Press.

1947 *Management and Morale*. Cambridge, Mass.: Harvard University Press.

1958 *The Motivation, Productivity, and Satisfaction of Workers: A Prediction Study*. With A. Zalesznik and C. R. Christensen. Boston: Division of Research, Harvard University Graduate School of Business Administration.

1966 *Counseling in an Organization: A Sequel to the Hawthorne Researches*. With William J. Dickson. Boston: Division of Research, Harvard University Graduate School of Business Administration.

1968 *Man-in-Organization*. Cambridge, Mass.: The Belknap Press of the Harvard University Press.

1977 *The Elusive Phenomena.* Edited by G. F. F. Lombard. Cambridge, Mass.: Division of Research, Harvard University Graduate School of Business Administration.

Articles:

1930 "Mechanization in Industry," *Harvard Business Review*, Vol. 9, October, pp. 124–127

1938 "Social Behavior in Industry," *Harvard Business Review*, Vol. 16, No. 4, Summer, pp. 424–435.

1948 "Human Relations: Rare, Medium, or Well-Done," *Harvard Business Review*, Vol. 26, No. 1, January, pp. 89–107.

1949 "Efficiency and Cooperative Behavior," *Journal of Engineering Education*, December.

1951 "Human Relations Training for Supervision," BACIE *Journal*, Vol. 5, July–August, pp. 98–108.

—— "Training Supervisors in Human Relations," *Harvard Business Review*, Vol. 29, No. 5, September, pp. 47–57.

1952 "Barriers and Gateways to Communication." With Carl R. Rogers. *Harvard Business Review*, Vol. 30, No. 4, p. 46.

1953 "The Administrator's Skill: Communication," *Harvard Business Review*, Vol. 31, November–December, pp. 55–62.

1954 "The Territory and Skill of the Administrator," *Michigan Business Review*, Vol. 6, November, pp. 1–9.

—— "Training for Human Relations: An Interim Report of a Program for Advanced Training and Research in Human Relations, 1951–1954." Boston: Division of Research, Harvard University Graduate School of Business Administration.

1957 "A Revolution in Thought," *Advanced Management*, March.

1962 "The Impact of Psychiatry on Management," *Journal of Industrial Medicine and Surgery*, November.

—— "What Is Guff and Not Guff?" Harvard Business School *Bulletin*, October–November.

1963 "Twenty Years of Management Development," *Training Directors Journal*, Vol. 17, September, pp. 4–14.

1965 "The Foreman: Master and Victim of Double Talk," *Harvard Business Review*, Vol. 43, No. 5, September–October, pp. 22–26.

Curriculum Vitae

1898 Born on October 29th in New York City.

1913–1917 Attended Staten Island Academy.

1917–1920 Attended Columbia College.

1920–1922 Attended Massachusetts Institute of Technology. Received B.S. in 1921.

1922 After a summer course, received A.B. from Columbia.

1922–1923 Worked as an assistant chemist, American Smelting & Refining Co., El Paso, Tex.
1923–1924 Worked as a sales correspondent, American Book Co., New York City.
1924–1927 Attended Graduate School of Arts and Sciences, Harvard University; received M.A. in 1925.
1927 Named Instructor in Industrial Research, Harvard University Graduate School of Business Administration.
1927–1932 Did planning and field work for the Hawthorne and Yankee City studies.
1927–1936 Active in student counseling, Department of Hygiene and Department of Industrial Research, Harvard University.
1930 Named Assistant Professor of Industrial Research by Harvard.
1933–1936 Writing *Management and the Worker* with William J. Dickson.
1936–1941 Participated in Cabot weekend-discussion groups for business executives.
1937–1942 Developed and taught course in "Human Problems of Administration" for second-year students.
1938 Became Associate Professor of Business Administration.
1938–1947 Taught in Radcliffe Management Training Program.
1941–1942 Served as Consultant to the Office of Production Management, Training Within Industry.
1942–1946 Taught in Trade Union Program, Harvard University.
1943–1946 Developed and taught personnel and management controls in retraining program for war-production supervisors (later Advanced Management Program).
1946 Named Professor of Human Relations.
1946–1947 Developed and taught first-year course on "Administrative Practices."
1949–1952 Developed and taught new second-year course called "Human Relations."
1950 Named Wallace Brett Donham Professor of Human Relations.
1951–1954 Headed program for advanced training and research in human relations.
1957 Developed and taught organizational behavior as a special field in the Doctoral Program.
1967 Retired from Harvard, becoming Wallace Brett Donham Professor Emeritus of Human Relations.
1974 Died on May 17th, aged 75, in Cambridge.

Fritz J. Roethlisberger was awarded the Taylor Key of the Society for the Advancement of Management in 1956 and the Ledlie Prize of Harvard University in 1959. In 1963 he received the honorary degree of Doctor of Economic Sciences from the St. Gal School of Economics, Business, and Public Administration in Switzerland.

Courtesy General Electric.

Ralph Jarron Cordiner
(1900–1973)
United States

RALPH Cordiner secured himself a place in managerial history through his accomplishments in behalf of the General Electric Company. Not only did he see GE through its decentralization and restructuring during the 1950s, but he laid a philosophical foundation for the firm which was matched by no other company of its time. Eminent management scholar Alfred Chandler claims, "Cordiner's reorganization went further than those in any other company . . . both in the erection of a large number of relatively small administrative units, and in the methods developed to administer these units."[1]

In 1943, Ralph Cordiner became Assistant to General Electric's President Gerard Swope. His major assignment was to develop a plan for overhauling the management and the organization structure of the corporation. He later noted, "Unless we could now put the responsibility and authority for decision making in each case closer to the scene of the problem, the company would not be able to compete with the hundreds of nimble competitors."

To Cordiner, decentralization meant keeping the strengths enjoyed by large organizations and adding to those strengths the flexibility of smaller firms. He became President of General Electric in December 1950, and within two years General Electric had been reorganized. Some two thousand

[1] Alfred Chandler, Jr., *Strategy and Structure: Chapters in the History of the Industrial Enterprise* (Cambridge, Mass.: The M.I.T. Press, 1962), p. 365.

top management jobs were created or redefined; 20 divisions and about 70 departments were established. In the process, the functional organization was abolished, while staff and service employees were cut to a relatively small number of highly experienced specialists who would provide assistance and advice.

These decentralization activities followed the well-conceived plan that Cordiner and Vice-President Harold F. Smiddy[2] had developed in the late 1940s and early 1950s. This plan reflected the beliefs of the generation that was inspired by the human relations movement; it brought to General Electric new concepts of delegated authority, responsibility, and accountability. Concern for people was to be the hallmark of the new corporate philosophy. Cordiner wrote:

> In 30 years the areas most seriously demanding management's immediate attention have gone through more than a complete cycle. First, it was the customer and the employee, and these two should have continued first. Then, it was the production backlog itself. Then, it was the customer—in the severest buyer's market of all times. Then, with war, it was production again. Now the equipment and facility problems are largely answered, and the personnel problems rising to an all-time high. In the belief that the personnel problem—or opportunity—is a series of intimate, personal, local cases, we are looking to decentralization to bring top management close to the employee.[3]

And, in a later paper, Cordiner noted that

> The problem in all larger companies is to have the members of the organization generally understand that the real test of a good manager is not the multitude of details and the amount of functional operations he performs, but, rather, how well he can visualize the over-all responsibility, assign the work to qualified people, and then see that the employee who is given the assignment, his associates, and the entire organization understand the organization structure and adhere to it.
>
> Our joint objective should be the continual study to simplify, streamline, and strengthen our organization, which means our human relations and their interdependence.[4]

Cordiner developed the philosophy of the new organization over a period of several years and documented his management philosophy in writing long before implementing his program. He firmly believed that management theory is a basic part of business practice, not something separate from it. This belief led Cordiner to establish an internal component at General

[2] See profile of Harold F. Smiddy in Part Two.

[3] Ralph J. Cordiner, "The Implications of Industrial Decentralization," American Management Association General Management Series, No. 134, 1945, p. 26.

[4] "Professional Management in General Electric" (Book One), *General Electric: Growth* (New York: General Electric Co., 1953), p. 42.

Electric, the Management Research and Development Institute, whose mission was to study and to advance the theoretical foundations upon which to build managerial practice.

It was the Institute that spent millions of man-hours and dollars in studying, testing, and retesting management theory as it was translated into practice. This was one of the earliest and most influential management laboratories of the period. It developed training programs for the entire company, set up a continuing training center, conducted executive development courses, and produced numerous management textbooks. Under Cordiner and Smiddy, too, the Institute published *Professional Management in General Electric*. This four-volume text reflects the Cordiner philosophy in depth and demonstrates the scope of the management research he supported.

Ralph Cordiner has been characterized by his associates as a man with a vision. He seemed to have a clear view of what the future could be. He saw the future and planned to reach it; he was a *long-term* planner. Also, as a result of having spent most of his career in senior management positions, Cordiner stressed the loneliness of these positions. Although he skillfully built outstanding management teams, he himself remained very much an individual. Even his hobbies, golfing and fishing, stressed individuality.—RONALD G. GREENWOOD

SELECTED PUBLICATIONS

Book:

1956 *New Frontiers for Professional Managers*. New York: McGraw-Hill (© Trustees of Columbia University, New York).

Articles:

1945 "The Implications of Industrial Decentralization," American Management Association General Management Series, No. 134.

1952 "Problems of Management in a Large Decentralized Organization," American Management Association General Management Series, No. 159.

Curriculum Vitae

1900 Born on March 20th in Walla Walla, Wash.

1922 Graduated from Whitman College with high honors, majoring in economics. Employed as a commercial district manageer, Pacific Power and Light Co.

1922–1932 Employed by General Electric Appliance Co., Portland, Oreg.

1932–1934 Employed by General Electric Co., Bridgeport, Conn.

1938 Became head of Appliances and Merchandising, General Electric Co., Bridgeport.

1939–1942 Employed as President, Schick, Inc., Stamford, Conn.

1942–1943 Contributed to wartime effort as Vice-Chairman, War Production Board.
1943–1945 Employed as Assistant to President, General Electric Co.
1945–1949 Served as Vice-President, General Electric Co.
1949–1950 Served as Executive Vice-President, General Electric Co.
1950–1958 Held office as President, General Electric Co.
1958–1963 Held office as Chairman of the Board and Chief Executive Officer, General Electric Co.
1963 Retired.
1973 Died on December 5th, aged 73, in Clearwater, Fla.

Ralph Cordiner was a member of the Business Council and a Fellow of the American Academy of Arts and Science.

Courtesy R. Greenwood.

Harold Francis Smiddy
(1900–1978)
United States

VERY few men of his generation made a greater impact on industrial management than Harold F. Smiddy. Although he was a scholar and a philosopher, he was first and foremost a manager. His individual concept of management is legendary at the General Electric Co.

During his days at General Electric's New York headquarters, Smiddy's emphasis was heaviest on managerial research and organization structuring. As Vice-President of GE's Management Consultation Service, he led a team whose function was to think through management theory, express it in a written document, and test it in day-to-day operations. It was here that the "eight key result areas" concept was developed along with the related project, costing many millions of dollars, which investigated ways of measuring the performance of the company, divisions, managers, and individual contributors. And it was also through this team that Smiddy, in the early 1950s, organized the first operation research and synthesis department in private industry. His inspiration was rewarded by the authority to purchase the Harry Hopf estate, 35 miles from New York City, and there to house what was originally called the Crotonville Human Resources Training Center, private industry's first major formal executive development facility.

Although Harold Smiddy was concerned with research to an unusual

See the profile of Ralph J. Cordiner in Part Two for another view of General Electric at this time.

degree for a manager in industry, he was most conscious of the need to transform theory into practice. As he once said in conversation:

> The time for laboratory testing is over. I enjoy study, research, and testing as much as anyone, but if you wait for all the questions to be answered the project will never get out of the lab. The best testing ground for lab work is at the customer level. I never met a researcher who was willing to let a study go; he will always find a reason to keep on researching. There comes a time when the research, to date, should be tested in operational practice. If you can't be practical, I can't use you.

In other words, Harold was work-oriented and demanded that those working with him devote full time and energy to their jobs. He believed in the "doctrine of completed work."

This doctrine of completed work was an aspect of the Smiddy philosophy that was learned at a very early date by anyone who reported to him. It simply meant that whoever took on a task must have full authority, commensurate with the responsibility, to make decisions. Once you understood and accepted an assignment, you were not expected to return for further instructions or with a host of questions. After the job had been delegated, the manager should keep "hands off" and allow the individual to complete his or her work and to learn from it, thereby freeing the manager for other tasks. A completed job was expected—not one that was closely directed or, above all, one that required any redoing. The philosophy of completed work, in brief, could be summed up as the willingness to accept responsibility, to make decisions, to be held accountable for achieving certain results, and to stand by those results if necessary.

Harold disapproved of decision-making committees. He was responsible for GE President Ralph Cordiner's decision to discontinue them. He abhorred the words "coordinate," "coordinator," and "liaison," particularly "liaison." "A liaison man," he said, "is one who is placed between two men who are paid to work together." Harold would have none of that. Furthermore, he was opposed to the terms "assistant to" and "administrative assistant," and the corresponding "assistant to" and "administrative assistant" positions were special targets in his management philosophy. He did not believe that a well-managed organization should have any such positions; in his opinion, they violated a number of sound principles of delegation in that their responsibility was not clearly defined, their accountability was therefore unclear, and assistants frequently added an extra—and superfluous—level of management. Thus individuals reporting either to the assistant or to the person being "assisted" might be unable to identify the relationships between them and, at times, believe they had more than one boss. Such a structure, Smiddy believed, inhibited self-development. The Smiddy philosophy was, of course, in conflict with that of Lyndall F. Urwick, and these two close friends had many a spirited debate on the subject.

Peter Drucker claims that the godfather of his now classic *The Practice of*

Management was Harold F. Smiddy. He gives Harold credit for originating or at least anticipating the concept of management by objectives that is generally attributed to Drucker himself. Harold did not write a book that has his name affixed to it, yet under his leadership a number of books have been produced. The four-volume set *Professional Management in General Electric* was for the most part developed under his leadership. In fact, every word in those books was either written by Harold Smiddy or approved by him—they have the stamp of his philosophy. Although they were technically team-produced, the concepts represent a thinking-through of that philosophy. Furthermore, Harold edited the two-volume set *Some Classic Contributions to Professional Managing* and *New Perspectives in Management: The Works of Harry Hopf*. And, in addition, he wrote countless articles and speeches for the President of the General Electric Co. which still are often quoted as outstanding contributions to the literature of managing.

The reputation that General Electric enjoys today in the field of manager development stems back to these many volumes which Harold Smiddy produced and which served as the very foundation for the Crotonville Human Resources Training Center, later the Crotonville Management Institute. Prior to his contributions in this field, General Electric had no component doing research and development in manager development. Today it leads the field.

In the five volumes of *Professional Management in General Electric,* four published and one unpublished, Harold Smiddy developed for General Electric the first well-documented philosophy of any corporate structure. The series was meant not only to set the corporate philosophy down on paper but also to be a guide on how to manage, to help further the study of management, and to help organize the investigation of management practice so as to upgrade understanding through greater in-depth reasoning. The series forced a logical analysis and thinking-through of the work of both manager and individual contributor. It was this thinking-through process which resulted in the conviction that management is leadership through inspiration and persuasion.

While Harold was developing the philosophy that provided the basis for the reorganization and decentralization of General Electric in the early 1950s, he often called on the services of Peter Drucker. He himself had brought to GE from Booz, Allen and Hamilton the concept of the "manager's letter"; Drucker had noted a similar concept at General Motors under Alfred P. Sloan, Jr. This was debated over a period of many weeks. Harold invited his associates to sit in on several discussions of the principles behind the "letter" as he and Drucker thought it through. Later he had the results written up. From these beginnings came management by objectives, perhaps the single most-discussed philosophy of management since Drucker first introduced it to the literature in 1954.

With management by objectives providing the central theme in Smiddy's philosophy of leadership, his advocacy of "self-control"—as opposed to control from above—followed naturally. He was most adamant that one should control one's own work. He even dropped the word "control" to describe a function of management in favor of the word "measure." For Harold Smiddy, "control" connoted restrictions or coercion; hence, one should measure one's own work. If anybody inadvertently, in Harold's presence, used the word "control" to describe a manager's leadership of others, a rather lengthy sermon was likely to follow on the evils of "domination from above," "management by direction," and other negative aspects of the word. Each of us has words that make shivers run up our spines. In Harold's vocabulary, "control" was such a word.

Harold Smiddy's philosophy is best summed up in his own words: "Management is leadership through inspiration and persuasion." It is persuasion rather than control which is the key here. Being the practitioner he was, he went on to say: "It is recognized that there may be emergency conditions, where persuasion has failed, and results of continued effort at persuasion—in the judgment of the manager—would be worse than temporary use of 'control' to get on with the job. In so doing, the manager is acknowledging temporary failure as a 'professional manager.'"

With eyes that pierced through unimportant realities and penetrated to essentials, Harold Smiddy saw that the inevitability of growth and change requires unyielding maintenance of the principle of open discussion—for ideas and persons we like and those we dislike.

Harold Smiddy is best characterized by his peers and co-workers—he detested the word subordinates—for his sincerity, dedication, unlimited drive, comprehension, vision, and especially his ability to develop the potentialities of others. He spent countless hours with many young managers and made opportunities available to those who were willing to pay the demanding price of success. He never failed to sense the need to challenge or inspire anyone who was not quite aware of his or her potential.

Harold was a compulsive reader. With his enormous retentive powers, he was able to absorb up to several hundred pages of information every day. Yet his mind was so active, so completely filled with diverse ideas gleaned by his very creative, analytical mind, that he really could not listen without taking over the conversation and then supplying, with machine-gun rapidity, a virtual library of knowledge pertaining to the subject being considered. If you wanted him to "listen," your safest recourse was the written word. Every man has a weakness, and overly long listening was not Smiddy's forte.

The respect Harold received from fellow managers was great, but even those who did not know of his managerial ability were drawn to him for other reasons. Although he and his wife, Lois, did not have children of their own, Harold could and would "adopt" any number. He was never too busy to fix a bicycle or help build a "camp" in the outer garden or explain a problem in a textbook. He was a born teacher in such a gifted way that children—or adults, for that matter—never realized they were being taught. He was "Smiddy" to his neighbors in Frankfort, the upstate New York community where he frequently spent his summers.

Harold Smiddy was always besieged with requests for favors. People felt, most of the time correctly, that he could do anything. He would usually accept any request, promise twice as much as had been requested, and deliver twice again that much.—RONALD G. GREENWOOD

SELECTED PUBLICATIONS

Books:

1979 *A Science of Management.* Edited by Ronald Greenwood under the supervision of Harold F. Smiddy and published posthumously. New York: AMACOM.

In addition, Harold F. Smiddy conceptualized and directed a number of books on management to be written and published by the General Electric Co. As is customary for books written inside corporations, these are anonymous publications and represent the work of many people, yet every word was either written or approved by Smiddy and reflects his management philosophy. The following are some of these books published in the 1950s:

Professional Management in General Electric:

Book One, *General Electric: Growth* (1953).

Book Two, *General Electric: Organization* (1955).

Book Three, *The Work of a Professional Manager* (1954).

Book Four, *The Work of a Functional Individual Contributor* (1959).

Book Five, *Professional Work* (drafted but never published).

"Manager Development Workbooks," a seven-book series (1954, 1956).

Some Classic Contributors to Professional Managing (2 vols., 1956).

Articles:

1952 "Why Write a Description of Your Position?" *GE Review*, July.

1954 "Evolution of a 'Science of Managing' in America," with Lionel Naum, *Management Science*, Vol. 1, October, pp. 1–31.

—— "Scientific Management of the Distribution Process," *Advanced Management*, January.

1955 "Do Industrial Engineers Need Executive Development?" *Advanced Management*, Vol. 24, May.

—— "General Electric's Philosophy and Approach for Manager Development," American Management Association General Management Series, No. 174.

1957 "Self-Growth Provides Base for GE's Executive Development," *American Business Magazine*, November.

1959 "Opportunities for New Contributions to the Future of Management by SAM Members," *Advanced Management*, Vol. 24, July.

—— "Research—and Shaping the Future of Management," in *Proceedings* of the Academy of Management, pp. 23–40.

1960 "Deciding," in *Top Management Handbook.* Harold B. Maynard, ed. New York: McGraw-Hill, pp. 266–300.

—— "Management as a Profession," in *50 Years' Progress in Management,*

1910–1960. New York: American Society of Mechanical Engineers, pp. 26–41.

1967 "Principles of Organization," in *Handbook of Business Administration*. Harold B. Maynard, ed. New York: McGraw-Hill, pp. 2-3 to 2-17.

1970 "Managerial Progress in the Sixties—Some Summary Reactions," American Society of Mechanical Engineers Paper No. 70-WA/Mgt.-10.

1978 "The Indispensability of Voluntary Teamwork," in *Managers for the Year 2000*, William H. Newman, ed. New York: Prentice-Hall.

Curriculum Vitae

1900 Born on June 3rd in Southborough, Mass.
1920 Received B.S. from Massachusetts Institute of Technology.
1920–1921 Began career as Cadet Engineer, Public Service Electric Co., Newark, N.J.
1921 Became Service Manager, West Penn Power Co., Pittsburgh, Pa.
1922 Became Assistant Distribution Engineer.
1923 Became Assistant to Commercial Manager.
1927 Became Assistant to Vice-President.
1928 Named Assistant Commercial Manager.
1928–1930 Functioned as Operation Manager.
1930 Became Assistant to Vice-President, Operation Department, Electric Bond and Share Co., New York City.
1931 Appointed Assistant to Executive Vice-President.
1933 Headed Commercial Department.
1935 Employed as head of Sales Department, Ebasco Services.
1937 Became Operation Sponsor, South Central Region.
1940 Became Chief Operating Sponsor.
1941 Became Director of Operating Section.
1943 Joined Booz, Allen and Hamilton, Chicago, as Consulting Engineer.
1944–1948 Served as General Partner, Booz, Allen and Hamilton.
1945 Opened New York office of Booz, Allen and Hamilton.
1948 Named Special Assistant, President's Staff, General Electric Co., New York.
1948–1951 Served as Vice-President and General Manager, Chemical Department and Air Conditioning Department.
1951–1961 Served as Vice-President, Management Consultation Service, and Director, International General Electric Co.
1961 Retired from General Electric Co. Began private consulting.
1978 Died on September 8th, aged 78, in New York City.

Harold F. Smiddy was a Fellow of the American Academy of Management (President, 1963), the Society for the Advancement of Management (Vice-President, 1948–1953), and the International Academy of Management (elected 1960). He held membership in the Academy of Political Science, the American Institute of Electric Engineers, The American Society of Mechanical Engineers, the Council for International Progress in Management, U.S.A. (Director, 1951–1960), the International Committee of Scientific Management (member of Executive Committee, 1951–1957), the Pan-American Council (First Vice-President, 1954–1956; member of Honorary Council, 1957–1960), the Institute of Management Sciences, and the Advertising and Sales Executives Association, New York and Chicago.

In 1953, Smiddy received the Taylor Key of the Society for the Advancement of Management; in 1957, the Gantt Medal, awarded in that year by ASME, and also the Wallace Clark Medal of the Council for International Progress in Management. He was awarded honorary degrees by Ithaca College (LL.D., 1960) and Manhattan College (LL.D., 1974). In 1976 he was elected to the Tau Beta Pi Association National Honor Society at Union College, Schenectady, N.Y.

Courtesy Olivetti Company.

Adriano Olivetti
(1901–1960)
Italy

ADRIANO Olivetti was a pioneer of modern industrial management in Italy, concerned with the organization of the manufacturing enterprise and the establishment of human relations within the company. As an industrialist and humanist, he saw his role as that of a capitalist setting a unique example of how full and coherent a role industry can play in the social and cultural life of the community.

Olivetti believed that the aims of industry could not be stated simply in terms of profits; rather, he sought a situation where industry worked for society. He refused to follow what he called the business world's "tragic march toward efficiency and profit." His emphasis on social service, town planning, and aesthetics fostered the development of what has been termed the "tocco Olivetti," or the "Olivetti touch," which was inspired by two fundamental convictions: first, that industry, in view of its great influence in the community, ought to have a code of ethics and a system of objectives beyond the purely economic; and, second, that present-day mass civilization should make every effort to achieve a society so organized that individuals may give their best by expressing themselves fully and constructively.

Olivetti's philosophy was most visible in the areas of company advertising, product design, company architecture, and social services. With respect to advertising, he refused to conform to the so-called public taste at the expense of aesthetics. Also, this same desire to bring aesthetics into industry was evident in machine design under his direction, which stressed clarity, unity, and logic. He believed that unconventional forms and language were required to convey the idea of special quality. Morevoer, the architecture of the Olivetti factories was unique for its time in that it aimed at a unified environment which would allow buildings and workers to fit harmoniously into their surroundings. And, finally, to ensure that the workers would feel happy and secure, Olivetti pioneered in the development of social services for his employees. "If," he stated, "the material and moral aims of our work are upheld, one day this factory will be an integral part of a new and authentic civilization directed toward a freer, happier, and more conscious development of the individual."

For all these social and philosophical concerns, Adriano Olivetti gave full attention to production, operations, and technology. As a direct result of his 1925 trip to the United States to make a survey of American factories, he began a radical transformation of the Olivetti organization structure. He was among the first to recognize both the need to hire young managers with scientific backgrounds and the need to expand into foreign markets. His efforts to improve Olivetti's products through research, combined with his bold reorganization moves, increased productivity considerably, made it possible for the firm to survive the Great Depression of the 1930s unscathed, and eventually established it as a company of international importance.

Adriano, who became Managing Director in 1933 and President in 1938, was very different from his father; however, their close cooperation for almost 20 years resulted in a substantial continuity of approach and purpose. While Camillo Olivetti had concentrated his energies on putting the right man in the right place, his son saw that the progress of the company required not only suitable personnel but a rational organization structure suited to prospective growth as forecast by objective analysis. Adriano was very much a thinker and a theoretician—indeed, his father had sometimes doubted his practicality—and his enthusiastic study of all problems, technical and social, grew into a vision of overall reform on the broadest scale. As an early Italian industrialist, the father brought out new human and social potential in a backward country still rooted in the nineteenth century. The son, for his part, was as responsive to the new needs produced by changing times. He played a decisive historical role in the expansion of the firm on many levels, closely interrelating technical, aesthetic, ethical, social, and political factors in a "moral" overview of the duties and responsibilities of industry in the modern world.

With his Socialist outlook, tempered by Federalist and Autonomist ideas, Adriano from 1922 on was a contributor to the weekly *Tempi nuovi.* He even helped the old Socialist leader Filippo Turati escape to France in September 1926—an exploit that made it advisable for him to leave Italy himself for a time.

Then, in 1937, Adriano founded the review *Tecnica ed organizzazione*, for which he wrote and edited articles on technology, economy, and sociology that introduced new ideas of great social consequence to Italy, which in many respects was lagging in these fields. He had a keen intuition of the place that industrial design, town planning, architecture, and industrial sociology would assume in the next few years. He also gave much attention to problems of advertising and in-house communication, adopting the latest methods for Olivetti; he gathered around himself a group of artists both Italian and foreign, encouraging them to develop a distinctive formal language and establishing the Olivetti touch or style that would emerge a few decades later. Directed by Renato Zveteremich, the group included graphic artists, architects, and interior designers—along with others outside the company who eventually were commissioned to do special designs for it. Operating in their own independent space within the firm, the development and advertising offices thus became a center for the creation of art forms that, during these years, promoted a taste for the contemporary in Italy and abroad. At the same time the company was being physically renewed and expanded in all areas: factories, office buildings, residential districts for clerical and production staff, cafeterias, kindergartens, and welfare centers of various types.

Beginning in 1938, Adriano Olivetti gradually built up a comprehensive system of social assistance, as well as cultural and recreational activities, that helped make Olivetti one of the most progressive companies in Italy. This experience, together with an intensive study of the relationship between industry and community, had created in him a predominant interest in town and country planning seen, not just as a technical and aesthetic issue, but also as a vehicle for decent community life and social progress. As early as 1937, he had directed a team of planners in preparing studies for the regional master plan of the Valle d'Aosta, the first scientific regional plan completed in Italy and still a model of advanced planning.

During the Second World War, Adriano kept in touch with the anti-Fascist forces that were working to break Italy's alliance with Germany and bring down Mussolini's regime. In 1943 he made a vain attempt to persuade General Badoglio to make a separate peace with the Allies, and in July he was arrested and confined in Regina Coeli, the notorious Roman prison. Released in September, a few hours before the Germans occupied Rome and issued a warrant for his rearrest, he managed to escape to Switzerland. There he remained till the end of hostilities.

In 1948 Adriano Olivetti was an active participant in the first postwar congress of the Istituto Nazionale di Urbanistica (National Town Planning Institute), of which he was a founder, and the following year he became the editor of *Urbanistica,* the Institute's official review. Like the other publications he created, the magazine brought before the Italian public the ideas and debates stimulated by such books as Lewis Mumford's *The Culture of Cities,* Frank Lloyd Wright's *When Democracy Builds,* and Richard Neutra's *Survival Through Design.* The principles of organic design that they spelled out gave concrete form to the vision of articulated democracy that appealed to Adriano Olivetti in the Catholic personalism of Maritain and Mounier, two of the social thinkers whose writing constantly absorbed him.

As President of INU and of UNRRA-Casas, organized to further the reconstruction of war-damaged housing, Adriano energetically advanced community projects and sought to overcome the bureaucratic obstacles in their way. In Italian politics and the social sciences, however, his name is most closely associated with the Movimento Comunità, the community movement which he founded in 1948 and which aimed at a complete reform of society. The movement's ideas were set forth in *L'Ordine politico delle comunità* (The Political System in Communities), the book he wrote while living in Switzerland. Like his other books and his articles, *L'Ordine politico delle comunità* analyzed the inadequacies of present-day Western democracy and the organization of political functions. Adriano Olivetti proposed a new balance between centralized power and local autonomy in which democratic representation would be achieved by institutionalizing the presence of representatives of the trade unions and cultural forces. To promote these views, he created the periodical *Comunità* and the publishing house Edizioni di Comunità, still active today, which has brought out more than 600 books on political and social science, architecture, philosophy, and contemporary thought in general.

Adriano Olivetti died suddenly in 1960. He is remembered as being unpretentious in appearance and manner. He was robust, of medium height, with blue eyes and—in his later years—graying hair. His smile is said to have been shy but pleasant. He and the company he rejuvenated and expanded so remarkably are held in the greatest respect the world over.—OLIVETTI COMPANY

SELECTED PUBLICATIONS

Books:

1945 *L'Ordine politico delle comunità. Le Garanzie di libertà in uno stato socialista* (The Political System in Communities. Guarantees of Freedom in a Socialist State). Ivrea: Nuove Edizioni Ivrea. Also editions by Edizioni di Comunità in 1946 and, edited by Renzo Zozzi with author's own revisions, in 1970.

1952 *Società, stato, comunità* (Society, State, Community). Milan: Edizioni di Comunità. Also, in 1954, English translation by Milton Gendel, giving view of earlier book's contents and synthesizing its historical and ideological antecedents.

1960 *Città dell' uomo* (City of Man). With preface by Gino Pampaloni. Milan: Edizioni di Comunità. Also, in Spanish translation by Assunta Fratelli de Innocenti, *Ciudad del hombre*. Buenos Aires: Emecé Editores, 1962.

Articles:

Many pamphlets and papers on Movimento Comunità published in Italy and abroad repeat passages or entire chapters of these books. In addition, numerous commentaries and essays by Adriano Olivetti appeared in the weekly *Tempi nuovi*, from 1922 on, and in the magazines *Tecnica ed organizzazione* (founded by Olivetti and published 1937–1944), *Comunità* (founded by Olivetti in connection with the establishment of the Comunità movement in 1948), and *Urbanistica* (official organ of the Istituto Nazionale di Urbanistica). Among the most notable are the following:

1937 "Considerazioni sulla direzione di industrie complesse di massa" (Reflections on the Management of Complex Mass-Production Industries), in *Tecnica ed organizzazione*, No. 3, May.

—— "Criterio scientifico e realità industriale" (Scientific Criterion and Industrial Reality), in *Tecnica ed organizzazione*, No. 1, January.

1943 "Il Piano regolatore della Valle d'Aosta" (The Master Plan for the Valle d'Aosta). Written in collaboration with others. Ivrea: Nuove Edizioni Ivrea.

1955 "L'Industrializziazione dell' Italia Meridionale" (The Industrialization of Southern Italy), in *Prospettivi Meridionali*, November.

1957 "Dal comunismo al socialismo" (From Communism to Socialism), in *Comunità*, January.

Curriculum Vitae

1901 Born on April 11, 1901, in Ivrea, Italy.

1924 Awarded degree in industrial chemistry by Politecnico di Torino. Joined Olivetti Co., founded by father in 1908, as factory apprentice.

1925–1926 Visited United States to study plant management and industrial methods.

1926 Returned home; radically reorganized Olivetti plant and introduced new procedures, with emphasis on scientifically trained teams in design and research.

1931 Created development and advertising offices at Olivetti, including graphic artists, architects, and interior designers.

1933 Made Managing Director, Olivetti Co.

1937 Directed preparation of studies for Valle d'Aosta master plan, first scientific regional plan completed in Italy. Founded review *Tecnica ed organizzazione*, writing and editing articles on technology, economics, and sociology.

1938 Became President of Olivetti after father's retirement.

1943 Imprisoned July–September in Rome; escaped to Switzerland after release, remaining till end of war.

1948 Active in first postwar congress, Istituto Nazionale di Urbanistica (National Town Planning Institute). Launched Comunità movement, dedicated to social, cultural, and political improvement in democratic tradition. Later added periodical *Comunità* and Edizioni di Comunità, publishing house.

1949 Became Editor of *Urbanistica*, INU's official review.

1950 Became President, Istituto Nazionale di Urbanistica.

1956 Elected Mayor of Ivrea.

1958 Elected to Italian Parliament in Rome.

1959 Became President, UNRRA-Casas, engaged in reconstruction of war-damaged housing.

1960 Died suddenly of a heart attack on February 27th, aged 58, at Aigle, Switzerland.

Adriano Olivetti served on the Upper Council of Public Works; the Technical Advisory Council for Increasing Employment; and the Board of Directors, Institute of Economic Studies, Milan. He was a corresponding member of the Academy of Science, Turin. In 1956, Olivetti was made a honorary member of the American Institute of Planners and Vice-President for 1956–1957 of the International Federation for Housing and Town Planning. In 1957 the National Management Association (Dayton, Ohio) gave him its Edward O. Seits Memorial Award for international management and free-enterprise leadership. The Olivetti Lettera 22 typewriter won the 1954 Compasso d'Oro for the high level of its design and quality, and in 1955 Adriano Olivetti himself was awarded the Gran Premio Nazionale Compasso d'Oro. In addition, he received the Grand Prix d'Architecture from the Cercle d'Etudes Architecturales of Paris (1956) and the Palma d'Oro for high-quality advertising style and copy (1950).

Olivetti was named cavaliere del lavoro (Italy) in 1952 and officier de la Légion d'Honneur (France) in 1954. In memoriam, he received an honorary degree in political and social science from the University of Florence and the Kaufman Award in design.

Courtesy Rensis Likert Associates, Inc.

Rensis Likert
(1903–1981)
United States

IF ever a definitive history of management thought in the twentieth century is written, the name of Rensis Likert will certainly emerge as preeminent. His professional life spanned five decades of almost convulsive change in American society and management practices. He was perhaps the foremost leader in the movement of management theory away from armchair dicta toward a basis in rigorous research. From the beginning, his approach was to collect evidence from the real world of work, analyze that evidence, and then integrate the resulting findings into a parsimonious statement of principles.

Ren Likert was born in Cheyenne, Wyoming on August 5, 1903. He began undergraduate work at The University of Michigan in the fall of 1922, majoring in civil engineering. During his first three years of study, however, he found that his interests were gravitating more toward the human component than toward the technical. He therefore transferred during his senior year to the Department of Sociology, receiving his bachelor's degree in 1926. Shortly after graduation, he registered at Columbia University as a graduate student in psychology. He received his Ph.D. from Columbia in 1932.

Ren's contributions to the field of organizational management stem from contributions to social science in general that may be even more fundamental. These contributions are of four distinct types: the development of (1) a method for measuring attitudes, (2) methods and procedures for use in survey research, (3) organizational entities to perform the needed research and facilitate its utilization, and (4) the meta-theoretical statement of participative management with which the Likert name eventually came to be linked most closely.

During his doctoral work at Columbia University, Ren worked closely with Gardner Murphy, who subsequently became the chairman of his dissertation committee. The research represented by that dissertation, which was published in 1932 under the title *A Technique for the Measurement of Attitudes*, dealt with a number of attitude scales, and in the course of that research Ren developed what has become the most widely used method of attitude measurement: the so-called Likert scale.

Late in the 1920s Leon Thurstone, at the University of Chicago, had developed a method of measuring attitudes by means of a procedure based on the psychophysical method of equal-appearing intervals. Ren found that a much simpler method, in which respondents were asked to place themselves on a scale of favorability to unfavorability, with a neutral midpoint, produced results that were nearly identical to those of the much more complicated Thurstone procedure. In a very real sense, therefore, he made possible the rigorous measurement of attitudes and perceptions with potential for broad-scale application.

Upon completing his graduate work and a short teaching stint in the Department of Psychology at New York University, Rensis Likert accepted the position of Director of Research for the Life Insurance Sales Research Bureau in Hartford, Connecticut. It was in this capacity that he undertook his first studies of management practices. These seminal studies, published under the title *Morale and Agency Management*, first identified what he and others would later find repeatedly and in amplified form: namely, that managers—in this case of insurance agencies—whose groups were productive and effective displayed a leadership style quite different from that displayed by managers whose groups were poorer performers. Managers of effective groups were more supportive, had higher performance goals, and did more to organize and facilitate the work than did their counterparts in the low-performing groups. These latter managers were more likely to be inconsiderate, demanding—in the negative sense of exerting undue pressure—and more concerned with the work itself than with those employed to perform the work.

These studies, it should be remembered, were performed in the mid-1930s. Yet the underlying issue was to be a lifelong interest for Ren.

Meanwhile, in September 1939, he moved from the Life Insurance Sales Research Bureau to become Director of Program Surveys in the Bureau of Agricultural Economics of the U.S. Department of Agriculture in Washington, D.C. The rationale for establishing a Division of Program Surveys was simple. The federal government was then, as in previous years, trying desperately to pull the farmers out of the Dust Bowl depression. It found, however, that it had no reliable, systematic way of knowing what the farmers needed or experienced or felt.

The data-gathering devices that Ren encountered in the Division were primitive, to say the least. Government agencies had customarily used a reporting form which specified the types of information desired but left to the interviewers the task of choosing whatever questions they thought appropriate. It was apparent to one and all that a serious degree of interviewer bias was inherent in this procedure, and under Ren's direction the Division of Program Surveys adopted formalized questionnaires to which the interviewer was instructed to adhere without deviation. In situations where it was desired that respondents interpret one or more questions in light of their own experience, open-end queries were used to supplement the closed-end, highly structured interview protocol. With careful content analysis, data of comparable reliability could then be obtained; in fact, together with the Likert scale, these procedures have become standard practice wherever surveys are used systematically in management.

With the start of the Second World War, of course, the attention of the Division turned from agriculture to a broader array of topics. Its personnel were used by the Office of War Information and a number of other agencies to gather a wide range of information on public attitudes, experiences, and behavior. Ren collaborated with Morris Hansen, Ray Jessen, Arnold King, and other individuals from the Department of Agriculture, the Bureau of the Census, and Iowa State University in developing a method of sampling households that was based on identifying and listing small units of land throughout the country. This procedure, along with the specific techniques of selection used, became the basis of what later became known as probability sampling.

After the close of the war, Ren and his associates decided to move their activities to a college or university setting in which more substantive research could be done. In the summer of 1946 the Regents of The University of Michigan invited the group to come to Ann Arbor to establish an interdisciplinary center for social science research. And the Institute for Social Research, which Ren founded and which he directed for its first 22 years, became unique among such enterprises. Intended to be truly interdisciplinary, it was administratively located outside the established University schools, colleges, and departments; that is, its research staff received their primary appointments from the Institute itself, not from a teaching department. As a result, although most of them held professorial appointments as well and taught part-time in the departments, their basic commitment was to the Institute. Moreover, from the beginning and by design, the Institute was self-supporting through research contracts and grants.

Ren's role in the early years of the Institute was particularly contributive. He was a developer of people and a creator of situations in which they could grow and develop themselves. He was an eternal optimist; he believed in the worth of human beings and believed that almost all difficult situations would ultimately work themselves out. Obstacles were problems to be solved, not reasons for precipitate action or despair. If his predictions or expectations at the time seemed unrealistic, they proved in fact to be quite realistic and attainable. Under his direction the Institute for Social Research grew and within a very few years became the country's largest university-based research organization in the social sciences.

It is in the area of management theory, however, that Ren Likert made his greatest contributions. In 1946 he picked up at ISR the theme of his earlier work at the Life Insurance Sales Research Bureau and began a lengthy program of research in organizational management and behavior. Initially, it was funded in part by a grant from the Office of Naval Research and supported to some extent by contracts with private corporations. With this backing, Ren launched a series of studies in business, industrial, and government organizations.

The first studies—like those of the 1930s—sought to identify managerial and supervisory characteristics that distinguished high- and low-performing organizational units. In the years between 1946 and the mid-1950s, Ren and his colleagues expanded both the spread of characteristics examined and the methodology used to a much broader body of substance. Performance in terms of operating record replaced categorical high-low judgments of effectiveness as the criteria to which characteristics were to be related. Organization- and group-level processes, communication flow, decision-making practices, and teamwork in the organization became the foci of investigation.

By 1960, it became apparent that a coherent body of management thought had emerged from these studies. Ren then began one of those exercises in which he excelled: integrating this coherent body of findings into a clear theoretical statement about effective management. He distinguished three bodies of variables in the management process: one labeled "causal," another "intervening," and a third "end-result." He separated the causal from the broader array of independent variables to mean those independent variables over which managements—in principle at least—have control. The most important of these, he felt, are the varying behaviors of managers and supervisors in the organization. From these behaviors there emerges an array of processes dealing with communication, coordination, control, and decision making that characterizes the management system. In combination with the different management behaviors, these intervening processes then determine the conditions that will prevail within the organization and produce such end results as satisfaction and productivity—or their opposites.

In his 1961 book *New Patterns of Management,* Rensis Likert presented this comprehensive theoretical statement of participative management for the first time in its full-blown form. He saw organizational management in his terms as capable of being located along a continuum which ranged from System 1 (an exploitive, authoritarian system) through System 2 (benevolent-authoritative) and System 3 (consultative) to System 4 (participative). In his view, System 1 was infrequently used in the United States. System 4 appeared at that time to be an emerging norm or desirable standard; and System 2, he believed, had characterized most managements in the decades immediately preceding the 1960s. System 3, which was consultative in nature, Ren described as a "way station" to System 4. He felt that a System 3 management was inherently unstable. Either it would move on to System 4 in its practices, or it would most likely revert to System 2.

In later years this theoretical statement of Ren's on participative management developed further. For example, he recognized that Systems 1 through 4 all assume a relatively high level of control in the organization; however, organizations are encountered in which little or no control or predictability exists, and so he added in his later writings the notion of System 0 as an essentially laissez-faire or underdeveloped management system. He extended the principles underlying the System 4 model to complex problems of coordination in highly functionalized systems. And finally he began a body of thought and work leading to human resources accounting—the valuation of the human organization in the same terms which are customarily used in setting basic corporate objectives and in making capital decisions.

To those who have followed Ren's ideas and his published work over the years, it is noteworthy that he seemed to encounter remarkably few dead ends. Issues would surface in the early stages of research, and Ren would write about them. Then—and often it would be several years downstream—the issues would emerge again and be integrated into the broader conceptual framework. Ren was an accumulator and a builder.

If one were to list the most critical management concepts articulated by Rensis Likert, they would be these: Effective leaders are supportive, close to their people, and egalitarian—not aloof, remote, and preoccupied with status. The face-to-face work group, not the individual occupant of a given role, is the basic building block of the human organization. Supervisors and managers are individuals with dual or multiple memberships within the organization whose role is that of the linking pin, the mechanism by which the organization is held together and its efforts become coherent. Being supportive and linking effectively will not in themselves produce high performance; instead, effective leaders must themselves have and communicate to others a contagious enthusiasm for high performance goals.

In the last months of his life, Ren spoke and wrote about yet another system, beyond System 4, which he saw beginning to emerge in American organizational life. He labeled it System 5. Although he never fully articulated it, he saw it as much like System 4, but with mutual accountability replacing the hierarchy of authority as the organizing substance.

When, in 1970, Rensis Likert retired as Director of the Institute for Social Research, he had spent almost a quarter of a century in that position. In 1971 he founded an organization of his own—Rensis Likert Associates—to apply research findings in the management and organizational areas. From then until his death in 1981 he collaborated with his wife, Jane Gibson Likert, in extending research-based principles and processes of management to educational settings. With her he published the third of his three major books, *New Ways of Managing Conflict*, in 1976.

As the management profession approaches the beginning of a new century and faces increasing needs for productivity and the efficient use of resources, it will more and more realize its debt to Rensis Likert. He discovered, integrated, articulated, and began the implementation of the principles and the insights which they must now use.—DAVID G. BOWERS

SELECTED PUBLICATIONS

Books:

1961 *New Patterns of Management.* New York: McGraw-Hill.

1967 *The Human Organization: Its Management and Value.* New York: McGraw-Hill.

1976 *New Ways of Managing Conflict.* With Jane Gibson Likert. New York: McGraw-Hill.

Articles:

1932 "A Technique for the Measurement of Attitudes," *Archives of Psychology* No. 140 (Ph.D. dissertation, Columbia University). Reprinted in E. P. Hollander and R. G. Hunt (eds.), *Classic Contributions to Social Psychology.* New York: Oxford University Press, 1972. See also G. F. Summers (ed.), *Attitude Measurement.* Chicago: Rand McNally, 1970.

1948 "Public Opinion Polls," *Scientific American,* Vol. 179, No. 6.

1957 "Behavioral Research: A Guide for Effective Action," in *Some Applications of Behavioral Research.* Paris: UNESCO Publications Division, 1957.

1958 "Measuring Organizational Performance," *Harvard Business Review,* Vol. 36, No. 2. Reprinted in H. Koontz and C. O'Donnell (eds.), *Management: A Book of Readings,* 3rd edition. New York: McGraw-Hill, 1972.

1960 "The Dual Function of Statistics," *Journal* of the American Statistical Association, 1960, Vol. 55.

1969 "Organizational Theory and Human Resource Accounting" (with David G. Bowers), *American Psychologist,* Vol. 24, No. 6, June.

—— "The Relationship Between Management Behavior and Social Structure—Improving Human Performance: Better Theory, More Accurate Accounting," *Proceedings* of the 15th International Management Congress, Tokyo, November. Reprinted as "Comportamento direttivo e misure umane nell'azienda" (*Studi organizzativi,* Vol. 3, 1970) and as *Readings in Management* (Fort Lee: U.S. Army Logistics Management Center, 1971, Vol. I, pp. 1.7–1.11).

Curriculum Vitae

1903 Born on August 5th in Cheyenne, Wyo.

1926 Awarded B.A. degree by The University of Michigan.

1932 Received Ph.D. degree in psychology from Columbia University.

1930–1935 Served as Instructor and Assistant Professor, New York University.
1935–1936 Taught at Sarah Lawrence College, Bronxville, N.Y.
1935–1939 Employed as Director of Research, Life Insurance Agency Management Association, Hartford, Conn.
1939–1944 Headed Division of Program Surveys, U.S. Department of Agriculture, Washington, D.C.
1944–1946 Active as Director of Morale Division, U.S. Strategic Bombing Survey.
1946–1948 Employed as Director of Survey Research Center and Professor of Psychology and Sociology, The University of Michigan.
1948–1970 Employed as Director of the Institute for Social Research, The University of Michigan.
1971 Named Director Emeritus, Institute for Social Research; Professor Emeritus of Sociology; and Professor Emeritus of Psychology.
1971–1981 Served as Chairman of the Board, Rensis Likert Associates, Inc.
1981 Died on September 3rd, at age of 78, in Ann Arbor, Mich.

Rensis Likert was a Fellow of the American Psychological Society. In 1959 he was elected President of the American Statistical Association.

Courtesy La Vie du Rail.

Louis-François Armand
(1905–1971)
France

LOUIS Armand achieved distinction in a wide variety of fields, supporting the cause of improved management in all of them. He was perhaps first of all a railroad man, but he was also an engineer and scientist, an academician, an economist, a writer, a shrewd management consultant, a pioneer of great causes, and a promoter of projects heroic in scale—notably the concept of pan-Europeanism. His interests ranged from oil in the Sahara and a tunnel under the English Channel to the proper use of atomic energy.

In short, Armand was one of those rare individuals whose talents, inclinations, and activities in an era of specialization were so numerous, so widespread as almost to be termed universal. Technician and technologist though he might be, he nevertheless remained sensitive to the slightest needs and feelings of the individual.

Louis Armand's railroad career began in 1934 with the Compagnie des Chemins de Fer P.L.M. (Paris-Lyons-Mediterranean Railway Company). Four years later he became Chief Engineer of the Société Nationale des Chemins de Fer Français (French National Railway System). During the Occupation his position made him an important figure in the resistance movement; he gave the Allies much valuable information on the railroads and, in 1943, established the group known as Résistance-Fer, whose exploits eventually brought about his arrest by the Germans. Released upon the liberation of Paris in the summer of 1944, he again took up his work with SNCF. Now in management, he rose rapidly to become General Manager in 1949 and President in 1955.

Louis Armand had immense faith in his railroads even though public opinion for the most part held that this form of transportation had no future. A true champion of the system, he succeeded in restoring the prestige it deserved: With the help of a remarkable team of engineers and technicians, he modernized the French railways completely. To quote *Popular Science*, "the French system today is not only the fastest, safest, and most punctual in Europe, but it is in the vanguard of the worldwide search for the push-button trains of tomorrow."[1] Armand's trains used an inexpensive type of alternating current, his solid half-mile rails provided both greater passenger comfort and increased roadbed economies, and there were such forms of automation as remote-control dispatching and electronic control of pilotless trains to make service more efficient and save taxpayers' money.

Louis Armand, with his engineering background, was particularly interested in the high speeds which electrification made possible, thereby helping to increase the quality and regularity of service at less cost. In 1954, between Dijon and Beaune, one of his locomotives reached a speed of 243 kilometers an hour; and in 1955, on a stretch of track in Landes, another achieved the amazing record of 331 kilometers an hour. Such was Armand's integrity and sense of responsibility, moreover, that he repeated the run with a second locomotive, different in design, with the same result. Thus he had the satisfaction of knowing that the first trial was valid, not a mere fluke or an isolated phenomenon.

But improving rail service within France was by no means the whole task as Armand saw it. He firmly believed that the future of Europe lay in its unification—economically if not, in time, politically. And the railroads, to his way of thinking, were responsible for bringing people together on an international basis, not keeping them apart. As President of the Union Internationale des Chemins de Fer (International Union of Railways), he was in a unique position to realize his dream of an international railway system through two organizations: Trans Europe Express, of which he was a strong advocate, and his own Société EUROFIMA—that is, the Société Européenne pour le Financement du Matériel Ferroviaire (European Society for the Financing of Railway Materiel). Today these two coordinate and control a joint pool of hundreds and thousands of freight cars, all labeled "Europ," which can be sent anywhere and used by any member country. Under this plan, the productivity of West European rolling stock has increased at least 50 percent; communication between countries is correspondingly easier, and economic development has benefited tremendously. In Armand's words, "The humble box car . . . points the way to a united Europe."[2]

Despite his faith in the railroads and his efforts to renew their popularity

[1] *Popular Science*, February 1957; printed simultaneously in *Reader's Digest*.
[2] *Rotarian*, May 1953.

as a means of transportation, Armand took the benefits of technological progress for granted; that was, after all, his approach to improving the efficiency of the combined network of European railways. At the same time, he was a proponent of atomic energy, wisely used. His was the first presidency of EURATOM, the Commission Européenne d l'Energie Atomique (European Atomic Energy Commission). Furthermore, his observations and experience as engineer and scientist made him keenly aware of the potential hazards along with the benefits of technological advancement—and not in terms solely of atomic power. In 1960 he became President of the Comité d'Action contre la Pollution Atmosphérique (Committee for the Control of Atmospheric Pollution). His work has been universally recognized as the greatest sort of contribution: He labored not only to solve the problems of modern times, and make life easier and more pleasant for today's generation, but to secure the safety of generations to come.

In his 1961 book *Plaidoyer pour l'avenir* (Plea for the Future), written in collaboration with Michel Drancourt, Louis Armand defines the first industrial revolution as that of coal and the steam engine. The second, he says, was touched off by the harnessing of electricity and is still in progress. But for him the Year Zero was 1942, when Enrico Fermi succeeded in building the first atomic pile. The hour had struck for the third industrial revolution and the era of information.

Louis Armand received much acclaim in France for the widely debated *Rueff-Armand Report*—more often known unofficially as the *Armand-Rueff Report*—upon its publication in 1960. Jacques Rueff, the previous year, had proposed to then Premier Michel Debré that a committee be set up to recommend reforms that would eliminate obstacles in the way of expanding the French economy. Debré himself headed the resulting group, with Rueff and Armand—in that order—serving under him. However, Armand's influence on the group's thinking and decision making appears to have been so pronounced that the matter of precedence was all but forgotten.

So far as management is concerned, Louis Armand's contribution did not end with his skilled planning, organizing, staffing, directing, and controlling of his railroads and the countless associations, committees, and other groups he found time to preside over. He taught at the Ecole Nationale d'Administration (National School of Administration), soon after its founding, and later joined its board. He spoke at the Eleventh International Congress on Scientific Management, held in Paris in June 1957, and also at the Thirteenth Congress in New York in September 1963. Nor did he limit his teaching and his concern for education to the field of management. He taught at the Ecole Nationale des Ponts et Chaussées, and later he not only became a board member there and at the Ecole Supérieure des Mines but also headed the Conseil de Perfectionnement at the Ecole Polytechnique in Paris. To other engineers, throughout his life, he was a model and a guide.

One of Armand's contemporaries has recalled that Armand summed up the qualities that make a great engineer as force of character, enthusiasm, sincerity, and knowledge. Those who knew Louis Armand declare that he lacked none of these four essentials. His wife, said to have influenced his important decisions, cannot be faulted for having chosen—for him and with him—a career in engineering at the expense of one in teaching, since this great engineer was able to become a marvelous teacher as well.

Louis Armand was naturally generous, full of good common sense, accessible to the humblest individual as readily as the richest and most powerful. He was also an eternally youthful man, brown-eyed and auburn-haired. He set his children and grandchildren an example of splendid zest for living. Quite naturally, with no great effort, he found his way into young hearts and minds. He trusted young people, counted on them to take care of the future. To his way of thinking, people in general—especially managers in the Western countries—were too attached to the past, either because they were afraid of what the future might bring or because they dreaded becoming obsolete themselves and losing the privileges they had enjoyed for so long. Louis Armand neither feared nor scorned the past; he merely thought it should not be regarded as the sole model for the present or, above all, for the future. We are entering into an era of abundance and therefore, he considered, into a period of greater sharing. Today, in contrast to yesterday, the problem is no longer one of producing more but one of better distribution.

Moreover, Armand was passionately devoted to freedom. No one knew more intimately than he the dangers of bureaucracy—he wished that government could modify its contacts with its citizens, that they might have greater confidence in it as the organizer and regulator of their collective efforts. Information, too, was a necessary element in the exercise of democracy, and journalists—that is, the press and the other media of communication—must be conscious at all times of their responsibilities and duties in the molding of public opinion.

Louis Armand was a great admirer of Teilhard de Chardin, whom he called one of the great French thinkers and one of those who had influenced his life most markedly. He especially treasured these Teilhard words: "Vers la convergence par l'élévation" (toward convergence through elevation). And on the obverse of the medal struck in his honor there appears the following motto, equally dear to him: Tout est carrefours (All life is a crossroads).—ELIZABETH MARTING

SELECTED PUBLICATIONS

Books:

1960 *Rapport sur les obstacles à l'expansion économique* présidé par le comité institué par le decret du 13 novembre 1959 (Report on Obstacles to Economic Expansion Prepared Under the Direction of the Committee Established by Decree No. 59-1284, November 13, 1959). The so-called *Rapport Armand-Rueff*, a collaboration. Paris: Imprimerie Nationale.

1961 *Plaidoyer pour l'avenir* (Plea for the Future). With Michel Drancourt. Paris: Editions Calmann-Lévy.

1968 *Le Pari européen* (The European Wager). With Michel Drancourt. Paris: Editions Fayard. Translated into 13 languages, including Japanese.
—— *Simples propos* (Plain Talk). Paris: Editions Fayard.
1970 *Propos ferroviaires* (Railroad Talk). Paris: Editions Fayard.

Articles:
1957 "Les Méthodes d'organisation scientifique dans l'orientation de l'avenir," in *Compte rendu* des travaux du XIème Congrès International de l'Organisation Scientifique; and, as "Methods of Scientific Management and the Future," in *Proceedings*, Eleventh International Congress on Scientific Management, Paris, June 24–28. Paris: Comité National de l'Organisation Française, pp. 37–50.
1963 "Les Fondements de l'autorité dans l'entreprise," in *Compte rendu*, XIIIème Congrès International de l'Organisation Scientifique; and, as "Bases of Authority in the Organization," in *Proceedings*, Thirteenth International Congress on Scientific Management, New York, September 16–20. New York: Council for International Progress in Management, pp. 13–14.
1965 "Il faut promouvoir l'idée d'industrie européenne" (We Must Promote the Concept of European Industry), in Communauté Européenne, No. 2, February, pp. 8–9.
1967 "Pour une association des entreprises transnationals" (For an Association of Transnational Companies), in *Entreprise*, No. 597, February 16, pp. 22–23.
—— "Concentration, dimension: est-ce vraiment l'efficacité? Réponse de L. Armand (Concentration, Size: Is This Really Efficiency? Reply by L. Armand), in *Entreprise*, No. 603, March 30, pp. 22–23.
1968 "Productivité et participation; editorial par L. Armand" (Productivity and Participation; editorial by L. Armand), in *Publicis Information*, No. 124, July–August–September, pp. 2–8.
1969 "Un Liberalisme progressiste?" (A Progressivist Liberalism?), address to the Association de Cadres Dirigeants de l'Industrie pour le Progrès Social et Economique (Association of Industrial Managers for Social and Economic Progress), in *Bulletin ACADI*, No. 243, May, pp. 197–216.

Curriculum Vitae

1905 Born on January 17th at Cruseilles (Haute-Savoie).
1922 Completed secondary education at lycées in Annecy and Lyons.
1924 Entered Ecole Polytechnique in Paris, graduating second in class; subsequently, attended Ecole Nationale Supérieure des Mines, graduating first in class.
1926 Served as second lieutenant in French artillery.
1929–1934 Was engineer in Corps de Mines at Clermont-Ferrand.

1934	Joined headquarters office of Compagnie des Chemins de Fer P.L.M. (Paris-Lyons-Mediterranean Railway Company).
1938	Became Chief Engineer, Société Nationale des Chemins de Fer Français (French National Railway System).
1939–1945	During war, active in several resistance networks, giving Allies valuable information on railways. In February 1943 organized well-known Résistance-Fer. Arrested by Gestapo in June 1944 and imprisoned at Fresnes; freed August 18, 1944, upon liberation of Paris.
1940–1949	Taught at Ecole Nationale des Ponts et Chaussées.
1946	Became Assistant General Manager, SNCF.
1947	Became teacher at newly established Ecole Nationale d'Administration (National School of Administration), Paris.
1947–1955	Active as board member, Ecole Nationale Supérieure des Mines, Paris.
1949	Became General Manager, SNCF.
1951–1959	Served as President, Union Internationale des Chemins de Fer (International Union of Railways), representing 36 countries.
1953–1958	Served as President, Bureau Industriel Africain (African Industrial Office), responsible for promoting development of the Sahara.
1955	Became board member, Ecole National d'Administration.
1955–1957	Held office as President, SNCF.
1956	Created EUROFIMA, Société Européenne pour le Financement du Matériel Ferroviaire (European Society for the Financing of Railway Materiel).
1956–1968	Was President, Conseil de Perfectionnement (Council on Advanced Study), Ecole Polytechnique.
1958–1959	Held first presidency of EURATOM, Commission Européenne de l'Energie Atomique (European Atomic Energy Commission).
1959	Named to serve as Vice-President, Comité Rueff-Armand, charged with proposing economic reforms. Signed name to famous report published in following year.
1960	Became President, Comité d'Action contre la Pollution Atmosphérique (Committee for the Control of Atmospheric Pollution).
1961	Became Secretary General, Union Internationale des Chemins de Fer (International Union of Railways).
1962	Became President, Association Française de Normalisation (French Association for Uniform Standards).
1963	Became President, La Protectrice (insurance company).
1971	Died on August 30th, aged 66, at Villers-sur-Mer (Calvados).

Louis Armand was known for a number of scientific studies. In 1953 he received the Louis Ancel Prize of the Société des Ingénieurs Civils (Society of Civil Engineers) for his work on locomotive boilers. In 1955, during his studies of the steadiness of cars on rails at high speeds, a record railway speed of 331 kilometers per hour was achieved. He also was cited by the Academy of Medicine and the Collège de France for studies of mineral waters and, by the Société des Ingénieurs Civils, for work on the chemistry of boiler waters, which won him the Felix Robin Prize, and on the electrification of the railroads, for which he again received the Prix Louis Ancel.

Armand was a frequent speaker before learned societies, as well as conferences in France and abroad, on topics relating to economics, political science, and sociology. At the opening of the XIème Congrès International de l'Organisation Scientifique (Eleventh Congress on Scientific Management), in June 1957, he spoke on "Les méthodes de l'organisation scientifique dans l'orientation de l'avenir" (Methods of Scientific Management and the Future). And in September 1963, at the Thirteenth Congress, his topic was "Les fondements de l'autorité dans l'entreprise" (Bases of Authority in the Organization).

Louis Armand was elected to the Académie des Sciences Morales et Politiques in 1960 and to the Académie Française—as geologist, physicist, chemist, and biologist—in 1963. Among his many other honors, he was awarded the Croix de la Libération, the Croix de Guerre 1939–1945, and the Medal of Freedom; he was a grand officier of the Légion d'honneur and a knight of the British Empire; and he was named to the Order of Merit of the Italian Republic, the Order of Orange-Nassau (Netherlands), and the Order of Léopold of Belgium. In addition, he was decorated by the United States, Sweden, Spain, the German Federal Republic, and Yugoslavia.

Douglas McGregor
(1906–1964)
United States

DOUGLAS McGregor was an academic, an administrator, and a consultant. He came from a family steeped in traditions of industriousness and service to mankind, all of which fused to bring about his major contribution to management.

McGregor was one of those who actively advanced and synthesized a humanistic approach to the management of organizations. *The Human Side of Enterprise,* the book which he published in 1960, captures this contribution. In it he delineates two different cosmologies which executives may hold. One he labeled "Theory X." It encompasses the assumptions about human nature which are associated with authoritarian leadership—for example, people dislike work; tend to avoid it; have to be controlled, directed, and coerced to do their jobs properly; and prefer to avoid responsibilities. The second he labeled "Theory Y." It assumes that work is as natural as rest or play; that people will exercise self-direction and self-control in the service of objectives to which they are committed; that commitment is a function of the rewards associated with achievement; and that people, under proper conditions, seek responsibility and generally are capable of creative solutions to organizational problems.

Theory X and Theory Y have become part of the lexicon of management. Unfortunately, they are often misused. Too often they are considered opposite poles in a continuum, whereas McGregor was really writing about two different theories of the universe as a whole and the laws governing it.

The point he emphasized was that managerial strategies are based upon the manager's view of the world and that the view taken in Theory X necessitates authoritarian management under which workers are treated in ways that frustrate the satisfaction of their social, egotistic, self-fulfillment, and other higher-order needs. In short, declared McGregor, much human behavior in formal organizations is a function of the Theory X views held by executives, and these beliefs are in effect self-fulfilling. They actually bring about the behavior which they assume.

Theory Y, in contrast, leads to individual growth and development. The individual is a resource with potential for problem solving and efficient adaptation. Hence McGregor's conclusion that many of the problems encountered in organizations are a function of the beliefs about workers held by managers.

McGregor's contribution to management has been increasingly recognized. From 1943 to 1948 he was Executive Director of the Industrial Relations Section at Massachusetts Institute of Technology, in which capacity he was instrumental in bringing to M.I.T. Professor Kurt Lewin and his Center for Group Dynamics. In particular, McGregor's writing, teaching, and consulting did much to contribute to the growth of the field identified as organization development. It is through his work in this area that many of the concepts essential to a Theory Y cosmology were invented and refined.

In summary, Douglas McGregor clearly delineated a basic problem—that is, the fact that the imposition by executives of a Theory X cosmology is a self-fulfilling prophecy. However, he also was a leader in the development of tools and mechanisms to facilitate the dissemination of Theory Y beliefs.

Douglas McGregor was a warm, robust individual with a crop of bristly hair. He had humor, vitality, and a variety of interests ranging from music to gardening and from active involvement in business reorganizations to education in India. He believed in the essential goodness of man and dedicated his professional life to the development of the "human side of enterprise." In a sense, he was a crusader who valued the individual and his or her potential and who sought ways of preserving the individual's autonomy and growth in an organizational setting.

McGregor took his work seriously but never himself. He understood himself and recognized his foibles. He learned from his own experiences and willingly confronted his problems.

McGregor had an aura that expanded to include those around him. He was a born innovator, a man who questioned tradition. One of his colleagues stated, "A large segment of his professional field operated in an environment which he created. Much of the work that goes on now couldn't have happened if he had never been."—WILLIAM B. WOLF

SELECTED PUBLICATIONS

Books:

1960 *The Human Side of Enterprise.* New York: McGraw-Hill.

1966 *Leadership and Motivation: Essays of Douglas McGregor.* Warren Bennis and Edgar H. Schein, eds. Cambridge, Mass.: The M.I.T. Press.
1967 *The Professional Manager.* New York: McGraw-Hill.

Articles:
1939 "The Attitudes of Workers Toward Layoff Policy," *Journal of Abnormal and Social Psychology,* Vol. 34, pp. 179–199.
1940 "The Genesis of Attitudes Toward Management." With Conrad M. Arensberg. *Psychological Bulletin,* Vol. 37, pp. 433–434.
—— "Motives as a Tool of Market Research," *Harvard Business Review,* Vol. 19, No. 1, pp. 42–51.
1941 "Industrial Relations and National Defense: A Challenge to Management." With Irving Knickerbocker. *Personnel,* Vol. 18, No. 1, pp. 49–63.
1942 "Determination of Morale in an Industrial Company." With Conrad M. Arensberg. *Applied Anthropology,* Vol. 1, No. 2, pp. 12–34.
—— "Union-Management Cooperation: A Psychological Analysis." With Irving Knickerbocker. *Personnel,* Vol. 19, No. 3, pp. 520–539.
1944 "Conditions of Effective Leadership in the Industrial Organization," *Journal of Consulting Psychology,* Vol. 8, pp. 55–63; *Advanced Management,* Vol. 9, No. 4, pp. 148–153; and S. D. Hoslett, ed., *Human Factors in Management,* New York: Harper, pp. 23–35.
1946 "The Foreman's Responsibilities in the Industrial Organization," *Personnel,* Vol. 22, No. 5, pp. 296–304.
—— "The Nature and Use of Authority," in University of Michigan, Bureau of Industrial Relations, *Addresses on Industrial Relations,* pp. 85–87.
—— "Re-evaluation of Training for Management Skills," in *Training for Management Skills,* American Management Association Personnel Series No. 104.
1948 *The Dewey and Almy Chemical Company: A Case Study.* With Joseph N. Scanlon. National Planning Association. Case Studies in Causes of Industrial Peace Under Collective Bargaining No. 3.
—— Foreword, "The Consultant Role and Organizational Leadership: Improving Human Relations in Industry," *Journal of Social Issues,* Vol. 4, No. 3, pp. 2–4.
—— "The Staff Function in Human Relations," *Journal of Social Issues,* Vol. 4, No. 3, pp. 5–22.
1949 "Toward a Theory of Organized Human Effort in Industry," in *Psychology of Labor-Management Relations, Proceedings of the Meeting.* Champaign, Ill.: Industrial Relations Research Association, pp. 111–122.
1950 "Changing Patterns in Human Relations," in *Conference Board Management Record,* Vol. 12, No. 9, pp. 322, 323, and M. deV. Richards and W. A. Nielander, eds., *Readings in Management.* Cincinnati, Ohio: South-Western Publishing.

—— "How Can We Go Forward? Panel Discussion on 'The Untapped Potential in Labor-Management Relations,'" in *Mobilizing America's Strength for World Security.* Report of 19th Annual New York Herald-Tribune Forum, October 23rd–25th. New York: Herald Tribune, pp. 65–68.

1953 "Line Management's Responsibility for Human Relations," in *Building Up the Supervisor's Job,* American Management Association Manufacturing Series No. 213, pp. 27–35.

1955 "The Changing Role of Management," *The Technology Review,* Vol. 57, No. 6, pp. 287–290, and H. C. Thole and C. C. Gibbons, eds., *Business Action in a Changing World.* Chicago: Public Administration Service, pp. 9–16.

1957 "The Human Side of Enterprise," in *Adventure in Thought and Action,* Proceedings of Fifth Anniversary Convocation of M.I.T. School of Industrial Management, June, pp. 23–30, and (in condensed form) in *Management Review,* Vol. 46, No. 11, pp. 22–28.

—— "An Uneasy Look at Performance Appraisal," *Harvard Business Review,* Vol. 35, No. 3, pp. 89–94.

1958 "The Scanlon Plan Through a Psychologist's Eyes." Chapter 8 in Frederick G. Lesieur, ed., *The Scanlon Plan: A Frontier in Labor-Management Cooperation.* New York: The Technology Press and John Wiley & Sons, pp. 89–99. Fifth printing by The M.I.T. Press, Cambridge, Mass., 1964.

—— "The Significance of Scanlon's Contribution," Chapter 2 in Frederick G. Lesieur, ed., *The Scanlon Plan: A Frontier in Labor-Management Cooperation.* New York: The Technology Press and John Wiley & Sons, pp. 7–15. Fifth printing by The M.I.T. Press, Cambridge, Mass., 1964.

1959 "Management Development: The Hope and the Reality," in *Proceedings of the American Petroleum Institute,* Section III, Division of Refining, Addresses and Reports, New York, May 28, pp. 272–277.

1960 "The Role of Staff in Modern Industry," Chapter 1 of Part III in George P. Shultz and Thomas L. Whisler, eds., *Management Organization and the Computer.* Glencoe, Ill.: The Free Press.

1961 "New Concepts of Management," *The Technology Review,* Vol. 63, No. 4, pp. 25–27, and *The Executive,* Vol. 4, No. 12, 13–15.

1963 "Behavioral Science—What's in It for Management?" *Business Management Record* (National Industrial Conference Board), Vol. 25, pp. 32–44.

1964 "Can You Measure Executive Performance? *International Management,* Vol. 19, No. 6, pp. 59–61.

Curriculum Vitae

1906 Born on September 16th in Detroit, Mich.

1923–1926 Attended City College of Detroit, now Wayne University.

1926	Attended Oberlin College.
1927–1930	Worked for Buffalo Grey Auto Stations as District Manager, Albany and Detroit.
1930–1932	With McGregor Institute, Detroit (transient laborers' shelter).
1931–1932	Attended City College of Detroit again; received B.A. in 1932.
1932–1935	Did graduate work in psychology at Harvard University. Awarded master's degree in 1933 and Ph.D. in 1935.
1935–1937	Employed as Instructor in Social Psychology, Harvard University.
1937–1948	Employed successively as Instructor, Assistant Professor, Associate Professor, and Professor of Psychology, Massachusetts Institute of Technology. Was a founder of M.I.T.'s Industrial Relations Section.
1943–1948	Was Executive Director of Industrial Relations Section, M.I.T.
1948–1954	Was President of Antioch College, Yellow Springs, Ohio.
1954–1964	Returned to M.I.T. as Professor of Industrial Management.
1961	Went to India as Visiting Lecturer at Summer Advanced Management Program sponsored at Kashmir by Indian Institute of Management.
1962–1964	Was Sloan Fellows Professor at M.I.T.
1963–1964	Headed Board of Governors, Endicott House.
1964	Returned as Visiting Lecturer at Winter Advanced Management Program sponsored by Indian Institute of Management, Calcutta, India.
____	Died on October 13th, aged 58, in Concord, Mass.

Douglas McGregor received the honorary degree of Doctor of Laws from Wayne University in 1949. He served as a Trustee of Antioch College (1960–1963) and was a member of the Visiting Committee to the Psychology Department at Harvard University (1960–1964), the Board of the Social Science Research Council (1952–1959), and the Board of the Foundation for Research in Human Behavior (1954–1964).

Courtesy Myrna Bustani.

Emile Bustani
(1907–1963)
Lebanon

EMILE Bustani played a major role in the spread of modern management by showing the Middle East that it could not only handle its own needs for competence in the various managerial fields but compete with the West on even terms both at home and internationally. It did not need to rely on foreigners for managers and technical specialists; it was entirely capable of developing the necessary expertise. Moreover, the Bustani career had a flamboyance calculated to fire the ambition of any young Arab.

Emile's widowed mother, with a precarious living to earn for her family in the Lebanon hills, sent him to a nearby American orphanage "for his own good" when he was nine years old. There this future "spokesman for the Arab world"—although the Bustanis were Christians—received his initial education. Emile Bustani was grateful all his life to his American teachers—first at the orphanage, then at the American University of Beirut, and finally at the Massachusetts Institute of Technology—for the knowledge and training that were to make him head of the largest industrial concern in the Middle East.

As a young student, Emile Bustani's interests lay in mathematics and astronomy; he was the author of a small volume entitled *Convection Currents in the Chromosphere*—his M.A. thesis at AUB, actually. He was thinking of an academic career in the abstract sciences when his wife-to-be, a member of a prosperous Beirut family of traders, persuaded him to try engineering. So for two years, after earning his degree from M.I.T., he worked as an engineer in Haifa for the Iraq Petroleum Co. Then, in 1935, he began contracting for IPC. It was another two years before he founded, still in Haifa, the organization known as CAT (Contracting and Trading Co.) with Kamel Abdel Rahman as partner.

The outbreak of the Second World War made the new company's prospects bright. CAT, in fact, "emerged as a major contractor, extending its activities from Palestine into Lebanon in the wake of the British army. Between 1941 and the end of the war, the partnership undertook work worth more than $10 million for the British and Allied forces, including timber works, buildings, fortifications, drainage and irrigation schemes, and camp, airfield, and road construction."[1] To expedite all this business, Bustani opened a CAT office in Beirut, taking Abdallah Khoury and, later, Shukri Shammas as partners. And in 1948 CAT moved its headquarters to Beirut.

By this time the war was over and the partners were extending their activities to oil.

> . . . CAT became the first company in the Arab world to undertake pipeline ditching contracts and other turnkey projects.
>
> The problems that had to be overcome were not only engineering ones. In 1947–1948 the company dug the ditch for the Iraq Petroleum Company's Kirkuk-Tripoli and Kirkuk-Haifa pipeline projects. On reaching the Palestine border the pipeline contractor stopped work on the Haifa line as dissension between Jews, Arabs, and British reached its climax.
>
> Undaunted, CAT undertook to continue the works and reached Nassira before the 1948 war broke out—a clear demonstration that a local company could get results in conditions that were virtually impossible for a foreign contractor."[2]

In 1951 CAT formed its major associate company in a joint venture with the Motherwell Bridge & Engineering Co. of Scotland. The unwieldy title—Motherwell Bridge Contracting & Trading Co.—was soon abbreviated to Mothercat in spite of the implication that Mothercat was the parent rather than the associate company. Because Mothercat could be registered in Glasgow as a nonresident British company, CAT could now handle projects for the British government in the Middle East and other areas. In 1966 CAT therefore acquired a controlling interest in Mothercat, and in 1967 it registered the familiar shortened name of its associate.

CAT operations had long since been prominent in Bahrein; in Kuwait, Qatar, and Aden; in Saudi Arabia; in Pakistan; in Libya, Ghana, Nigeria, and Guinea; and in Somalia and Ethiopia—to name only a few of the 25 countries and more with which it has contracted. It has built not only pipelines and oil tanks but schools, hospitals, airports, roads, and hotels. At

[1] Tim Henshaw, "The Bustani Legacy," in *The Arab World,* Spring 1975.
[2] *Ibid.*

home in Lebanon, its interests have included hotels like the Al-Bustan overlooking Beirut, built and owned by CAT; the Banque de l'Industrie et du Travail (Bank of Industry and Labor); a piece of Middle East Airlines; and a chocolate factory. In addition, the CAT group has bolstered the Lebanese economy through the repatriation of funds by Lebanon nationals employed abroad. Bustani has also attracted capital from other Arab countries by inducing people there to invest money in Lebanon and thereby making it the banking center of the Middle East.

To have built the largest industrial firm in the Middle East, Emile Bustani would have had to possess remarkable managerial talents, together with a boldness of vision that might almost be termed audacity. It goes without saying that he also was self-reliant, resourceful, and highly intelligent—qualities which were rewarded by fantastic material success. We are told, also, that he was a good and honorable man. But the driving force behind his career was his strong belief in the need for economic development in the Arab countries and for cooperation between the Arabs and the West—which to him, personally, meant proving that an Arab could create and manage an enterprise capable of taking on the big international companies and beating them at their own game.[3]

Emile Bustani's interest in Lebanese politics, then, grew out of his hopes and aspirations as much as the need to open up business opportunities not only with Arabs but with British, French, and other "intruders." As early as 1941, he set up a CAT office in Beirut, and in 1948 he moved CAT headquarters there from Haifa, having already opened a political office in Beirut for the express purpose of promoting Lebanese independence and putting an end to the French mandate. In 1951 Bustani was elected to the Lebanese Parliament for the first time, and in 1956 he was appointed Minister of Reconstruction. He seemed headed for the country's presidency, according to his biographer,[4] if he had not crashed to death in his own plane over Beirut harbor on March 15, 1963.

The Bustani managerial abilities undoubtedly were sharpened by the year he spent at M.I.T. Or perhaps it would be more accurate to say that he became aware, during those months, not only of scientific management but—more important—of his own latent management skills. We are fond of saying that good managers are not born but, rather, are developed. Yet some of the greatest are born, and surely Emile Bustani was one of them. Moreover, he used his gifts to do more than simply build his enormous industrial empire. He saw, and demonstrated to the Middle East, the possibilities of world leadership inherent in management excellence as the key to economic development. At the same time, he recognized the problems confronting ambitious Arab managers.

One of these problems, in the beginning, was the scarcity of skilled

[3] *The New Statesman*, March 1963.

[4] Desmond Stewart, *Orphan with a Hoop: The Life of Emile Bustani*. London: Chapman and Hall, 1967.

technical workers, and Bustani was quick to realize that CAT must develop its own. There was the case, for example, where a Lloyd's inspector was inveigled into lecturing evenings on welding. Since this was at a time when there were literally no Arab welders, CAT in effect trained practically all of the many now working on pipelines in that part of the world. Today CAT devotes a sizable training budget to developing not only technicians but also engineers and accountants, both Lebanese and non-Lebanese. In addition, it makes scholarships available at schools in Lebanon, Great Britain, and the United States to likely students from Lebanon and such countries as Pakistan, Iraq, Iran, and the Ivory Coast. In so doing, the company is steadily increasing the supply of trained personnel in both the Middle East and Africa—thus contributing to the advancement of the developing countries of the world.[5]

Bustani lectured on several occasions before the Lebanese Management Association and at the American University of Beirut, expounding his philosophy and his views on the future of Arabian management. The need for more technical people was of course only part of the basic difficulty, and that need was slowly being met. However, the backward attitudes of many business leaders in the Middle East would have to change, and enlightenment would come only as professional training and development staffs were brought into companies and new young managers, exposed to modern management theory and methods, began to infiltrate each organization.

Emile Bustani had to leave some of his dreams unrealized. When he died, he was thinking in terms of an Arab economic community along the lines of the European Common Market. And he was helping to lay the plans for a Middle East development fund to which each Arab country would contribute 2 percent of its oil revenues.

His was truly an exhilarating spirit.—ELIZABETH MARTING

PUBLICATIONS

1932 *Convection Currents in the Chromosphere* (M.A. thesis, American University of Beirut). Publisher unknown.
1958 *Doubts and Dynamite: The Middle East Today.* London: Allen Wingate.
1961 *March Arabesque.* London: Robert Hale Ltd. Second edition, 1963.

Curriculum Vitae

1907 Born in Dibbiyeh, Lebanon.
1929 Graduated from American University of Beirut with B.A. degree.
1932 Received M.A. in astrophysics, also from American University of Beirut.
1933 Received B.Sc. (Engineering) from Massachusetts Institute of Technology.

[5] Henshaw, *op. cit.*

1933–1935	Worked for Iraq Petroleum Co. (IPC) as engineer at Haifa Line Station H-1.
1935	Started contracting for IPC in Haifa.
1937	Founded Contracting and Trading Co. (CAT) with Kamel Abdel Rahman as partner.
1941	Opened CAT office in Beirut, taking Abdallah Khoury and, later, Shukri Shammas as partners. Did work for British army.
1943	Opened political office in Beirut. Main purpose: Lebanon's independence and end to French mandate.
1948	Moved CAT headquarters to Beirut.
1951	Elected Deputy in Lebanese Parliament for first time. Saw CAT enter into joint venture with Motherwell Bridge & Engineering Co. of Scotland to form major associate company: Motherwell Bridge Contracting & Trading Co. (Mothercat).
1956	Appointed Minister for Reconstruction in Lebanese Cabinet. During Suez war, asked by Nasser to make contract with French and British friends and pave way for cease-fire.
1963	Died on March 15, aged 56, in crash of own plane in Beirut harbor.

Barry M. Richman
(1936–1978)
Canada/United States

BARRY Richman represented a growth and expansion of concepts in the management movement. He was one of the pioneers in the development of the "comparative" approach to international management. Along with his friend and co-author, Richard Farmer, he brought into focus the relationship of management to international factors such as government, economic organizations, and culture. In emphasizing a comparative approach to management, they were, in many ways, precursors to the development of "contingency" theory.

Barry Richman was active as a consultant to governments and businesses as well as a writer and a teacher. He contributed to both the theoretical and the tangible aspects of international comparative management. He developed a theoretical construct which allows one to grasp what appears to be almost unmanageable—that is, the complexity of a comparative international approach. Moreover, through his field studies, research, and publications, he contributed significantly to the Western world's understanding of management in the U.S.S.R., India, and China. His *Industrial Society in Communist China* stands as a landmark in the field. In many ways its success arises from the fact that Richman had a well-developed theoretical framework. When he visited the Peoples Republic of China, he could quite readily categorize data and ask the "right" questions. He was in the process of updating and rewriting this book when he died of a heart attack at the age of 42.

Despite his short life span, Barry Richman accomplished more management research and published more than most world-renowned management scholars do in a life span twice as long. He was the author or co-author of 12 books and 45 scholarly papers, many of which were based on firsthand studies in various countries.

Richman was significantly honored for his accomplishments. Coming to the University of California in 1962 as an acting assistant professor, he rapidly rose through the professorial ranks to become a full professor at the University in 1968 at the age of 32. He was then the youngest person to achieve the rank of professor in the entire University of California system. He was elected a Fellow of the U.S. Academy of Management in 1970—the youngest person ever to be selected. Likewise, he was elected a Fellow of the International Academy of Management in 1973, when, at the age of 37, he was probably the youngest person ever to receive this high honor.

Richman combined his admirable research record with considerable practical experience. Before coming to the University of California, he was a systems analyst and project director with a firm of management consultants in Montreal, spending two years as an operations planning analyst with Air Canada Airlines in that city. Also, during his years as a professor and dean, Richman maintained close relationships with business and government organizations through his work as a consultant.

Over all, Barry M. Richman made his unique contribution to management by highlighting the dynamics of management in different national settings. He gave speeches and led seminars not only in the United States but in many foreign countries besides the U.S.S.R. and China, particularly those of the so-called Third World. Both in his research and in his writing, he displayed considerable interest in the economic problems of the developing countries and, above all, in the development of skilled management in those countries. And he was similarly interested in the problems of management in American colleges and universities.

Richman was an exceptionally hard worker, giving his colleagues the impression that he must be writing books and papers with both hands. A dedicated scholar and researcher, an original thinker, and an excellent teacher, he packed into his few years a large volume of accomplishments almost too numerous to summarize. His indomitable spirit is illustrated by the fact that he picked the Soviet Union in which to do his doctoral research in management, realizing that in order to achieve any degree of success he must live there for a considerable period and learn a new and difficult language.

Travel and research aside, Richman was fortunate in having a happy home life with his wife Vivian, who is herself an active researcher, and their daughter and son. He liked the ocean front at Malibu and the hills rising behind it. Yet, though he spent most of his working life in the United States, Barry maintained his Canadian citizenship—principally, his friends suspected, because this allowed him to spend time in the Soviet Union and, later, in Communist China during those years when citizens of the United States were not particularly welcome in either country.

For those who were privileged to be colleagues of Barry Richman in business, the academic world, research, or travel, he was a person to be enjoyed as well as admired. True, while writing a book or a paper, Richman would concentrate single-mindedly on his task; however, he could and did count it part of the good life to socialize informally, as opportunities arose, with his many friends all over the world. He loved tennis, swimming, good food, good cigars. He had a contagious laugh, and his hospitality was genuine.

Barry's youth made it inevitable that he would now and then cause envy among his academic colleagues. He was the typical "young man in a hurry," and occasionally it was hard not to feel a compulsion to criticize him for seeming to ride roughshod over one or another of his associates. He was impatient with anyone who, he thought, wasted time; often, in committee meetings, he would sketch out ideas for research or problem analyses during a tedious discussion. But, as intense and hard-working as Barry was, he was never dull. What he had to say was invariably provocative and stimulating.

One can barely imagine what additional contributions to management theory and science might have flowed from Barry Richman's fertile mind—and there would have been many of them—had he been allowed man's normal life span. Instead, he lived a mere 16 years between his doctorate and his death. But suppose he had lived three times 16 years, which would have given him just over the biblical three score and ten? A man who deliberately chose to do important work in both the U.S.S.R. and China, who learned two complex languages for that express purpose, surely would have tripled his far from insignificant outstanding achievements.—HAROLD KOONTZ AND WILLIAM B. WOLF

SELECTED PUBLICATIONS

Books:

1965 *Comparative Management and Economic Progress.* With Richard M. Farmer. Homewood, Ill.: Richard D. Irwin. Revised editions, Bloomington, Ind.: Cedarwood Press, 1970 and 1976.

—— *Soviet Management: With Significant American Comparisons.* Englewood Cliffs, N.J.: Prentice-Hall.

1966 *Incidents in Applying Management Theory.* With Richard M. Farmer and William Ryan. Belmont, Calif.: Wadsworth.

—— *International Business: An Operational Theory.* With Richard M. Farmer. Homewood, Ill.: Richard D. Irwin.

1967 *Management Development and Education in the Soviet Union.* East Lansing, Mich.: Michigan State University.

1969 *Industrial Management in India.* With Melvin Copen and Arvind Phatak. Reading, Mass.: Addison-Wesley.

—— *Industrial Society in Communist China: A First-Hand Study of China's Economic Development and Management.* New York: Random House. Second edition, New York: Vintage Paperback.

1970 *Incidents for Studying Management and Organization.* With Richard M. Farmer and William Ryan. Belmont, Calif.: Wadsworth.

1972 *International Management and Economic Development with Particular Reference to India and Other Developing Countries.* With Melvin Copen. New York: McGraw-Hill.

1974 *International Business.* With Richard M. Farmer. Bloomington, Ind.: Cedarwood Press.

—— *Leadership, Goals and Power in Higher Education: A Contingency and Open-Systems Approach to Effective Management.* With Richard M. Farmer. San Francisco: Jossey-Bass.

1975 *Management and Organizations.* With Richard M. Farmer. New York: Random House.

Papers and Articles:

1962 "A Rating Scale for Product Innovation," *Business Horizons,* Vol. 5, No. 4, pp. 37–44.

1963 "Employee Motivation in Soviet Industry," *Annals of Collective Economy,* Vol. 34, No. 4, pp. 551–571.

—— "Formulation of Enterprise Operating Plans in Soviet Industry," *Soviet Studies,* Vol. 15, No. 1.

—— "Innovation Problems in Soviet Industry," *Management International,* Vol. 3, No. 6, pp. 67–95.

—— "A Managerial Motivation in Soviet and Czechoslovakian Industries: A Comparison," *Journal* of the Academy of Management, Vol. 6, No. 2, pp. 107–128.

—— "Managerial Opposition to Product Innovation in Soviet Industry," *California Management Review,* Vol. 6, No. 2, pp. 11–26.

—— "The Red Profit Motive: Soviet Industry in Transition" (with Richard M. Farmer), *Business Horizons,* Vol. 6, No. 2, pp. 21–28.

1964 "Increasing Worker Productivity: How the Soviets Do It," *Personnel,* Vol. 41, No. 1, pp. 8–21.

—— "L'Incoraggiamento agli innovatori nell' USSR" (Encouragement of Innovators in the USSR), *Mercurio,* Vol. 7, No. 8, pp. 87–90.

—— "A Model for Research in Comparative Management" (with Richard M. Farmer), *California Management Review,* Vol. 7, No. 2, pp. 55–68.

1965 "Ownership and Management: The Real Issues" (with Richard M. Farmer), *Management International,* Vol. 4, No. 6, pp. 31–43.

1967 "Capitalists and Managers in Communist China," *Harvard Business Review,* Vol. 45, No. 1, pp. 57–78.

1968 "China Organizes Foreign Trade to Accelerate Development," *Columbia Journal of World Business,* Vol. 7, pp. 27–38.

1970 "A First-Hand Study of Marketing in Communist China," *Journal of Retailing,* Vol. 46, No. 2, pp. 27–47.

1971 "Ideology and Management: The Chinese Oscillate," *Columbia Journal of World Business,* Vol. 6, No. 1, pp. 33–71.

—— "Ideology and Management: The Soviet Evolution," *Columbia Journal of World Business,* Vol. 6, No. 2, pp. 62–72.

1973 "Corporate Social Responsibility and Enlightened Management," *The Business Quarterly,* Vol. 38, No. 1, pp. 44–53.

—— "Management Techniques in the Developing Nations" (with Melvin Copen), *Columbia Journal of World Business,* Vol. 8, No. 2, pp. 49–58.

—— "New Paths to Corporate Social Responsibility," *California Management Review,* Vol. 15, No. 3, pp. 20–36.

1974 "Implementing Competitive Policy in Communist Countries," *California Management Review,* Vol. 16, No. 4, pp. 104–111.

1975 "Chinese and Indian Development: An Interdisciplinary Environmental Analysis," *American Economic Review,* Vol. 65, No. 2, pp. 345–355.

1976 "Multinational Corporations and the Communist Nations," *Management International Review,* Vol. 16, No. 3, pp. 9–22.

Curriculum Vitae

1936 Born on March 18th in Montreal, Canada.

1958 Awarded Bachelor of Commerce degree by McGill University, Quebec.

1959 Awarded Master of Science degree by Columbia University, New York City.

1960–1962 Lectured on management and marketing at Columbia.

1962 Awarded Ph.D. by Columbia University.

1962–1978 Successively, was Assistant Professor, Associate Professor, and Professor, University of California, Los Angeles.

1965–1966 In India as Visiting M.I.T. Professor of Industrial Management at the Indian Institute of Management, Calcutta.

1972–1973 Served as Dean, Faculty of Administrative Studies, York University, Toronto, Canada.

1975–1977 Returning to UCLA, was for two years Chairman, Department of Management, Graduate School of Management.

1977 Addressed Joint Economic Committee of U.S. Congress on Managerial Decision Making and Performance at the Enterprise Level in Communist China.

1978 Named Director, Graduate School of Management, Pacific Basin Center, University of California, Los Angeles.

—— Died on June 5th, aged 42, in Malibu, Calif.

Barry Richman was a Fellow of the Academy of Management, a Fellow of the International Academy of Management, and a member of Beta Gamma Sigma, the national business academic honorary society. He held the Samuel Bronfman Doctoral Fellowship at Columbia University for the year 1959–1960 and received the Columbia University Doctoral Award for dissertation research on Soviet industry from 1961 to 1962. He was a member of the American Economic Association and the American Sociological Association.

Appendix

Publications Listed by Pioneer Name
(used in preparing Part Two of the expanded *Golden Book of Management*)

ARMAND, LOUIS-FRANÇOIS

Baruzy, Jacques, Association Française de Management, Paris, special biographical materials.

Current Biography, 1957

Lecler, René, in *Popular Science,* February 1957 (reprinted in *Reader's Digest,* February 1957).

"Louis Armand," *Cour. de la Norm,* No. 221, ix–x, 1971.

Millet, Roger, "Notice sur la vie et les travaux de Louis Armand," *Vie Sociale,* No. 4, 1973.

Qui est qui en France (Who's Who in France), 1969–1970.

Who's Who in Europe.

BABA, KEIJI

Published Japanese sources and several unpublished materials available to the author.

BARNARD, CHESTER IRVING

Boulding, Kenneth, "The Pioneer Work of Chester I. Barnard, in *The Image* (Ann Arbor: University of Michigan Press), 1956.

Fortune, June 1948, p. 188.

Wolf, William B., *The Basic Barnard.* Ithaca, N.Y.: New York State School of Industrial and Labor Relations, Publications Division, 1974.

BROWN, ALVIN McCREARY

Brown, Alvin McCreary, "The Case (or Bootstrap) Method," *Advanced Management,* Vol. 21, No. 7, July.

Mee, John F., unpublished letters and personal conversations during Brown's term as President, Academy of Management.

Who's Who in Commerce and Industry, 1957.

BROWN, F. DONALDSON

Brown, F. Donaldson, *Some Reminiscences of an Industrialist.* New York: Hive Publishing Co., 1958.

Chandler, Alfred D., *Strategy and Structure: Chapters in the History of the Enterprise.* Cambridge, Mass.: The M.I.T. Press, 1962, pp. 238, 390–392.

Drucker, Peter F., *Adventures of a Bystander.* New York: Harper & Row, 1978.

———, interview with William B. Wolf, March 16, 1966.

New York Herald-Tribune, October 3, 1965. Obituary.

The Wall Street Journal, December 31, 1941.

Washington Evening Star, October 2, 1965 (second edition). Obituary.

BUSTANI, EMILE

Hutchinson, George, "Arabian Knight" (review of *Orphan with a Hoop: The Life of Emile Bustani*), *Spectator,* June 9, 1967.

Henshaw, Tim, "The Bustani Legacy," *The Arab World,* Spring 1975.

Stewart, Desmond, *Orphan with a Hoop: The Life of Emile Bustani.* London: Chapman and Hall, 1967.

Who's Who in Lebanon (under the spelling "Boustany").

COOKE, MORRIS LLEWELLYN

Current Biography, 1950

"Famous Firsts: Extending the Scientific Gospel," *Business Week,* April 8, 1964, pp. 132–136.

The New York Times, March 6, 1960. Obituary.

Trombley, Kenneth E., *The Life and Times of a Happy Liberal: A Biography of Morris Llewellyn Cooke.* New York: Harper, 1954.

"Trouble-Shooter Extraordinary," *New Republic,* Vol. 112, February 12, 1945, pp. 220–223.

Wrege, Charles D., School of Administrative Sciences, Rutgers University, material in files.

CORDINER, RALPH JARRON

Cordiner, Ralph, "Address of Acceptance," *The Henry Laurence Gantt Memorial Gold Medal: Ralph J. Cordiner, 1965 Medalist.* New York: American Management Association, 1965, pp. 8–13.

———, "When a Man Looks Back," *GE Monogram,* Vol. 12, December 1963, pp. 11–18.

General Electric Co., *The Source Book—Biographies.*

Drucker, Peter F., personal reminiscences.

"New Appliance Manager," *GE Monogram,* February 1938, p. 13.

Smiddy, Harold F., interviews with Ronald G. Greenwood.

The New York Times, December 6, 1973. Obituary.

DUBREUIL, HYACINTHE JOSEPH

Richard, Max, "Hyacinthe Dubreuil—mon maître et mon ami," October 12, 1981. Made available by Comité Hyacinthe Dubreuil, Paris.

Travail et méthodes, No. 308, December 1974 (Editions Entreprise et Techniques, Paris).

Who's Who in France 1969–1970.

Larousse encyclopédique.

GILBRETH, LILLIAN MOLLER

Current Biography, 1951

Gilbreth, Frank B., Jr., and Ernestine Gilbreth Carey, *Belles on Their Toes.* New York: T. Y. Crowell, 1950.

——————, *Cheaper by the Dozen* (New York: T. Y. Crowell, 1949).

Journal of the Academy of Management, Vol. 15, March.

Koontz, Harold, personal reminiscences.

The New York Times, January 3, 1972. Obituary.

Who Was Who, Vol. II, 1974–1976.

Wolf, William B., interview with Mrs. Gilbreth.

GOTTL-OTTLILIENFELD, FRIEDRICH EDLER VON

Standard *Who's Who* listings and biographical dictionaries (international, European, German). But see also Hunke, Heinrich, and Wiskemann-Erwin (publishers), *Gegenwartsfragen der Wirtschaftswissenschaft. Festschrift zum 70. Geburtstag von Friedrich von Gottl-Ottlilienfeld* (Present-Day Questions About Economics. Commemorative Volume in Honor of the 70th Birthday of Friedrich von Gottl-Ottlilienfeld). Berlin: 1939.

HELLERN, BERNHARD

Hellern, Eyvind, personal correspondence, 1980, 1981.

Hvem er hvem? (Who's Who). Oslo: 1968.

Stoltz, Gerhard, Rector, Norges Handelshøyskole, Bergen, letter of information, 1980.

HIRAI, YASUTARO

Hax, Karl, "Hirai Yasutaro kjoju no omoide" (Reminiscences of Professor Yasutaro Hirai), in *Tane o maku hito* (The Sower). Yasutaro Hirai Memorial Association, 1974.

Hirai keieigaku ronshu (Collected Articles on business Administration by Yasutaro Hirai). Bibliography included. Tokyo: Chikura Shobo, 1972.

"Hirai Yasutaro sensei nempu" (Yasutaro Hirai Chronology), *Tane o maku hito* (The Sower). Afterword included. Yasutaro Hirai Memorial Association, 1974.

Yamamoto, Yasujiro, *50 Years of Business Administration in Japan.* Tokyo: Toyo Keizai Shimposha, 1977. See Chapter 7, Part 1.

KENDALL, HENRY PLIMPTON

Allen, Robert L., personal correspondence, 1975–1976.

Kendall, John Plimpton, personal correspondence, 1972, 1975–1976.

National Cyclopaedia of American Biography.

Young, Marjorie W., editor, *Textile Leaders of the South.* Anderson, S.C.: James R. Young, 1963, pp. 121, 770–775.

Who's Who in America, 1959.

LEWIN, KURT

Marrow, Alfred, J., *The Practical Theorist: The Life and Work of Kurt Lewin.* New York: Basic Books, 1969.

Wolf, William B., interview with Mrs. Gertrude Weiss Lewin.

LIKERT, RENSIS

Bowers, D. G., *Systems of Organization: Management of the Human Resource.* Ann Arbor, Mich.: The University of Michigan Press, 1976.

Consultants and Consulting Organizations Directory. Detroit: Gale Research Co., 1979.

Men of Achievement, Vol. 7, Cambridge (England): International Biographical Centre, 1980.

Who's Who in America, 40th edition (1978–1979), Vol. 2.

MASUCHI, YOJIRO

Information from son. Also published Japanese sources and unpublished materials available to the author.

McCORMICK, CHARLES PERRY

McCormick, Charles Perry, "Address of Acceptance," *The Henry Laurence Gantt Memorial Gold Medal: Charles Perry McCormick, Medalist.* New York: American Management Association, 1960.

Who's Who in America, 1968–1969.

McGREGOR, DOUGLAS

Bennis, Warren, introduction to Douglas McGregor, *Leadership and Motivation.* Cambridge, Mass., and London, England: The M.I.T. Press, 1966, pp. ix–xv.

Chambers, Peter, "The Man Who Created Theory 'Y,'" *International Management,* June 1973.

The New York Times, October 14, 1964. Obituary.

Picker, Walt, interview with Caroline McGregor, 1967.

Wolf, William B., interview with Charles Myers (Professor, M.I.T.), 1975.

———, interview with Patricia McPherson (secretary to McGregor at M.I.T.), 1975.

MOONEY, JAMES DAVID

"Drawing the Rules from History," *Business Week,* August 3, 1963, pp. 46–57. Reprinted in *Milestones of Management* (New York: *Business Week,* 1964).

The New York Times, September 22, 1957. Obituary.

Who's Who in America, 1954–1955.

MURAMOTO, FUKUMATSU

Keieigaku jiten (A Dictionary of Business Administration). Edited by Y. Hirai. Entry on Fukumatsu Muramoto. Tokyo: Diamond-sha.

NAKANISHI, TORAO

Published Japanese sources and unpublished materials available to the author.

NORDLING, ROLF

"Rolf Nordling 9 octobre 1893–9 octobre 1974." Paris: Comité National de l'Organisation Française, 1974.

"Rolf Nordling 1893–1974," *Management France,* January 1975.

OLIVETTI, ADRIANO

Chi e? (*Who's Who*), 1957

Current Biography, 1959

Dizionario enciclopedico labor (Encyclopedic Dictionary of Labor), 1950

The New York Times Magazine, June 19, 1955, p. 28.

The New Yorker, Vol. 38, September 27, 1958, p. 93 *et seq.*

Panorama biografico degli italiani d'oggi, 1956.

Reader's Digest, Vol. 70, January 1957, p. 169 *et seq.*

Time, Vol. 63, February 8, 1954, p. 84.

Olivetti Company (Ivrea, Italy), especially prepared bibliographical material.

PERSON, HARLOW STAFFORD

National Cyclopaedia of American Biography.

The New York Times, November 8, 1955. Obituary.

RICHMAN, BARRY M.

Koontz, Harold, experiences as colleague of Richman at UCLA.

Who's Who in America, 1978–1979

ROETHLISBERGER, FRITZ J.

Academy of Management (Management History Division), "Fritz J. Roethlisberger's Contributions to Management Thinking and Practice," August 1975. Contributors: George F. F. Lombard, James R. Surface, James V. Clark, Daniel A. Wren, and Jay W. Lorsch.

Roethlisberger, Fritz J., *The Elusive Phenomena.* Edited by G. F. F. Lombard. Cambridge, Mass.: Harvard University Press, for Division of Research, Harvard University Graduate School of Business Administration, 1977.

Lombard, George F. F., personal conversations with Roethlisberger.

SCHELL, ERWIN HASKELL

Who's Who in America, 1956–1957.

Wolf, William B., interview with G. B. Tallman, formerly Professor of Marketing at M.I.T., June 27, 1978.

————, interview with Frank Gilmore, February 24, 1974.

SCHMALENBACH, EUGEN

Standard "Who's Who" listings and biographical dictionaries (international, European, German).

SCOTT, WALTER DILL

Ferguson, Leonard W., *The Heritage of Industrial Psychology.* Provincetown, Me.: Leonard W. Ferguson, 1962. Published privately.

Jacobsen, J. Z., *Scott of Northwestern.* Chicago: Louis Mariano, 1951.

Lynch, Edmund C., *Walter Dill Scott: Pioneer in Personnel Management.* Austin: Bureau of Business Research, University of Texas, 1968.

SIEMENS, CARL FRIEDRICH VON

Siemens, Georg, *Carl Friedrich von Siemens: Ein grosser Unternehmer* (Carl Friedrich von Siemens: A Great Entrepreneur). Freiburg and Munich: Verlag Carl Alber, 1960.

————, *History of the House of Siemens,* Vol. I: The Era of the Free Enterprise; Vol. II, The Era of World Wars. Freiburg and Munich: Verlag Karl Alber, 1961 (German-language edition published in 1960).

Schmölders, G., *Carl Friedrich von Siemens—Vom Leitbild des grossindustriellen Unternehmens* (Carl Friedrich von Siemens—Model of the "Big Business" Entrepreneur). Commemorative address at the Carl Friedrich von Siemens Foundation in Munich-Nymphenburg on October 23, 1972. With an introduction by Dr. Peter von Siemens. Published by the Foundation. 59 pp.

Weiher, Sigfrid, and Herbert Goetzler, *Weg und Wirken der Siemens-Werke im Fortschritt der Elektrotechnik.* Munich: F. Bruckmann KG, 1972. Also published in English as *The Siemens Family: Its Historical Role in the Progress of Electrical Engineering.* Berlin and Munich: Siemens Aktiengesellschaft, 1977.

See also the heading "Siemens" in most standard encyclopedias.

SLOAN, ALFRED PRITCHARD, JR.

Dale, Ernest, *The Great Organizers.* New York: McGraw-Hill, 1960.

Drucker, Peter F., *Adventures of a Bystander.* New York: Harper & Row, 1978.

The New York Times, February 18, 1966.

SMIDDY, HAROLD FRANCIS

Drucker, Peter F., interviews with Ronald G. Greenwood.

Greenwood, Ronald G., "Crotonville: The Origins of Industry's Best Management Training Institute," *Proceedings* of the 17th Annual Conference, Eastern Academy of Management, May 1980, pp. 18–22.

————, "Harold Smiddy: Manager by Inspiration and Persuasion," Academy of Management *Proceedings,* 1979, pp. 12–16.

————, "In Memoriam—Harold Smiddy," Academy of Management *Newsletter,* Vol. 9, No. 1, January 1979, p. 5.

————, interviews with Harold Smiddy.

————, "Management Objectives: As Developed by Peter Drucker, Assisted by Harold Smiddy," Academy of Management *Review,* Vol. 6, No. 2, April 1981, pp. 225–230.

Zimet, Melvin, and Ronald G. Greenwood, eds., *The Evolving Science of Management: The Collected Papers of Harold Smiddy and Papers by Others in His Honor.* New York: AMACOM, for the Trustees of Manhattan College of Business, 1979. See Chapter 1 on Smiddy and his work.

TEAD, ORDWAY

Chamberlain, Neil, unpublished remarks, 1973.

Current Biography, May 1942, pp. 77–78.

Exman, Eugene, Century Club obituary, 1973. Unpublished.

Gallagher, Buell G., "Remarks in memoriam of Ordway Tead," January 9, 1974. Unpublished.

McAdoo, Richard, "Remarks in Memoriam of Ordway Tead," January 9, 1974. Unpublished.

Michaelis, Diana Tead, personal correspondence, 1973, 1975–1976.

The New York Times, November 17, 1973. Obituary.

Tead, Ordway, autobiographical chapter in Louis Frankelstein, ed., *Thirteen Americans: Their Spiritual Autobiography.* New York: The Institute for Religious and Social Studies (distributed by Harper & Row), 1953, pp. 15–30.

————, personal correspondence, 1973.

Who's Who in America, 1972–1973.

THOMPSON, CLARENCE BERTRAND

Dale, Ernest, personal papers concerning Thompson, with whom he corresponded for many years.

Greenwood, Ronald G., and Regina A. Greenwood, "C. Bertrand Thompson—Pioneer Management Bibliographer," *Proceedings* of the Academy of Management, 1976, pp. 3–6.

Planus, "A propos de ma rencontre avec Clarence Bertrand Thompson" (About My Meeting with Clarence Bertrand Thompson), *L'Etude du travail,* No. 164, July–August, 1965, pp. 33–34.

UEDA, TEIJIRO

Compiled from Japanese sources sent by Professor Kisou Tasugi, Kyoto. See, however:

Keiei keizai no shomondai (Problems of Business Administration), commemorative publication in honor of Teijiro Ueda. See Preface.

Keieigaku jiten (Dictionary of Business Administration). Edited by Y. Hirai. Tokyo: Diamond-sha.

Ueda Teijiro zenshi (Collected Works of Teijiro Ueda). Chronology, bibliography, and promotion pamphlet. Tokyo: Diamond-sha, 1976.

UENO, YOICHI

Published Japanese sources and unpublished materials available to the author. But see also: Greenwood, Ronald G., Regina A. Greenwood, and Robert H. Ross, "History of Japanese Management, 1911 to World War II," Academy of Management *Proceedings,* 1981, pp. 107–110.

WEBER, ALFRED

Standard "Who's Who" listings and biographical dictionaries (international, European, German). But see also: Niederhauser, Elisabeth, *Die Standorttheorie Webers* (Weber's Theory of Industry Location). Diss. Basel, 1944; and *Synopsis. Festschrift für Alfred Weber* (Synopsis: Commemorative Volume for Alfred Weber). Heidelberg: E. Salin, 1948.

Index of Names

Names of pioneers and the pages where their entries appear are given in boldface type.